Get the eBook FREE!

(PDF, ePub, Kindle, and liveBook all included)

We believe that once you buy a book from us, you should be able to read it in any format we have available. To get electronic versions of this book at no additional cost to you, purchase and then register this book at the Manning website.

Go to https://www.manning.com/freebook and follow the instructions to complete your pBook registration.

That's it!
Thanks from Manning!

Data-Oriented Programming

Data-Oriented Programming

REDUCE SOFTWARE COMPLEXITY

YEHONATHAN SHARVIT

Forewords by MICHAEL T. NYGARD and RYAN SINGER

MANNING
SHELTER ISLAND

For online information and ordering of this and other Manning books, please visit www.manning.com. The publisher offers discounts on this book when ordered in quantity. For more information, please contact

Special Sales Department
Manning Publications Co.
20 Baldwin Road
PO Box 761
Shelter Island, NY 11964
Email: orders@manning.com

Manning Publications Co.
20 Baldwin Road
PO Box 761
Shelter Island, NY 11964

Development editor: Elesha Hyde
Technical development editor: Marius Butuc
Review editors: Aleksandar Dragosavljević
Production editor: Andy Marinkovich
Copy editor: Frances Buran
Proofreader: Keri Hales
Technical proofreader: Karsten Strøbaek
Typesetter: Dennis Dalinnik
Cover designer: Marija Tudor

ISBN: 9781617298578
Printed in the United States of America

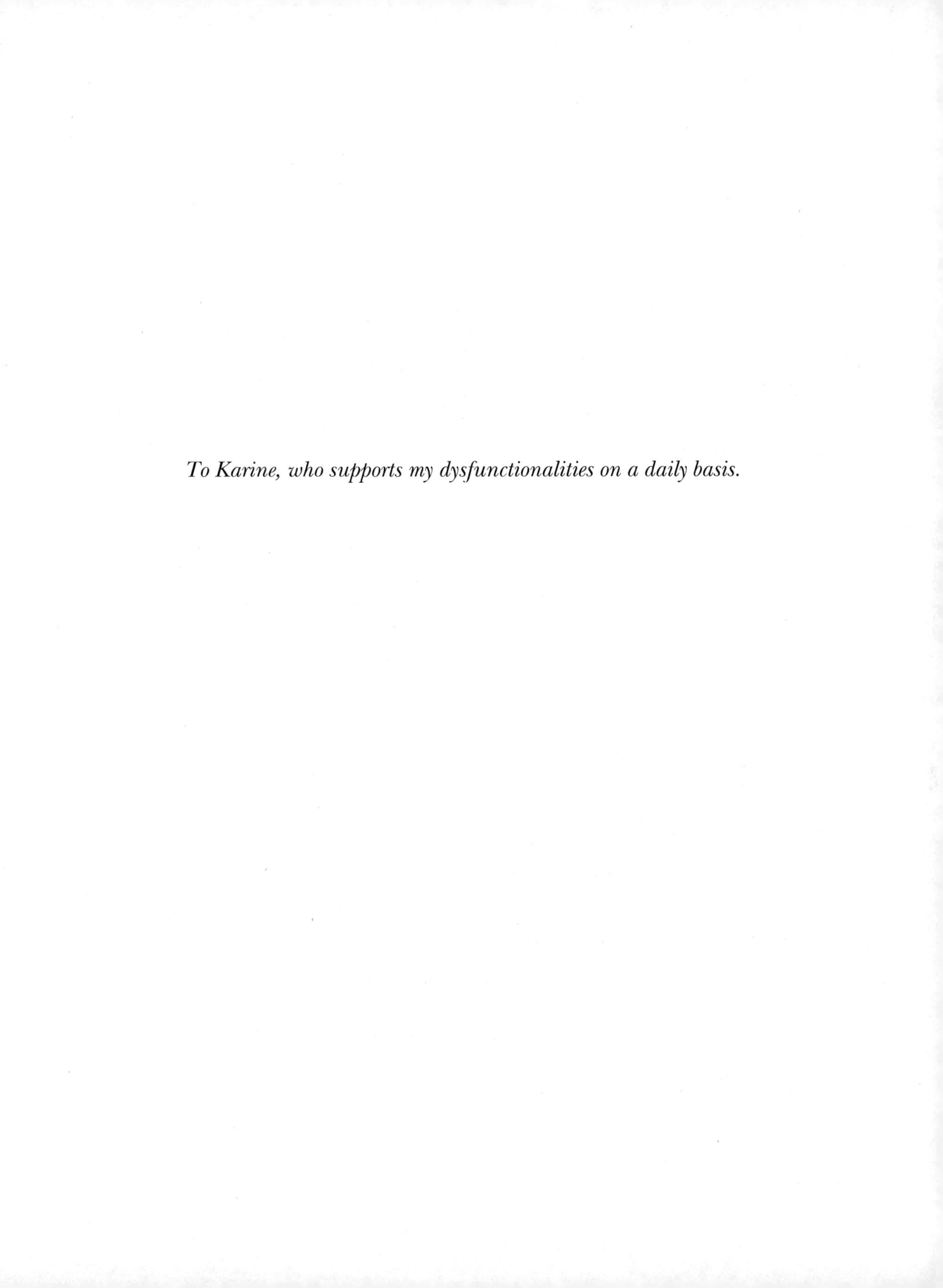

To Karine, who supports my dysfunctionalities on a daily basis.

brief contents

contents

forewords

Every programming principle, every design method, every architecture style, and even most language features are about organizing complexity while allowing adaptation. Two characteristics—immutable data and turning parts of the program into data inside the program itself—drew me to Clojure in 2009 and more recently to Yehonathan Sharvit's *Data-Oriented Programming*.

In 2005, I worked on one of my favorite projects with some of my favorite people. It was a Java project, but we did two things that were not common practice in the Java world at that time. First, we made our core data values immutable. It wasn't easy but it worked extraordinarily well. We hand-rolled `clone` and `deepClone` methods in many classes. The payoff was huge. Just as one example, suppose you need template documents for users to instantiate. When you can make copies of entire object trees, the objects themselves don't need to "know" whether they are template data or instance data. That decision is up to whatever object holds the reference. Another big benefit came from comparison: when values are immutable, equality of identity indicates equality of value. This can make for very fast equality checks.

Our second technique was to take advantage of generic data—though not to the extent Yehonathan will show you in this book. Where one layer had a hierarchy of classes, its adjoining layer would represent those as instances of a more general class. What would be a member variable in one layer would be described by a field in a map in another layer. I am certain this style was influenced by the several small talkers on our team. It also paid off immediately, as we were able to compose and recompose objects in different configurations.

Data-oriented programming, as you will see, promises to reduce accidental complexity, and raise the level of abstraction you work at. You will start to see repeated behavior in your programs as artificial, a result of carving generic functions into classes, which act like little namespaces that operate only on a subset of your program's values (their instances). We can "fold together" almost all of those values into maps and lists. We can turn member names (data available only with difficulty via reflective APIs) into map keys. As we do that, code simply melts away. This is the first level of enlightenment.

At this point, you might object that the compiler uses those member names at compile time for correctness checking. Indeed it does. But have faith, for Yehonathan will guide you to the next level of enlightenment: that those compile-time checks are a small subset of possible correctness checks on values. We can make the *correctness checks themselves* into data, too! We can make schemas into values inside our programs. What's more, we can enforce criteria that researchers on the forefront of type systems are still trying to figure out. This is the second level of enlightenment.

Data-oriented programming especially shines when working with web APIs. There is no type of system on the wire, so attempting to map a request payload directly into a domain class guarantees a brittle, complex implementation. If we let data be data, we get simpler code and far fewer dependencies on hundred-megabyte framework libraries.

So, whatever happened to the OOP virtues of encapsulation, inheritance, and polymorphism? It turns out we can decomplect these and get each of them à la carte. (In my opinion, inheritance of implementations is the least important of these, even though it is often the first one taught. I now prefer inheritance of *interfaces* via protocols and shared function signatures.) Data-oriented programming offers polymorphism of the "traditional" kind: dispatch to one of many functions based on the type of the first argument (in an OO language, `this` is a disguise for the method's first argument. It just happens it goes before the "`.`"). However, as with schema checking, DOP allows more dynamism. Imagine dispatching based on the types of the first two arguments. Or based on whether the argument has a "birthday" field with today's date in it! This is the third level of enlightenment.

And as for encapsulation, we must still apply it to the organizing logic of our program. We encapsulate subsystems, not values. This encapsulation embodies the decision-hiding of David Parnas. Inside a subsystem, we can stop walling off our data into the disjointed namespaces that classes impose. In the words of Alan Perlis, "It is better to have one hundred functions operate on one data structure than ten functions on ten data structures."

In our unending battle with entropy, we can use data-oriented programming to both reduce the volume of code to keep up and raise the level of abstraction to make our program's logic and meaning precise and evident. Enjoy the journey and pause at each new plateau to enjoy the view and say to yourself, "It's just data!"

—MICHAEL T. NYGARD
author of *Release It!: Design and Deploy Production-Ready Software*

This book hit me at just the right time. I had been building web apps for nearly 20 years in an object-oriented framework. I never considered myself an expert programmer, but I knew my tools well enough to look at a typical business problem, sketch out a data model, and build an MVC-style app to get the job done.

Projects were thrilling at the start. I loved the feeling of plugging pieces together and seeing the app come to life. But once I got it working, I ran into problems. I couldn't change one part without keeping all the other models in mind. I knew I should write tests, but I had to set up so much state to test things that it didn't feel worth it—I didn't want to write more code that would be hard to change. Even running bits of code in the console was tedious because I had to create database state to call the method. I thought I was probably doing it wrong, but the solutions I knew about, such as sophisticated testing frameworks, seemed to add to the complexity instead of making things easier.

Then one day, I saw a talk on YouTube by Rich Hickey, the creator of Clojure. He was explaining functional programming and contrasting it with OO, which he derisively called "place-oriented programming." I wasn't sure if he was right, but I heard a hidden message that intrigued me: "It's not you, it's your language." I watched all the videos I could find and started to think Clojure might be the answer.

Years went by. I kept watching Clojure videos and trying to apply functional principles when I could. But whenever it was time to start on a new project, I fell back on my familiar framework. Changing to another language with a totally different ecosystem of libraries was too big of a leap.

Then, just as I was about to start work on a new product, I found this book. The words "Data-Oriented" in the title rang a bell. I heard programmers in those Clojure videos use the words before, but I hadn't really understood what they meant. Something about how it's easier to build systems that manipulate data literals (like maps and arrays) instead of custom objects. The languages I knew had good support for data literals, so I thought I might learn something to hold me over until that magical day when I might switch to Clojure.

My first a-ha moment came right in the introduction. In the first few pages, Yehonathan explains that, though he's written Clojure for 10 years, the book isn't language-specific, and the examples will be in JavaScript. Wait!—I thought. Could it really be that I don't have to change languages to deeply improve the way I write programs?

I was so excited by this prospect that I devoured the book in one sitting. My eyes opened to something that had been right in front of me all along. Of course my code was hard to test! Because of the ORM I used, all my functionality was written in objects that assumed a bunch of database state! When I saw it spelled out with examples in the book, I couldn't unsee it. I didn't need a new language, I just needed to approach programming differently!

The designers I consider great all point to the same thing: good design is about pulling things apart. It's not just about getting the code to work, no matter how ugly.

It's about untangling the parts from each other so you can change one thing without breaking everything else.

This book pulls apart code and data, with surprising and exciting results. For me, it also went further. It pulled apart a *way of programming* from a specific *language.* I might never make that switch to Clojure, and I don't feel like I have to anymore. *Data-Oriented Programming* helped me see new possibilities in the languages I know and the multitude of new frameworks appearing every day.

—RYAN SINGER
author of *Shape Up: Stop Running in Circles and Ship Work that Matters*

preface

I have been a software engineer since 2000. For me, there is clearly a "before" and an "after" 2012. Why 2012? Because 2012 is the year I discovered Clojure. Before Clojure, programming was my job. After Clojure, programming has been my passion.

A few years ago, I wondered what features of Clojure made this programming language such a great source of pleasure for me. I shared my questions with other members of the Clojure community who have the same passion for it that I do. Together, we discovered that what was so special about Clojure was not features, but principles.

When we set out to distill the core principles of Clojure, we realized that they were, in fact, applicable to other programming languages. It was then that the idea for this book began to emerge. I wanted to share what I like so much about Clojure with the global community of developers. For that, I would need a means of clearly expressing ideas that are mostly unfamiliar to developers who do not know Clojure.

I've always loved inventing stories, but would my invented dialogues be taken seriously by programmers? Certainly, Plato had invented stories with his "Socratic Dialogues" to transmit the teachings of his teacher. Likewise, Rabbi Judah Halevi had invented the story of the king of the Khazars to explain the foundations of Judaism. But these two works are in the realm of thought, not practice!

I then remembered a management book I had read a few years ago, called *The Goal* (North River Press, 2014). In this book, Eliyahu Goldratt invents the story of a plant manager who manages to save his factory thanks to the principles coming from the theory of constraints. Plato, Judah Halevi, and Eliyahu Goldratt legitimized my crazy desire to write a story to share ideas.

acknowledgments

First and foremost, I want to thank my beloved, Karine. You believed in me since the beginning of this project. You always manage to see the light, even when it hides behind several layers of darkness. To my wonderful children, Odaya, Orel, Advah, Nehoray, and Yair, who were the first audience for the stories I invented when I was a young daddy. You are the most beautiful story I ever wrote!

There are numerous other folks to whom I want to also extend my thanks, including Joel Klein, for all the fascinating and enriching discussions on the art and the soul; to Meir Armon for helping me clarify what content should not be included in the book; to Rich Hickey for inventing Clojure, such a beautiful language, which embraced data-oriented programming before it even had a name; to Christophe Grand, whose precious advice helped me to distill the first three principles of data-oriented programming; to Mark Champine, for reviewing the manuscript so carefully and providing many valuable suggestions; to Eric Normand, for your encouragement and, in particular, your advice on the application of data-oriented programming in Java; to Bert Bates, for teaching me the secrets of writing a good book; and to Ben Button, for reviewing the chapters that deal with JSON Schema.

My thanks to all the folks at Manning Publications, especially Mike Stephens, for agreeing to continue working with me despite the failure of my first book; Elesha Hyde, for your availability and your attention to the smallest details; Marius Butuc, for your enthusiastic positive feedback from reading the first chapter; Linda Kotlyarsky, for formulating the chapter descriptions in such a fun way; and to Frances Buran for improving the clarity of the text and the flow of the story.

To all the reviewers, Alex Gout, Allen Ding, Andreas Schabus, Andrew Jennings, Andy Kirsch, Anne Epstein, Berthold Frank, Christian Kreutzer-Beck, Christopher Kardell, Dane Balia, Dr. Davide Cadamuro, Elias Ilmari Liinamaa, Ezra Simeloff, George Thomas, Giri S., Giuliano Araujo Bertoti, Gregor Rayman, J. M. Borovina Josko, Jerome Meyer, Jesús A. Juárez Guerrero, John D. Lewis, Jon Guenther, Kelum Prabath Senanayake, Kelvin Johnson, Kent R. Spillner, Kim Gabrielsen, Konstantin Eremin, Marcus Geselle, Mark Elston, Matthew Proctor, Maurizio Tomasi, Michael Aydinbas, Milorad Imbra, Özay Duman, Raffaella Ventaglio, Ramanan Nararajan, Rambabu Posa, Saurabh Singh, Seth MacPherson, Shiloh Morris, Victor Durán, Vincent Theron, William E. Wheeler, Yogesh Shetty, and Yvan Phelizot, your suggestions helped make this a better book.

Finally, I'd like to mention my cousin Nissim, whom a band of barbarians did not allow to flourish.

about this book

Data-Oriented Programming was written to help developers reduce the complexity of the systems they build. The ideas in this book are mostly applicable to systems that manipulate information—systems like frontend applications, backend web servers, or web services.

Who should read this book?

Data-Oriented Programming is for frontend, backend, and full stack developers with a couple of years of experience in a high-level programming language like Java, C#, C++, Ruby, or Python. For object-oriented programming developers, some ideas presented in this book might take them out of their comfort zone and require them to unlearn some of the programming paradigms they feel so much at ease with. For functional programming developers, this book will be a little easier to digest but should deliver some nice surprises as well.

How this book is organized: A road map

This book tells a story that illustrates the value of data-oriented programming (DOP) and how to apply its principles in real-life production systems. My suggestion is to follow the story and read the chapters in order. However, if some chapters trigger your curiosity more than the others, be aware that the material in part 1 and in chapter 7 are required to understand part 2 and part 3.

Throughout the book, we use Lodash (https://lodash.com/) to illustrate how to manipulate data with generic functions. In case you are reading a code snippet that uses a Lodash function that you are unfamiliar with, you can refer to appendix D to understand the behavior of the function.

Part 1, *Flexibility*, contains six chapters and shines a spotlight on the challenges of traditional object-oriented programming (OOP) and puts data-oriented programming (DOP) center stage, revealing how to build flexible systems by using DOP's basic principles. The chapters line up this way:

- In chapter 1, *Complexity of object-oriented programming*, we look at the complexity of OOP. Then, our DOP saga begins! Listen in on a conversation between Theo, a senior developer, and his up-and-coming colleague, Dave. Feel empathy for Theo struggling with OOP complexity and discover an excellent reason for trying a different programming paradigm.
- Chapter 2, *Separation between code and data*, finds our friend Theo searching for a solution that will reduce complexity and increase the flexibility of systems. His job is on the line. Enter Joe, an experienced developer who has an answer for him—DOP. Discover how DOP Principle #1 helps to reduce complexity of information systems.
- Chapter 3, *Basic data manipulation*, explores how we can liberate our data from its encapsulation in class rigidity and manipulate it freely with generic functions by applying DOP Principle #2. Vive la révolution!
- Chapter 4, *State management*, explores state management with a multiversion approach that lets us go back in time by restoring the system to a previous state because, in DOP, state is nothing more than data. Time travel is real—in DOP!
- Chapter 5, *Basic concurrency control*, helps us to get high throughput of reads and writes in a concurrent system by applying an optimistic concurrency control strategy. No rose-colored glasses required!
- Chapter 6, *Unit tests*, offers a cup of joe . . . with Joe! Our friend Joe proves that unit testing data-oriented code is so easy you can tackle it in a coffee shop. Grab a cuppa and learn why it's so straightforward—even for mutations!—as you write a DOP unit test hands-on with Joe. It's cool beans!

Part 2, *Scalability*, illustrates how to build a DOP system at scale with a focus on data validation, multi-threaded environments, large data collections, and database access and web services. Need to supersize your system? No problem!

- Chapter 7, *Basic data validation*, teaches us how to ensure that data going in and out of our systems is valid, just in case . . . because, as Joe says, you are not forced to validate data in DOP, but you can when you need to. To validate or not to validate, that is the question!
- Chapter 8, *Advanced concurrency control*, discusses how, after our friend Joe breaks down the implementation details of the atom mechanism, we'll learn to manage the whole system state in a thread-safe way without using any locks. You won't know complexity from atom—up and atom!

- Chapter 9, *Persistent data structures*, moves to a more academic setting where our friend Joe unveils the internal details of a safer and more scalable way to preserve data immutability as well as how to implement it efficiently, no matter the data size. Class is now in session!
- Chapter 10, *Database operations*, teaches us how to represent, access, and manipulate data from the database in a way that offers added flexibility, and—you guessed it!—less complexity.
- Chapter 11, *Web services*, lets us discover the simplicity of communicating with web services. We'll learn what Joe means when he says, "We should build the insides of our systems like we build the outsides."

Part 3, *Maintainability*, levels up to the DOP techniques of advanced data validation, polymorphism, eloquent code, and debugging techniques, which are vital when you're working in a team. Welcome to the team!

- Chapter 12, *Advanced data validation*, allows us to discover the shape of things to come. Here, you'll learn how to validate data when it flows inside the system, allowing you to ease development by defining the expected shape of function arguments and return values.
- Chapter 13, *Polymorphism*, takes us along with Theo and Dave for a class in the countryside—a fitting place to play with animals and learn about polymorphism without objects via multimethods.
- Chapter 14, *Advanced data manipulation*, lets us see how Dave and Theo apply Joe's sage advice to turn tedious code into eloquent code as they create their own data manipulation tools. "Put the cart before the horse."—another gem from Joe!
- Chapter 15, *Debugging*, takes Dave and Theo to the museum for one last "hurrah" as they create an innovative solution for reproducing and fixing bugs.

This book also has four appendices:

- Appendix A, *Principles of data-oriented programming*, summarizes each of the four DOP principles that are covered in detail in part 1 and illustrates how each principle can be applied to both FP and OOP languages. It also describes the benefits of each principle and the costs of adherence to each.
- Appendix B, *Generic data access in statically-typed languages*, presents various ways to provide generic data access in statically-typed programming languages like Java and C#.
- Appendix C, *Data-oriented programming: A link in the chain of programming paradigms*, explores the ideas and trends that have inspired DOP. We look at the discoveries that make it applicable in production systems at scale.
- Appendix D, *Lodash reference*, summarizes the Lodash functions that we use throughout the book to illustrate how to manipulate data with generic functions without mutating it.

About the code

Most of the code snippets in this book are in JavaScript. We chose JavaScript for two reasons:

- JavaScript supports both functional programming and object-oriented programming styles.
- The syntax of JavaScript is easy to read in the sense that, even if you are not familiar with JavaScript, you can read a piece of JavaScript code at a high level as though it were pseudocode.

To make it easy for readers from any programming language to read the code snippets, we have limited ourselves to basic JavaScript syntax and have avoided the use of advanced language features like arrow functions and async notation. Where there was a conceptual challenge in applying an idea to a statically-typed language, we have added code snippets in Java.

Code appears throughout the text and as separate code snippets in a `fixed-width font like this`. In many cases, the original source code has been reformatted. We've added line breaks and reworked indentation to accommodate the available page space in the book. Code annotations also accompany some of the listings, highlighting important concepts.

You can get executable snippets of code from the liveBook (online) version of this book at https://livebook.manning.com/book/data-oriented-programming, or from the book's Github link here: https://github.com/viebel/data-oriented-programming.

liveBook discussion forum

Purchase of *Data-Oriented Programming* includes free access to liveBook, Manning's online reading platform. Using liveBook's exclusive discussion features, you can attach comments to the book globally or to specific sections or paragraphs. It's a snap to make notes for yourself, ask and answer technical questions, and receive help from the author and other users. To access the forum, go to https://livebook.manning.com/book/data-oriented-programming/discussion. You can also learn more about Manning's forums and the rules of conduct at https://livebook.manning.com/discussion.

Manning's commitment to our readers is to provide a venue where a meaningful dialogue between individual readers and between readers and the author can take place. It is not a commitment to any specific amount of participation on the part of the author, whose contribution to the forum remains voluntary (and unpaid). We suggest you try asking the author some challenging questions lest his interest stray! The forum and the archives of previous discussions will be accessible from the publisher's website as long as the book is in print.

about the author

YEHONATHAN SHARVIT has over 20 years of experience as a software engineer, programming with C++, Java, Ruby, JavaScript, Clojure, and ClojureScript, both in the backend and the frontend. At the time of writing this book, he works as a software architect at Cycognito, building software infrastructures for high-scale data pipelines. He shares his passion about programming on his blog (https://blog.klipse.tech/) and at tech conferences. You can follow him on Twitter (https://twitter.com/viebel).

about the cover illustration

The figure on the cover of *Data-Oriented Programming* is "Fille de l'Isle Santorin," or "Girl from the island of Santorini," taken from a collection by Jacques Grasset de Saint-Sauveur, published in 1797. Each illustration is finely drawn and colored by hand.

In those days, it was easy to identify where people lived and what their trade or station in life was just by their dress. Manning celebrates the inventiveness and initiative of the computer business with book covers based on the rich diversity of regional culture centuries ago, brought back to life by pictures from collections such as this one.

dramatis personae

THEO, *senior developer*

NANCY, *entrepreneur*

MONICA, *manager, Theo's boss*

DAVE, *junior developer, Theo's colleague*

JOE, *independent programmer*

KAY, *therapist, Joe's wife*

JANE, *Theo's wife*

NERIAH, *Joe's son*

AURELIA, *Joe's daughter*

The story takes place in San Francisco.

Part 1

Flexibility

It's Monday morning. Theodore is sitting with Nancy on the terrace of La Vita è Bella, an Italian coffee shop near the San Francisco Zoo. Nancy is an entrepreneur looking for a development agency for her startup company, Klafim. Theo works for Albatross, a software development agency that seeks to regain the trust of startups.

Nancy and her business partner have raised seed money for Klafim, a social network for books. Klafim's unique value proposition is to combine the online world with the physical world by allowing users to borrow books from local libraries and then to meet online to discuss the books. Most parts of the product rely on the integration of already existing online services. The only piece that requires software development is what Nancy calls a Global Library Management System. Their discussion is momentarily interrupted by the waiter who brings Theo his tight espresso and Nancy her Americano with milk on the side.

Theo In your mind, what's a Global Library Management System?

Nancy It's a software system that handles the basic housekeeping functions of a library, mainly around the book catalog and the library members.

Theo Could you be a little bit more specific?

Nancy Sure. For the moment, we need a quick prototype. If the market response to Klafim is positive, we will move forward with a big project.

Theo What features do you need for the prototype phase?

Nancy grabs the napkin under her coffee mug and writes down a couple of bulleted points on the napkin.

The requirements for the Klafim prototype

- Two kinds of library users are members and librarians.
- Users log in to the system via email and password.
- Members can borrow books.
- Members and librarians can search books by title or by author.
- Librarians can block and unblock members (e.g., when they are late in returning a book).
- Librarians can list the books currently lent to a member.
- There could be several copies of a book.
- The book belongs to a physical library.

Theo Well, that's pretty clear.

Nancy How much time would it take for your company to deliver the prototype?

Theo I think we should be able to deliver within a month. Let's say Wednesday the 30th.

Nancy That's too long. We need it in two weeks!

Theo That's tough! Can you cut a feature or two?

Nancy Unfortunately, we cannot cut any feature, but if you like, you can make the search very basic.

(Theo really doesn't want to lose this contract, so he's willing to work hard and sleep later.)

Theo I think it should be doable by Wednesday the 16th.

Nancy Perfect!

1 Complexity of object-oriented programming

A capricious entrepreneur

This chapter covers

- The tendency of OOP to increase system complexity
- What makes OOP systems hard to understand
- The cost of mixing code and data together into objects

In this chapter, we'll explore why *object-oriented programming* (OOP) systems tend to be complex. This complexity is not related to the syntax or the semantics of a specific OOP language. It is something that is inherent to OOP's fundamental insight—programs should be composed from objects, which consist of some state, together with methods for accessing and manipulating that state.

Over the years, OOP ecosystems have alleviated this complexity by adding new features to the language (e.g., anonymous classes and anonymous functions) and by developing frameworks that hide some of this complexity, providing a simpler interface for developers (e.g., Spring and Jackson in Java). Internally, the frameworks rely on the advanced features of the language such as reflection and custom annotations.

This chapter is not meant to be read as a critical analysis of OOP. Its purpose is to raise your awareness of the tendency towards OOP's increased complexity as a programming paradigm. Hopefully, it will motivate you to discover a different programming paradigm, where system complexity tends to be reduced. This paradigm is known as *data-oriented programming* (DOP).

1.1 OOP design: Classic or classical?

▶ **NOTE** Theo, Nancy, and their new project were introduced in the opener for part 1. Take a moment to read the opener if you missed it.

Theo gets back to the office with Nancy's napkin in his pocket and a lot of anxiety in his heart because he knows he has committed to a tough deadline. But he had no choice! Last week, Monica, his boss, told him quite clearly that he had to close the deal with Nancy no matter what.

Albatross, where Theo works, is a software consulting company with customers all over the world. It originally had lots of customers among startups. Over the last year, however, many projects were badly managed, and the Startup department lost the trust of its customers. That's why management moved Theo from the Enterprise department to the Startup department as a Senior Tech lead. His job is to close deals and to deliver on time.

1.1.1 The design phase

Before rushing to his laptop to code the system, Theo grabs a sheet of paper, much bigger than a napkin, and starts to draw a UML class diagram of the system that will implement the Klafim prototype. Theo is an object-oriented programmer. For him, there is no question—every business entity is represented by an object, and every object is made from a class.

The requirements for the Klafim prototype

- There are two kinds of users: library members and librarians.
- Users log in to the system via email and password.
- Members can borrow books.
- Members and librarians can search books by title or by author.
- Librarians can block and unblock members (e.g., when they are late in returning a book).
- Librarians can list the books currently lent to a member.
- There can be several copies of a book.
- A book belongs to a physical library.

Theo spends some time thinking about the organization of the system. He identifies the main classes for the Klafim Global Library Management System.

The main classes of the library management system

- `Library`—The central part of the system design.
- `Book`—A book.
- `BookItem`—A book can have multiple copies, and each copy is considered as a book item.
- `BookLending`—When a book is lent, a book lending object is created.
- `Member`—A member of the library.
- `Librarian`—A librarian.
- `User`—A base class for `Librarian` and `Member`.
- `Catalog`—Contains a list of books.
- `Author`—A book author.

That was the easy part. Now comes the difficult part: the relations between the classes. After two hours or so, Theo comes up with a first draft of a design for the Global Library Management System. It looks like the diagram in figure 1.1.

▶ **NOTE** The design presented here doesn't pretend to be the smartest OOP design: experienced OOP developers would probably use a couple of design patterns to suggest a much better design. This design is meant to be naive and by no means covers all the features of the system. It serves two purposes:

- For Theo, *the developer*, it is rich enough to start coding.
- For me, *the author of the book*, it is rich enough to illustrate the complexity of a typical OOP system.

Theo feels proud of himself and of the design diagram he just produced. He definitely deserves a cup of coffee!

Near the coffee machine, Theo meets Dave, a junior software developer who joined Albatross a couple of weeks ago. Theo and Dave appreciate each other, as Dave's curiosity leads him to ask challenging questions. Meetings near the coffee machine often turn into interesting discussions about programming.

Theo Hey Dave! How's it going?

Dave Today? Not great. I'm trying to fix a bug in my code! I can't understand why the state of my objects always changes. I'll figure it out though, I'm sure. How's your day going?

Theo I just finished the design of a system for a new customer.

Dave Cool! Would it be OK for me to see it? I'm trying to improve my design skills.

Theo Sure! I have the diagram on my desk. We can take a look now if you like.

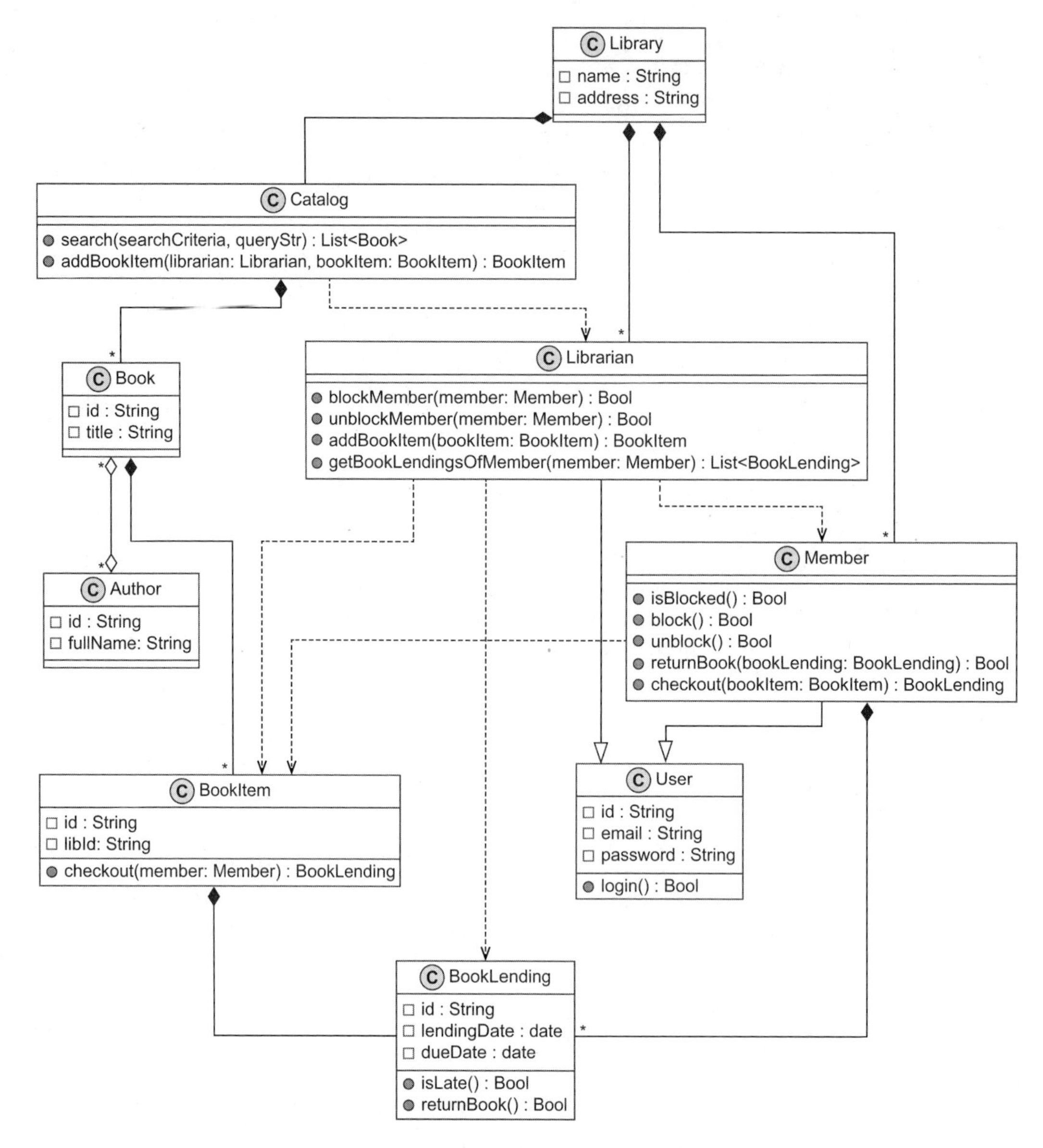

Figure 1.1 A class diagram for Klafim's Global Library Management System

1.1.2 UML 101

Latte in hand, Dave follows Theo to his desk. Theo proudly shows Dave his piece of art: the UML diagram for the Library Management System (figure 1.1). Dave seems really excited.

Dave Wow! Such a detailed class diagram.

Theo Yeah. I'm pretty happy with it.

Dave The thing is that I can never remember the meaning of the different arrows.

Theo There are four types of arrows in my class diagram: *composition*, *association*, *inheritance*, and *usage*.

Dave What's the difference between composition and association?

▶ **NOTE** Don't worry if you're not familiar with OOP jargon. We're going to leave it aside in the next chapter.

Theo It's all about whether the objects can live without each other. With composition, when one object dies, the other one dies too. While in an association relation, each object has an independent life.

TIP In a composition relation, when one object dies, the other one also dies. While in an association relation, each object has an independent life cycle.

In the class diagram, there are two kinds of composition symbolized by an arrow with a plain diamond at one edge and an optional star at the other edge. Figure 1.2 shows the relation between:

- A `Library` that owns a `Catalog`—A one-to-one composition. If a `Library` object dies, then its `Catalog` object dies with it.
- A `Library` that owns many `Members`—A one-to-many composition. If a `Library` object dies, then all its `Member` objects die with it.

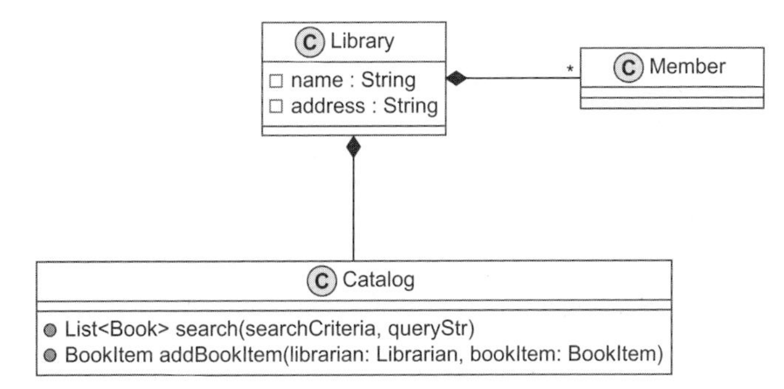

Figure 1.2 The two kinds of composition: one-to-one and one-to-many. In both cases, when an object dies, the composed object dies with it.

TIP A composition relation is represented by a plain diamond at one edge and an optional star at the other edge.

Dave Do you have association relations in your diagram?

Theo Take a look at the arrow between `Book` and `Author`. It has an empty diamond and a star at both edges, so it's a many-to-many association relation.

A book can be written by multiple authors, and an author can write multiple books. Moreover, `Book` and `Author` objects can live independently. The relation between books and authors is a many-to-many association (figure 1.3).

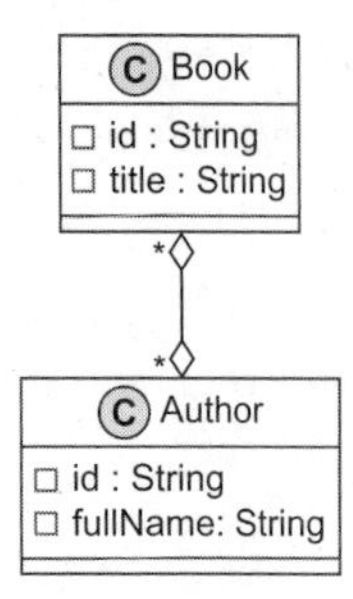

Figure 1.3 Many-to-many association relation: each object lives independently.

TIP A *many-to-many* association relation is represented by an empty diamond and a star at both edges.

Dave I also see a bunch of dashed arrows in your diagram.

Theo Dashed arrows are for usage relations: when a class uses a method of another class. Consider, for example, the `Librarian::blockMember` method. It calls `Member::block`.

TIP Dashed arrows indicate *usage* relations (figure 1.4), for instance, when a class uses a method of another class.

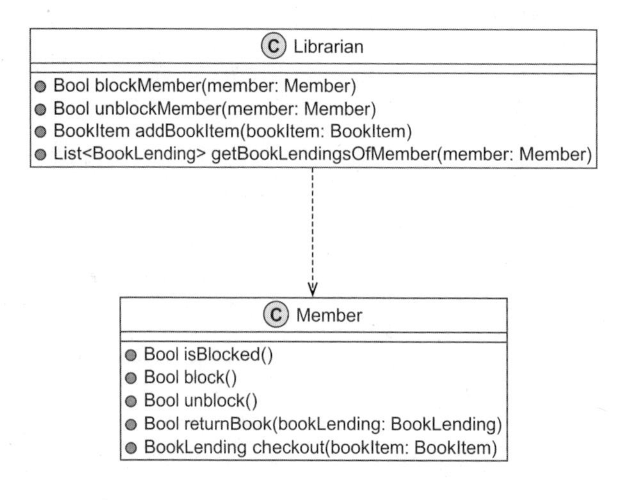

Figure 1.4 Usage relation: a class uses a method of another class.

Dave I see. And I guess a plain arrow with an empty triangle, like the one between `Member` and `User`, represents inheritance.

Theo Absolutely!

TIP Plain arrows with empty triangles represent *class inheritance* (figure 1.5), where the arrow points towards the superclass.

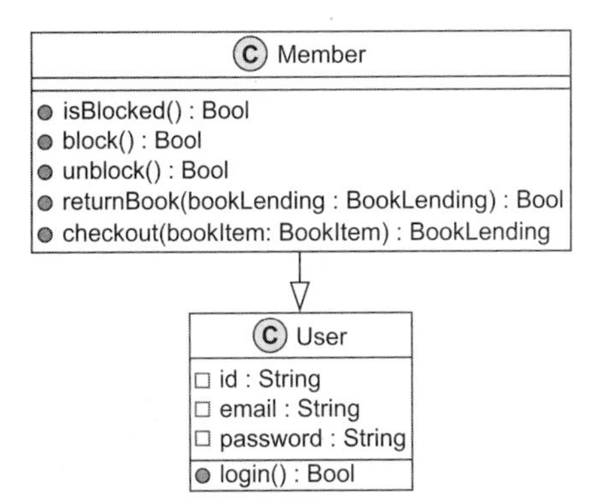

Figure 1.5 Inheritance relation: a class derives from another class.

1.1.3 *Explaining each piece of the class diagram*

Dave Thanks for the UML refresher! Now I think I can remember what the different arrows mean.

Theo My pleasure. Want to see how it all fits together?

Dave What class should we look at first?

Theo I think we should start with `Library`.

THE LIBRARY CLASS

The `Library` is the root class of the library system. Figure 1.6 shows the system structure.

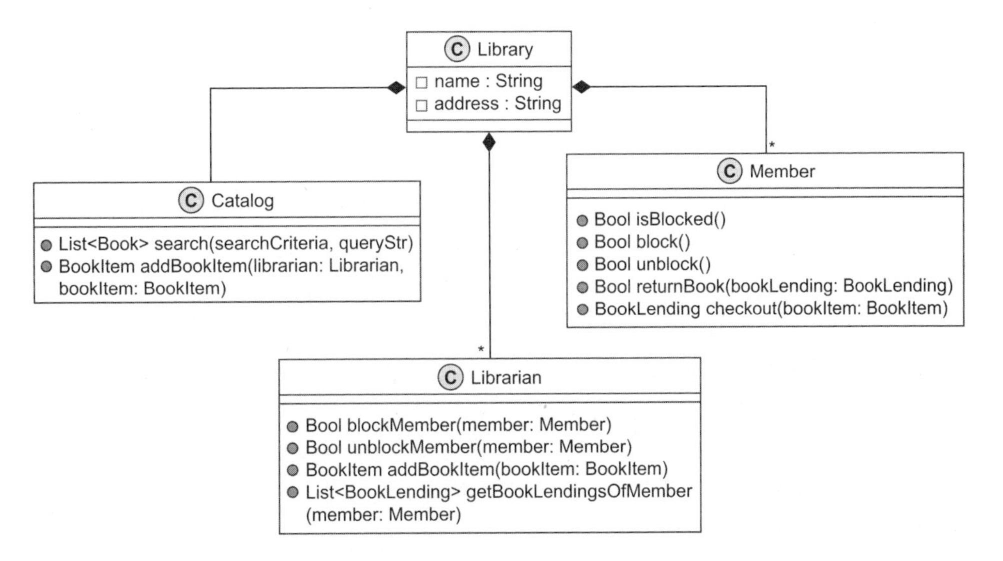

Figure 1.6 The `Library` class

In terms of code (behavior), a `Library` object does nothing on its own. It delegates everything to the objects it owns. In terms of data, a `Library` object owns

- Multiple `Member` objects
- Multiple `Librarian` objects
- A single `Catalog` object

▶ **NOTE** In this book, we use the terms *code* and *behavior* interchangeably.

LIBRARIAN, MEMBER, AND USER CLASSES

`Librarian` and `Member` both derive from `User`. Figure 1.7 shows this relation.

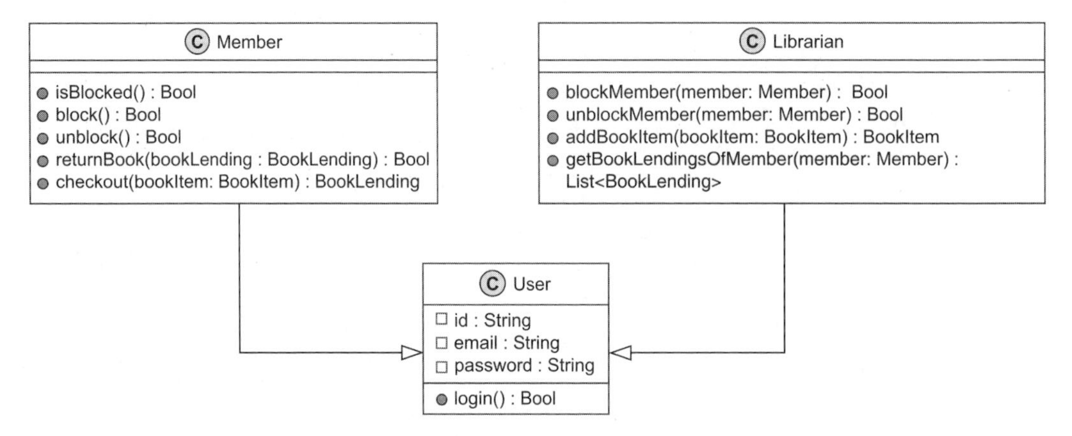

Figure 1.7 **`Librarian` and `Member` derive from `User`.**

The `User` class represents a user of the library:

- In terms of data members, it sticks to the bare minimum: it has an `id`, `email`, and `password` (with no security and encryption for now).
- In terms of code, it can log in via `login`.

The `Member` class represents a member of the library:

- It inherits from `User`.
- In terms of data members, it has nothing more than `User`.
- In terms of code, it can
  - Check out a book via `checkout`.
  - Return a book via `returnBook`.
  - Block itself via `block`.
  - Unblock itself via `unblock`.
  - Answer if it is blocked via `isBlocked`.
- It owns multiple `BookLending` objects.
- It uses `BookItem` in order to implement `checkout`.

The Librarian class represents a librarian:

- It derives from User.
- In terms of data members, it has nothing more than User.
- In terms of code, it can
  - Block and unblock a Member.
  - List the member's book lendings via getBookLendings.
  - Add book items to the library via addBookItem.
- It uses Member to implement blockMember, unblockMember, and getBookLendings.
- It uses BookItem to implement checkout.
- It uses BookLending to implement getBookLendings.

The Catalog class

The Catalog class is responsible for the management of the books. Figure 1.8 shows the relation among the Catalog, Librarian, and Book classes. In terms of code, a Catalog object can

- Search books via search.
- Add book items to the library via addBookItem.

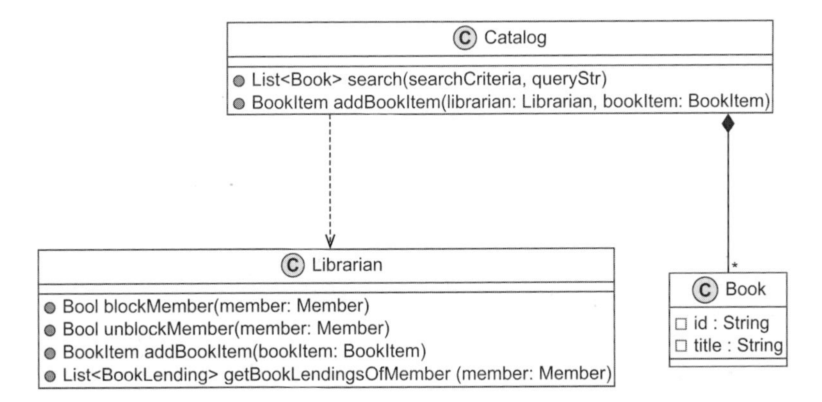

Figure 1.8 The Catalog class

A Catalog object uses Librarian in order to implement addBookItem. In terms of data, a Catalog owns multiple Book objects.

The Book class

Figure 1.9 presents the Book class. In terms of data, a Book object

- Should have as its bare minimum an id and a title.
- Is associated with multiple Author objects (a book might have multiple authors).
- Owns multiple BookItem objects, one for each copy of the book.

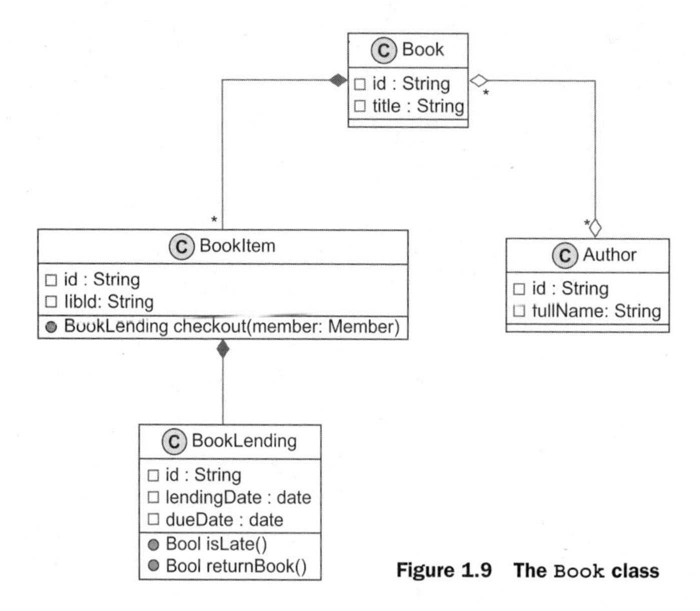

Figure 1.9 The `Book` class

The BookItem class

The `BookItem` class represents a book copy, and a book could have many copies. In terms of data, a `BookItem` object

- Should have as its bare minimum data for members: an `id` and a `libId` (for its physical library ID).
- Owns multiple `BookLending` objects, one for each time the book is lent.

In terms of code, a `BookItem` object can be checked out via `checkout`.

1.1.4 *The implementation phase*

After this detailed investigation of Theo's diagrams, Dave lets it sink in as he slowly sips his coffee. He then expresses his admiration to Theo.

Dave Wow! That's amazing!

Theo Thank you.

Dave I didn't realize people were really spending the time to write down their design in such detail before coding.

Theo I always do that. It saves me lot of time during the coding phase.

Dave When will you start coding?

Theo When I finish my latte.

Theo grabs his coffee mug and notices that his hot latte has become an iced latte. He was so excited to show his class diagram to Dave that he forgot to drink it!

1.2 Sources of complexity

While Theo is getting himself another cup of coffee (a cappuccino this time), I would like to challenge his design. It might look beautiful and clear on the paper, but I claim that this design makes the system hard to understand. It's not that Theo picked the wrong classes or that he misunderstood the relations among the classes. It goes much deeper:

- It's about the programming paradigm he chose to implement the system.
- It's about the object-oriented paradigm.
- It's about the tendency of OOP to increase the complexity of a system.

TIP OOP has a tendency to create complex systems.

Throughout this book, the type of *complexity* I refer to is that which makes systems hard to understand as defined in the paper, "Out of the Tar Pit," by Ben Moseley and Peter Marks (2006), available at http://mng.bz/enzq. It has nothing to do with the type of complexity that deals with the amount of resources consumed by a program. Similarly, when I refer to *simplicity*, I mean not complex (in other words, easy to understand).

Keep in mind that complexity and simplicity (like hard and easy) are not absolute but relative concepts. We can compare the complexity of two systems and determine whether system *A* is more complex (or simpler) than system *B*.

▶ **NOTE** Complexity in the context of this book means *hard to understand.*

As mentioned in the introduction of this chapter, there are many ways in OOP to alleviate complexity. The purpose of this book is not be critical of OOP, but rather to present a programming paradigm called *data-oriented programming* (DOP) that tends to build systems that are less complex. In fact, the DOP paradigm is compatible with OOP.

If one chooses to build an OOP system that adheres to DOP principles, the system will be less complex. According to DOP, the main sources of complexity in Theo's system (and of many traditional OOP systems) are that

- Code and data are mixed.
- Objects are mutable.
- Data is locked in objects as members.
- Code is locked into classes as methods.

This analysis is similar to what functional programming (FP) thinks about traditional OOP. However, as we will see throughout the book, the data approach that DOP takes in order to reduce system complexity differs from the FP approach. In appendix A, we illustrate how to apply DOP principles both in OOP and in FP styles.

TIP DOP is compatible both with OOP and FP.

In the remaining sections of this chapter, we will illustrate each of the previous aspects, summarized in table 1.1. We'll look at this in the context of the Klafim project and explain in what sense these aspects are a source of complexity.

Table 1.1 Aspects of OOP and their impact on system complexity

Aspect	Impact on complexity
Code and data are mixed.	Classes tend to be involved in many relations.
Objects are mutable.	Extra thinking is needed when reading code.
Objects are mutable.	Explicit synchronization is required on multi-threaded environments.
Data is locked in objects.	Data serialization is not trivial.
Code is locked in classes.	Class hierarchies are complex.

1.2.1 Many relations between classes

One way to assess the complexity of a class diagram is to look only at the entities and their relations, ignoring members and methods, as in figure 1.10. When we design a system, we have to define the relations between different pieces of code and data. That's unavoidable.

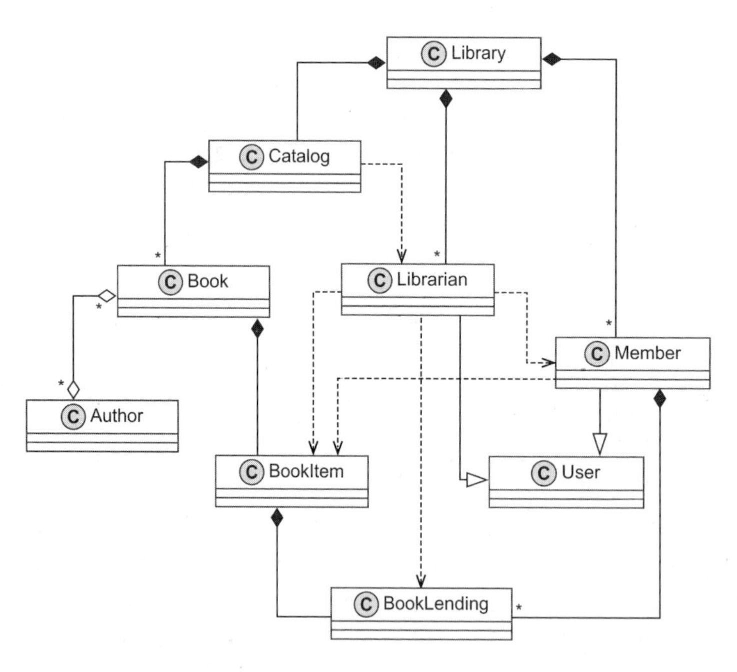

Figure 1.10 A class diagram overview for Klafim's Library Management System

TIP In OOP, code and data are mixed together in classes: data as *members* and code as *methods.*

From a system analysis perspective, the fact that code and data are mixed together makes the system complex in the sense that entities tend to be involved in many relations. In figure 1.11, we take a closer look at the Member class. Member is involved in five relations: two data relations and three code relations.

- Data relations:
  - Library has many Members.
  - Member has many BookLendings.
- Code relations:
  - Member extends User.
  - Librarian uses Member.
  - Member uses BookItem.

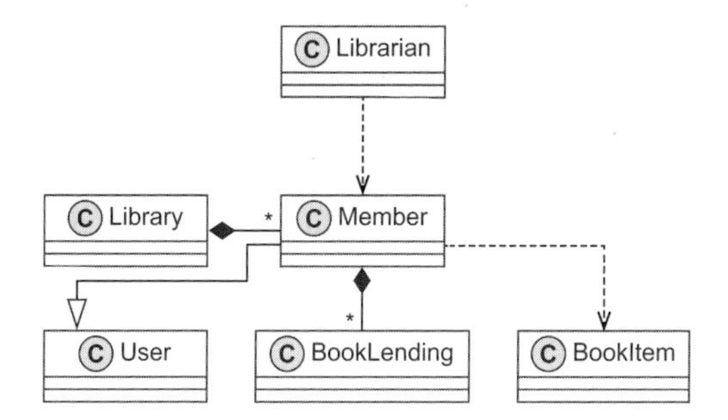

Figure 1.11 The class Member is involved in five relations.

Imagine for a moment that we were able, somehow, to split the Member class into two separate entities:

- MemberCode for the code
- MemberData for the data

Instead of a Member class with five relations, we would have the diagram shown in figure 1.12 with:

- A MemberCode entity and three relations.
- A MemberData entity and two relations.

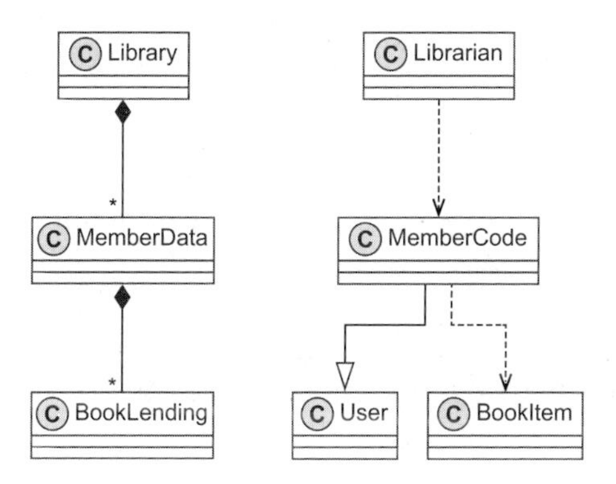

Figure 1.12 A class diagram where Member is split into code and data entities

The class diagram where `Member` is split into `MemberCode` and `MemberData` is made of two independent parts. Each part is easier to understand than the original diagram.

Let's split every class of our original class diagram into code and data entities. Figure 1.13 shows the resulting diagram. Now the system is made of two independent parts:

- A part that involves only data entities.
- A part that involves only code entities.

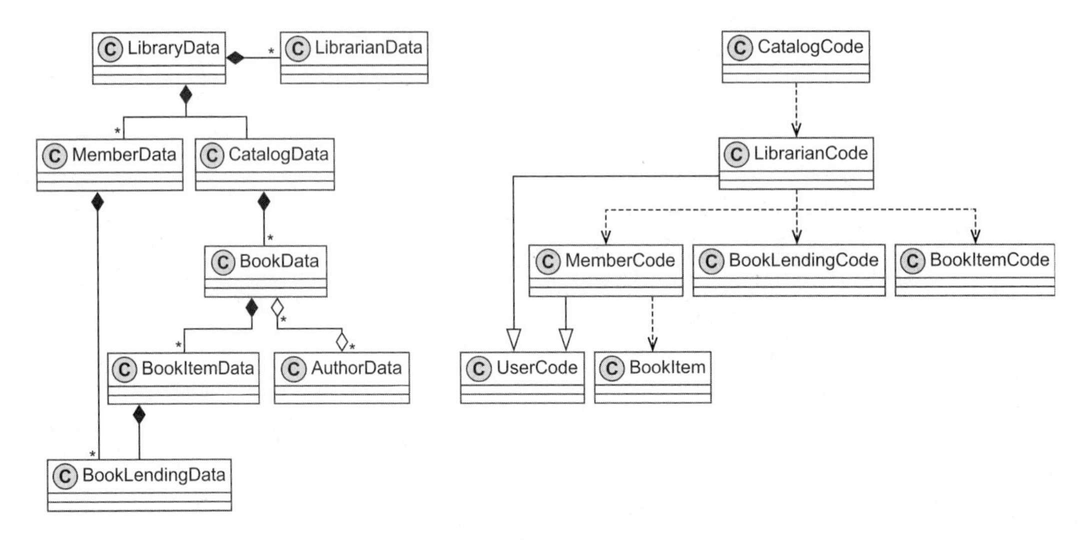

Figure 1.13 A class diagram where every class is split into code and data entities

TIP A system where every class is split into two independent parts, code and data, is simpler than a system where code and data are mixed.

The resulting system, made up of two independent subsystems, is easier to understand than the original system. The fact that the two subsystems are independent means that each subsystem can be understood separately and in any order. The resulting system not simpler by *accident*; it is a *logical consequence* of separating code from data.

TIP A system made of multiple simple independent parts is less complex than a system made of a single complex part.

1.2.2 Unpredictable code behavior

You might be a bit tired after the system-level analysis that we presented in the previous section. Let's get refreshed and look at some code.

Take a look at the code in listing 1.1, where we get the blocked status of a member and display it twice. If I tell you that when I called `displayBlockedStatusTwice`, the program displayed `true` on the first `console.log` call, can you tell me what the program displayed on the second `console.log` call?

Listing 1.1 Really simple code

```
class Member {
  isBlocked;

  displayBlockedStatusTwice() {
    var isBlocked = this.isBlocked;
    console.log(isBlocked);
    console.log(isBlocked);
  }
}

member.displayBlockedStatusTwice();
```

"Of course, it displayed `true` again," you say. And you are right!

Now, take a look at a slightly different pseudocode as shown in listing 1.2. Here we display, twice, the blocked status of a member without assigning a variable. Same question as before: if I tell you that when I called `displayBlockedStatusTwice`, the program displayed `true` on the first `console.log` call, can you tell me what the program displayed on the second `console.log` call?

Listing 1.2 Apparently simple code

```
class Member {
  isBlocked;

  displayBlockedStatusTwice() {
    console.log(this.isBlocked);
    console.log(this.isBlocked);
  }
}

member.displayBlockedStatusTwice();
```

Wow

The correct answer is . . . in a single-threaded environment, it displays `true`, while in a multi-threaded environment, it's unpredictable. Indeed, in a multi-threaded environment between the two `console.log` calls, there could be a context switch that changes the state of the object (e.g., a librarian unblocked the member). In fact, with a slight modification, the same kind of code unpredictability could occur even in a single-threaded environment like JavaScript, when data is modified via asynchronous code (see the section about Principle #3 in appendix A). The difference between the two code snippets is that

- In the first listing (listing 1.1), we access a Boolean value twice, which is a primitive value.
- In the second listing (listing 1.2), we access a member of an object twice.

TIP When data is mutable, code is unpredictable.

This unpredictable behavior of the second listing is one of the annoying consequences of OOP. Unlike primitive types, which are usually immutable, object members are mutable. One way to solve this problem in OOP is to protect sensitive code with concurrency safety mechanisms like mutexes, but that introduces issues like a performance hit and a risk of deadlocks.

We will see later in the book that DOP treats every piece of data in the same way: both primitive types and collection types are immutable values. This *value treatment for all citizens* brings serenity to DOP developers' minds, and more brain cells are available to handle the interesting pieces of the applications they build.

Haha

TIP Data immutability brings serenity to DOP developers' minds.

1.2.3 Not trivial data serialization

Theo is really tired, and he falls asleep at his desk. He's having dream. In his dream, Nancy asks him to make Klafim's Library Management System accessible via a REST API using JSON as a transport layer. Theo has to implement a `/search` endpoint that receives a query in JSON format and returns the results in JSON format. Listing 1.3 shows an input example of the `/search` endpoint, and listing 1.4 shows an output example of the `/search` endpoint.

Listing 1.3 A JSON input of the `/search` endpoint

```
{
  "searchCriteria": "author",
  "query": "albert"
}
```

Listing 1.4 A JSON output of the `/search` endpoint

```
[
  {
    "title": "The world as I see it",
    "authors": [
      {
        "fullName": "Albert Einstein"
      }
    ]
  },
  {
    "title": "The Stranger",
    "authors": [
      {
        "fullName": "Albert Camus"
      }
    ]
  }
]
```

Theo would probably implement the /search endpoint by creating three classes similarly to what is shown in the following list and in figure 1.14. (Not surprisingly, everything in OOP has to be wrapped in a class. Right?)

- SearchController is responsible for handling the query.
- SearchQuery converts the JSON query string into data.
- SearchResult converts the search result data into a JSON string.

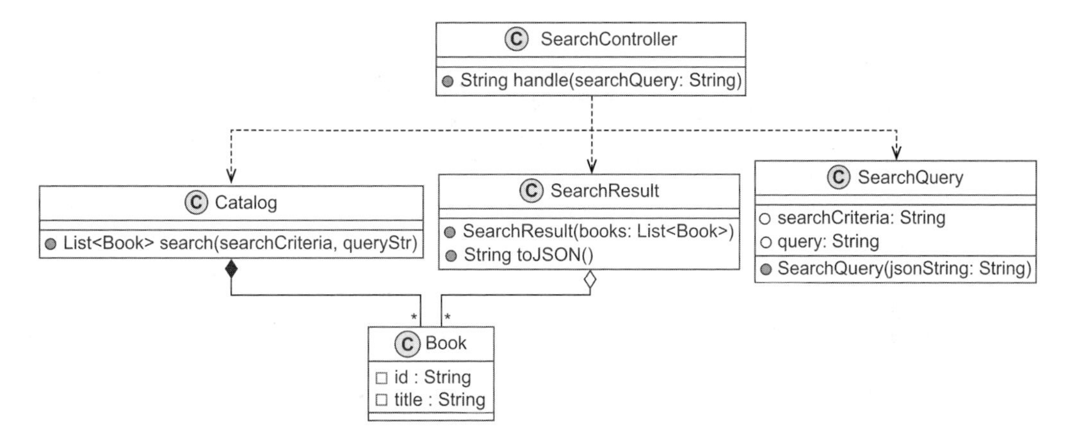

Figure 1.14 The class diagram for SearchController

The SearchController (see figure 1.14) would have a single handle method with the following flow:

- Creates a SearchQuery object from the JSON query string.
- Retrieves searchCriteria and queryStr from the SearchQuery object.
- Calls the search method of the catalog:Catalog with searchCriteria and queryStr and receives books:List<Book>.
- Creates a SearchResult object with books.
- Converts the SearchResult object to a JSON string.

What about other endpoints, for instance, those allowing librarians to add book items through /add-book-item? Theo would have to repeat the exact same process and create three classes:

- AddBookItemController to handle the query
- BookItemQuery to convert the JSON query string into data
- BookItemResult to convert the search result data into a JSON string

The code that deals with JSON deserialization that Theo wrote previously in SearchQuery would have to be rewritten in BookItemQuery. Same thing for the code that deals with JSON serialization he wrote previously in SearchResult; it would have to be rewritten in BookItemResult.

The bad news is that Theo would have to repeat the same process for every endpoint of the system. Each time he encounters a new kind of JSON input or output, he would have to create a new class and write code. Theo's dream is turning into a nightmare!

Suddenly, his phone rings, next to where he was resting his head on the desk. As Theo wakes up, he realizes that Nancy never asked for JSON. It was all a dream . . . a really bad dream!

TIP In OOP, data serialization is difficult.

It's quite frustrating that handling JSON serialization and deserialization in OOP requires the addition of so many classes and writing so much code—again and again! The frustration grows when you consider that serializing a search query, a book item query, or *any* query is quite similar. It comes down to

- Going over data fields.
- Concatenating the name of the data fields and the value of the data fields, separated by a comma.

Why is such a simple thing so hard to achieve in OOP? In OOP, data has to follow a rigid shape defined in classes, which means that data is locked in members. There is no simple way to access data generically.

TIP In OOP, data is locked in classes as members.

We will refine later what we mean by generic access to the data, and we will see how DOP provides a generic way to handle JSON serialization and deserialization. Until then, you will have to continue suffering. But at least you are starting to become aware of this suffering, and you know that it is avoidable.

▶ **NOTE** Most OOP programming languages alleviate a bit of the difficulty involved in the conversion from and to JSON. It either involves reflection, which is definitely a complex thing, or code verbosity.

1.2.4 Complex class hierarchies

One way to avoid writing the same code twice in OOP involves class inheritance. Indeed, when every requirement of the system is known up front, you design your class hierarchy is such a way that classes with common behavior derive from a base class.

Figure 1.15 shows an example of this pattern that focuses on the part of our class diagram that deals with members and librarians. Both `Librarians` and `Members` need the ability to log in, and they inherit this ability from the `User` class.

So far, so good, but when new requirements are introduced after the system is implemented, it's a completely different story. Fast forward to Monday, March 29th, at 11:00 AM, where two days are left before the deadline (Wednesday at midnight).

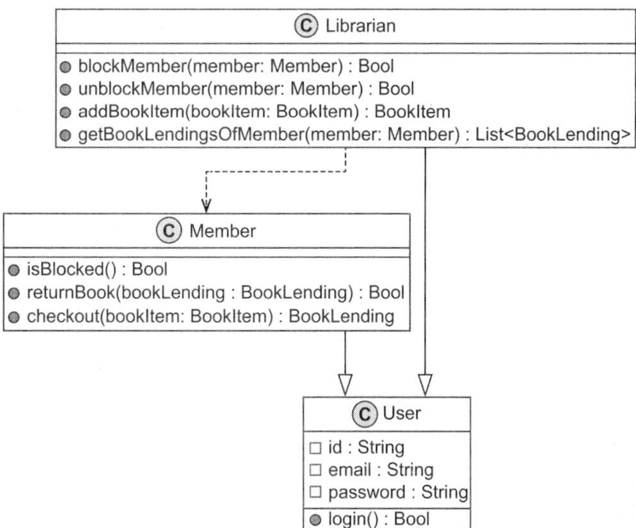

Figure 1.15 The part of the class diagram that deals with members and librarians

Nancy calls Theo with an urgent request. Theo is not sure if it's a dream or reality. He pinches himself and he can feel the jolt. It's definitely reality!

Nancy How is the project doing?

Theo Fine, Nancy. We're on schedule to meet the deadline. We're running our last round of regression tests now.

Nancy Fantastic! It means we have time for adding a tiny feature to the system, right?

Theo Depends what you mean by "tiny."

Nancy We need to add VIP members to the system.

Theo What do you mean by VIP members?

Nancy VIP members are allowed to add book items to the library by themselves.

Theo Hmm . . .

Nancy What?

Theo That's not a tiny change!

Nancy Why?

I'll ask you the same question Nancy asked Theo: why is adding VIP members to our system not a tiny task? After all, Theo has already written the code that allows librarians to add book items to the library (it's in `Librarian::addBookItem`). What prevents him from reusing this code for VIP members? The reason is that, in OOP, the code is locked into classes as methods.

TIP In OOP, code is locked into classes.

VIP members are members that are allowed to add book items to the library by themselves. Theo decomposes the customer requirements into two pieces:

- VIP members are library members.
- VIP members are allowed to add book items to the library by themselves.

Theo then decides that he needs a new class, `VIPMember`. For the first requirement (VIP members are library members), it seems reasonable to make `VIPMember` derive from `Member`. However, handling the second requirement (VIP members are allowed to add book items) is more complex. He cannot make a `VIPMember` derive from `Librarian` because the relation between `VIPMember` and `Librarian` is not linear:

- On one hand, VIP members are like librarians in that they are allowed to add book items.
- On the other hand, VIP members are *not* like librarians in that they are not allowed to block members or list the books lent to a member.

The problem is that the code that adds book items is locked in the `Librarian` class. There is no way for the `VIPMember` class to use this code.

Figure 1.16 shows one possible solution that makes the code of `Librarian::addBookItem` available to both `Librarian` and `VIPMember` classes. Here are the changes to the previous class diagram:

- A base class `UserWithBookItemRight` extends `User`.
- `addBookItem` moves from `Librarian` to `UserWithBookItemRight`.
- Both `VIPMember` and `Librarian` extend `UserWithBookItemRight`.

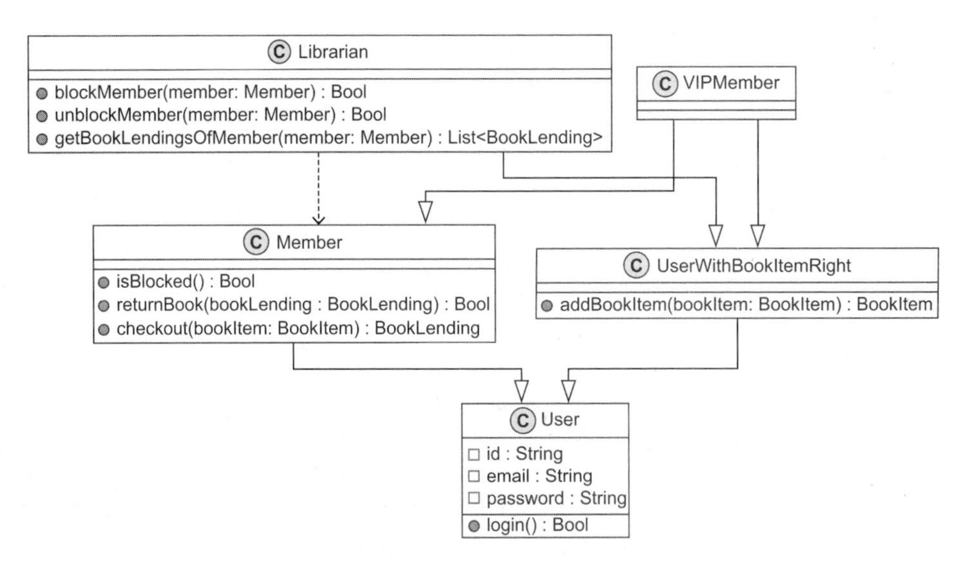

Figure 1.16 A class diagram for a system with VIP members

It wasn't easy, but Theo manages to handle the change on time, thanks to an all nighter coding on his laptop. He was even able to add new tests to the system and run the regression tests again. However, he was so excited that he didn't pay attention to the diamond problem `VIPMember` introduced in his class diagram due to multiple inheritance: `VIPMember` extends both `Member` and `UserWithBookItemRight`, which both extend `User`.

Wednesday, March 31, at 10:00 AM (14 hours before the deadline), Theo calls Nancy to tell her the good news.

Theo We were able to add VIP members to the system on time, Nancy.

Nancy Fantastic! I told you it was a tiny feature.

Theo Yeah, well . . .

Nancy Look, I was going to call you anyway. I just finished a meeting with my business partner, and we realized that we need another tiny feature before the launch. Will you be able to handle it before the deadline?

Theo Again, it depends what you mean by "tiny."

Nancy We need to add Super members to the system.

Theo What do you mean by Super members?

Nancy Super members are allowed to list the books lent to other members.

Theo Err . . .

Nancy What?

Theo That's not a tiny change!

Nancy Why?

As with VIP members, adding Super members to the system requires changes to Theo's class hierarchy. Figure 1.17 shows the solution Theo has in mind.

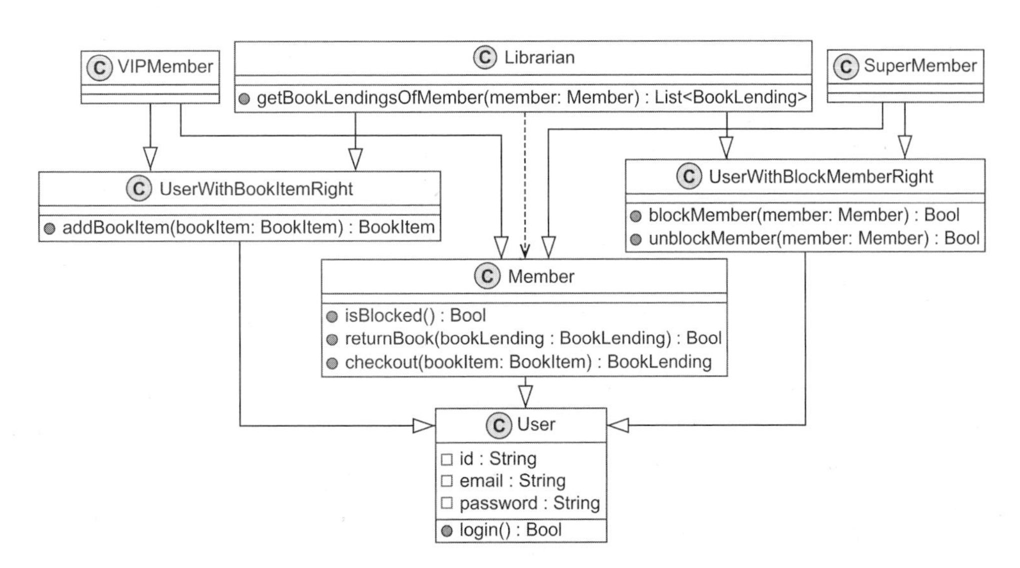

Figure 1.17 A class diagram for a system with Super and VIP members

The addition of Super members has made the system really complex. Theo suddenly notices that he has three diamonds in his class diagram—not gemstones but three "Deadly

Diamonds of Death" as OOP developers sometimes name the ambiguity that arises when a class *D* inherits from two classes *B* and *C*, where both inherit from class *A*!

He tries to avoid the diamonds by transforming the `User` class into an interface and using the composition over inheritance design pattern. But with the stress of the deadline looming, he isn't able to use all of his brain cells. In fact, the system has become so complex, he's unable to deliver the system by the deadline. Theo tells himself that he should have used composition instead of class inheritance. But, it's too late now.

TIP In OOP, prefer composition over class inheritance.

At 10:00 PM, two hours before the deadline, Theo calls Nancy to explain the situation.

Theo Look Nancy, we really did our best, but we won't be able to add Super members to the system before the deadline.

Nancy No worries, my business partner and I decided to omit this feature for now. We'll add it later.

With mixed feelings of anger and relief, Theo stops pacing around his office. He realizes he will be spending tonight in his own bed, rather than plowing away on his computer at the office. That should make his wife happy.

Theo I guess that means we're ready for the launch tomorrow morning.

Nancy Yes. We'll offer this new product for a month or so, and if we get good market traction, we'll move forward with a bigger project.

Theo Cool. Let's be in touch in a month then. Good luck on the launch!

Summary

- Complexity in the context of this book means *hard to understand*.
- We use the terms *code* and *behavior* interchangeably.
- DOP stands for data-oriented programming.
- OOP stands for object-oriented programming.
- FP stands for functional programming.
- In a *composition relation*, when one object dies, the other one also dies.
- A composition relation is represented by a plain diamond at one edge and an optional star at the other edge.
- In an *association relation*, each object has an independent life cycle.
- A *many-to-many association relation* is represented by an empty diamond and a star at both edges.
- Dashed arrows indicate a *usage relation*; for instance, when a class uses a method of another class.
- Plain arrows with empty triangles represent *class inheritance*, where the arrow points towards the superclass.
- The design presented in this chapter doesn't pretend to be the smartest OOP design. Experienced OOP developers would probably use a couple of design patterns and suggest a much better diagram.

- Traditional OOP systems tend to increase system complexity, in the sense that OOP systems are hard to understand.
- In traditional OOP, code and data are mixed together in classes: data as members and code as methods.
- In traditional OOP, data is mutable.
- The root cause of the increase in complexity is related to the mixing of code and data together into objects.
- When code and data are mixed, classes tend to be involved in many relations.
- When objects are mutable, extra thinking is required in order to understand how the code behaves.
- When objects are mutable, explicit synchronization mechanisms are required on multi-threaded environments.
- When data is locked in objects, data *serialization* is not trivial.
- When code is locked in classes, class hierarchies tend to be complex.
- A system where every class is split into two independent parts, code and data, is simpler than a system where code and data are mixed.
- A system made of multiple simple independent parts is less complex than a system made of a single complex part.
- When data is mutable, code is unpredictable.
- A strategic use of design patterns can help mitigate complexity in traditional OOP to some degree.
- Data immutability brings serenity to DOP developers' minds.
- Most OOP programming languages alleviate slightly the difficulty involved the conversion from and to JSON. It either involves *reflection*, which is definitely a complex thing, or code verbosity.
- In traditional OOP, data *serialization* is difficult.
- In traditional OOP, data is locked in classes as members.
- In traditional OOP, code is locked into classes.
- DOP reduces complexity by rethinking data.
- DOP is compatible both with OOP and FP.

Separation between code and data

A whole new world

2

This chapter covers

- The benefits of separating code from data
- Designing a system where code and data are separate
- Implementing a system that respects the separation between code and data

The first insight of DOP is that we can decrease the complexity of our systems by separating code from data. Indeed, when code is separated from data, our systems are made of two main pieces that can be thought about separately: data entities and code modules. This chapter is a deep dive in the first principle of DOP (summarized in figure 2.1).

PRINCIPLE #1 Separate code from data such that the code resides in functions, whose behavior doesn't depend on data that is somehow encapsulated in the function's context.

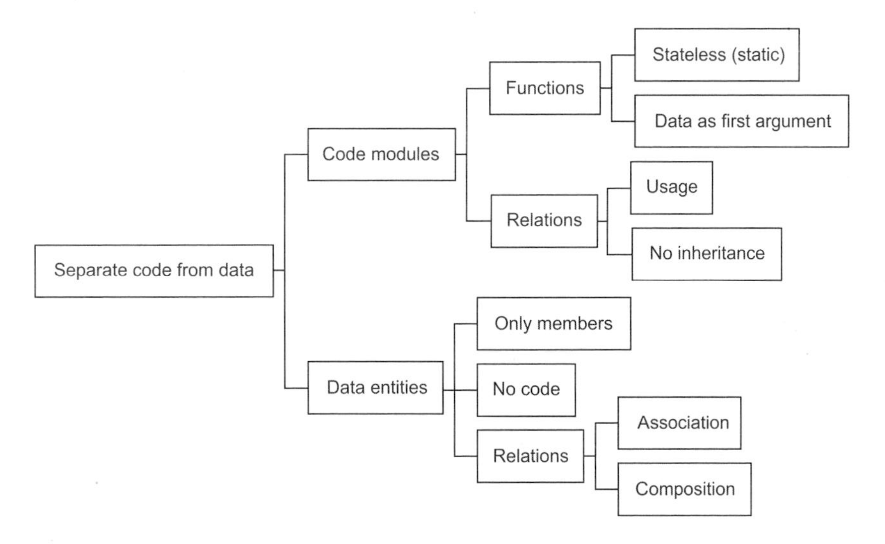

Figure 2.1 DOP principle #1 summarized: Separate code from data.

In this chapter, we'll illustrate the separation between code and data in the context of Klafim's Library Management System that we introduced in chapter 1. We'll also unveil the benefits that this separation brings to the system:

- *The system is simple.* It is easy to understand.
- *The system is flexible and extensible.* Quite often, it requires no design changes to adapt to changing requirements.

This chapter focuses on the design of the code in a system where code and data are separate. In the next chapter, we'll focus on the design of the data. As we progress in the book, we'll discover other benefits of separating code from data.

2.1 The two parts of a DOP system

While Theo is driving home after delivering the prototype, he asks himself whether the Klafim project was a success or not. Sure, he was able to satisfy the customer, but it was more luck than brains. He wouldn't have made it on time if Nancy had decided to keep the Super members feature. Why was it so complicated to add tiny features to the system? Why was the system he built so complex? He thought there should be a way to build more flexible systems!

The next morning, Theo asks on Hacker News and on Reddit for ways to reduce system complexity and build flexible systems. Some folks mention using different programming languages, while others talk about advanced design patterns. Finally, Theo's attention gets captured by a comment from a user named Joe. He mentions *data-oriented programming* and claims that its main goal is to reduce system complexity. Theo has never heard this term before. Out of curiosity, he decides to contact Joe by email. What a coincidence! Joe lives in San Francisco too. Theo invites him to a meeting in his office.

Joe is a 40-year-old developer. He was a Java developer for nearly a decade before adopting Clojure around 7 years ago. When Theo tells Joe about the Library Management System he designed and built, and about his struggles to adapt to changing requirements, Joe is not surprised.

Joe tells Theo that the systems that he and his team have built in Clojure over the last 7 years are less complex and more flexible than the systems he used to build in Java. According to Joe, the systems they build now tend to be much simpler because they follow the principles of DOP.

Theo I've never heard of data-oriented programming. Is it a new concept?

Joe Yes and no. Most of the foundational ideas of data-oriented programming, or DOP as we like to call it, are well known to programmers as best practices. The novelty of DOP, however, is that it combines best practices into a cohesive whole.

Theo That's a bit abstract for me. Can you give me an example?

Joe Sure! Take, for instance, the first insight of DOP. It's about the relations between code and data.

Theo You mean the encapsulation of data in objects?

Joe Actually, DOP is against data encapsulation.

Theo Why is that? I thought data encapsulation was a positive programming paradigm.

Joe Data encapsulation has both merits and drawbacks. Think about the way you designed the Library Management System. According to DOP, the main cause of complexity and inflexibility in systems is that code and data are mixed together in objects.

TIP DOP is *against* data encapsulation.

Theo It sounds similar to what I've heard about functional programming. So, if I want to adopt DOP, do I need to get rid of object-oriented programming and learn functional programming?

Joe No, DOP principles are language-agnostic. They can be applied in both object-oriented and functional programming languages.

Theo That's a relief! I was afraid that you were going to teach me about monads, algebraic data types, and higher order functions.

Joe No, none of that is required in DOP.

TIP DOP principles are *language-agnostic.*

Theo What does the separation between code and data look like in DOP then?

Joe Data is represented by data entities that only hold members. Code is aggregated into modules where all functions are stateless.

Theo What do you mean by stateless functions?

Joe Instead of having the state encapsulated in the object, the data entity is passed as an argument.

Theo I don't get that.

Joe Here, let's make it visual.

Joe steps up to a whiteboard and quickly draws a diagram to illustrate his comment. Figure 2.2 shows Joe's drawing.

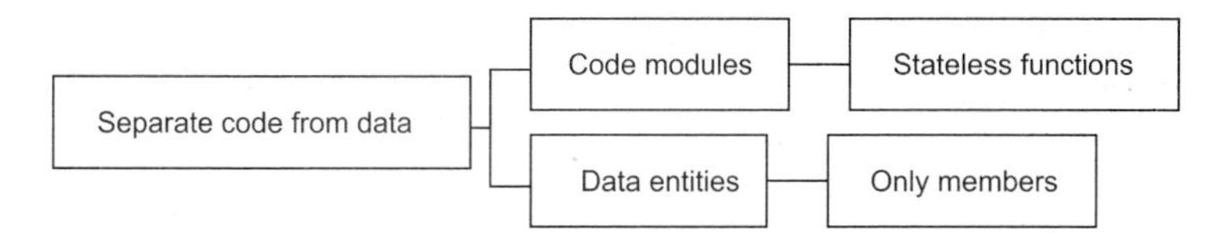

Figure 2.2 The separation between code and data

Theo It's still not clear.

Joe It will become clearer when I show you how it looks in the context of your Library Management System.

Theo OK. Shall we start with code or with data?

Joe Well, it's data-oriented programming, so let's start with data.

2.2 Data entities

In DOP, we start the design process by discovering the *data entities* of our system. Here's what Joe and Theo have to say about data entities.

Joe What are the data entities of your system?

Theo What do you mean by data entities?

Joe I mean the parts of your system that hold information.

▶ **NOTE** Data entities are the parts of your system that hold information.

Theo Well, it's a Library Management System, so we have books and members.

Joe Of course, but there are more. One way to discover the data entities of a system is to look for nouns and noun phrases in the requirements of the system.

Theo looks at Nancy's requirement napkin. He highlights the nouns and noun phrases that seem to represent data entities.

Highlighting terms in the requirements that correspond to data entities

- There are two kinds of users: library *members* and *librarians*.
- *Users* log in to the system via email and password.
- *Members* can borrow *books*.
- *Members* and *librarians* can search *books* by *title* or by *author*.
- *Librarians* can block and unblock *members* (e.g., when they are late in returning a book).
- *Librarians* can list the *books currently lent* to a member.
- There could be several *copies of a book*.

Joe Excellent. Can you see a natural way to group these entities?

Theo Not sure, but it seems to me that users, members, and librarians form one group, whereas books, authors, and book copies form another group.

Joe Sounds good to me. What would you call each group?

Theo Probably user management for the first group and catalog for the second group.

The data entities of the system organized in a nested list

- The catalog data
  - Data about books
  - Data about authors
  - Data about book items
  - Data about book lendings
- The user management data
  - Data about users
  - Data about members
  - Data about librarians

Theo I'm not sure about the relations between books and authors. Should it be association or composition?

Joe Don't worry too much about the details for the moment. We'll refine our data entity design later. For now, let's visualize the two groups in a mind map.

Theo and Joe confer for a bit. Figure 2.3 shows the mind map they come up with.

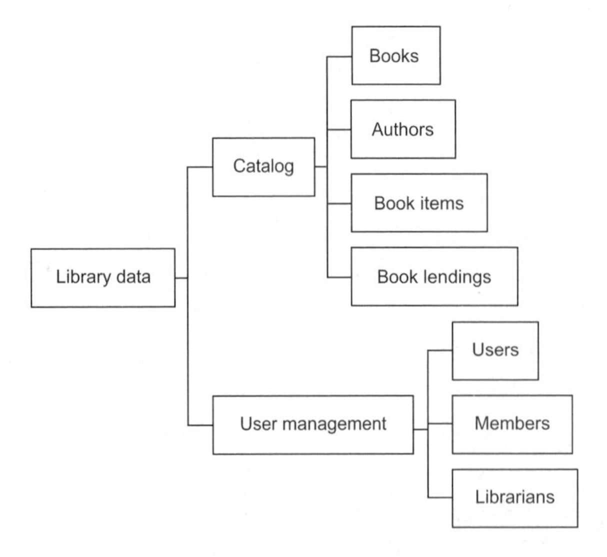

Figure 2.3 The data entities of the system organized in a mind map

The most precise way to visualize the data entities of a DOP system is to draw a data entity diagram with different arrows for association and composition. We will come back to data entity diagrams later.

TIP Discover the data entities of your system and then sort them into high-level groups, either as a nested list or as a mind map.

We will dive deeper into the design and representation of data entities in the next chapter. For now, let's simplify things and say that the data of our library system is made of two high-level groups: user management and catalog.

2.3 Code modules

The second step of the design process in DOP is to define the code modules. Let's listen in on Joe and Theo again.

Joe Now that you have identified the data entities of your system and have arranged them into high-level groups, it's time to think about the code part of your system.

Theo What do you mean by the code part?

Joe One way to think about that is to identity the functionality of your system.

Theo looks again at Nancy's requirements. This time he highlights the verb phrases that represent functionality.

Highlighting terms in the requirements that correspond to functionality

- There are two kinds of users: library members and librarians.
- Users *log in to the system* via email and password.
- Members can *borrow books*.
- Members and librarians can *search books* by title or by author.
- Librarians can *block* and *unblock members* (e.g., when they are late in returning a book).
- Librarians can *list the books currently lent to a member*.
- There could be several copies of a book.

In addition, it's obvious to Theo that members can also return a book. Moreover, there should be a way to detect whether a user is a librarian or not. He adds those to the requirements and then lists the functionality of the system.

The functionality of the library system

- Search for a book.
- Add a book item.
- Block a member.

(continued)

- Unblock a member.
- Log a user into the system.
- List the books currently lent to a member.
- Borrow a book.
- Return a book.
- Check whether a user is a librarian.

Joe Excellent! Now, tell me what functionality needs to be exposed to the outside world?

Theo What do you mean by exposed to the outside world?

Joe Imagine that the Library Management System exposes an API over HTTP. What functionality would be exposed by the HTTP endpoints?

Theo Well, all system functionality would be exposed except checking to see if a user is a librarian.

Joe OK. Now give each exposed function a short name and gather them together in a module box called `Library`.

That takes Theo less than a minute. Figure 2.4 shows the module that contains the exposed functions of the library devised by Theo.

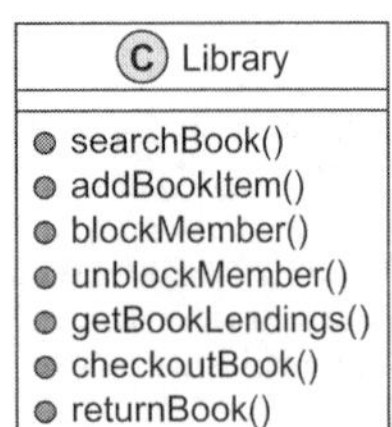

Figure 2.4 The `Library` module contains the exposed functions of the Library Management System.

TIP The first step in designing the code part of a DOP system is to aggregate the exposed functions into a single module.

Joe Beautiful! You just created your first code module.

Theo To me it looks like a class. What's the difference between a module and a class?

Joe A module is an aggregation of functions. In OOP, a module is represented by a class, but in other programming languages, it might be a package or a namespace.

Theo I see.

Joe The important thing about DOP code modules is that they contain only stateless functions.

Theo You mean like static methods in Java?

Joe Yes, and the classes of these static methods should not have any data members.

Theo So, how do the functions know what piece of information they operate on?

Joe Easy. We pass that as the first argument to the function.

Theo OK. Can you give me an example?

Joe, biting his nails, takes a look at the list of functions of the `Library` module in figure 2.4. He spots a likely candidate.

Joe Let's take, for example, `getBookLendings`. In classic OOP, what would its arguments be?

Theo A librarian ID and a member ID.

Joe So, in traditional OOP, `getBookLendings` would be a method of a `Library` class that receives two arguments: `librarianId` and `memberId`.

Theo Yep.

Joe Now comes the subtle part. In DOP, `getBookLendings` is part of the `Library` module, and it receives the `LibraryData` as an argument.

Theo Could you show me what you mean?

Joe Sure.

Joe goes over to Theo's keyboard and starts typing. He enters an example of what a class method looks like in OOP:

```
class Library {
  catalog
  userManagement

  getBookLendings(userId, memberId) {
    // accesses library state via this.catalog and this.userManagement
  }
}
```

Theo Right! The method accesses the state of the object (in our case, the library data) via `this`.

Joe Would you say that the object's state is an argument of the object's methods?

Theo I'd say that the object's state is an implicit argument to the object's methods.

TIP In traditional OOP, the state of the object is an implicit argument to the methods of the object.

Joe Well, in DOP, we pass data as an explicit argument. The signature of `getBookLendings` would look like this.

Listing 2.1 The signature of `getBookLendings`

```
class Library {
  static getBookLendings(libraryData, userId, memberId) {
  }
}
```

Joe The state of the library is stored in `libraryData`, and `libraryData` is passed to the `getBookLendings` static method as an explicit argument.

Theo Is that a general rule?

Joe Absolutely! The same rule applies to the other functions of the `Library` module and to other modules as well. All of the modules are stateless—they receive the library data that they manipulate as an argument.

TIP In DOP, functions of a code module are stateless. They receive the data that they manipulate as an explicit argument, which is usually the first argument.

▶ **NOTE** A module is an aggregation of functions. In DOP, the module functions are stateless.

Theo It reminds me of Python and the way the `self` argument appears in method signatures. Here, let me show you an example.

Listing 2.2 A Python object as an explicit argument in method signatures

```
class Library:
  catalog = {}
  userManagement = {}

  def getBookLendings(self, userId, memberId):
  # accesses library state via self.catalog and self.userManagement
```

Joe Indeed, but the difference I'm talking about is much deeper than a syntax change. It's about the fact that data lives outside the modules.

Theo I got that. As you said, module functions are stateless.

Joe Exactly! Would you like to try and apply this principle across the whole `Library` module?

Theo Sure.

Theo refines the design of the `Library` module by including the details about the functions' arguments. He presents the diagram in figure 2.5 to Joe.

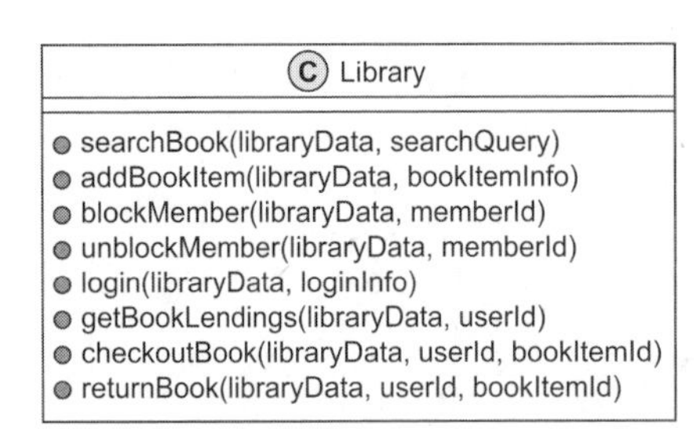

Figure 2.5 The `Library` module with the functions' arguments

Joe Perfect. Now, we're ready to tackle the high-level design of our system.

Theo What's a high-level design in DOP?

Joe A high-level design in DOP is the definition of modules and the interaction between them.

Theo I see. Are there any guidelines to help me define the modules?

Joe Definitely. The high-level modules of the system correspond to the high-level data entities.

Theo You mean the data entities that appear in the data mind map?

Joe Exactly!

Theo looks again at the data mind map (figure 2.6). He focuses on the high-level data entities library, catalog, and user management. This means that in the system, besides the `Library` module, we have two high-level modules:

- The `Catalog` module deals with catalog data.
- The `UserManagement` module deals with user management data.

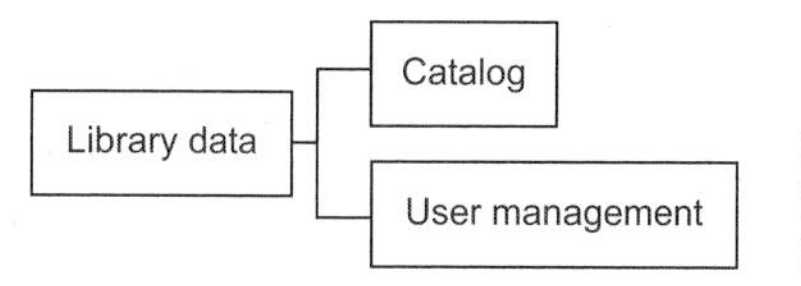

Figure 2.6 A mind map of the high-level data entities of the Library Management System

Theo then draws the high-level design of the Library Management System with the `Catalog` and `UserManagement` modules. Figure 2.7 shows the addition of these modules, where:

- Functions of `Catalog` receive `catalogData` as their first argument.
- Functions of `UserManagement` receive `userManagementData` as their first argument.

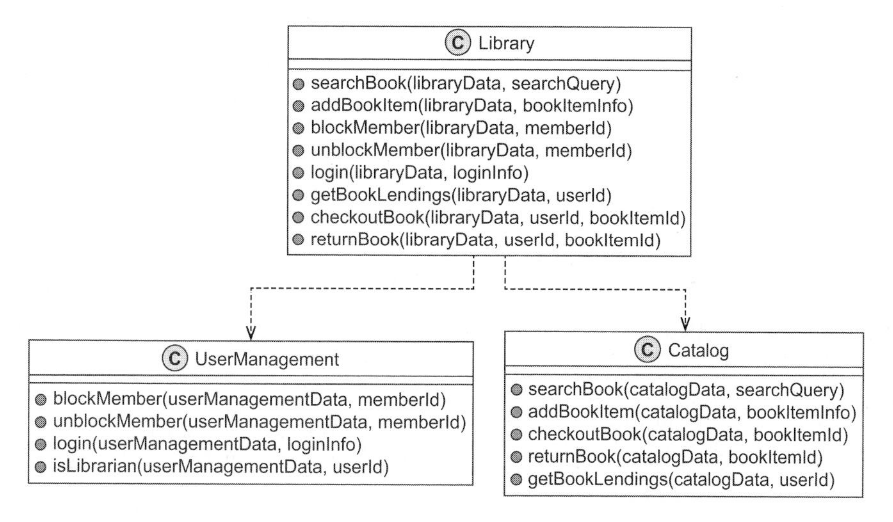

Figure 2.7 The modules of the Library Management System with their functions' arguments

It's not 100% clear for Theo at this point how the data entities get passed between modules. For the moment, he thinks of `libraryData` as a class with two members:

- `catalog` holds the catalog data.
- `userManagement` holds the user management data.

Theo also sees that the functions of `Library` share a common pattern. (Later on in this chapter, we'll see the code for some functions of the `Library` module.)

- They receive `libraryData` as an argument.
- They pass `libraryData.catalog` to the functions of `Catalog`.
- They pass `libraryData.userManagement` to the functions of `UserManagement`.

TIP The high-level modules of a DOP system correspond to the high-level data entities.

2.4 DOP systems are easy to understand

Theo takes a look at the two diagrams that represent the high-level design of his system:

- The data entities in the data mind map in figure 2.8
- The code modules in the module diagram in figure 2.9

A bit perplexed, Theo asks Joe:

Theo I'm not sure that this system is better than a traditional OOP system where objects encapsulate data.

Joe The main benefit of a DOP system over a traditional OOP system is that it's easier to understand.

Theo What makes it easier to understand?

Joe The fact that the system is split cleanly into code modules and data entities.

Theo How does that help?

Joe When you try to understand the data entities of the system, you don't have to think about the details of the code that manipulates the data entities.

Theo So, when I look at the data mind map of my Library Management System, I can understand it on its own?

Joe Exactly, and similarly, when you try to understand the code modules of the system, you don't have to think about the details of the data entities manipulated by the code. There is a clear separation of concerns between the code and the data.

Theo looks again at the data mind map in figure 2.8. He has kind of an *Aha!* moment:

Data lives on its own!

▶ **NOTE** A DOP system is easier to understand because the system is split into two parts: data entities and code modules.

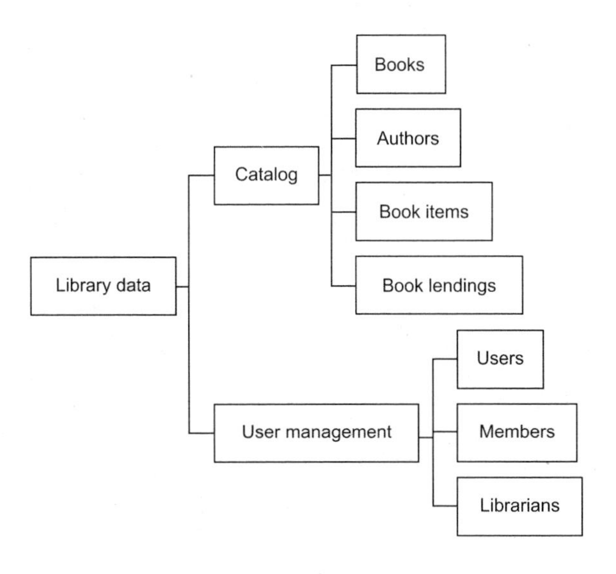

Figure 2.8 A data mind map of the Library Management System

Now, Theo looks at the module diagram in figure 2.9. He feels a bit confused and asks Joe for clarification:

- On one hand, the module diagram looks similar to the class diagrams from classic OOP, boxes for classes and arrows for relations between classes.
- On the other hand, the code module diagram looks much simpler than the class diagrams from classic OOP, but he cannot explain why.

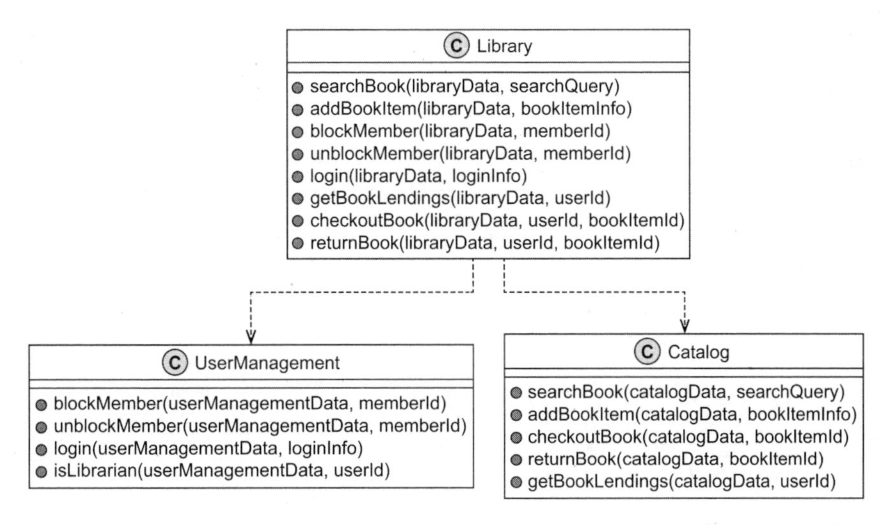

Figure 2.9 The modules of the Library Management System with the function arguments

Theo The module diagram seems much simpler than the class diagrams I am used to in OOP. I feel it, but I can't put it into words.

Joe The reason is that module diagrams have constraints.

Theo What kind of constraints?

Joe Constraints on the functions we saw before. All the functions are static (or stateless), but there's also constraints on the relations between the modules.

TIP All the functions in a DOP module are *stateless.*

Theo In what way are the relations between modules constrained?

Joe There is a single kind of relation between DOP modules—the usage relation. A module uses code from another module. There's no association, no composition, and no inheritance between modules. That's what makes a DOP module diagram easy to understand.

Theo I understand why there is no association and no composition between DOP modules. After all, association and composition are data relations. But why no inheritance relation? Does that mean that DOP is against polymorphism?

Joe That's a great question! The quick answer is that in DOP, we achieve polymorphism with a different mechanism than class inheritance. We will talk about it some day.

▶ **NOTE** For a discussion of polymorphism in DOP, see chapter 13.

Theo Now, you've piqued my curiosity. I thought inheritance was the only way to achieve polymorphism.

Theo looks again at the module diagram in figure 2.9. Now he not only feels that this diagram is simpler than traditional OOP class diagrams, he understands *why* it's simpler: all the functions are static, and all the relations between modules are of type usage. Table 2.1 summarizes Theo's perception.

TIP The only kind of relation between DOP modules is the usage relation.

Table 2.1 What makes each part of a DOP system easy to understand

System part	Constraint on entities	Constraints on relations
Data entities	Members only (no code)	Association and composition
Code modules	Stateless functions (no members)	Usage (no inheritance)

TIP Each part of a DOP system is easy to understand because it provides constraints.

2.5 DOP systems are flexible

Theo I see how a sharp separation between code and data makes DOP systems easier to understand than classic OOP systems. But what about adapting to changes in requirements?

Joe Another benefit of DOP systems is that it is easy to extend them and to adapt to changing requirements.

Theo I remember that, when Nancy asked me to add Super members and VIP members to the system, it was hard to adapt my OOP system. I had to introduce a few base classes, and the class hierarchy became really complex.

Joe I know exactly what you mean. I've experienced the same kind of struggle so many times. Describe the changes in the requirements for Super members and VIP members, and I'm quite sure that you'll see how easy it would be to extend your DOP system.

The requirements for Super members and VIP members

- Super members are members that are allowed to list the book lendings to other members.
- VIP members are members that are allowed to add book items to the library.

Theo opens his IDE and starts to code the `getBookLendings` function of the `Library` module (see listing 2.3), first without addressing the requirements for Super members. Theo remembers what Joe told him about module functions in DOP:

- Functions are stateless.
- Functions receive the data they manipulate as their first argument.

In terms of functionality, `getBookLendings` has two parts:

- Checks that the user is a librarian.
- Retrieves the book lendings from the catalog.

Basically, the code of `getBookLendings` has two parts as well:

- Calls the `isLibrarian` function from the `UserManagement` module and passes it the `UserManagementData`.
- Calls the `getBookLendings` function from the `Catalog` module and passes it the `CatalogData`.

Listing 2.3 Getting the book lendings of a member

```
class Library {
  static getBookLendings(libraryData, userId, memberId) {
    if(UserManagement.isLibrarian(libraryData.userManagement, userId)) {
      return Catalog.getBookLendings(libraryData.catalog, memberId);
    } else {
      throw "Not allowed to get book lendings";    // There are other ways to manage errors.
    }
  }
}

class UserManagement {
  static isLibrarian(userManagementData, userId) {
    // will be implemented later    // In chapter 3, we will see how to manage permissions with generic data collections.
  }
}
```

```
class Catalog {
  static getBookLendings(catalogData, memberId) {
    // will be implemented later
  }
}
```

In chapter 3, we will see how to query data with generic data collections.

It's Theo's first piece of DOP code and passing around all those data objects—`libraryData`, `libraryData.userManagement`, and `libraryData.catalog`—feels a bit awkward. But he did it! Joe looks at Theo's code and seems satisfied.

Joe Now, how would you adapt your code to Super members?

Theo I would add a function `isSuperMember` to the `UserManagement` module and call it from `Library.getBookLendings`.

Joe Exactly! It's as simple as that.

Theo types the code on his laptop so that he can show it to Joe. Here's how Theo adapts his code for Super members.

Listing 2.4 Allowing Super members to get the book lendings of a member

```
class Library {
  static getBookLendings(libraryData, userId, memberId) {
    if(Usermanagement.isLibrarian(libraryData.userManagement, userId) ||
      Usermanagement.isSuperMember(libraryData.userManagement, userId)) {
      return Catalog.getBookLendings(libraryData.catalog, memberId);
    } else {
      throw "Not allowed to get book lendings";
    }
  }
}

class UserManagement {
  static isLibrarian(userManagementData, userId) {
    // will be implemented later
  }
  static isSuperMember(userManagementData, userId) {
    // will be implemented later
  }
}

class Catalog {
  static getBookLendings(catalogData, memberId) {
    // will be implemented later
  }
}
```

There are other ways to manage errors.

In chapter 3, we will see how to manage permissions with generic data collections.

In chapter 3, we will see how to query data with generic data collections.

Now, the awkward feeling caused by passing around all those data objects is dominated by a feeling of relief. Adapting to this change in requirements takes only a few lines of code and requires no changes in the system design. Once again, Joe seems satisfied.

TIP DOP systems are flexible. Quite often they adapt to changing requirements without changing the system design.

Theo starts coding addBookItem. He looks at the signature of Library.addBookItem, and the meaning of the third argument bookItemInfo isn't clear to him. He asks Joe for clarification.

Listing 2.5 The signature of Library.addBookItem

```
class Library {
  static addBookItem(libraryData, userId, bookItemInfo) {
  }
}
```

Theo What is bookItemInfo?

Joe Let's call it the book item information. Imagine we have a way to represent this information in a data entity named bookItemInfo.

Theo You mean an object?

Joe For now, it's OK to think about bookItemInfo as an object. Later on, I will show you how to we represent data in DOP.

Besides this subtlety about how the book item information is represented by bookItemInfo, the code for Library.addBookItem in listing 2.6 is quite similar to the code Theo wrote for Library.getBookLendings in listing 2.4. Once again, Theo is amazed by the fact that adding support for VIP members requires no design change.

Listing 2.6 Allowing VIP members to add a book item to the library

```
class Library {
  static addBookItem(libraryData, userId, bookItemInfo) {
    if(UserManagement.isLibrarian(libraryData.userManagement, userId) ||
      UserManagement.isVIPMember(libraryData.userManagement, userId)) {
      return Catalog.addBookItem(libraryData.catalog, bookItemInfo);
    } else {
      throw "Not allowed to add a book item";
    }
  }
}

class UserManagement {
  static isLibrarian(userManagementData, userId) {
    // will be implemented later
  }
  static isVIPMember(userManagementData, userId) {
    // will be implemented later
  }
}

class Catalog {
  static addBookItem(catalogData, memberId) {
    // will be implemented later
  }
}
```

There are other ways to manage errors. (annotates `throw "Not allowed to add a book item";`)

In chapter 3, we will see how to manage permissions with generic data collections. (annotates both `// will be implemented later` lines in UserManagement)

In chapter 4, we will see how to manage state of the system with immutable data. (annotates `// will be implemented later` in Catalog.addBookItem)

Theo It takes a big mindset shift to learn how to separate code from data!

Joe What was the most challenging thing to accept?

Theo The fact that data is not encapsulated in objects.

Joe It was the same for me when I switched from OOP to DOP.

Now it's time to eat! Theo takes Joe for lunch at Simple, a nice, small restaurant near the office.

Summary

- DOP principles are *language-agnostic.*
- DOP principle #1 is to separate code from data.
- The separation between code and data in DOP systems makes them simpler (easier to understand) than traditional OOP systems.
- *Data entities* are the parts of your system that hold information.
- DOP is against *data encapsulation.*
- The more flexible a system is, the easier it is to adapt to changing requirements.
- The separation between code and data in DOP systems makes them more flexible than traditional OOP systems.
- When code is separated from data, we have the freedom to design code and data in isolation.
- We represent data as *data entities.*
- We discover the data entities of our system and sort them into high-level groups, either as a nested list or as a mind map.
- A DOP system is easier to understand than a traditional OOP system because the system is split into two parts: *data entities* and *code modules.*
- In DOP, a *code module* is an aggregation of stateless functions.
- DOP systems are flexible. Quite often they adapt to changing requirements without changing the system design.
- In traditional OOP, the state of the object is an implicit argument to the methods of the object.
- Stateless functions receive data they manipulate as an explicit argument.
- The high-level modules of a DOP system correspond to high-level data entities.
- The only kind of relation between *code modules* is the *usage relation.*
- The only kinds of relation between *data entities* are the *association* and the *composition* relation.
- For a discussion of *polymorphism* in DOP, see chapter 13.

Basic data manipulation

Meditation and programming

3

This chapter covers

- Representing records with string maps to improve flexibility
- Manipulating data with generic functions
- Accessing each piece of information via its information path
- Gaining JSON serialization for free

After learning why and how to separate code from data in the previous chapter, let's talk about data on its own. In contrast to traditional OOP, where system design tends to involve a rigid class hierarchy, DOP prescribes that we represent our data model as a flexible combination of maps and arrays (or lists), where we can access each piece of information via an information path. This chapter is a deep dive into the second principle of DOP.

PRINCIPLE #2 Represent data entities with generic data structures.

We increase system flexibility when we represent records as string maps and not as objects instantiated from classes. This liberates data from the rigidity of a class-based system. Data becomes a first-class citizen powered by generic functions to add, remove, or rename fields.

▶ **NOTE** We refer to maps that have strings as keys as *string maps.*

The dependency between the code that manipulates data and the data is a weak dependency. The code only needs to know the keys of specific fields in the record it wants to manipulate. The code doesn't even need to know about all the keys in the record, only the ones relevant to it. In this chapter, we'll deal only with data query. We'll discuss managing changes in system state in the next chapter.

3.1 Designing a data model

During lunch at Simple, Theo and Joe don't talk about programming. Instead, they start getting to know each other on a personal level. Theo discovers that Joe is married to Kay, who has just opened her creative therapy practice after many years of studying various fields related to well-being. Neriah, their 14-year-old son, is passionate about drones, whereas Aurelia, their 12-year-old daughter, plays the transverse flute.

Joe tells Theo that he's been practicing meditation for 10 years. Meditation, he says, has taught him how to break away from being continually lost in a "storm thought" (especially negative thoughts, which can be the source of great suffering) to achieve a more direct relationship with reality. The more he learns to experience reality as it is, the calmer his mind. When he first started to practice meditation, it was sometimes difficult and even weird, but by persevering, he has increased his feeling of well-being with each passing year.

When they're back at the office, Joe tells Theo that his next step in their DOP journey will be about data models. This includes data representation.

Joe When we design the data part of our system, we're free to do it in isolation.

Theo What do you mean by isolation?

Joe I mean that you don't have to bother with code, only data.

Theo Oh, right. I remember you telling me how that makes a DOP system simpler than OOP. Separation of concerns is a design principle I'm used to in OOP.

Joe Indeed.

Theo And, when we think about data, the only relations we have to think about are association and composition.

Joe Correct.

Theo Will the data model design be significantly different than the data model I'm used to designing as an OOP developer?

Joe Not so much.

Theo OK. Let me see if I can draw a DOP-style data entity diagram.

Theo takes a look at the data mind map that he drew earlier in the morning. He then draws the diagram in figure 3.1.

He refines the details of the fields of each data entity and the kind of relations between entities. Figure 3.2 shows the result of this redefined data entity diagram.

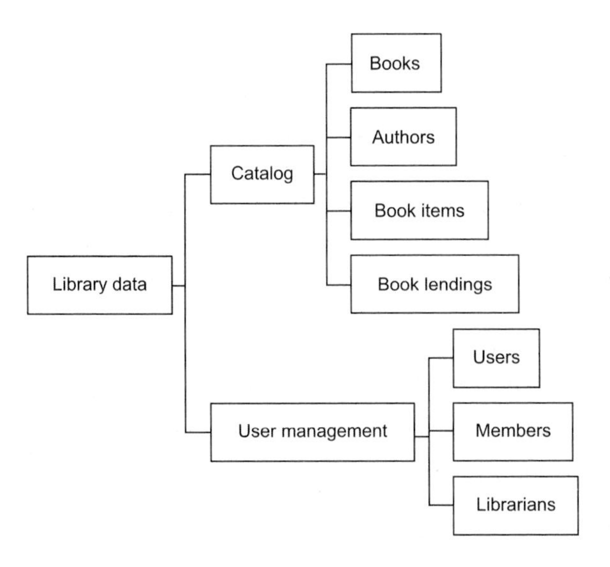

Figure 3.1 A data mind map of the Library Management System

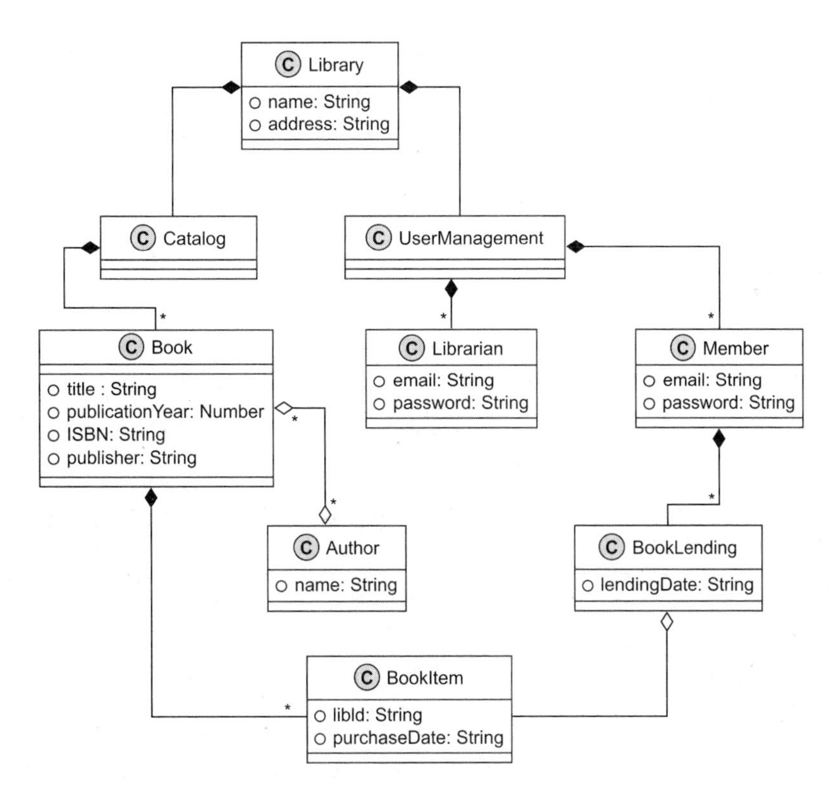

Figure 3.2 A data model of the Library Management System

Joe The next step is to be more explicit about the relations between entities.

Theo What do you mean?

Joe For example, in your entity diagram, `Book` and `Author` are connected by a many-to-many association relation. How is this relation going to be represented in your program?

Theo In the `Book` entity, there will be a collection of author IDs, and in the `Author` entity, there will be a collection of book IDs.

Joe Sounds good. And what will the book ID be?

Theo The book ISBN.

▶ **NOTE** The International Standard Book Number (ISBN) is a numeric commercial book identifier that is intended to be unique.

Joe And where will you hold the index that enables you to retrieve a `Book` from its ISBN?

Theo In the `Catalog` because the catalog holds a `bookByISBN` index.

Joe What about author ID?

Theo Author ID is the author name in lowercase and with dashes instead of white spaces (assuming that we don't have two authors with the same name).

Joe And I guess that you also hold the author index in the `Catalog`?

Theo Exactly!

Joe Excellent. You've been 100% explicit about the relation between `Book` and `Author`. I'll ask you to do the same with the other relations of the system.

It's quite easy for Theo to do, as he has done that so many times as an OOP developer. Figure 3.3 provides the detailed entity diagram of Theo's system.

▶ **NOTE** By *positional collection*, we mean a collection where the elements are in order (like a list or an array). By *index*, we mean a collection where the elements are accessible via a key (like a hash map or a dictionary).

The `Catalog` entity contains two indexes:

- `booksByIsbn`—The keys are book ISBNs, and the values are `Book` entities. Its type is noted as `{Book}`.
- `authorsById`—The keys are author IDs, and the values are `Author` entities. Its type is noted as `{Author}`.

Inside a `Book` entity, we have `authors`, which is a positional collection of author IDs of type `[String]`. Inside an `Author` entity, we have `books`, which is a collection of book IDs of type `[String]`.

▶ **NOTE** For the notation for collections and index types, a positional collection of `String`s is noted as `[String]`. An index of `Book`s is noted as `{Book}`. In the context of a data model, the index keys are always strings.

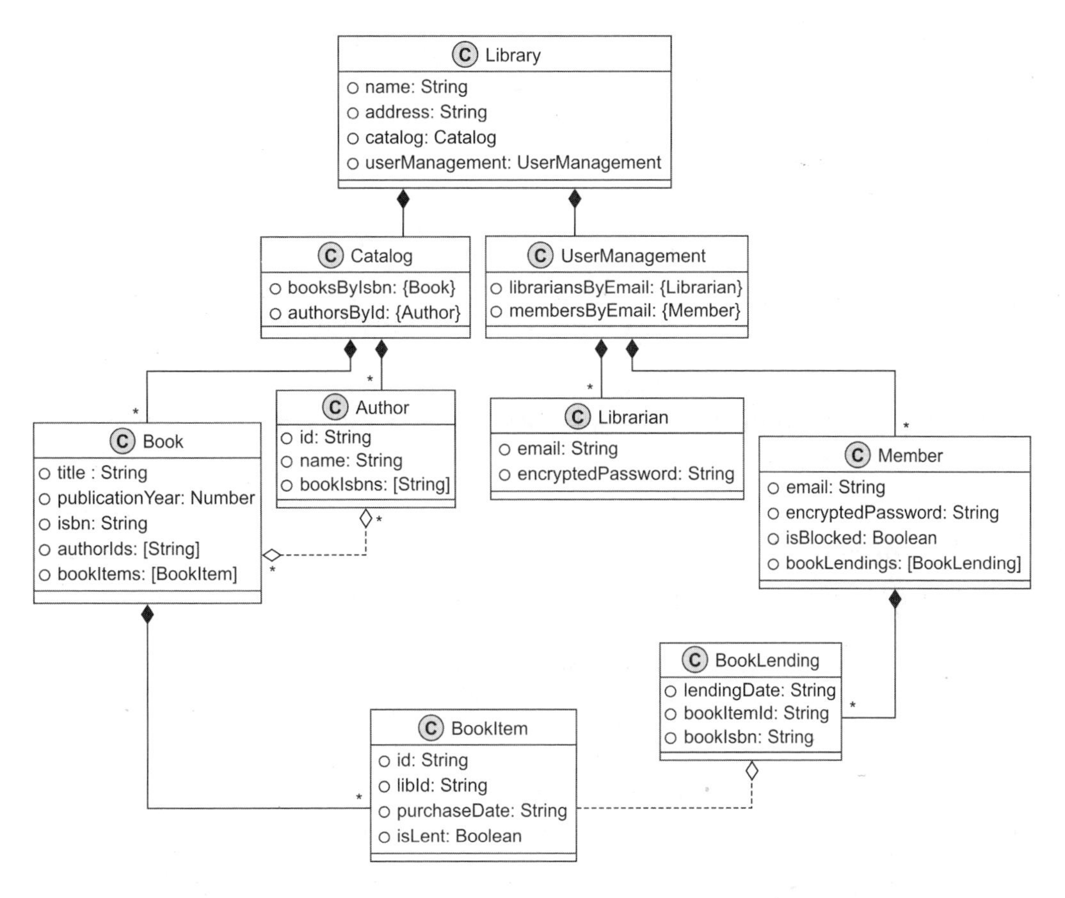

Figure 3.3 Library management relation model. Dashed lines (e.g., between `Book` and `Author`) denote indirect relations, `[String]` denotes a positional collection of strings, and `{Book}` denotes an index of `Books`.

There is a dashed line between `Book` and `Author`, which means that the relation between `Book` and `Author` is indirect. To access the collection of `Author` entities from a `Book` entity, we'll use the `authorById` index defined in the `Catalog` entity.

Joe I like your data entity diagram.

Theo Thank you.

Joe Can you tell me what the three kinds of data aggregations are in your diagram (and, in fact, in any data entity diagram)?

Theo Let's see . . . we have positional collections like `authors` in `Book`. We have indexes like `booksByIsbn` in `Catalog`. I can't find the third one.

Joe The third kind of data aggregation is what we've called, until now, an "entity" (like `Library`, `Catalog`, `Book`, etc.), and the common term for entity in computer science is record.

▶ **NOTE** A *record* is a data structure that groups together related data items. It's a collection of fields, possibly of different data types.

Theo Is it correct to say that a data entity diagram consists only of records, positional collections, and indexes?

Joe That's correct. Can you make a similar statement about the relations between entities?

Theo The relations in a data entity diagram are either composition (solid line with a full diamond) or association (dashed line with an empty diamond). Both types of relations can be either one-to-one, one-to-many, or many-to-many.

Joe Excellent!

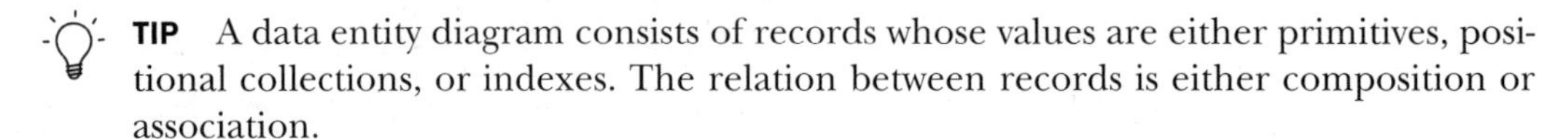

TIP A data entity diagram consists of records whose values are either primitives, positional collections, or indexes. The relation between records is either composition or association.

3.2 Representing records as maps

So far, we've illustrated the benefits we gain from the separation between code and data at a high-system level. There's a separation of concerns between code and data, and each part has clear constraints:

- Code consists of static functions that receive data as an explicit argument.
- Data entities are modeled as records, and the relations between records are represented by positional collections and indexes.

Now comes the question of the representation of the data. DOP has nothing special to say about collections and indexes. However, it's strongly opinionated about the representation of records: records should be represented by generic data structures such as maps.

This applies to both OOP and FP languages. In dynamically-typed languages like JavaScript, Python, and Ruby, data representation feels natural. While in statically-typed languages like Java and C#, it is a bit more cumbersome.

Theo I'm really curious to know how we represent positional collections, indexes, and records in DOP.

Joe Let's start with positional collections. DOP has nothing special to say about the representation of collections. They can be linked lists, arrays, vectors, sets, or other collections best suited for the use case.

Theo It's like in OOP.

Joe Right! For now, to keep things simple, we'll use arrays to represent positional collections.

Theo What about indexes?

Joe Indexes are represented as homogeneous string maps.

Theo What do you mean by a homogeneous map?

Joe I mean that all the values of the map are of the same kind. For example, in a `Book` index, all the values are `Book`, and in an author index, all the values are `Author`, and so forth.

Theo Again, it's like in OOP.

▶ **NOTE** A *homogeneous map* is a map where all the values are of the same type. A *heterogeneous map* is a map where the values are of different types.

Joe Now, here's the big surprise. In DOP, records are represented as maps, more precisely, heterogeneous string maps.

Joe goes to the whiteboard and begins to draw. When he's finished, he shows Theo the diagram in figure 3.4.

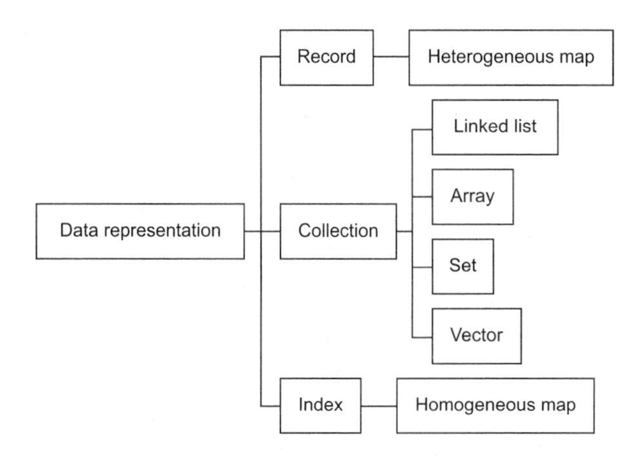

Figure 3.4 The building blocks of data representation

Theo stays silent for a while. He is shocked to hear that the data entities of a system can be represented as a generic data structure, where the field names and value types are not specified in a class. Then, Theo asks Joe:

Theo What are the benefits of this folly?

Joe Flexibility and genericity.

Theo Could you explain, please?

Joe I'll explain in a moment, but before that, I'd like to show you what an instance of a record in a DOP system looks like.

Theo OK.

Joe Let's take as an example, *Watchmen*, by Alan Moore and Dave Gibbons, which is my favorite graphic novel. This masterpiece was published in 1987. I'm going to assume that, in a physical library, there are two copies of this book, whose ID is `nyc-central-lib`, and that one of the two copies is currently out. Here's how I'd represent the `Book` record for *Watchmen* in DOP.

Joe comes closer to Theo's laptop. He opens a text editor (not an IDE!) and types the `Book` record for Theo.

Listing 3.1 An instance of a Book record represented as a map

```
{
  "isbn": "978-1779501127",
  "title": "Watchmen",
  "publicationYear": 1987,
  "authors": ["alan-moore", "dave-gibbons"],
  "bookItems": [
    {
      "id": "book-item-1",
      "libId": "nyc-central-lib",
      "isLent": true
    },
    {
      "id": "book-item-2",
      "libId": "nyc-central-lib",
      "isLent": false
    }
  ]
}
```

Theo looks at the laptop screen. He has a question.

Theo How am I supposed to instantiate the Book record for *Watchmen* programmatically?

Joe It depends on the facilities that your programming language offers to instantiate maps. With dynamic languages like JavaScript, Ruby, or Python, it's straightforward, because we can use literals for maps and arrays. Here, let me show you how.

Joe jots down the JavaScript code that creates an instance of a Book record, which represents as a map in JavaScript. He shows the code to Theo.

Listing 3.2 A Book record represented as a map in JavaScript

```
var watchmenBook = {
  "isbn": "978-1779501127",
  "title": "Watchmen",
  "publicationYear": 1987,
  "authors": ["alan-moore", "dave-gibbons"],
  "bookItems": [
    {
      "id": "book-item-1",
      "libId": "nyc-central-lib",
      "isLent": true
    },
    {
      "id": "book-item-2",
      "libId": "nyc-central-lib",
      "isLent": false
    }
  ]
}
```

Theo And, if I'm in Java?

Joe It's a bit more tedious, but still doable with the immutable `Map` and `List` static factory methods.

▶ **NOTE** See "Creating Immutable Lists, Sets, and Maps" at http://mng.bz/voGm for more information on this Java core library.

Joe types the Java code to create an instance of a `Book` record represented as a map. He shows Theo the Java code.

Listing 3.3 A `Book` record represented as a map in Java

```
Map watchmen = Map.of(
  "isbn", "978-1779501127",
  "title", "Watchmen",
  "publicationYear", 1987,
  "authors", List.of("alan-moore", "dave-gibbons"),
  "bookItems", List.of(
    Map.of(
      "id", "book-item-1",
      "libId", "nyc-central-lib",
      "isLent", true
    ),
    Map.of (
      "id", "book-item-2",
      "libId", "nyc-central-lib",
      "isLent", false
    )
  )
);
```

TIP In DOP, we represent a record as a heterogeneous string map.

Theo I'd definitely prefer to create a `Book` record using a `Book` class and a `BookItem` class.

Theo opens his IDE. He types the JavaScript code to represent a `Book` record as an instance of a `Book` class.

Listing 3.4 A `Book` record as an instance of a `Book` class in JavaScript

```
class Book {
  isbn;
  title;
  publicationYear;
  authors;
  bookItems;
  constructor(isbn, title, publicationYear, authors, bookItems) {
    this.isbn = isbn;
    this.title = title;
    this.publicationYear = publicationYear;
    this.authors = authors;
    this.bookItems = bookItems;
```

```
  }
}

class BookItem {
  id;
  libId;
  isLent;
  constructor(id, libId, isLent) {
    this.id = id;
    this.libId = libId;
    this.isLent = isLent;
  }
}

var watchmenBook = new Book("978-1779501127",
  "Watchmen",
  1987,
  ["alan-moore", "dave-gibbons"],
  [new BookItem("book-item-1", "nyc-central-lib", true),
    new BookItem("book-item-2", "nyc-central-lib", false)]);
```

Joe Theo, why do you prefer classes over maps for representing records?

Theo It makes the data shape of the record part of my program. As a result, the IDE can auto-complete field names, and errors are caught at compile time.

Joe Fair enough. Can I show you some drawbacks for this approach?

Theo Sure.

Joe Imagine that you want to display the information about a book in the context of search results. In that case, instead of author IDs, you want to display author names, and you don't need the book item information. How would you handle that?

Theo I'd create a class `BookInSearchResults` without a `bookItems` member and with an `authorNames` member instead of the `authorIds` member of the `Book` class. Also, I would need to write a copy constructor that receives a `Book` object.

Joe In classic OOP, the fact that data is instantiated only via classes brings safety. But this safety comes at the cost of flexibility.

TIP There's a tradeoff between flexibility and safety in a data model.

Theo So, how can it be different?

Joe In the DOP approach, where records are represented as maps, we don't need to create a class for each variation of the data. We're free to add, remove, and rename record fields dynamically. Our data model is flexible.

Theo Interesting!

TIP In DOP, the data model is flexible. We're free to add, remove, and rename record fields dynamically at run time.

Joe Now, let me talk about genericity. How would you serialize the content of a `Book` object to JSON?

TIP In DOP, records are manipulated with generic functions.

Theo Oh no! I remember that while working on the Klafim prototype, I had a nightmare about JSON serialization when I was developing the first version of the Library Management System.

Joe Well, in DOP, serializing a record to JSON is super easy.

Theo Does it require the usage of reflection in order to go over the fields of the record like the Gson Java library does?

▶ **NOTE** See https://github.com/google/gson for more information on Gson.

Joe Not at all! Remember that in DOP, a record is nothing more than data. We can write a generic JSON serialization function that works with any record. It can be a `Book`, an `Author`, a `BookItem`, or anything else.

Theo Amazing!

TIP In DOP, you get JSON serialization for free.

Joe Actually, as I'll show you in a moment, lots of data manipulation stuff can be done using generic functions.

Theo Are the generic functions part of the language?

Joe It depends on the functions and on the language. For example, JavaScript provides a JSON serialization function called `JSON.stringify` out of the box, but none for omitting multiple keys or for renaming keys.

Theo That's annoying.

Joe Not so much; there are third-party libraries that provide data-manipulation facilities. A popular data manipulation library in the JavaScript ecosystem is Lodash.

▶ **NOTE** See https://lodash.com/ to find out more about Lodash.

Theo What about other languages?

Joe Lodash has been ported to Java, C#, Python, and Ruby. Let me bookmark some sites for you.

Joe bookmarks these sites for Theo:

- https://javalibs.com/artifact/com.github.javadev/underscore-lodash for Java
- https://www.nuget.org/packages/lodash/ for C#
- https://github.com/dgilland/pydash for Python
- https://rudash-website.now.sh/ for Ruby

▶ **NOTE** Throughout the book, we use Lodash to show how to manipulate data with generic functions, but there is nothing special about Lodash. The exact same approach could be implemented via other data manipulation libraries or custom code.

Theo Cool!

Joe Actually, Lodash and its rich set of data manipulation functions can be ported to any language. That's why it's so beneficial to represent records as maps.

TIP DOP compromises on data safety to gain flexibility and genericity.

At the whiteboard, Joe quickly sketches the tradeoffs (see table 3.1).

Table 3.1 The tradeoff among safety, flexibility, and genericity

	OOP	DOP
Safety	High	Low
Flexibility	Low	High
Genericity	Low	High

3.3 Manipulating data with generic functions

Joe Now let me show you how to manipulate data in DOP with generic functions.

Theo Yes, I'm quite curious to see how you'll implement the search functionality of the Library Management System.

Joe OK. First, let's instantiate a `Catalog` record for the catalog data of a library, where we have a single book, *Watchmen*.

Joe instantiates a `Catalog` record according to Theo's data model in figure 3.3. Here's what Joe shows to Theo.

Listing 3.5 A `Catalog` record

```
var catalogData = {
  "booksByIsbn": {
    "978-1779501127": {
      "isbn": "978-1779501127",
      "title": "Watchmen",
      "publicationYear": 1987,
      "authorIds": ["alan-moore", "dave-gibbons"],
      "bookItems": [
        {
          "id": "book-item-1",
          "libId": "nyc-central-lib",
          "isLent": true
        },
        {
          "id": "book-item-2",
          "libId": "nyc-central-lib",
          "isLent": false
        }
      ]
    }
  },
  "authorsById": {
    "alan-moore": {
      "name": "Alan Moore",
      "bookIsbns": ["978-1779501127"]
    },
```

```
      "dave-gibbons": {
        "name": "Dave Gibbons",
        "bookIsbns": ["978-1779501127"]
      }
    }
  }
```

Theo I see the two indexes we talked about, `booksByIsbn` and `authorsById`. How do you differentiate a record from an index in DOP?

Joe In an entity diagram, there's a clear distinction between records and indexes. But in our code, both are plain data.

Theo I guess that's why this approach is called data-oriented programming.

Joe See how straightforward it is to visualize any part of the system data inside a program? The reason is that data is represented as data!

 **TIP** In DOP, data is represented as data.

Theo That sounds like a lapalissade.[1]

Joe Oh, does it? I'm not so sure! In OOP, data is usually represented by objects, which makes it more challenging to visualize data inside a program.

 **TIP** In DOP, we can visualize any part of the system data.

Theo How would you retrieve the title of a specific book from the catalog data?

Joe Great question! In fact, in a DOP system, every piece of information has an information path from which we can retrieve the information.

Theo Information path?

Joe For example, the information path to the title of the *Watchmen* book in the catalog is `["booksByIsbn", "978-1779501127", "title"]`.

Theo Ah, I see. So, is an information path sort of like a file path, but that names in an information path correspond to nested entities?

Joe You're exactly right. And once we have the path of a piece of information, we can retrieve the information with Lodash's `_.get` function.

Joe types a few characters on Theo's laptop. Theo is amazed at how little code is needed to get the book title.

Listing 3.6 Retrieving the title of a book from its information path

```
_.get(catalogData, ["booksByIsbn", "978-1779501127", "title"])
// → "Watchmen"
```

Theo Neat. I wonder how hard it would be to implement a function like `_.get` myself.

[1] A lapalissade is an obvious truth—a truism or tautology—that produces a comical effect.

After a few minutes of trial and error, Theo is able to produce his implementation. He shows Joe the code.

Listing 3.7 Custom implementation of `get`

```
function get(m, path) {
  var res = m;
  for(var i = 0; i < path.length; i++) {     <-- We could use forEach instead of a for loop.
    var key = path[i];
    res = res[key];
  }
  return res;
}
```

After testing Theo's implementation of `get`, Joe compliments Theo. He's grateful that Theo is catching on so quickly.

Listing 3.8 Testing the custom implementation of `get`

```
get(catalogData, ["booksByIsbn", "978-1779501127", "title"]);
// → "Watchmen"
```

Joe Well done!

Theo I wonder if a function like `_.get` works smoothly in a statically-typed language like Java?

Joe It depends on whether you only need to pass the value around or to access the value concretely.

Theo I don't follow.

Joe Imagine that once you get the title of a book, you want to convert the string into an uppercase string. You need to do a static cast to `String`, right? Here, let me show you an example that casts a field value to a string, then we can manipulate it as a string.

Listing 3.9 Casting a field value to a string

```
((String)watchmen.get("title")).toUpperCase()
```

Theo That makes sense. The values of the map are of different types, so the compiler declares it as a `Map<String,Object>`. The information of the type of the field is lost.

Joe It's a bit annoying, but quite often our code just passes the data around. In that case, we don't have to deal with static casting. Moreover, in a language like C#, when using the `dynamic` data type, type casting can be avoided.[2,3]

[2] See http://mng.bz/4jo5 for the C# documentation on the built-in reference to dynamic types.

[3] See appendix A for details about dynamic fields and type casting in C#.

 **TIP** In statically-typed languages, we sometimes need to statically cast the field values.

Theo What about performance?

Joe In most programming languages, maps are quite efficient. Accessing a field in a map is slightly slower than accessing a class member. Usually, it's not significant.

 **TIP** There's no significant performance hit for accessing a field in a map instead of as a class member.

Theo Let's get back to this idea of information path. It works in OOP too. I could access the title of the *Watchmen* book with `catalogData.booksByIsbn["978-1779501127"].title`. I'd use class members for record fields and strings for index keys.

Joe There's a fundamental difference, though. When records are represented as maps, the information can be retrieved via its information path using a generic function like `_.get`. But when records are represented as objects, you need to write specific code for each type of information path.

Theo What do you mean by specific code? What's specific in `catalogData.booksByIsbn["978-1779501127"].title`?

Joe In a statically-typed language like Java, you'd need to import the class definitions for `Catalog` and `Book`.

Theo And, in a dynamically-typed language like JavaScript . . . ?

Joe Even in JavaScript, when you represent records with objects instantiated from classes, you can't easily write a function that receives a path as an argument and display the information that corresponds to this path. You would have to write specific code for each kind of path. You'd access class members with dot notation and map fields with bracket notation.

Theo Would you say that in DOP, the information path is a first-class citizen?

Joe Absolutely! The information path can be stored in a variable and passed as an argument to a function.

 **TIP** In DOP, you can retrieve every piece of information via a path and a generic function.

Joe goes to the whiteboard. He draws a diagram like that in figure 3.5, which shows the catalog data as a tree.

Joe You see, Theo, each piece of information is accessible via a path made of strings and integers. For example, the path of Alan Moore's first book is `["catalog", "authorsById", "alan-moore", "bookIsbns", 0]`.

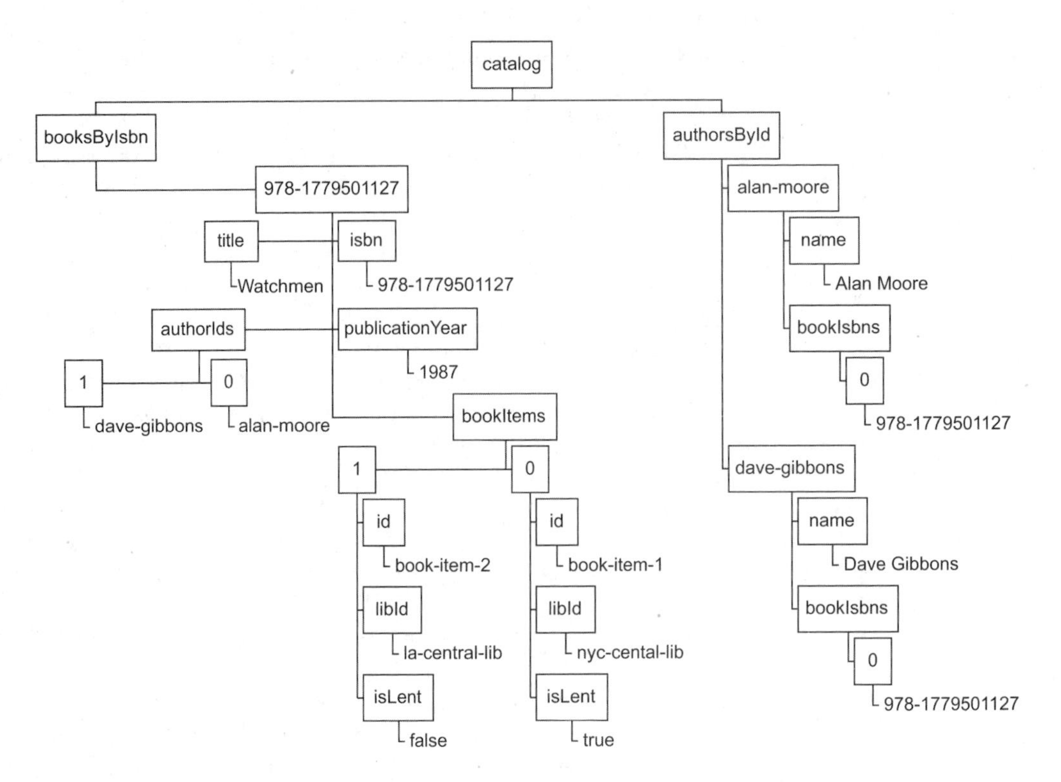

Figure 3.5 The catalog data as a tree

3.4 Calculating search results

Theo Interesting. I'm starting to feel the power of expression of DOP!

Joe Wait, that's just the beginning. Let me show you how simple it is to write code that retrieves book information and displays it in search results. Can you tell me exactly what information has to appear in the search results?

Theo Searching for book information should return `isbn`, `title`, and `authorNames`.

Joe And what would a `BookInfo` record look like for *Watchmen*?

Theo quickly enters the code on his laptop. He then shows it to Joe.

Listing 3.10 A `BookInfo` record for *Watchmen* in the context of search result

```
{
  "title": "Watchmen",
  "isbn": "978-1779501127",
  "authorNames": [
    "Alan Moore",
    "Dave Gibbons",
  ]
}
```

Joe Now I'll show you step by step how to write a function that returns search results matching a title in JSON format. I'll use generic data manipulation functions from Lodash.

Theo I'm ready!

Joe Let's start with an `authorNames` function that calculates the author names of a `Book` record by looking at the `authorsById` index. Could you tell me what's the information path for the name of an author whose ID is `authorId`?

Theo It's `["authorsById", authorId, "name"]`.

Joe Now, let me show you how to retrieve the name of several authors using `_.map`.

Joe types the code to map the author IDs to the author names. Theo nonchalantly peeks over Joe's shoulder.

Listing 3.11 Mapping author IDs to author names

```
_.map(["alan-moore", "dave-gibbons"],
  function(authorId) {
    return _.get(catalogData, ["authorsById", authorId, "name"]);
  });
// → [ "Alan Moore", "Dave Gibbons"]
```

Theo What's this `_.map` function? It smells like functional programming! You said I wouldn't have to learn FP to implement DOP!

Joe No need to learn functional programming in order to use `_.map`, which is a function that transforms the values of a collection. You can implement it with a simple `for` loop.

Theo spends a couple of minutes in front of his computer figuring out how to implement `_.map`. Now he's got it!

Listing 3.12 Custom implementation of `map`

```
function map(coll, f) {
  var res = [];
  for(var i = 0; i < coll.length; i++) {      <-- We could use forEach instead of a for loop.
    res[i] = f(coll[i]);
  }
  return res;
}
```

After testing Theo's implementation of `map`, Joe shows Theo the test. Joe again compliments Theo.

Listing 3.13 Testing the custom implementation of `map`

```
map(["alan-moore", "dave-gibbons"],
  function(authorId) {
    return _.get(catalogData, ["authorsById", authorId, "name"]);
  });
// → [ "Alan Moore", "Dave Gibbons"]
```

Joe Well done!

Theo You were right! It wasn't hard.

Joe Now, let's implement `authorNames` using `_.map`.

It takes a few minutes for Theo to come up with the implementation of `authorNames`. When he's finished, he turns his laptop to Joe.

Listing 3.14 Calculating the author names of a book

```
function authorNames(catalogData, book) {
  var authorIds = _.get(book, "authorIds");
  var names = _.map(authorIds, function(authorId) {
    return _.get(catalogData, ["authorsById", authorId, "name"]);
  });
  return names;
}
```

Joe We also need a `bookInfo` function that converts a `Book` record into a `BookInfo` record. Let me show you the code for that.

Listing 3.15 Converting a `Book` record into a `BookInfo` record

```
function bookInfo(catalogData, book) {
  var bookInfo = {
    "title": _.get(book, "title"),
    "isbn": _.get(book, "isbn"),
    "authorNames": authorNames(catalogData, book)
  };
  return bookInfo;        <-- There's no need to create
}                             a class for bookInfo.
```

Theo Looking at the code, I see that a `BookInfo` record has three fields: `title`, `isbn`, and `authorNames`. Is there a way to get this information without looking at the code?

Joe You can either add it to the data entity diagram or write it in the documentation of the `bookInfo` function, or both.

Theo I have to get used to the idea that in DOP, the record field information is not part of the program.

Joe Indeed, it's not part of the program, but it gives us a lot of flexibility.

Theo Is there any way for me to have my cake and eat it too?

Joe Yes, and someday I'll show you how to make record field information part of a DOP program (see chapters 7 and 12).

Theo Sounds intriguing!

Joe Now that we have all the pieces in place, we can write our `searchBooksByTitle` function, which returns the book information about the books that match the query. First, we find the `Book` records that match the query with `_.filter` and then we transform each `Book` record into a `BookInfo` record with `_.map` and `bookInfo`.

Listing 3.16 Searching books that match a query

```
function searchBooksByTitle(catalogData, query) {
  var allBooks = _.values(_.get(catalogData, "booksByIsbn"));
  var matchingBooks = _.filter(allBooks, function(book) {
    return _.get(book, "title").includes(query);
  });

  var bookInfos = _.map(matchingBooks, function(book) {
    return bookInfo(catalogData, book);
  });
  return bookInfos;
}
```

The includes JavaScript function checks whether a string includes a string as a substring.

Theo You're using Lodash functions without any explanation again!

Joe Sorry about that. I am so used to basic data manipulation functions that I consider them as part of the language. What functions are new to you?

Theo `_.values` and `_.filter`

Joe Well, `_.values` returns a collection made of the values of a map, and `_.filter` returns a collection made of the values that satisfy a predicate.

Theo `_.values` seems trivial. Let me try to implement `_.filter`.

The implementation of `_.filter` takes a bit more time. Eventually, Theo manages to get it right, then he is able to test it.

Listing 3.17 Custom implementation of `filter`

```
function filter(coll, f) {
  var res = [];
  for(var i = 0; i < coll.length; i++) {
    if(f(coll[i])) {
      res.push(coll[i]);
    }
  }
  return res;
}
```

We could use forEach instead of a for loop.

Listing 3.18 Testing the custom implementation of `filter`

```
filter(["Watchmen", "Batman"], function (title) {
  return title.includes("Watch");
});
// → ["Watchmen"]
```

Theo To me, it's a bit weird that to access the title of a book record, I need to write `_.get(book, "title")`. I'd expect it to be `book.title` in dot notation or `book["title"]` in bracket notation.

Joe Remember that book is a record that's not represented as an object. It's a map. Indeed, in JavaScript, you can write `_.get(book, "title")`, `book.title`, or `book["title"]`. But I prefer to use Lodash's `_.get` function. In some languages, the dot and the bracket notations might not work on maps.

Theo Being language-agnostic has a price!

Joe Right, would you like to test `searchBooksByTitle`?

Theo Absolutely! Let me call `searchBooksByTitle` to search the books whose title contain the string `Watch`.

Listing 3.19 Testing `searchBooksByTitle`

```
searchBooksByTitle(catalogData, "Wat");
//[
//  {
//    "authorNames": [
//      "Alan Moore",
//      "Dave Gibbons"
//    ],
//    "isbn": "978-1779501127",
//    "title": "Watchmen"
//  }
//]
```

Theo It seems to work! Are we done with the search implementation?

Joe Almost. The `searchBooksByTitle` function we wrote is going to be part of the `Catalog` module, and it returns a collection of records. We have to write a function that's part of the `Library` module, and that returns a JSON string.

Theo You told me earlier that JSON serialization was straightforward in DOP.

Joe Correct. The code for `searchBooksByTitleJSON` retrieves the `Catalog` record, passes it to `searchBooksByTitle`, and converts the results to JSON with `JSON.stringify`. That's part of JavaScript. Here, let me show you.

Listing 3.20 Implementation of searching books in a library as JSON

```
function searchBooksByTitleJSON(libraryData, query) {
  var results = searchBooksByTitle(_.get(libraryData, "catalog"), query);
  var resultsJSON = JSON.stringify(results);
  return resultsJSON;
}
```

Joe In order to test our code, we need to create a `Library` record that contains our `Catalog` record. Could you do that for me, please?

Theo Should the `Library` record contain all the `Library` fields (`name`, `address`, and `UserManagement`)?

Joe That's not necessary. For now, we only need the `catalog` field, then the test for searching books.

Listing 3.21 A `Library` record

```
var libraryData = {
  "catalog": {
    "booksByIsbn": {
      "978-1779501127": {
        "isbn": "978-1779501127",
        "title": "Watchmen",
```

```
        "publicationYear": 1987,
        "authorIds": ["alan-moore",
          "dave-gibbons"],
        "bookItems": [
          {
            "id": "book-item-1",
            "libId": "nyc-central-lib",
            "isLent": true
          },
          {
            "id": "book-item-2",
            "libId": "nyc-central-lib",
            "isLent": false
          }
        ]
      }
    },
    "authorsById": {
      "alan-moore": {
        "name": "Alan Moore",
        "bookIsbns": ["978-1779501127"]
      },
      "dave-gibbons": {
        "name": "Dave Gibbons",
        "bookIsbns": ["978-1779501127"]
      }
    }
  }
};
```

Listing 3.22 Test for searching books in a library as JSON

```
searchBooksByTitleJSON(libraryData, "Wat");
```

Theo How are we going to combine the four functions that we've written so far?

Joe The functions `authorNames`, `bookInfo`, and `searchBooksByTitle` go into the `Catalog` module, and `searchBooksByTitleJSON` goes into the `Library` module.

Theo looks at the resulting code of the two modules, `Library` and `Catalog`. He's quite amazed by its conciseness.

Listing 3.23 Calculating search results for `Library` and `Catalog`

```
class Catalog {
  static authorNames(catalogData, book) {
    var authorIds = _.get(book, "authorIds");
    var names = _.map(authorIds, function(authorId) {
      return _.get(catalogData, ["authorsById", authorId, "name"]);
    });
    return names;
  }
```

```
  static bookInfo(catalogData, book) {
    var bookInfo =  {
      "title": _.get(book, "title"),
      "isbn": _.get(book, "isbn"),
      "authorNames": Catalog.authorNames(catalogData, book)
    };                                    <-- There's no need
    return bookInfo;                          to create a class
  }                                           for bookInfo.

  static searchBooksByTitle(catalogData, query) {
    var allBooks = _.get(catalogData, "booksByIsbn");
    var matchingBooks = _.filter(allBooks,
      function(book) {                         <-- When _.filter is passed a map, it
        return _.get(book, "title").includes(query);   goes over the values of the map.
    });
    var bookInfos = _.map(matchingBooks, function(book) {
      return Catalog.bookInfo(catalogData, book);
    });
    return bookInfos;
  }
}

class Library {
  static searchBooksByTitleJSON(libraryData, query) {
    var catalogData = _.get(libraryData, "catalog");
    var results = Catalog.searchBooksByTitle(catalogData, query);
    var resultsJSON = JSON.stringify(results);    <-- Converts data
    return resultsJSON;                               to JSON (part
  }                                                   of JavaScript)
}
```

After testing the final code in listing 3.24, Theo looks again at the source code from listing 3.23. After a few seconds, he feels like he's having another *Aha!* moment.

Listing 3.24 Search results in JSON

```
Library.searchBooksByTitleJSON(libraryData, "Watchmen");
// → "[{\"title\":\"Watchmen\",\"isbn\":\"978-1779501127\",
// → \"authorNames\":[\"Alan Moore\",\"Dave Gibbons\"]}]"
```

Theo The important thing is not that the code is concise, but that the code contains no abstractions. It's just data manipulation!

Joe responds with a smile that says, "You got it, my friend!"

Joe It reminds me of what my first meditation teacher told me 10 years ago: meditation guides the mind to grasp the reality as it is without the abstractions created by our thoughts.

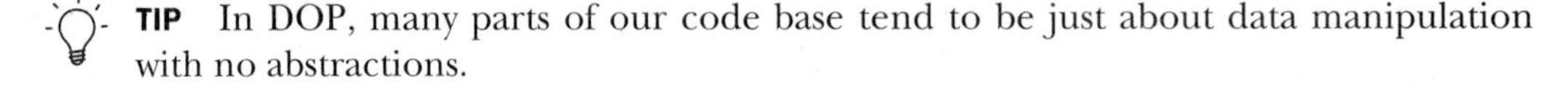

TIP In DOP, many parts of our code base tend to be just about data manipulation with no abstractions.

3.5 Handling records of different types

We've seen how DOP enables us to treat records as first-class citizens that can be manipulated in a flexible way using generic functions. But if a record is nothing more than an aggregation of fields, how do we know what the type of the record is? DOP has a surprising answer to this question.

Theo I have a question. If a record is nothing more than a map, how do you know the type of the record?

Joe That's a great question with a surprising answer.

Theo I'm curious.

Joe Most of the time, there's no need to know the record type.

Theo What! What do you mean?

Joe I mean that what matters most are the values of the fields. For example, take a look at the `Catalog.authorNames` source code. It operates on a `Book` record, but the only thing that matters is the value of the `authorIds` field.

Doubtful, Theo looks at the source code for `Catalog.authorNames`. This is what Theo sees.

Listing 3.25 Calculating the author names of a book

```
function authorNames(catalogData, book) {
  var authorIds = _.get(book, "authorIds");
  var names = _.map(authorIds, function(authorId) {
    return _.get(catalogData, ["authorsById", authorId, "name"]);
  });
  return names;
}
```

Theo What about differentiating between various user types like `Member` versus `Librarian`? I mean, they both have `email` and `encryptedPassword`. How do you know if a record represents a `Member` or a `Librarian`?

Joe Simple. You check to see if the record is found in the `librariansByEmail` index or in the `membersByEmail` index of the `Catalog`.

Theo Could you be more specific?

Joe Sure! Let me write what the user management data of our tiny library might look like, assuming we have one librarian and one member. To keep things simple, I'm encrypting passwords through naive base-64 encoding for the `User-Management` record.

Listing 3.26 A `UserManagement` record

```
var userManagementData = {
  "librariansByEmail": {
    "franck@gmail.com" : {
      "email": "franck@gmail.com",
      "encryptedPassword": "bXlwYXNzd29yZA=="    // The base-64 encoding of "mypassword"
    }
  },
```

```
    "membersByEmail": {
      "samantha@gmail.com": {
        "email": "samantha@gmail.com",
        "encryptedPassword": "c2VjcmV0",       ◁ The base-64 encoding of "secret"
        "isBlocked": false,
        "bookLendings": [
          {
            "bookItemId": "book-item-1",
            "bookIsbn": "978-1779501127",
            "lendingDate": "2020-04-23"
          }
        ]
      }
    }
}
```

TIP Most of the time, there's no need to know the record type.

Theo This morning, you told me you'd show me the code for `UserManagement.isLibrarian` function this afternoon.

Joe So, here we are. It's afternoon, and I'm going to fulfill my promise.

Joe implements `isLibrarian`. With a slight pause, he then issues the test for `isLibrarian`.

Listing 3.27 Checking if a user is a librarian

```
function isLibrarian(userManagement, email) {
  return _.has(_.get(userManagement, "librariansByEmail"), email);
}
```

Listing 3.28 Testing `isLibrarian`

```
isLibrarian(userManagementData, "franck@gmail.com");
// → true
```

Theo I'm assuming that `_.has` is a function that checks whether a key exists in a map. Right?

Joe Correct.

Theo OK. You simply check whether the `librariansByEmail` map contains the `email` field.

Joe Yep.

Theo Would you use the same pattern to check whether a member is a Super member or a VIP member?

Joe Sure. We could have `SuperMembersByEmail` and `VIPMembersByEmail` indexes. But there's a better way.

Theo How?

Joe When a member is a VIP member, we add a field, `isVIP`, with the value `true` to its record. To check if a member is a VIP member, we check whether the `isVIP` field is set to `true` in the member record. Here's how I would code `isVIPMember`.

Listing 3.29 Checking whether a member is a VIP member

```
function isVIPMember(userManagement, email) {
  return _.get(userManagement, ["membersByEmail", email, "isVIP"]) == true;
}
```

Theo I see that you access the `isVIP` field via its information path, `["membersByEmail", email, "isVIP"]`.

Joe Yes, I think it makes the code crystal clear.

Theo I agree. I guess we can do the same for `isSuperMember` and set an `isSuper` field to `true` when a member is a Super member?

Joe Yes, just like this.

Joe assembles all the pieces in a `UserManagement` class. He then shows the code to Theo.

Listing 3.30 The code of `UserManagement` module

```
class UserManagement {
  isLibrarian(userManagement, email) {
    return _.has(_.get(userManagement, "librariansByEmail"), email);
  }

  isVIPMember(userManagement, email) {
    return _.get(userManagement,
      ["membersByEmail", email, "isVIP"]) == true;
  }

  isSuperMember(userManagement, email) {
    return _.get(userManagement,
      ["membersByEmail", email, "isSuper"]) == true;
  }
}
```

Theo looks at the `UserManagement` module code for a couple of seconds. Suddenly, an idea comes to his mind.

Theo Why not have a `type` field in member record whose value would be either `VIP` or `Super`?

Joe I assume that, according to the product requirements, a member can be both a VIP and a Super member.

Theo Hmm . . . then the `types` field could be a collection containing `VIP` or `Super` or both.

Joe In some situations, having a `types` field is helpful, but I find it simpler to have a Boolean field for each feature that the record supports.

Theo Is there a name for fields like `isVIP` and `isSuper`?

Joe I call them *feature fields*.

TIP Instead of maintaining type information about a record, use a feature field (e.g., `isVIP`).

Theo Can we use feature fields to differentiate between librarians and members?

Joe You mean having an `isLibrarian` and an `isMember` field?

Theo Yes, and having a common `User` record type for both librarians and members.

Joe We can, but I think it's simpler to have different record types for librarians and members: `Librarian` for librarians and `Member` for members.

Theo Why?

Joe Because there's a clear distinction between librarians and members in terms of data. For example, members can have book lendings but librarians don't.

Theo I agree. Now, we need to mention the two `Member` feature fields in our entity diagram.

With that, Theo adds these fields to his diagram on the whiteboard. When he's finished, he shows Joe his additions (figure 3.6).

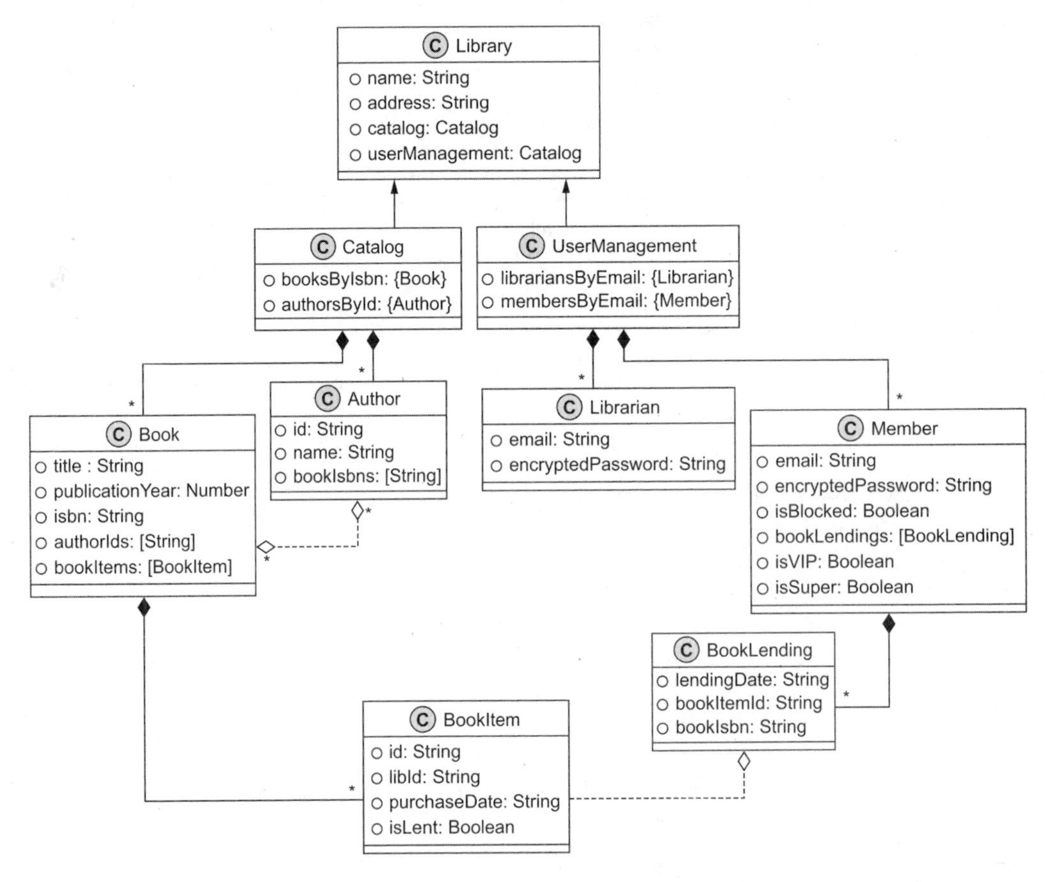

Figure 3.6 A library management data model with the `Member` feature fields `isVIP` and `isSuper`

Joe Do you like the data model that we have designed together?

Theo I find it quite simple and clear.

Joe That's the main goal of DOP.

Theo Also, I'm pleasantly surprised how easy it is to adapt to changing requirements, both in terms of code and the data model.

Joe I suppose you're also happy to get rid of complex class hierarchy diagrams.

Theo Absolutely! Also, I think I've found an interesting connection between DOP and meditation.

Joe Really?

Theo When we were eating at Simple, you told me that meditation helped you experience reality as it is without the filter of your thoughts.

Joe Right.

Theo From what you taught me today, I understand that in DOP, we are encouraged to treat data as data without the filter of our classes.

Joe Clever! I never noticed that connection between those two disciplines that are so important for me. I guess you'd like to continue your journey in the realm of DOP.

Theo Definitely. Let's meet again tomorrow.

Joe Unfortunately, tomorrow I'm taking my family to the beach to celebrate the twelfth birthday of my eldest daughter, Aurelia.

Theo Happy birthday, Aurelia!

Joe We could meet again next Monday, if that's OK with you.

Theo With pleasure!

Summary

- DOP principle #2 is to represent data entities with generic data structures.
- We refer to maps that have strings as keys as *string maps*.
- Representing data as data means representing records with string maps.
- By *positional collection*, we mean a collection where the elements are in order (like a list or an array).
- A positional collection of `Strings` is noted as `[String]`.
- By *index*, we mean a collection where the elements are accessible via a key (like a hash map or a dictionary).
- An index of `Books` is noted as `{Book}`.
- In the context of a data model, the index keys are always strings.
- A *record* is a data structure that groups together related data items. It's a collection of fields, possibly of different data types.
- A *homogeneous map* is a map where all the values are of the same type.
- A *heterogeneous map* is a map where the values are of different types.
- In DOP, we represent a record as a heterogeneous string map.
- A *data entity diagram* consists of records whose values are either primitives, positional collections, or indexes.
- The relation between records in a data entity diagram is either *composition* or *association*.

- The data part of a DOP system is flexible, and each piece of information is accessible via its information path.
- There is a tradeoff between flexibility and safety in a data model.
- DOP compromises on data safety to gain flexibility and genericity.
- In DOP, the data model is flexible. We're free to add, remove, and rename record fields dynamically at run time.
- We manipulate data with generic functions.
- Generic functions are provided either by the language itself or by third-party libraries like Lodash.
- JSON *serialization* is implemented in terms of a generic function.
- On the one hand, we've lost the safety of accessing record fields via members defined at compile time. On the other hand, we've liberated data from the limitation of classes and objects. Data is represented as data!
- The weak dependency between code and data makes it is easier to adapt to changing requirements.
- When data is represented as data, it is straightforward to visualize system data.
- Usually, we do not need to maintain type information about a record.
- We can visualize any part of the system data.
- In statically-typed languages, we sometimes need to statically cast the field values.
- Instead of maintaining type information about a record, we use a *feature field*.
- There is no significant performance hit for accessing a field in a map instead of a class member.
- In DOP, you can retrieve every piece of information via an *information path* and a generic function.
- In DOP, many parts of our code base tend to be just about data manipulation with no abstractions.

Lodash functions introduced in this chapter

Function	Description
`get(map, path)`	Gets the value of `map` at `path`
`has(map, path)`	Checks if `map` has a field at `path`
`merge(mapA, mapB)`	Creates a map resulting from the recursive merges between `mapA` and `mapB`
`values(map)`	Creates an array of values of `map`
`filter(coll, pred)`	Iterates over elements of `coll`, returning an array of all elements for which `pred` returns `true`
`map(coll, f)`	Creates an array of values by running each element in `coll` through `f`

4 State management

Time travel

This chapter covers

- A multi-version approach to state management
- The calculation phase of a mutation
- The commit phase of a mutation
- Keeping a history of previous state versions

So far, we have seen how DOP handles queries via generic functions that access system data, which is represented as a hash map. In this chapter, we illustrate how DOP deals with *mutations* (requests that change the system state). Instead of updating the state in place, we maintain multiple versions of the system data. At a specific point in time, the *system state* refers to a specific version of the system data. This chapter is a deep dive in the third principle of DOP.

> PRINCIPLE #3 Data is immutable.

The maintenance of multiple versions of the system data requires the data to be immutable. This is made efficient both in terms of computation and memory via a technique called *structural sharing*, where parts of the data that are common between two versions are shared instead of being copied. In DOP, a mutation is split into two distinct phases:

- In the calculation phase, we compute the next version of the system data.
- In the commit phase, we move the system state forward so that it refers to the version of the system data computed by the calculation phase.

This distinction between calculation and commit phases allows us to reduce the part of our system that is stateful to its bare minimum. Only the code of the commit phase is stateful, while the code in the calculation phase of a mutation is stateless and is made of generic functions similar to the code of a query. The implementation of the commit phase is common to all mutations. As a consequence, inside the commit phase, we have the ability to ensure that the state always refers to a valid version of the system data.

Another benefit of this state management approach is that we can keep track of the history of previous versions of the system data. Restoring the system to a previous state (if needed) becomes straightforward. Table 4.1 shows the two phases.

Table 4.1 The two phases of a mutation

Phase	Responsibility	State	Implementation
Calculation	Computes the next version of system data	Stateless	Specific
Commit	Moves the system state forward	Stateful	Common

In this chapter, we assume that no mutations occur concurrently in our system. In the next chapter, we will deal with concurrency control.

4.1 Multiple versions of the system data

When Joe comes in to the office on Monday, he tells Theo that he needs to exercise before starting to work with his mind. Theo and Joe go for a walk around the block, and the discussion turns toward version control systems. They discuss how Git keeps track of the whole commit history and how easy and fast it is to restore the code to a previous state. When Theo tells Joe that Git's ability to "time travel" reminds him one of his favorite movies, *Back to the Future*, Joe shares that a month ago he watched the *Back to the Future* trilogy with Neriah, his 14-year-old son.

Their walk complete, they arrive back at Theo's office. Theo and Joe partake of the espresso machine in the kitchen before they begin today's lesson.

Joe So far, we've seen how we manage queries that retrieve information from the system in DOP. Now I'm going to show you how we manage mutations. By a mutation, I mean an operation that changes the state of the system.

▶ **NOTE** A *mutation* is an operation that changes the state of the system.

Theo Is there a fundamental difference between queries and mutations in DOP? After all, the whole state of the system is represented as a hash map. I could easily write code that modifies part of the hash map, and it would be similar to the code that retrieves information from the hash map.

Joe You could mutate the data in place, but then it would be challenging to ensure that the code of a mutation doesn't put the system into an invalid date. You would also lose the ability to track previous versions of the system state.

Theo I see. So, how do you handle mutations in DOP?

Joe We adopt a multi-version state approach, similar to what a version control system like Git does; we manage different versions of the system data. At a specific point in time, the state of the system refers to a version of the system data. After a mutation is executed, we move the reference forward.

Theo I'm confused. Is the system state mutable or immutable?

Joe The data is immutable, but the state reference is mutable.

TIP The data is immutable, but the state reference is mutable.

Noticing the look of confusion on Theo's face, Joe draws a quick diagram on the whiteboard. He then shows Theo figure 4.1, hoping that it will clear up Theo's perplexity.

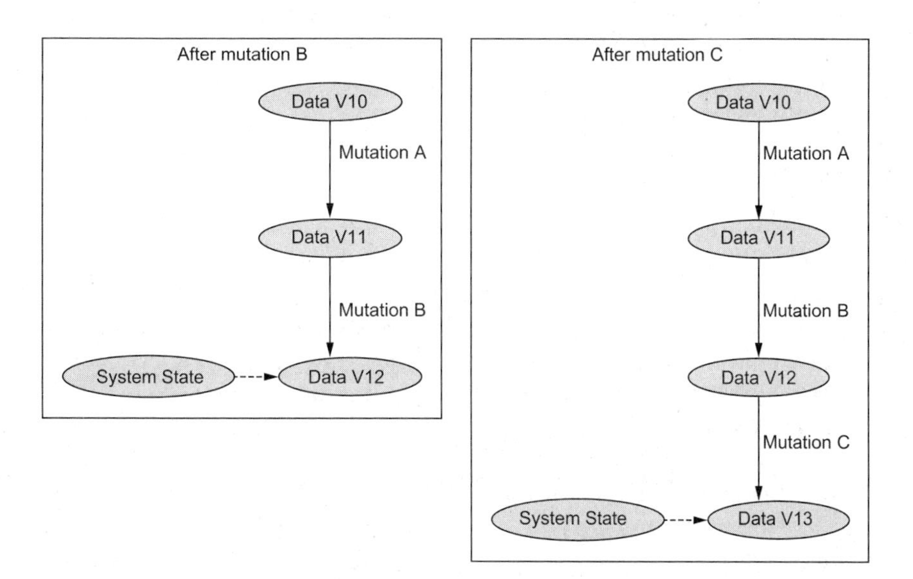

Figure 4.1 After `mutation B` is executed, the system state refers to `Data V12`. After `mutation C` is executed, the system state refers to `Data V13`.

Theo Does that mean that before the code of a mutation runs, we make a copy of the system data?

Joe No, that would be inefficient, as we would have to do a deep copy of the data.

Theo How does it work then?

Joe It works by using a technique called structural sharing, where most of the data between subsequent versions of the state is shared instead of being copied. This technique efficiently creates new versions of the system data, both in terms of memory and computation.

Theo I'm intrigued.

TIP With structural sharing, it's efficient (in terms of memory and computation) to create new versions of data.

Joe I'll explain in detail how structural sharing works in a moment.

Theo takes another look at the diagram in figure 4.1, which illustrates how the system state refers to a version of the system data. Suddenly, a question emerges.

Theo Are the previous versions of the system data kept?

Joe In a simple application, previous versions are automatically removed by the garbage collector. But, in some cases, we maintain historical references to previous versions of the data.

Theo What kind of cases?

Joe For example, if we want to support time travel in our system, as in Git, we can move the system back to a previous version of the state easily.

Theo Now I understand what you mean by data is immutable, but the state reference is mutable!

4.2 Structural sharing

As mentioned in the previous section, *structural sharing* enables the efficient creation of new versions of immutable data. In DOP, we use structural sharing in the calculation phase of a mutation to compute the next state of the system based on the current state of the system. Inside the calculation phase, we don't have to deal with state management; that is delayed to the commit phase. As a consequence, the code involved in the calculation phase of a mutation is stateless and is as simple as the code of a query.

Theo I'm really intrigued by this more efficient way to create new versions of data. How does it work?

Joe Let's take a simple example from our library system. Imagine that you want to modify the value of a field in a book in the catalog; for instance, the publication year of *Watchmen*. Can you tell me the information path for *Watchmen*'s publication year?

Theo takes a quick look at the catalog data in figure 4.2. Then he answers Joe's question.

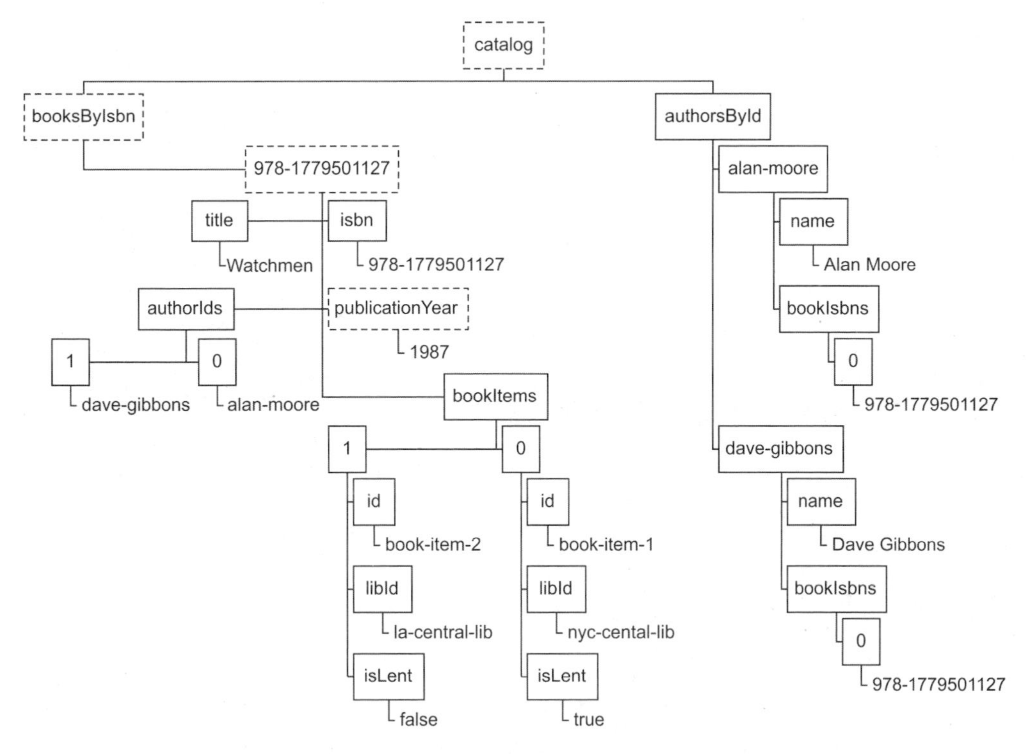

Figure 4.2 Visualization of the catalog data. The nodes in the information path to *Watchmen*'s publication year are marked with a dotted border.

Theo The information path for *Watchmen*'s publication year is `["catalog", "booksByIsbn", "978-1779501127", "publicationYear"]`.

Joe Now, let me show how you to use the immutable function `_.set` that Lodash also provides.

Theo Wait! What do you mean by an immutable function? When I looked at the Lodash documentation for `_.set` on their website, it said that it mutates the object.

Joe You're right, but the default Lodash functions are not immutable. In order to use an immutable version of the functions, we need to use the Lodash FP module as explained in the Lodash FP guide.

▶ **NOTE** See https://lodash.com/docs/4.17.15#set to view Lodash's documentation for `_.set`, and see https://github.com/lodash/lodash/wiki/FP-Guide to view the Lodash FP guide.

Theo Do the immutable functions have the same signature as the mutable functions?

Joe By default, the order of the arguments in immutable functions is shuffled. The Lodash FP guide explains how to resolve this. With this piece of code, the signature of the immutable functions is exactly the same as the mutable functions.

Listing 4.1 Configuring Lodash so immutable and mutable functions have same signature

```
_ = fp.convert({
  "cap": false,
  "curry": false,
  "fixed": false,
  "immutable": true,
  "rearg": false
});
```

TIP In order to use Lodash immutable functions, we use Lodash's FP module, and we configure it so that the signature of the immutable functions is the same as in the Lodash documentation web site.

Theo So basically, I can still rely on Lodash documentation when using immutable versions of the functions.

Joe Except for the piece in the documentation that says the function mutates the object.

Theo Of course!

Joe Now I'll show you how to write code that creates a version of the library data with the immutable function `_.set`.

Joe's fingers fly across Theo's keyboard. Theo then looks at Joe's code, which creates a version of the library data where the *Watchmen* publication year is set to 1986.

Listing 4.2 Using `_.set` as an immutable function

```
var nextLibraryData = _.set(libraryData,
  ["catalog", "booksByIsbn",
    "978-1779501127", "publicationYear"],
  1986);
```

▶ **NOTE** A function is said to be *immutable* when, instead of mutating the data, it creates a new version of the data without changing the data it receives.

Theo You told me earlier that structural sharing allowed immutable functions to be efficient in terms of memory and computation. Can you tell me what makes them efficient?

Joe With pleasure, but before that, you have to answer a series of questions. Are you ready?

Theo Yes, sure . . .

Joe What part of the library data is impacted by updating the *Watchmen* publication year: the `UserManagement` or the `Catalog`?

Theo Only the `Catalog`.

Joe What part of the `Catalog`?

Theo Only the `booksByIsbn` index.

Joe What part of the `booksByIsbn` index?

Theo Only the `Book` record that holds the information about *Watchmen*.

Joe What part of the `Book` record?

Theo Only the `publicationYear` field.

Joe Perfect! Now, suppose that the current version of the library data looks like this.

Joe goes to the whiteboard and draws a diagram. Figure 4.3 shows the result.

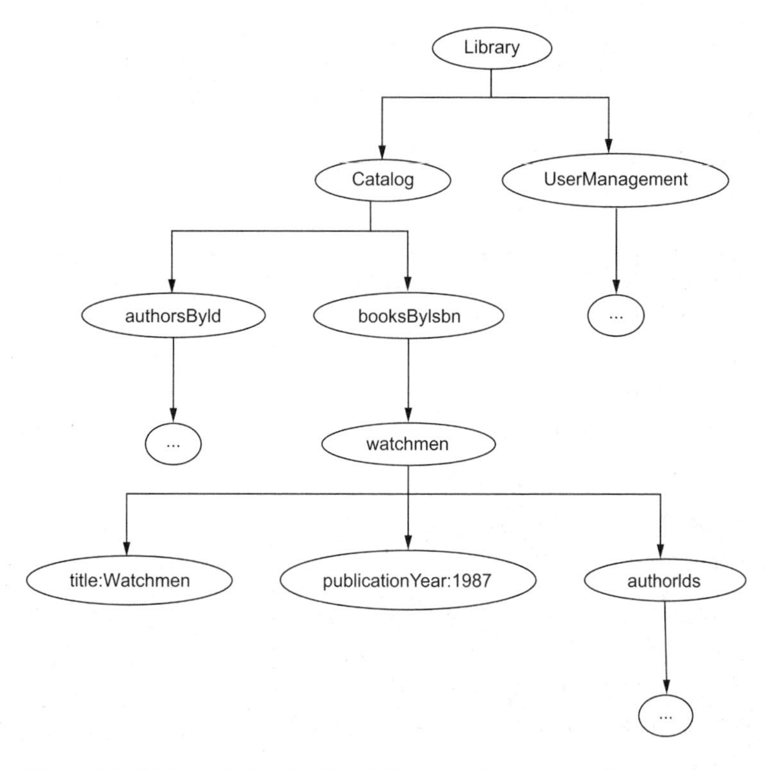

Figure 4.3 High-level visualization of the current version of `Library`

Theo So far, so good . . .

Joe Next, let me show you what an immutable function does when you use it to create a new version of `Library`, where the publication year of *Watchmen* is set to 1986 instead of 1987.

Joe updates his diagram on the whiteboard. It now looks like figure 4.4.

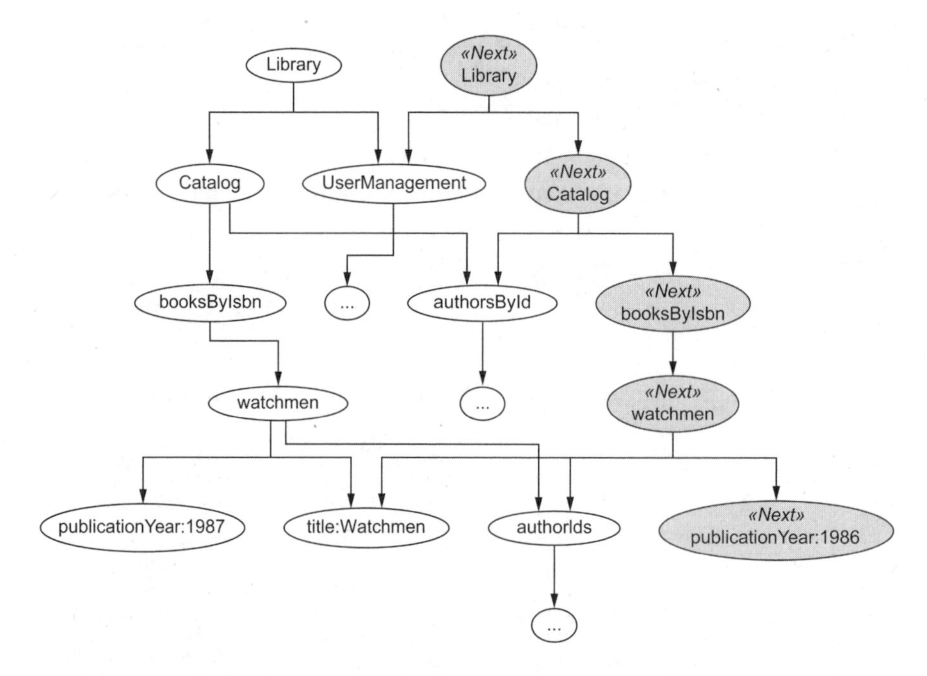

Figure 4.4 Structural sharing provides an efficient way to create a new version of the data. `Next Library` is recursively made of nodes that use the parts of `Library` that are common between the two.

Theo Could you explain?

Joe The immutable function creates a fresh `Library` hash map, which recursively uses the parts of the current `Library` that are common between the two versions instead of deeply copying them.

Theo It's a bit abstract for me.

Joe The next version of `Library` uses the same `UserManagement` hash map as the old one. The `Catalog` inside the next `Library` uses the same `authorsById` as the current `Catalog`. The *Watchmen* `Book` record inside the next `Catalog` uses all the fields of the current `Book` except for the `publicationYear` field.

Theo So, in fact, most parts of the data are shared between the two versions. Right?

Joe Exactly! That's why this technique is called *structural sharing*.

TIP Structural sharing provides an efficient way (both in terms of memory and computation) to create a new version of the data by recursively sharing the parts that don't need to change.

Theo That's very cool!

Joe Indeed. Now let's look at how to write a mutation for adding a member using immutable functions.

Once again, Joe goes to the whiteboard. Figure 4.5 shows the diagram that Joe draws to illustrate how structural sharing looks when we add a member.

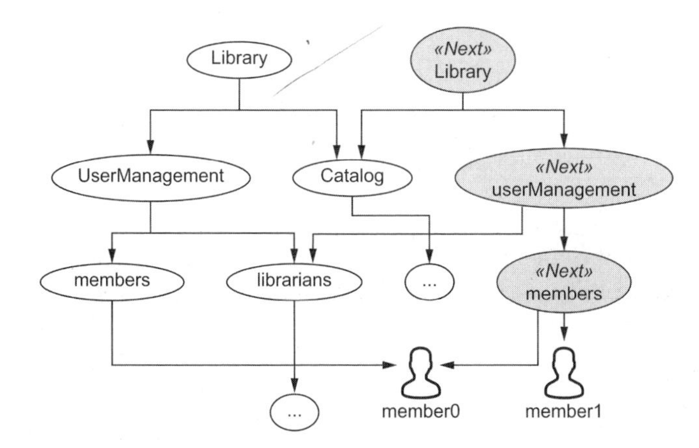

Figure 4.5 Adding a member with structural sharing. Most of the data is shared between the two versions.

Theo Awesome! The `Catalog` and the `librarians` hash maps don't have to be copied!

Joe Now, in terms of code, we have to write a `Library.addMember` function that delegates to `UserManagement.addMember`.

Theo I guess it's going to be similar to the code we wrote earlier to implement the search books query, where `Library.searchBooksByTitleJSON` delegates to `Catalog.searchBooksByTitle`.

Joe Similar in the sense that all the functions are static, and they receive the data they manipulate as an argument. But there are two differences. First, a mutation could fail, for instance, if the member to be added already exists. Second, the code for `Library.addMember` is a bit more elaborate than the code for `Library.searchBooksByTitleJSON` because we have to create a new version of `Library` that refers to the new version of `UserManagement`. Here, let me show you an example.

Listing 4.3 The code for the mutation that adds a member

```
UserManagement.addMember = function(userManagement, member) {
  var email = _.get(member, "email");
  var infoPath = ["membersByEmail", email];
  if(_.has(userManagement, infoPath)) {
    throw "Member already exists.";
  }
  var nextUserManagement =  _.set(
    userManagement,
    infoPath,
    member);
  return nextUserManagement;
};
```

- Checks if a member with the same email address already exists (annotates the `if(_.has(...))` line)
- Creates a new version of userManagement that includes the member (annotates the `_.set(` call)

```
Library.addMember = function(library, member) {
  var currentUserManagement = _.get(library, "userManagement");
  var nextUserManagement = UserManagement.addMember(
    currentUserManagement,
    member);
  var nextLibrary = _.set(library,
    "userManagement",
    nextUserManagement);
  return nextLibrary;
};
```

Creates a new version of library that contains the new version of userManagement

Theo To me, it's a bit weird that immutable functions return an updated version of the data instead of changing it in place.

Joe It was also weird for me when I first encountered immutable data in Clojure seven years ago.

Theo How long did it take you to get used to it?

Joe A couple of weeks.

4.3 Implementing structural sharing

When Joe leaves the office, Theo meets Dave near the coffee machine. Dave looks perplexed.

Dave Who's the guy that just left the office?

Theo It's Joe. My DOP mentor.

Dave What's DOP?

Theo DOP refers to data-oriented programming.

Dave I never heard that term before.

Theo It's not well-known by programmers yet, but it's quite a powerful programming paradigm. From what I've seen so far, it makes programming much simpler.

Dave Can you give me an example?

Theo I just learned about structural sharing and how it makes it possible to create new versions of data, effectively without copying.

Dave How does that work?

Theo takes Dave to his office and shows him Joe's diagram on the whiteboard (see figure 4.6). It takes Theo a few minutes to explain to Dave what it does exactly, but in the end, Dave gets it.

Dave What does the implementation of structural sharing look like?

Theo I don't know. I used the `_.set` function from Lodash.

Dave It sounds like an interesting challenge.

Theo Take the challenge if you want. Right now, I'm too tired for this recursive algorithmic stuff.

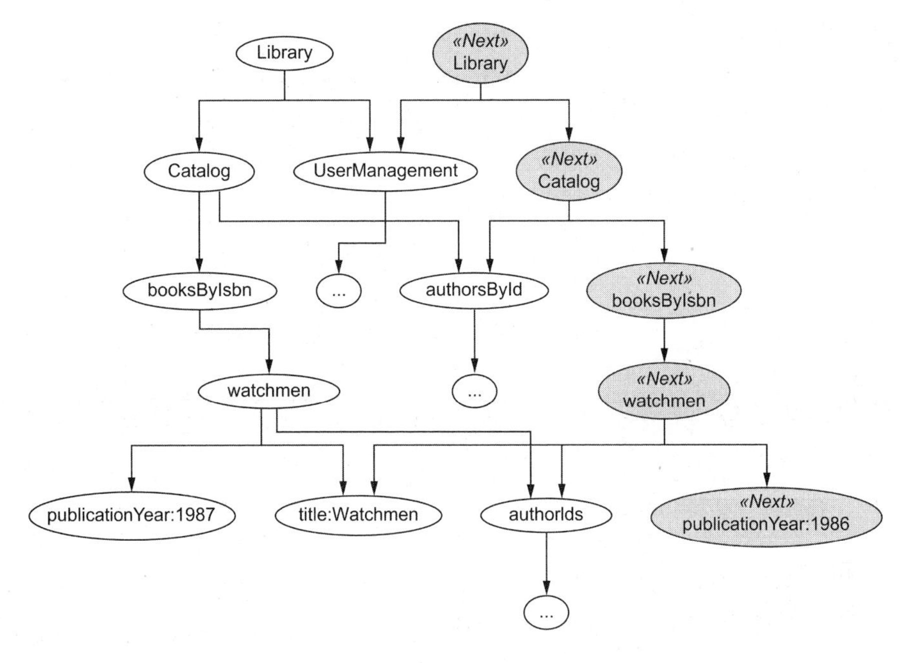

Figure 4.6 Structural sharing in action

The next day, Theo stops by Dave's cubicle before heading to his office. Dave, with a touch of pride, shows Theo his implementation of structural sharing. Theo is amazed by the fact that it's only 11 lines of JavaScript code!

Listing 4.4 The implementation of structural sharing

```
function setImmutable(map, path, v) {
  var modifiedNode = v;
  var k = path[0];
  var restOfPath = path.slice(1);
  if (restOfPath.length > 0) {
    modifiedNode = setImmutable(map[k], restOfPath, v);
  }
  var res = Object.assign({}, map);     <-- Shallow clones a map in JavaScript.
  res[k] = modifiedNode;
  return res;
}
```

Theo Dave, you're brilliant!

Dave (smiling) Aw, shucks.

Theo Oops, I have to go. I'm already late for my session with Joe! Joe is probably waiting in my office, biting his nails.

4.4 Data safety

Joe is about to start the day's lesson. Theo asks him a question about yesterday's material instead.

Theo Something isn't clear to me regarding this structural sharing stuff. What happens if we write code that modifies the data part that's shared between the two versions of the data? Does the change affect both versions?

Joe Could you please write a code snippet that illustrates your question?

Theo starts typing on his laptop. He comes up with this code to illustrate modifying a piece of data shared between two versions.

Listing 4.5 Modifying data that's shared between two versions

```
var books = {
  "978-1779501127": {
    "isbn": "978-1779501127",
    "title": "Watchmen",
    "publicationYear": 1987,
    "authorIds": ["alan-moore",
      "dave-gibbons"]
  }
};

var nextBooks = _.set(books, ["978-1779501127", "publicationYear"], 1986)

console.log("Before:", nextBooks["978-1779501127"]["authorIds"][1]);

books["978-1779501127"]["authorIds"][1] = "dave-chester-gibbons";

console.log("After:", nextBooks["978-1779501127"]["authorIds"][1]);
// → Before: dave-gibbons
// → After: dave-chester-gibbons
```

Theo My question is, what is the value of `isBlocked` in `updatedMember`?

Joe The answer is that mutating data via the native hash map setter is forbidden. All the data manipulation must be done via immutable functions.

▶ **NOTE** All data manipulation must be done with immutable functions. It is forbidden to use the native hash map setter.

Theo When you say "forbidden," you mean that it's up to the developer to make sure it doesn't happen. Right?

Joe Exactly.

Theo Is there a way to protect our system from a developer's mistake?

Joe Yes, there is a way to ensure the immutability of the data at the level of the data structure. It's called persistent data structures.

Theo Are persistent data structures also efficient in terms of memory and computation?

Joe Actually, the way data is organized inside persistent data structures make them even more efficient than immutable functions.

TIP Persistent data structures are immutable at the level of the data. There is no way to mutate them, even by mistake.

Theo Are there libraries providing persistent data structures?

Joe Definitely. I just happen to have a list of those libraries on my computer.

Joe, being well-organized for a programmer, quickly brings up his list. He shows it to Theo:

- Immutable.js in JavaScript at https://immutable-js.com/
- Paguro in Java at https://github.com/GlenKPeterson/Paguro
- Immutable Collections in C# at http://mng.bz/y4Ke
- Pyrsistent in Python at https://github.com/tobgu/pyrsistent
- Hamster in Ruby at https://github.com/hamstergem/hamster

Theo Why not use persistent data structures instead of immutable functions?

Joe The drawback of persistent data structures is that they are not native. This means that working with them requires conversion from native to persistent and from persistent to native.

Theo What approach would you recommend?

Joe If you want to play around a bit, then start with immutable functions. But for a production application, I'd recommend using persistent data structures.

Theo Too bad the native data structures aren't persistent!

Joe That's one of the reasons why I love Clojure—the native data structures of the language are immutable!

4.5 The commit phase of a mutation

So far, we saw how to implement the calculation phase of a mutation. The calculation phase is stateless in the sense that it doesn't make any change to the system. Now, let's see how to update the state of the system inside the commit phase.

Theo takes another look at the code for `Library.addMember`. Something bothers him: this function returns a new state of the library that contains an additional member, but it doesn't affect the current state of the library.

Listing 4.6 The commit phase moves the system state forward

```
Library.addMember = function(library, member) {
  var currentUserManagement = _.get(library, "userManagement");
  var nextUserManagement = UserManagement.addMember(
    currentUserManagement,
    member);
  var nextLibrary = _.set(library, "userManagement", nextUserManagement);
  return nextLibrary;
};
```

Theo I see that `Library.addMember` doesn't change the state of the library. How does the library state get updated?

Joe That's an excellent question. `Library.addMember` deals only with data calculation and is stateless. The state is updated in the commit phase by moving forward the version of the state that the system state refers to.

Theo What do you mean by that?

Joe Here's what happens when we add a member to the system. The calculation phase creates a version of the state that has two members. Before the commit phase, the system state refers to the version of the state with one member. The responsibility of the commit phase is to move the system state forward so that it refers to the version of the state with two members.

TIP The responsibility of the commit phase is to move the system state forward to the version of the state returned by the calculation phase.

Joe draws another illustration on the whiteboard (figure 4.7). He hopes it helps to clear up any misunderstanding Theo may have.

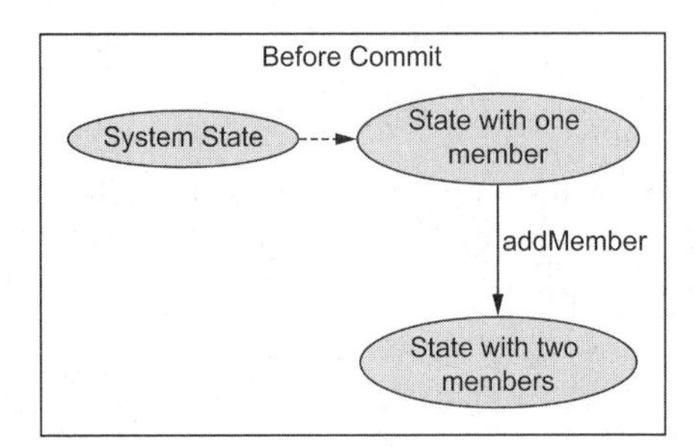

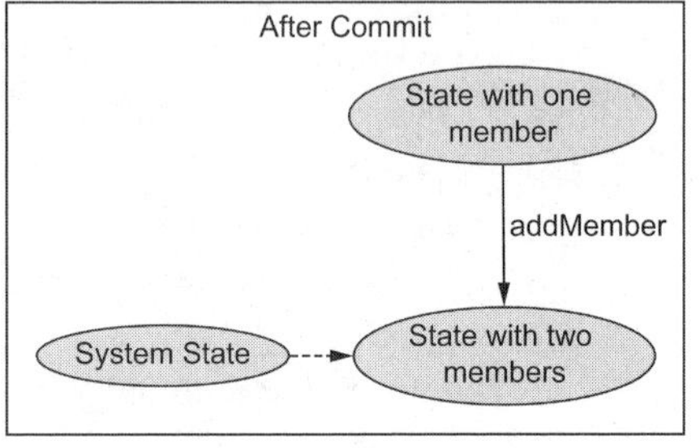

Figure 4.7 The commit phase moves the system state forward.

Theo How is this implemented?

Joe The code is made of two classes: `System`, a singleton stateful class that implements the mutations, and `SystemState`, a singleton stateful class that manages the system state.

Theo It sounds to me like classic OOP.

Joe Right, and this part of the system being stateful is OOP-like.

Theo I'm happy to see that you still find some utility in OOP.

Joe Meditation taught me that every part of our universe has a role to play.

Theo Nice! Could you show me some code?

Joe Sure.

Joe thinks for a moment before starting to type. He wants to show the `System` class and its implementation of the `addMember` mutation.

Listing 4.7 The `System` class

```
class System {
  addMember(member) {
    var previous = SystemState.get();
```

```
    var next = Library.addMember(previous, member);
    SystemState.commit(previous, next);
  }
}
```
SystemState is covered in listing 4.8.

Theo What does `SystemState` look like?

Joe I had a feeling you were going to ask that. Here's the code for the `SystemState` class, which is a stateful class!

Listing 4.8 The `SystemState` class

```
class SystemState {
  systemState;

  get() {
    return this.systemState;
  }

  commit(previous, next) {
    this.systemState = next;
  }
}
```

Theo I don't get the point of `SystemState`. It's a simple class with a getter and a commit function, right?

Joe In a moment, we are going to enrich the code of the `SystemState.commit` method so that it provides data validation and history tracking. For now, the important thing to notice is that the code of the calculation phase is stateless and is decoupled from the code of the commit phase, which is stateful.

 **TIP** The calculation phase is stateless. The commit phase is stateful.

4.6 Ensuring system state integrity

Theo Something still bothers me about the way functions manipulate immutable data in the calculation phase. How do we preserve data integrity?

Joe What do you mean?

Theo In OOP, data is manipulated only by methods that belong to the same class as the data. It prevents other classes from corrupting the inner state of the class.

Joe Could you give me an example of an invalid state of the library?

Theo For example, imagine that the code of a mutation adds a book item to the book lendings of a member without marking the book item as lent in the catalog. Then the system data would be corrupted.

Joe In DOP, we have the privilege of ensuring data integrity at the level of the whole system instead of scattering the validation among many classes.

Theo How does that work?

Joe The fact that the code for the commit phase is common to all the mutations allows us to validate the system data in a central place. At the beginning of the commit phase, there is a step that checks whether the version of the system state to be committed is valid. If the data is invalid, the commit is rejected. Here let me show you.

Listing 4.9 Data validation inside the commit phase

```
SystemState.commit = function(previous, next) {
  if(!SystemValidity.validate(previous, next)) { // not implemented for now
    throw "The system data to be committed is not valid!";
  };
  this.systemData = next;
};
```

Theo It sounds similar to a commit hook in Git.

Joe I like your analogy!

Theo Why are you passing the previous state in `previous` and the next state in `next` to `SystemValidity.validate`?

Joe Because it allows `SystemValidity.validate` to optimize the validation in terms of computation. For example, we could validate just the data that has changed.

TIP In DOP, we validate the system data as a whole. Data validation is decoupled from data manipulation.

Theo What does the code of `SystemValidity.validate` look like?

Joe Someday, I will show you how to define a data schema and to validate that a piece of data conforms to a schema.

▶ **NOTE** See chapters 7 and 12 to see how Joe defines this data schema.

4.7 Restoring previous states

Another advantage of the multi-version state approach with immutable data that is manipulated via structural sharing is that we can keep track of the history of all the versions of the data without exploding the memory of our program. It allows us, for instance, to restore the system back to an earlier state easily.

Theo You told me earlier that it was easy to restore the system to a previous state. Could you show me how?

Joe Happily, but before that, I'd like to make sure you understand why keeping track of all the versions of the data is efficient in terms of memory.

Theo I think it's related to the fact that immutable functions use structural sharing, and most of the data between subsequent versions of the state is shared.

TIP Structural sharing allows us to keep many versions of the system state without exploding memory use.

Joe Perfect! Now, I'll show you how simple it is to undo a mutation. In order to implement an undo mechanism, our `SystemState` class needs to have two references to the system data: `systemData` references the current state of the system, and `previousSystemData` references the previous state of the system.

Theo That makes sense.

Joe In the commit phase, we update both `previousSystemData` and `systemData`.

Theo What does it take to implement an undo mechanism?

Joe The undo is achieved by having `systemData` reference the same version of the system data as `previousSystemData`.

Theo Could you walk me through an example?

Joe To make things simple, I am going to give a number to each version of the system state. It starts at `V0`, and each time a mutation is committed, the version is incremented: `V1`, `V2`, `V3`, and so forth.

Theo OK.

Joe Let's say that currently our system state is at `V12` (see figure 4.8). In the `SystemState` object, `systemData` refers to `V12`, and `previousSystemData` refers to `V11`.

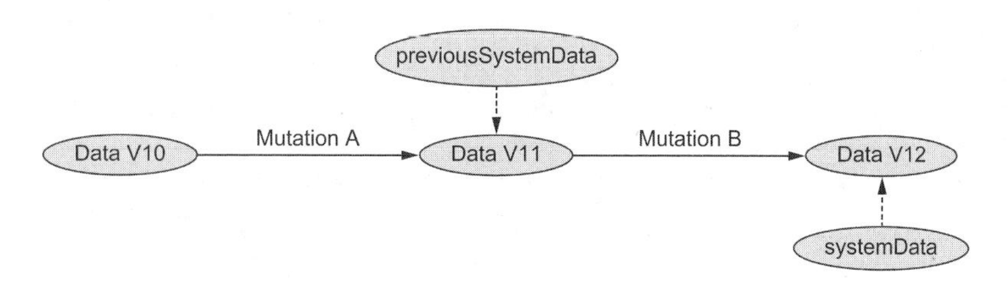

Figure 4.8 When the system state is at `V12`, `systemData` refers to `V12`, and `previousSystemData` refers to `V11`.

Theo So far, so good . . .

Joe Now, when a mutation is committed (for instance, adding a member), both references move forward: `systemData` refers to `V13`, and `previousSystemData` refers to `V12`.

Joe erases the whiteboard to make room for another diagram (figure 4.9). When he's through with his drawing, he shows it to Theo.

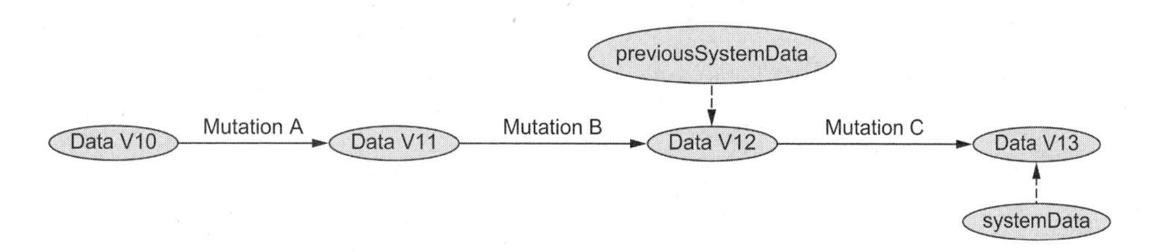

Figure 4.9 When a mutation is committed, `systemData` refers to `V13`, and `previousSystemData` refers to `V12`.

Theo I suppose that when we undo the mutation, both references move backward.

Joe In theory, yes, but in practice, it's necessary to maintain a stack of all the state references. For now, to simplify things, we'll maintain only a reference to the previous version. As a consequence, when we undo the mutation, both references refer to `V12`. Let me draw another diagram on the whiteboard that shows this state (see figure 4.10).

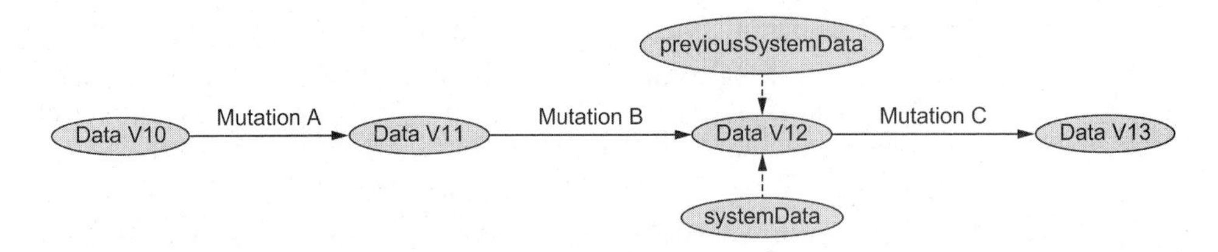

Figure 4.10 When a mutation is undone, both `systemData` and `previousSystemData` refer to `V12`.

Theo Could you show me how to implement this undo mechanism?

Joe Actually, it takes only a couple of changes to the `SystemState` class. Pay attention to the changes in the `commit` function. Inside `systemDataBeforeUpdate`, we keep a reference to the current state of the system. If the validation and the conflict resolution succeed, we update both `previousSystemData` and `systemData`.

Listing 4.10 The `SystemState` class with undo capability

```
class SystemState {
  systemData;
  previousSystemData;

  get() {
    return this.systemData;
  }

  commit(previous, next) {
    var systemDataBeforeUpdate = this.systemData;
    if(!Consistency.validate(previous, next)) {
      throw "The system data to be committed is not valid!";
    }
    this.systemData = next;
    this.previousSystemData = systemDataBeforeUpdate;
  }

  undoLastMutation() {
    this.systemData = this.previousSystemData;
  }
}
```

Theo I see that implementing `System.undoLastMutation` is simply a matter of having `systemData` refer the same value as `previousSystemData`.

Joe As I told you, if we need to allow multiple undos, the code would be a bit more complicated, but you get the idea.

Theo I think so. Although *Back to the Future* belongs to the realm of science fiction, in DOP, time travel is real.

Summary

- DOP principle #3 states that data is immutable.
- A *mutation* is an operation that changes the state of the system.
- In a multi-version approach to state management, mutations are split into calculation and commit phases.
- All data manipulation must be done via immutable functions. It is forbidden to use the native hash map setter.
- *Structural sharing* allows us to create new versions of data efficiently (in terms of memory and computation), where data that is common between the two versions is shared instead of being copied.
- Structural sharing creates a new version of the data by recursively sharing the parts that don't need to change.
- A mutation is split in two phases: calculation and commit.
- A function is said to be *immutable* when, instead of mutating the data, it creates a new version of the data without changing the data it receives.
- During the *calculation phase*, data is manipulated with immutable functions that use structural sharing.
- The calculation phase is stateless.
- During the *commit phase*, we update the system state.
- The responsibility of the commit phase is to move the system state forward to the version of the state returned by the calculation phase.
- The data is immutable, but the state reference is mutable.
- The *commit phase* is stateful.
- We validate the system data as a whole. Data validation is decoupled from data manipulation.
- The fact that the code for the commit phase is common to all the mutations allows us to validate the system state in a central place before we update the state.
- Keeping the history of the versions of the system data is memory efficient due to *structural sharing*.
- Restoring the system to one of its previous states is straightforward due to the clear separation between the calculation phase and the commit phase.

- In order to use Lodash immutable functions, we use the Lodash FP module (https://github.com/lodash/lodash/wiki/FP-Guide).

Lodash functions introduced in this chapter

Function	Description
set(map, path, value)	Creates a map with the same fields as map with the addition of a <path, value> field

5 Basic concurrency control

Conflicts at home

This chapter covers

- Managing concurrent mutations with a lock-free optimistic concurrency control strategy
- Supporting high throughput of reads and writes
- Reconciliation between concurrent mutations

The changes required for system manage concurrency are only in the commit phase. They involve a reconciliation algorithm that is universal, in the sense that it can be used in any system where data is represented as an immutable hash map. The implementation of the reconciliation algorithm is efficient because subsequent versions of the system state are created via structural sharing.

In the previous chapter, we illustrated the multiversion approach to state management, where a mutation is split into two distinct phases: the calculation phase that deals only with computation, and the commit phase that moves the state reference forward. Usually, in a production system, mutations occur concurrently. Moving the state forward naively like we did in the previous chapter is not appropriate. In the present chapter, we are going to learn how to handle concurrent mutations.

In DOP, because only the code of the commit phase is stateful, that allows us to use an *optimistic concurrency control* strategy that doesn't involve any locking mechanism. As a consequence, the throughput of reads and writes is high. The modifications to the code are not trivial, as we have to implement an algorithm that reconciles concurrent mutations. But the modifications impact only the commit phase. The code for the calculation phase stays the same as in the previous chapter.

▶ **NOTE** This chapter requires more of an effort to grasp. The flow of the reconciliation algorithm is definitely not trivial, and the implementation involves a nontrivial recursion.

5.1 Optimistic concurrency control

This morning, before getting to work, Theo takes Joe to the fitness room in the office and, while running on the step machine, the two men talk about their personal lives again. Joe talks about a fight he had last night with Kay, who thinks that he pays more attention to his work than to his family. Theo recounts the painful conflict he had with Jane, his wife, about house budget management. They went to see a therapist, an expert in Imago Relationship Therapy. Imago allowed them to transform their conflict into an opportunity to grow and heal.

Joe's ears perk up when he hears the word *conflict* because today's lesson is going to be about resolving conflicts and concurrent mutations. A different kind of conflict, though. . . . After a shower and a healthy breakfast, Theo and Joe get down to work.

Joe Yesterday, I showed you how to manage state with immutable data, assuming that no mutations occur concurrently. Today, I am going to show you how to deal with concurrency control in DOP.

Theo I'm curious to discover what kind of lock mechanisms you use in DOP to synchronize concurrent mutations.

Joe In fact, we don't use any lock mechanism!

Theo Why not?

Joe Locks hit performance, and if you're not careful, your system could get into a deadlock.

Theo So, how do you handle possible conflicts between concurrent mutations in DOP?

Joe In DOP, we use a lock-free strategy called optimistic concurrency control. It's a strategy that allows databases like Elasticsearch to be highly scalable.

▶ **NOTE** See https://www.elastic.co/elasticsearch/ to find out more about Elasticsearch.

Theo You sound like my couples therapist and her anger-free, optimistic conflict resolution strategy.

Joe Optimistic concurrency control and DOP fit together well. As you will see in a moment, optimistic concurrency control is super efficient when the system data is immutable.

TIP Optimistic concurrency control with immutable data is super efficient.

Theo How does it work?

Joe Optimistic concurrency control occurs when we let mutations ask forgiveness instead of permission.

TIP Optimistic concurrency control occurs when we let mutations ask forgiveness instead of permission.

Theo What do you mean?

Joe The calculation phase does its calculation as if it were the only mutation running. The commit phase is responsible for reconciling concurrent mutations when they don't conflict or for aborting the mutation.

TIP The *calculation phase* does its calculation as if it were the only mutation running. The *commit phase* is responsible for trying to reconcile concurrent mutations.

Theo That sounds quite challenging to implement.

Joe Dealing with state is never trivial. But the good news is that the code for the reconciliation logic in the commit phase is universal.

Theo Does that mean that the same code for the commit phase can be used in any DOP system?

Joe Definitely. The code that implements the commit phase assumes nothing about the details of the system except that the system data is represented as an immutable map.

TIP The implementation of the commit phase in optimistic concurrency control is universal. It can be used in any system where the data is represented by an immutable hash map.

Theo That's awesome!

Joe Another cool thing is that handling concurrency doesn't require any changes to the code in the calculation phase. From the calculation phase perspective, the next version of the system data is computed in isolation as if no other mutations were running concurrently.

Joe stands up to illustrate what he means on the whiteboard. While Theo looks at the drawing in figure 5.1, Joe summarizes the information in table 5.1.

Table 5.1 The two phases of a mutation with optimistic concurrency control

Phase	Responsibility	State	Implementation
Calculation	Compute next state in isolation	Stateless	Specific
Commit	Reconcile and update system state	Stateful	Common

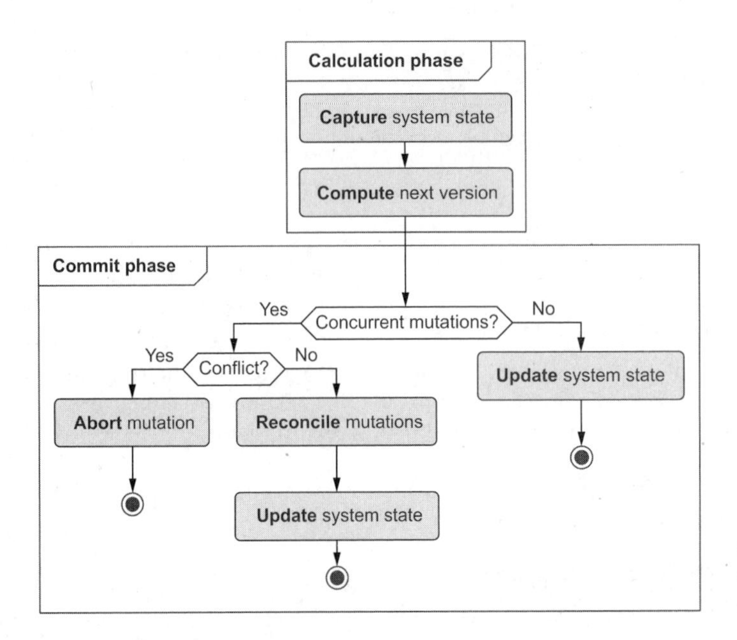

Figure 5.1 The logic flow of optimistic concurrency control

5.2 Reconciliation between concurrent mutations

Theo Could you give me some examples of conflicting concurrent mutations?

Joe Sure. One example would be two members trying to borrow the same book copy. Another example might be when two librarians update the publication year of the same book.

Theo You mentioned that the code for the reconciliation logic in the commit phase is universal. What do you mean exactly by reconciliation logic?

Joe It's quite similar to what could happen in Git when you merge a branch back into the main branch.

Theo I love it when the main branch stays the same.

Joe Yes, it's nice when the merge has no conflicts and can be done automatically. Do you remember how Git handles the merge in that case?

Theo Git does a fast-forward; it updates the main branch to be the same as the merge branch.

Joe Right! And what happens when you discover that, meanwhile, another developer has committed their code to the main branch?

Theo Then Git does a three-way merge, trying to combine all the changes from the two merge branches with the main branch.

Joe Does it always go smoothly?

Theo Usually, yes, but it's possible that two developers have modified the same line in the same file. I then have to manually resolve the conflict. I hate when that happens!

TIP In a production system, multiple mutations run concurrently. Before updating the state, we need to reconcile the conflicts between possible concurrent mutations.

Joe In DOP, the reconciliation algorithm in the commit phase is quite similar to a merge in Git, except instead of a manual conflict resolution, we abort the mutation. There are three possibilities to reconcile between possible concurrent mutations: fast-forward, three-way merge, or abort.

Joe goes to the whiteboard again. He draws the two diagrams shown in figures 5.2 and 5.3.

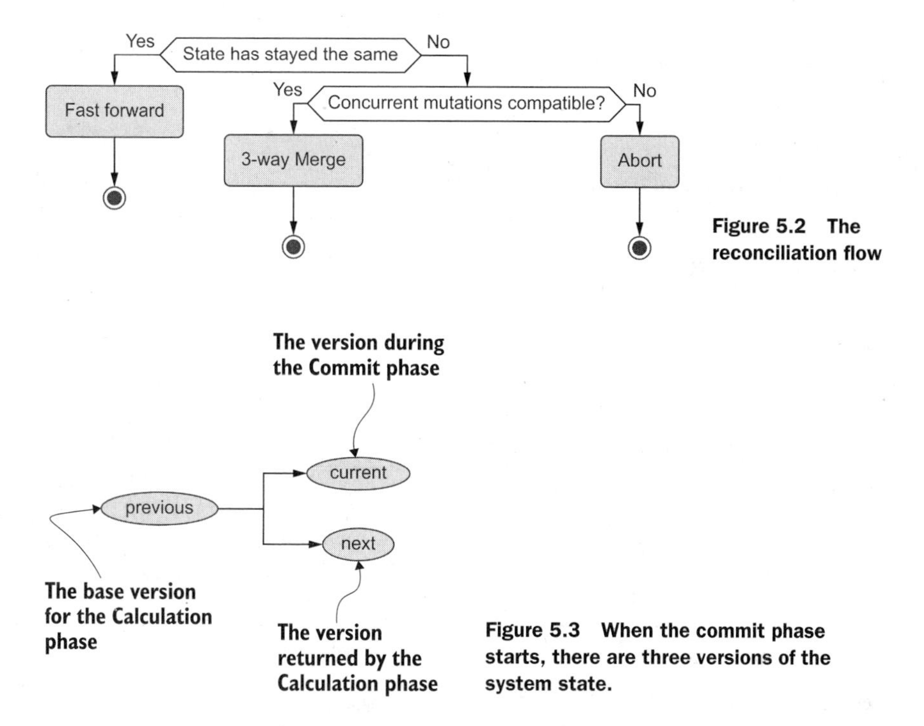

Figure 5.2 The reconciliation flow

Figure 5.3 When the commit phase starts, there are three versions of the system state.

Theo Could you explain in more detail?

Joe When the commit phase of a mutation starts, we have three versions of the system state: `previous`, which is the version on which the calculation phase based its computation; `current`, which is the current version during the commit phase; and `next`, which is the version returned by the calculation phase.

Theo Why would `current` be different than `previous`?

Joe It happens when other mutations have run concurrently with our mutation.

Theo I see.

Joe If we are in a situation where the current state is the same as the previous state, it means that no mutations run concurrently. Therefore, as in Git, we can safely fast-forward and update the state of the system with the next version.

Theo What if the state has not stayed the same?

Joe Then it means that mutations have run concurrently. We have to check for conflicts in a way similar to the three-way merge used by Git. The difference is that instead of comparing lines, we compare fields of the system hash map.

Theo Could you explain that?

Joe We calculate the diff between `previous` and `next` and between `previous` and `current`. If the two diffs have no fields in common, then there is no conflict between the mutations that have run concurrently. We can safely apply the changes from `previous` to `next` into `current`.

Joe makes his explanation visual with another diagram on the whiteboard. He then shows figure 5.4 to Theo.

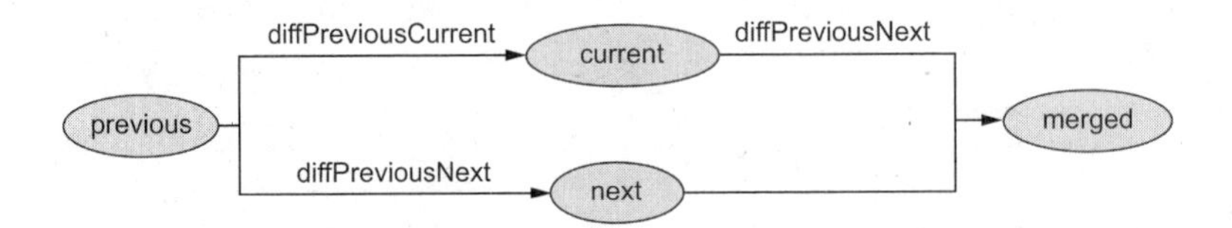

Figure 5.4 In a three-way merge, we calculate the diff between `previous` and `next`, and we apply it to `current`.

Theo What if there is a conflict?

Joe Then we abort the mutation.

Theo Aborting a user request seems unacceptable.

Joe In fact, in a user-facing system, conflicting concurrent mutations are fairly rare. That's why it's OK to abort and let the user run the mutation again. Here, let me draft a table to show you the differences between Git and DOP (table 5.2).

Table 5.2 The analogy between Git and data-oriented programming

Data-oriented programming	Git
Concurrent mutations	Different branches
A version of the system data	A commit
State	A reference
Calculation phase	Branching
Validation	Precommit hook
Reconciliation	Merge
Fast-forward	Fast-forward
Three-way merge	Three-way merge
Abort	Manual conflict resolution
Hash map	Tree (folder)
Leaf node	Blob (file)
Data field	Line of code

Theo Great! That helps, but in cases where two mutations update the same field of the same entity, I think it's fair enough to let the user know that the request can't be processed.

TIP In a user-facing system, conflicting concurrent mutations are fairly rare.

5.3 Reducing collections

Joe Are you ready to challenge your mind with the implementation of the diff algorithm?

Theo Let's take a short coffee break before, if you don't mind. Then, I'll be ready to tackle anything.

After enjoying large mug of hot coffee and a few butter cookies, Theo and Joe are back to work. Their discussion on the diff algorithm continues.

Joe In the implementation of the diff algorithm, we're going to reduce collections.

Theo I heard about reducing collections in a talk about FP, but I don't remember the details. Could you remind me how this works?

Joe Imagine you want to calculate the sum of the elements in a collection of numbers. With Lodash's `_.reduce`, it would look like this.

Listing 5.1 Summing numbers with `_.reduce`

```
_.reduce([1, 2, 3], function(res, elem) {
  return res + elem;
}, 0);
// → 6
```

Theo I don't understand.

Joe goes to the whiteboard and writes the description of `_.reduce`. Theo waits patiently until Joe puts the pen down before looking at the description.

Description of `_.reduce`

`_.reduce` receives three arguments:

- `coll`—A collection of elements
- `f`—A function that receives two arguments
- `initVal`—A value

Logic flow:

1. Initialize `currentRes` with `initVal`.
2. For each element `x` of `coll`, update `currentRes` with `f(currentRes, x)`.
3. Return `currentRes`.

Theo Would you mind if I manually expand the logic flow of that code you just wrote for `_.reduce`?

Joe I think it's a great idea!

Theo In our case, `initVal` is `0`. It means that the first call to `f` will be `f(0, 1)`. Then, we'll have `f(f(0, 1), 2)` and, finally, `f(f(f(0, 1), 2), 3)`.

Joe I like your manual expansion, Theo! Let's make it visual.

Now Theo goes to the whiteboard and draws a diagram. Figure 5.5 shows what that looks like.

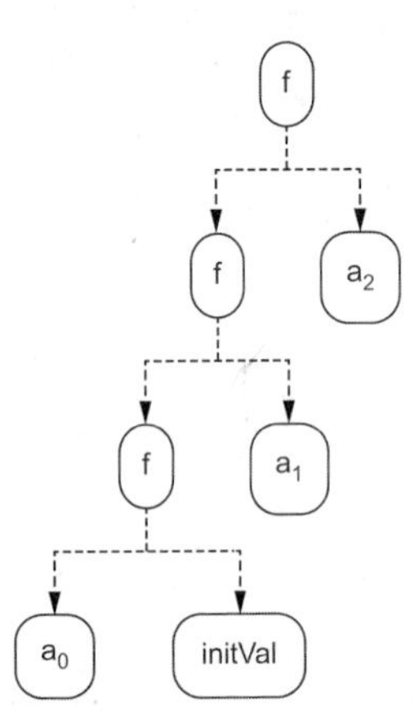

Figure 5.5 Visualization of `_.reduce`

Theo It's much clearer now. I think that by implementing my custom version of `_.reduce`, it will make things 100% clear.

It takes Theo much less time than he expected to implement `reduce()`. In no time at all, he shows Joe the code.

Listing 5.2 Custom implementation of `_.reduce`

```
function reduce(coll, f, initVal) {
  var currentRes = initVal;
  for (var i = 0; i < coll.length; i++) {
    currentRes = f(currentRes, coll[i])
  }
  return currentRes;
}
```

We could use forEach instead of a for loop.

After checking that Theo's code works as expected (see listing 5.3), Joe is proud of Theo. He seems to be catching on better than he anticipated.

Listing 5.3 Testing the custom implementation of `reduce()`

```
reduce([1, 2, 3], function(res, elem) {
  return res + elem;
}, 0);
// → 6
```

Joe Well done!

5.4 Structural difference

▶ **NOTE** This section deals with the implementation of a *structural diff algorithm*. Feel free to skip this section if you don't want to challenge your mind right now with the details of a sophisticated use of recursion. It won't prevent you from enjoying the rest of the book. You can come back to this section later.

Theo How do you calculate the diff between various versions of the system state?

Joe That's the most challenging part of the reconciliation algorithm. We need to implement a structural diff algorithm for hash maps.

Theo In what sense is the diff structural?

Joe The structural diff algorithm looks at the structure of the hash maps and ignores the order of the fields.

Theo Could you give me an example?

Joe Let's start with maps without nested fields. Basically, there are three kinds of diffs: field replacement, field addition, and field deletion. In order to make things not too complicated, for now, we'll deal only with replacement and addition.

Joe once again goes to the whiteboard and draws table 5.3, representing the three kinds of diffs. Theo is thinking the whiteboard is really starting to fill up today.

Table 5.3 Kinds of structural differences between maps without nested fields

Kind	First map	Second map	Diff
Replacement	`{"a": 1}`	`{"a": 2}`	`{"a": 2}`
Addition	`{"a": 1}`	`{"a": 1, "b": 2}`	`{"b": 2}`
Deletion	`{"a": 1, "b": 2}`	`{"a": 1}`	Not supported

Theo I notice that the order of the maps matters a lot. What about nested fields?

Joe It's the same idea, but the nesting makes it a bit more difficult to grasp.

Joe changes several of the columns in table 5.3. When he's through, he shows Theo the nested fields in table 5.4.

Table 5.4 Kinds of structural differences between maps with nested fields

Kind	First map	Second map	Diff

Replacement	`{`
	`  "a": {`
	`    "x": 1`
	`  }`
	`}`
		`{`
		`  "a": {`
		`    "x": 2`
		`  }`
		`}`
			`{`
			`  "a": {`
			`    "x": 2`
			`  }`
			`}`

Table 5.4 Kinds of structural differences between maps with nested fields *(continued)*

Kind	First map	Second map	Diff

Addition	{
	"a": {
	"x": 1
	}
	}
		{
		"a": {
		"x": 1,
		"y": 2,
		}
		}
			{
			"a": {
			"y": 2
			}
			}

Deletion	{
	"a": {
	"x": 1,
	"y": 2,
	}
	}
		{
		"a": {
		"y": 2
		}
		}
			Not supported

▶ **NOTE** The version of the structural diff algorithm illustrated in this chapter does not deal with deletions. Dealing with deletions is definitely possible, but it requires a more complicated algorithm.

Theo As you said, it's harder to grasp. What about arrays?

Joe We compare the elements of the arrays in order: if they are equal, the diff is `null`; if they differ, the diff has the value of the second array.

Joe summarizes the various kinds of diffs in another table on the whiteboard. Theo looks at the result in table 5.5.

Table 5.5 Kinds of structural differences between arrays without nested elements

Kind	First array	Second array	Diff
Replacement	`[1]`	`[2]`	`[2]`
Addition	`[1]`	`[1, 2]`	`[null, 2]`
Deletion	`[1, 2]`	`[1]`	Not supported

Theo This usage of `null` is a bit weird but OK. Is it complicated to implement the structural diff algorithm?

Joe Definitely! It took a good dose of mental gymnastics to come up with these 30 lines of code.

Joe downloads the code from one his personal repositories. Theo, with thumb and forefingers touching his chin and his forehead slightly tilted, studies the code.

Listing 5.4 The implementation of a structural diff

```
function diffObjects(data1, data2) {
  var emptyObject = _.isArray(data1) ? [] : {};
  if(data1 == data2) {
```

_.isArray checks whether its argument is an array.

```
    return emptyObject;
  }
  var keys = _.union(_.keys(data1), _.keys(data2));
  return _.reduce(keys,
    function (acc, k) {
      var res = diff(
        _.get(data1, k),
        _.get(data2, k));
      if((_.isObject(res) && _.isEmpty(res)) ||

        (res == "no-diff")) {
        return acc;
      }
      return _.set(acc, [k], res);
    },
    emptyObject);
}

function diff(data1, data2) {
  if(_.isObject(data1) && _.isObject(data2)) {
    return diffObjects(data1, data2);
  }
  if(data1 !== data2) {
    return data2;
  }
  return "no-diff";
}
```

_.union creates an array of unique values from two arrays (like union of two sets in Maths).

_.isObject checks whether its argument is a collection (either a map or an array).

_.isEmpty checks whether its argument is an empty collection.

"no-diff" is how we mark that two values are the same.

Theo Wow! It involves a recursion inside a reduce! I'm sure Dave will love this, but I'm too tired to understand this code right now. Let's focus on what it does instead of how it does it.

In order familiarize himself with the structural diff algorithm, Theo runs the algorithm with examples from the table that Joe drew on the whiteboard. While Theo occupies his fingers with more and more complicated examples, his mind wanders in the realm of performance.

Listing 5.5 An example of usage of a structural diff

```
var data1 = {
  "a": {
    "x": 1,
    "y": [2, 3],
    "z": 4
  }
};

var data2 = {
  "a": {
    "x": 2,
    "y": [2, 4],
    "z": 4
  }
}
```

```
diff(data1, data2);
//{
//  "a": {
//    "x": 2,
//    "y": [
//      undefined,
//      4
//    ]
//  }
//}
```

Theo What about the performance of the structural diff algorithm? It seems that the algorithm goes over the leaves of both pieces of data?

Joe In the general case, that's true. But, in the case of system data that's manipulated with structural sharing, the code is much more efficient.

Theo What do you mean?

Joe With structural sharing, most of the nested objects are shared between two versions of the system state. Therefore, most of the time, when the code enters `diffObjects`, it will immediately return because `data1` and `data2` are the same.

TIP Calculating the diff between two versions of the state is efficient because two hash maps created via structural sharing from the same hash map have most of their nodes in common.

Theo Another benefit of immutable data . . . Let me see how the diff algorithm behaves with concurrent mutations. I think I'll start with a tiny library with no users and a catalog with a single book, *Watchmen*.

Listing 5.6 The data for a tiny library

```
var library = {
  "catalog": {
    "booksByIsbn": {
      "978-1779501127": {
        "isbn": "978-1779501127",
        "title": "Watchmen",
        "publicationYear": 1987,
        "authorIds": ["alan-moore", "dave-gibbons"]
      }
    },
    "authorsById": {
      "alan-moore": {
        "name": "Alan Moore",
        "bookIsbns": ["978-1779501127"]
      },
      "dave-gibbons": {
        "name": "Dave Gibbons",
        "bookIsbns": ["978-1779501127"]
      }
    }
  }
};
```

Joe I suggest that we start with nonconflicting mutations. What do you suggest?

Theo A mutation that updates the publication year of *Watchmen* and a mutation that updates both the title of *Watchmen* and the name of the author of *Watchmen*.

On his laptop, Theo creates three versions of the library. He shows Joe his code, where one mutation updates the publication year of *Watchmen*, and the other one updates the title of *Watchmen* and the author's name.

Listing 5.7 Two nonconflicting mutations

```
var previous = library;

var next = _.set(
  library,
  ["catalog", "booksByIsbn", "978-1779501127", "publicationYear"],
  1986);

var libraryWithUpdatedTitle = _.set(
  library,
  ["catalog", "booksByIsbn", "978-1779501127", "title"],
  "The Watchmen");
var current = _.set(
  libraryWithUpdatedTitle,
  ["catalog", "authorsById", "dave-gibbons", "name"],
  "David Chester Gibbons");
```

Theo I'm curious to see what the diff between `previous` and `current` looks like.

Joe Run the code and you'll see.

Theo runs the code snippets for the structural diff between `previous` and `next` and for the structural diff between `previous` and `current`. His curiosity satisfied, Theo finds it's all beginning to make sense.

Listing 5.8 Structural diff between maps with a single difference

```
diff(previous, next);
//{
//    "catalog": {
//        "booksByIsbn": {
//            "978-1779501127": {
//                "publicationYear": 1986
//            }
//        }
//    }
//}
```

Listing 5.9 Structural diff between maps with two differences

```
diff(previous, current);
//{
//  "authorsById": {
//    "dave-gibbons": {
//      "name": "David Chester Gibbons",
```

```
//     }
//   },
//   "catalog": {
//     "booksByIsbn": {
//       "978-1779501127": {
//         "title": "The Watchmen"
//       }
//     }
//   }
//}
//
```

Joe Can you give me the information path of the single field in the structural diff between `previous` and `next`?

Theo It's `["catalog", "booksByIsbn", "978-1779501127", "publicationYear"]`.

Joe Right. And what are the information paths of the fields in the structural diff between `previous` and `current`?

Theo It's `["catalog", "booksByIsbn", "978-1779501127", "title"]` for the book title and `["authorsById", "dave-gibbons", "name"]` for the author's name.

Joe Perfect! Now, can you figure out how to detect conflicting mutations by inspecting the information paths of the structural diffs?

Theo We need to check if they have an information path in common or not.

Joe Exactly! If they have, it means the mutations are conflicting.

Theo But I have no idea how to write code that retrieves the information paths of a nested map.

Joe Once again, it's a nontrivial piece of code that involves a recursion inside a `reduce`. Let me download another piece of code from my repository and show it to you.

Listing 5.10 Calculating the information paths of a (nested) map

```
function informationPaths (obj, path = []) {
  return _.reduce(obj,
    function(acc, v, k) {
      if (_.isObject(v)) {
        return _.concat(acc,
          informationPaths(v,
            _.concat(path, k)));
      }
      return _.concat(acc, [_.concat(path, k)]);
    },
    []);
}
```

Theo Let me see if your code works as expected with the structural diffs of the mutations.

Theo tests Joe's code with two code snippets. The first shows the information paths of the structural diff between `previous` and `next`, and the second shows the information paths of the structural diff between `previous` and `current`.

Listing 5.11 Fields that differ between `previous` and `next`

```
informationPaths(diff(previous, next));
// → ["catalog.booksByIsbn.978-1779501127.publicationYear"]
```

Listing 5.12 Fields that differ between `previous` and `current`

```
informationPaths(diff(previous, current));
// [
//   [
//     "catalog",
//     "booksByIsbn",
//     "978-1779501127",
//     "title"
//   ],
//   [
//     "authorsById",
//     "dave-gibbons",
//     "name"
//   ]
//]
```

Theo Nice! I assume that Lodash has a function that checks whether two arrays have an element in common.

Joe Almost. There is `_.intersection`, which returns an array of the unique values that are in two given arrays. For our purpose, though, we need to check whether the intersection is empty. Here, look at this example.

Listing 5.13 Checking whether two diff maps have a common information path

```
function havePathInCommon(diff1, diff2) {
  return !_.isEmpty(_.intersection(informationPaths(diff1),
    informationPaths(diff2)));
}
```

Theo You told me earlier that in the case of nonconflicting mutations, we can safely patch the changes induced by the transition from `previous` to `next` into `current`. How do you implement that?

Joe We do a recursive merge between `current` and the diff between `previous` and `next`.

Theo Does Lodash provide an immutable version of recursive merge?

Joe Yes, here's another example. Take a look at this code.

Listing 5.14 Applying a patch

```
_.merge(current, (diff(previous, next)));
//{
// "authorsById": {
//   "dave-gibbons": {
//     "name": "David Chester Gibbons"
//   }
// },
```

```
// "catalog": {
//   "authorsById": {
//     "alan-moore": {
//       "bookIsbns": ["978-1779501127"]
//       "name": "Alan Moore"
//     },
//     "dave-gibbons": {
//       "bookIsbns": ["978-1779501127"],
//       "name": "Dave Gibbons"
//     },
//   },
//   "booksByIsbn": {
//     "978-1779501127": {
//       "authorIds": ["alan-moore", "dave-gibbons"],
//       "isbn": "978-1779501127",
//       "publicationYear": 1986,
//       "title": "The Watchmen"
//     }
//   }
// }
//}
```

Theo Could it be as simple as this?

Joe Indeed.

5.5 *Implementing the reconciliation algorithm*

Joe All the pieces are now in place to implement our reconciliation algorithm.

Theo What kind of changes are required?

Joe It only requires changes in the code of `SystemState.commit`. Here, look at this example on my laptop.

Listing 5.15 The `SystemState` class

```
class SystemState {
  systemData;

  get() {
    return this.systemData;
  }

  set(_systemData) {
    this.systemData = _systemData;
  }

  commit(previous, next) {
    var nextSystemData = SystemConsistency.reconcile(
      this.systemData,        <-- SystemConsistency class is
      previous,                   implemented in listing 5.16.
      next);
    if(!SystemValidity.validate(previous, nextSystemData)) {
      throw "The system data to be committed is not valid!";
    };
```

```
    this.systemData = nextSystemData;
  }
}
```

Theo How does `SystemConsistency` do the reconciliation?

Joe The `SystemConsistency` class starts the reconciliation process by comparing `previous` and `current`. If they are the same, then we fast-forward and return `next`. Look at this code for `SystemConsistency`.

Listing 5.16 The reconciliation flow in action

```
class SystemConsistency {
  static threeWayMerge(current, previous, next) {
    var previousToCurrent = diff(previous, current);
    var previousToNext = diff(previous, next);
    if(havePathInCommon(previousToCurrent, previousToNext)) {
      return _.merge(current, previousToNext);
    }
    throw "Conflicting concurrent mutations.";
  }
  static reconcile(current, previous, next) {
    if(current == previous) {
      return next;
    }
    return SystemConsistency.threeWayMerge(current,
      previous,
      next);
  }
}
```

When the system state is the same as the state used by the calculation phase, we fast-forward.

Theo Wait a minute! Why do you compare `previous` and `current` by reference? You should be comparing them by value, right? And, it would be quite expensive to compare all the leaves of the two nested hash maps!

Joe That's another benefit of immutable data. When the data is not mutated, it is safe to compare references. If they are the same, we know for sure that the data is the same.

TIP When data is immutable, it is safe to compare by reference, which is super fast. When the references are the same, it means that the data is the same.

Theo What about the implementation of the three-way merge algorithm?

Joe When `previous` differs from `current`, it means that concurrent mutations have run. In order to determine whether there is a conflict, we calculate two diffs: the diff between `previous` and `current` and the diff between `previous` and `next`. If the intersection between the two diffs is empty, it means there is no conflict. We can safely patch the changes between `previous` to `next` into `current`.

Theo takes a closer look at the code for the `SystemConsistency` class in listing 5.16. He tries to figure out if the code is thread-safe or not.

Theo I think the code for `SystemConsistency` class is not thread-safe! If there's a context switch between checking whether the system has changed in the `SystemConsistency` class and the updating of the state in `SystemData` class, a mutation might override the changes of a previous mutation.

Joe You are totally right! The code works fine in a single-threaded environment like JavaScript, where concurrency is handled via an event loop. However, in a multi-threaded environment, the code needs to be refined in order to be thread-safe. I'll show you some day.

▶ **NOTE** The `SystemConsistency` class is not thread-safe. We will make it thread-safe in chapter 8.

Theo I think I understand why you called it optimistic concurrency control. It's because we assume that conflicts don't occur too often. Right?

Joe Correct! It makes me wonder what your therapist would say about conflicts that cannot be resolved. Are there some cases where it's not possible to reconcile the couple?

Theo I don't think she ever mentioned such a possibility.

Joe She must be a very optimistic person.

Summary

- *Optimistic concurrency control* allows mutations to ask forgiveness instead of permission.
- Optimistic concurrency control is *lock-free*.
- Managing concurrent mutations of our system state with optimistic concurrency control allows our system to support a high throughput of reads and writes.
- Optimistic concurrency control with immutable data is super efficient.
- Before updating the state, we need to *reconcile* the conflicts between possible concurrent mutations.
- We reconcile between concurrent mutations in a way that is similar to how Git handles a merge between two branches: either a fast-forward or a three-way merge.
- The changes required to let our system manage concurrency are only in the commit phase.
- The *calculation phase* does its calculation as if it were the only mutation running.
- The *commit phase* is responsible for trying to reconcile concurrent mutations.
- The *reconciliation algorithm* is universal in the sense that it can be used in any system where the system data is represented as an immutable hash map.
- The implementation of the reconciliation algorithm is efficient, as it leverages the fact that subsequent versions of the system state are created via structural sharing.
- In a user-facing system, conflicting concurrent mutations are fairly rare.
- When we cannot safely reconcile between concurrent mutations, we abort the mutation and ask the user to try again.

- Calculating the *structural diff* between two versions of the state is efficient because two hash maps created via structural sharing from the same hash map have most of their nodes in common.
- When data is immutable, it is safe to compare by reference, which is fast. When the references are the same, it means that the data is the same.
- There are three kinds of structural differences between two nested hash maps: replacement, addition, and deletion.
- Our structural diff algorithm supports replacements and additions but not deletions.

Lodash functions introduced in this chapter

Function	Description
`concat(arrA, arrB)`	Creates an new array, concatenating `arrA` and `arrB`
`intersection(arrA, arrB)`	Creates an array of unique values both in `arrA` and `arrB`
`union(arrA, arrB)`	Creates an array of unique values from `arrA` and `arrB`
`find(coll, pred)`	Iterates over elements of `coll`, returning the first element for which `pred` returns `true`
`isEmpty(coll)`	Checks if `coll` is empty
`reduce(coll, f, initVal)`	Reduces `coll` to a value that is the accumulated result of running each element in `coll` through `f`, where each successive invocation is supplied the return value of the previous
`isArray(coll)`	Checks if `coll` is an array
`isObject(coll)`	Checks if `coll` is a collection

6 Unit tests

Programming at a coffee shop

This chapter covers

- Generation of the minimal data input for a test case
- Comparison of the output of a function with the expected output
- Guidance about the quality and the quantity of the test cases

In a data-oriented system, our code deals mainly with data manipulation: most of our functions receive data and return data. As a consequence, it's quite easy to write unit tests to check whether our code behaves as expected. A unit test is made of test cases that generate data input and compare the data output of the function with the expected data output. In this chapter, we write unit tests for the queries and mutations that we wrote in the previous chapters.

6.1 The simplicity of data-oriented test cases

Theo and Joe are seated around a large wooden table in a corner of "La vie est belle," a nice little French coffee shop, located near the Golden Gate Bridge. Theo orders a café au lait with a croissant, and Joe orders a tight espresso with a pain au chocolat. Instead of the usual general discussions about programming and life when they're out of the office, Joe leads the discussion towards a very concrete topic—unit tests. Theo asks Joe for an explanation.

Theo Are unit tests such a simple topic that we can tackle it here in a coffee shop?

Joe Unit tests in general, no. But unit tests for data-oriented code, yes!

Theo Why does that make a difference?

Joe The vast majority of the code base of a data-oriented system deals with data manipulation.

Theo Yeah. I noticed that almost all the functions we wrote so far receive data and return data.

TIP Most of the code in a data-oriented system deals with data manipulation.

Joe Writing a test case for functions that deal with data is only about generating data input and expected output, and comparing the output of the function with the expected output.

The steps of a test case

1. Generate data input: `dataIn`
2. Generate expected output: `dataOut`
3. Compare the output of the function with the expected output: `f(dataIn)` and `dataOut`

Theo That's it?

Joe Yes. As you'll see in a moment, in DOP, there's usually no need for mock functions.

Theo I understand how to compare primitive values like strings or numbers, but I'm not sure how I would compare data collections like maps.

Joe You compare field by field.

Theo Recursively?

Joe Yes!

Theo Oh no! I'm not able to write any recursive code in a coffee shop. I need the calm of my office for that kind of stuff.

Joe Don't worry. In DOP, data is represented in a generic way. There is a generic function in Lodash called `_.isEqual` for recursive comparison of data collections. It works with both maps and arrays.

Joe opens his laptop. He is able to convince Theo by executing a few code snippets with `_.isEqual` to compare an equal data collection with a non-equal one.

Listing 6.1 Comparing an equal data collection recursively

```
_.isEqual({
  "name": "Alan Moore",
  "bookIsbns": ["978-1779501127"]
```

```
}, {
    "name": "Alan Moore",
    "bookIsbns": ["978-1779501127"]
  });
// → true
```

Listing 6.2 Comparing a non-equal data collection recursively

```
_.isEqual({
  "name": "Alan Moore",
  "bookIsbns": ["978-1779501127"]
}, {
    "name": "Alan Moore",
    "bookIsbns": ["bad-isbn"]
  });
// → false
```

Theo Nice!

Joe Most of the test cases in DOP follow this pattern.

Theo decides he wants to try this out. He fires up his laptop and types a few lines of pseudocode.

Listing 6.3 The general pattern of a data-oriented test case

```
var dataIn = {
  // input
};

var dataOut = {
  // expected output
};

_.isEqual(f(dataIn), dataOut);
```

TIP It's straightforward to write unit tests for code that deals with data manipulation.

Theo Indeed, this looks like something we can tackle in a coffee shop!

6.2 Unit tests for data manipulation code

A waiter in an elegant bow tie brings Theo his croissant and Joe his pain au chocolat. The two friends momentarily interrupt their discussion to savor their French pastries. When they're done, they ask the waiter to bring them their drinks. Meanwhile, they resume the discussion.

Joe Do you remember the code flow of the implementation of the search query?

Theo Let me look again at the code that implements the search query.

Theo brings up the implementation of the search query on his laptop. Noticing that Joe is chewing on his nails again, he quickly checks out the code.

Listing 6.4 The code involved in the implementation of the search query

```
class Catalog {
  static authorNames(catalogData, authorIds) {
    return _.map(authorIds, function(authorId) {
      return _.get(catalogData, ["authorsById", authorId, "name"]);
    });
  }

  static bookInfo(catalogData, book) {
    var bookInfo =  {
      "title": _.get(book, "title"),
      "isbn": _.get(book, "isbn"),
      "authorNames": Catalog.authorNames(catalogData,
        _.get(book, "authorIds"))
    };
    return bookInfo;
  }

  static searchBooksByTitle(catalogData, query) {
    var allBooks = _.get(catalogData, "booksByIsbn");
    var matchingBooks = _.filter(allBooks, function(book) {
      return _.get(book, "title").includes(query);
    });
    var bookInfos = _.map(matchingBooks, function(book) {
      return Catalog.bookInfo(catalogData, book);
    });
    return bookInfos;
  }
}

class Library {
  static searchBooksByTitleJSON(libraryData, query) {
    var catalogData = _.get(libraryData, "catalog");
    var results = Catalog.searchBooksByTitle(catalogData, query);
    var resultsJSON = JSON.stringify(results);
    return resultsJSON;
  }
}
```

6.2.1 The tree of function calls

The waiter brings Theo his café au lait and Joe his tight espresso. They continue their discussion while enjoying their coffees.

Joe Before writing a unit test for a code flow, I find it useful to visualize the tree of function calls of the code flow.

Theo What do you mean by a tree of function calls?

Joe Here, I'll draw the tree of function calls for the `Library.searchBooksByTitleJSON` code flow.

Joe puts down his espresso and takes a napkin from the dispenser. He carefully places it flat on the table and starts to draw. When he is done, he shows the illustration to Theo (see figure 6.1).

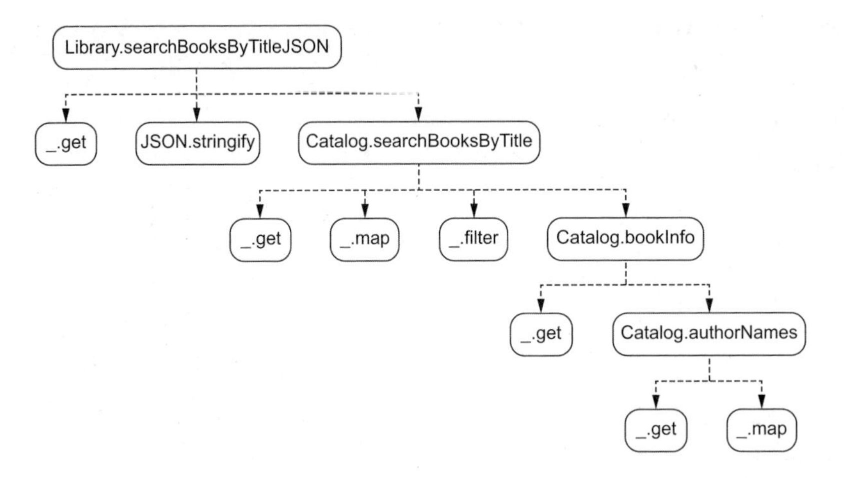

Figure 6.1 The tree of function calls for the search query code flow

Theo Nice! Can you teach me how to draw a tree of function calls like that?

Joe Sure. The root of the tree is the name of the function for which you draw the tree, in our case, `Library.searchBooksByTitleJSON`. The children of a node in the tree are the names of the functions called by the function. For example, if you look again at the code for `Library.searchBooksByTitleJSON` (listing 6.4), you'll see that it calls `Catalog.searchBooksByTitle`, `_.get`, and `JSON.stringify`.

Theo How long would I continue to recursively expand the tree?

Joe You continue until you reach a function that doesn't belong to the code base of your application. Those nodes are the leaves of our tree; for example, the functions from Lodash: `_.get`, `_.map`, and so forth.

Theo What if the code of a function doesn't call any other functions?

Joe A function that doesn't call any other function would be a leaf in the tree.

Theo What about functions that are called inside anonymous functions like `Catalog.bookInfo`?

Joe `Catalog.bookInfo` appears in the code of `Catalog.searchBooksByTitle`. Therefore, it is considered to be a child node of `Catalog.searchBooksByTitle`. The fact that it is nested inside an anonymous function is not relevant in the context of the tree of function calls.

▶ **NOTE** A tree of function calls for a function `f` is a tree where the root is `f`, and the children of a node `g` in the tree are the functions called by `g`. The leaves of the tree are functions that are not part of the code base of the application. These are functions that don't call any other functions.

Theo It's very cool to visualize my code as a tree, but I don't see how it relates to unit tests.

Joe The tree of function calls guides us about the quality and the quantity of test cases we should write.

Theo How?

Joe You'll see in a moment.

6.2.2 Unit tests for functions down the tree

Joe Let's start from the function that appears in the deepest node in our tree: `Catalog.authorNames`. Take a look at the code for `Catalog.authorNames` and tell me what are the input and the output of `Catalog.authorNames`.

Joe turns his laptop so Theo can a closer look at the code. Theo takes a sip of his café au lait as he looks over what's on Joe's laptop.

Listing 6.5 The code of `Catalog.authorNames`

```
Catalog.authorNames = function (catalogData, authorIds) {
  return _.map(authorIds, function(authorId) {
    return _.get(catalogData, ["authorsById", authorId, "name"]);
  });
};
```

Theo The input of `Catalog.authorNames` is `catalogData` and `authorIds`. The output is `authorNames`.

Joe Would you do me a favor and express it visually?

Theo Sure.

It's Theo's turn to grab a napkin. He draws a small rectangle with two inward arrows and one outward arrow as in figure 6.2.

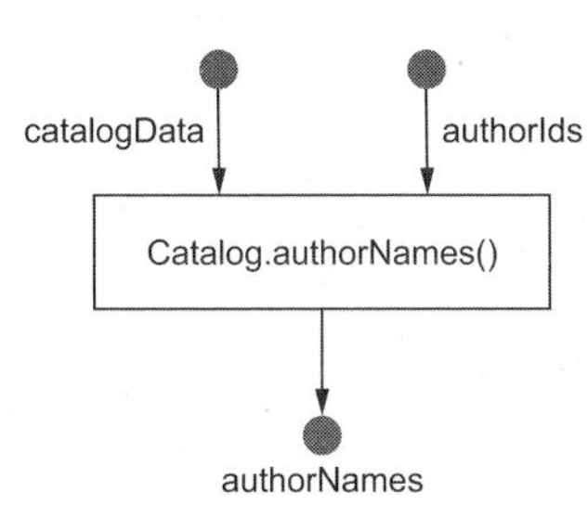

Figure 6.2 Visualization of the input and output of `Catalog.authorNames`

Joe Excellent! Now, how many combinations of input would you include in the unit test for `Catalog.authorNames`?

Theo Let me see.

Theo reaches for another napkin. This time he creates a table to gather his thoughts (table 6.1).

Table 6.1 The table of test cases for `Catalog.authorNames`

catalogData	authorIds	authorNames
Catalog with two authors	Empty array	Empty array
Catalog with two authors	Array with one author ID	Array with one author name
Catalog with two authors	Array with two author IDs	Array with two author names

Theo To begin with, I would have a `catalogData` with two author IDs and call `Catalog.authorNames` with three arguments: an empty array, an array with a single author ID, and an array with two author IDs.

Joe How would you generate the `catalogData`?

Theo Exactly as we generated it before.

Turning to his laptop, Theo writes the code for `catalogData`. He shows it to Joe.

Listing 6.6 A complete `catalogData` map

```
var catalogData = {
  "booksByIsbn": {
    "978-1779501127": {
      "isbn": "978-1779501127",
      "title": "Watchmen",
      "publicationYear": 1987,
      "authorIds": ["alan-moore", "dave-gibbons"],
      "bookItems": [
        {
          "id": "book-item-1",
          "libId": "nyc-central-lib",
          "isLent": true
        },
        {
          "id": "book-item-2",
          "libId": "nyc-central-lib",
          "isLent": false
        }
      ]
    }
  },
  "authorsById": {
    "alan-moore": {
      "name": "Alan Moore",
      "bookIsbns": ["978-1779501127"]
    },
    "dave-gibbons": {
      "name": "Dave Gibbons",
      "bookIsbns": ["978-1779501127"]
    }
  }
};
```

Joe You could use your big catalogData map for the unit test, but you could also use a smaller map in the context of Catalog.authorNames. You can get rid of the booksByIsbn field of the catalogData and the bookIsbns fields of the authors.

Joe deletes a few lines from catalogData and gets a much smaller map. He shows the revision to Theo.

Listing 6.7 A minimal version of catalogData

```
var catalogData = {
  "authorsById": {
    "alan-moore": {
      "name": "Alan Moore"
    },
    "dave-gibbons": {
      "name": "Dave Gibbons"
    }
  }
};
```

Theo Wait a minute! This catalogData is not valid.

Joe In DOP, data validity depends on the context. In the context of Library .searchBooksByTitleJSON and Catalog.searchBooksByTitle, the minimal version of catalogData is indeed not valid. However, in the context of Catalog.bookInfo and Catalog.authorNames, it is perfectly valid. The reason is that those two functions access only the authorsById field of catalogData.

TIP The validity of the data depends on the context.

Theo Why is it better to use a minimal version of the data in a test case?

Joe For a very simple reason—the smaller the data, the easier it is to manipulate.

TIP The smaller the data, the easier it is to manipulate.

Theo I'll appreciate that when I write the unit tests!

Joe Definitely! One last thing before we start coding: how would you check that the output of Catalog.authorNames is as expected?

Theo I would check that the value returned by Catalog.authorNames is an array with the expected author names.

Joe How would you handle the array comparison?

Theo Let me think. I want to compare by value, not by reference. I guess I'll have to check that the array is of the expected size and then check member by member, recursively.

Joe That's too much of a mental burden when you're in a coffee shop. As I showed you earlier (see listing 6.1), we can recursively compare two data collections by value with _.isEqual from Lodash.

TIP We can compare the output and the expected output of our functions with `_.isEqual`.

Theo Sounds good! Let me write the test cases.

Theo starts typing on his laptop. After a few minutes, he has some test cases for `Catalog.authorNames`, each made from a function call to `Catalog.authorNames` wrapped in `_.isEqual`.

Listing 6.8 Unit test for `Catalog.authorNames`

```
var catalogData = {
  "authorsById": {
    "alan-moore": {
      "name": "Alan Moore"
    },
    "dave-gibbons": {
      "name": "Dave Gibbons"
    }
  }
};

_.isEqual(Catalog.authorNames(catalogData, []), []);
_.isEqual(Catalog.authorNames(
  catalogData,
  ["alan-moore"]),
  ["Alan Moore"]);
_.isEqual(Catalog.authorNames(catalogData, ["alan-moore", "dave-gibbons"]),
  ["Alan Moore", "Dave Gibbons"]);
```

Joe Well done! Can you think of more test cases?

Theo Yes. There are test cases where the author ID doesn't appear in the catalog data, and test cases with empty catalog data. With minimal catalog data and `_.isEqual`, it's really easy to write lots of test cases!

Theo really enjoys this challenge. He creates a few more test cases to present to Joe.

Listing 6.9 More test cases for `Catalog.authorNames`

```
_.isEqual(Catalog.authorNames({}, []), []);
_.isEqual(Catalog.authorNames({}, ["alan-moore"]), [undefined]);

_.isEqual(Catalog.authorNames(catalogData, ["alan-moore",
  "albert-einstein"]), ["Alan Moore", undefined]);
_.isEqual(Catalog.authorNames(catalogData, []), []);
_.isEqual(Catalog.authorNames(catalogData, ["albert-einstein"]),
  [undefined]);
```

Theo How do I run these unit tests?

Joe You use your preferred test framework.

▶ **NOTE** We don't deal here with test runners and test frameworks. We deal only with the logic of the test cases.

6.2.3 Unit tests for nodes in the tree

Theo I'm curious to see what unit tests for an upper node in the tree of function calls look like.

Joe Sure. Let's write a unit test for `Catalog.bookInfo`. How many test cases would you have for `Catalog.bookInfo`?

Listing 6.10 The code of `Catalog.bookInfo`

```
Catalog.bookInfo = function (catalogData, book) {
  return {
    "title": _.get(book, "title"),
    "isbn": _.get(book, "isbn"),
    "authorNames": Catalog.authorNames(catalogData,
      _.get(book, "authorIds"))
  };
};
```

Theo takes another look at the code for `Catalog.bookInfo` on his laptop. Then, reaching for another napkin, he draws a diagram of its input and output (see figure 6.3).

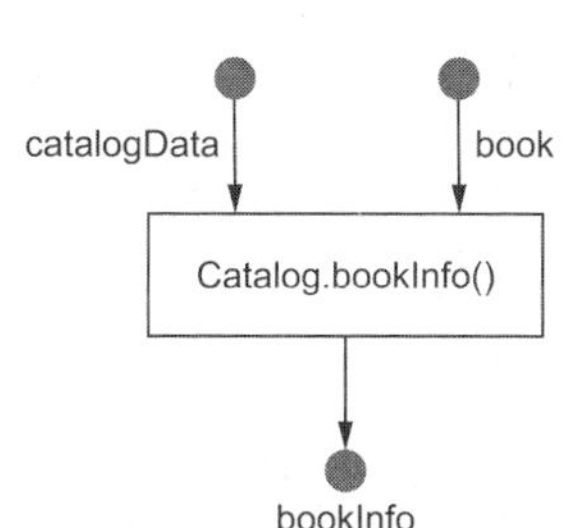

Figure 6.3 Visualization of the input and output of `Catalog.bookInfo`

Theo I would have a similar number of test cases for `Catalog.authorNames`: a book with a single author, with two authors, with existing authors, with non-existent authors, with . . .

Joe Whoa! That's not necessary. Given that we have already written unit tests for `Catalog.authorNames`, we don't need to check all the cases again. We simply need to write a minimal test case to confirm that the code works.

TIP When we write a unit test for a function, we assume that the functions called by this function are covered by unit tests and work as expected. It significantly reduces the quantity of test cases in our unit tests.

Theo That makes sense.

Joe How would you write a minimal test case for `Catalog.bookInfo`?

Theo once again takes a look at the code for `Catalog.bookInfo` (see listing 6.10). Now he can answer Joe's question.

Theo I would use the same catalog data as for `Catalog.authorNames` and a book record. I'd test that the function behaves as expected by comparing its return value with a book info record using `_.isEqual`. Here, let me show you.

It takes Theo a bit more time to write the unit test. The reason is that the input and the output of `Catalog.authorNames` are both records. Dealing with a record is more complex than dealing with an array of strings (as it was the case for `Catalog.authorNames`). Theo appreciates the fact that `_.isEqual` saves him from writing code that compares the two maps property by property. When he's through, he shows the result to Joe and takes a napkin to wipe his forehead.

Listing 6.11 Unit test for `Catalog.bookInfo`

```
var catalogData = {
  "authorsById": {
    "alan-moore": {
      "name": "Alan Moore"
    },
    "dave-gibbons": {
      "name": "Dave Gibbons"
    }
  }
};

var book = {
  "isbn": "978-1779501127",
  "title": "Watchmen",
  "publicationYear": 1987,
  "authorIds": ["alan-moore", "dave-gibbons"]
};

var expectedResult = {
  "authorNames": ["Alan Moore", "Dave Gibbons"],
  "isbn": "978-1779501127",
  "title": "Watchmen",
};

var result = Catalog.bookInfo(catalogData, book);

_.isEqual(result, expectedResult);
```

Joe Perfect! Now, how would you compare the kind of unit tests for `Catalog.bookInfo` with the unit tests for `Catalog.authorNames`?

Theo On one hand, there is only a single test case in the unit test for `Catalog.bookInfo`. On the other hand, the data involved in the test case is more complex than the data involved in the test cases for `Catalog.authorNames`.

Joe Exactly! Functions that appear in a deep node in the tree of function calls tend to require more test cases, but the data involved in the test cases is less complex.

TIP Functions that appear in a lower level in the tree of function calls tend to involve less complex data than functions that appear in a higher level in the tree (see table 6.2).

Table 6.2 The correlation between the depth of a function in the tree of function calls and the quality and quantity of the test cases

Depth in the tree	Complexity of the data	Number of test cases
Lower	Higher	Lower
Higher	Lower	Higher

6.3 Unit tests for queries

In the previous section, we saw how to write unit tests for utility functions like `Catalog.bookInfo` and `Catalog.authorNames`. Now, we are going to see how to write unit tests for the nodes of a query tree of function calls that are close to the root of the tree.

Joe Theo, how would you write a unit test for the code of the entry point of the search query?

To recall the particulars, Theo checks the code for `Library.searchBooksByTitleJSON`. Although Joe was right about today's topic being easy enough to enjoy the ambience of a coffee shop, he has been doing quite a lot of coding this morning.

Listing 6.12 The code of `Library.searchBooksByTitleJSON`

```
Library.searchBooksByTitleJSON = function (libraryData, query) {
  var catalogData = _.get(libraryData, "catalog");
  var results = Catalog.searchBooksByTitle(catalogData, query);
  var resultsJSON = JSON.stringify(results);
  return resultsJSON;
};
```

He then takes a moment to think about how he'd write a unit test for that code. After another *Aha!* moment, now he's got it.

Theo The inputs of `Library.searchBooksByTitleJSON` are library data and a query string, and the output is a JSON string (see figure 6.4). So, I would create a library data record with a single book and write tests with query strings that match the name of the book and ones that don't match.

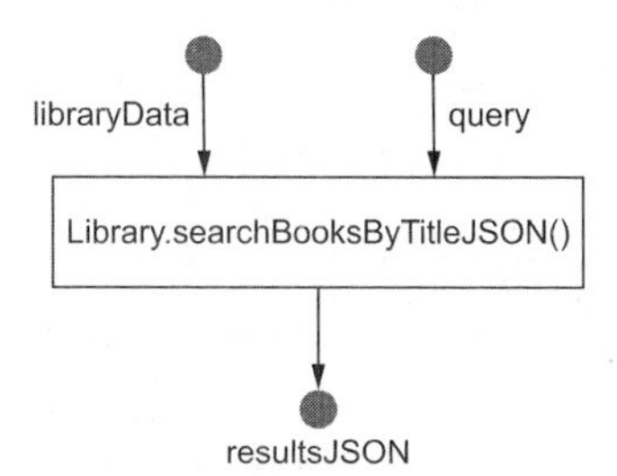

Figure 6.4 The input and output of `Library.searchBooksByTitleJSON`

Joe What about the expected results of the test cases?

Theo In cases where the query string matches, the expected result is a JSON string with the book info. In cases where the query string doesn't match, the expected result is a JSON string with an empty array.

Joe Hmm . . .

Theo What?

Joe I don't like your answer.

Theo Why?

Joe Because your test case relies on a string comparison instead of a data comparison.

Theo What difference does it make? After all, the strings I'm comparing come from the serialization of data.

Joe It's inherently much more complex to compare JSON strings than it is to compare data. For example, two different strings might be the serialization of the same piece of data.

Theo Really? How?

Joe Take a look at these two strings. They are the serialization of the same data. They're different strings because the fields appear in a different order, but in fact, they serialize the same data!

Joe turns his laptop to Theo. As Theo looks at the code, he realizes that, once again, Joe is correct.

Listing 6.13 Two different strings that serialize the same data

```
var stringA = "{\"title\":\"Watchmen\",\"publicationYear\":1987}";
var stringB = "{\"publicationYear\":1987,\"title\":\"Watchmen\"}";
```

TIP Avoid using a string comparison in unit tests for functions that deal with data.

Theo I see. . . . Well, what can I do instead?

Joe Instead of comparing the output of `Library.searchBooksByTitleJSON` with a string, you could deserialize the output and compare it to the expected data.

Theo What do you mean by deserialize a string?

Joe Deserializing a string `s`, for example, means to generate a piece of data whose serialization is `s`.

Theo Is there a Lodash function for string deserialization?

Joe Actually, there is a native JavaScript function for string deserialization; it's called `JSON.parse`.

Joe retrieves his laptop and shows Theo an example of string deserialization. The code illustrates a common usage of `JSON.parse`.

Listing 6.14 Example of string deserialization

```
var myString = "{\"publicationYear\":1987,\"title\":\"Watchmen\"}";
var myData = JSON.parse(myString);
```

```
_.get(myData, "title");
// → "Watchmen"
```

Theo Cool! Let me try writing a unit test for `Library.searchBooksByTitleJSON` using `JSON.parse`.

It doesn't take Theo too much time to come up with a piece of code. Using his laptop, he inputs the unit test.

Listing 6.15 Unit test for `Library.searchBooksByTitleJSON`

```
var libraryData = {
  "catalog": {
    "booksByIsbn": {
      "978-1779501127": {
        "isbn": "978-1779501127",
        "title": "Watchmen",
        "publicationYear": 1987,
        "authorIds": ["alan-moore",
          "dave-gibbons"]
      }
    },
    "authorsById": {
      "alan-moore": {
        "name": "Alan Moore",
        "bookIsbns": ["978-1779501127"]
      },
      "dave-gibbons": {
        "name": "Dave Gibbons",
        "bookIsbns": ["978-1779501127"]
      }
    }
  }
};


var bookInfo = {
  "isbn": "978-1779501127",
  "title": "Watchmen",
  "authorNames": ["Alan Moore",
    "Dave Gibbons"]
};


_.isEqual(JSON.parse(Library.searchBooksByTitleJSON(libraryData,
  "Watchmen")),
  [bookInfo]);

_.isEqual(JSON.parse(Library.searchBooksByTitleJSON(libraryData,
  "Batman")),
  []);
```

Joe Well done! I think you're ready to move on to the last piece of the puzzle and write the unit test for `Catalog.searchBooksByTitle`.

Because Theo and Joe have been discussing unit tests for quite some time, he asks Joe if he would like another espresso. They call the waiter and order, then Theo looks again at the code for `Catalog.searchBooksByTitle`.

Listing 6.16 The code of `Catalog.searchBooksByTitle`

```
Catalog.searchBooksByTitle = function(catalogData, query) {
  var allBooks = _.get(catalogData, "booksByIsbn");
  var matchingBooks = _.filter(allBooks, function(book) {
    return _.get(book, "title").includes(query);
  });
  var bookInfos = _.map(matchingBooks, function(book) {
    return Catalog.bookInfo(catalogData, book);
  });
  return bookInfos;
};
```

Writing the unit test for `Catalog.searchBooksByTitle` is a more pleasant experience for Theo than writing the unit test for `Library.searchBooksByTitleJSON`. He appreciates this for two reasons:

- It's not necessary to deserialize the output because the function returns data.
- It's not necessary to wrap the catalog data in a library data map.

Listing 6.17 Unit test for `Catalog.searchBooksByTitle`

```
var catalogData = {
  "booksByIsbn": {
    "978-1779501127": {
      "isbn": "978-1779501127",
      "title": "Watchmen",
      "publicationYear": 1987,
      "authorIds": ["alan-moore",
        "dave-gibbons"]
    }
  },
  "authorsById": {
    "alan-moore": {
      "name": "Alan Moore",
      "bookIsbns": ["978-1779501127"]
    },
    "dave-gibbons": {
      "name": "Dave Gibbons",
      "bookIsbns": ["978-1779501127"]
    }
  }
};

var bookInfo = {
  "isbn": "978-1779501127",
  "title": "Watchmen",
  "authorNames": ["Alan Moore",
    "Dave Gibbons"]
};
```

```
_.isEqual(Catalog.searchBooksByTitle(catalogData, "Watchmen"), [bookInfo]);
_.isEqual(Catalog.searchBooksByTitle(catalogData, "Batman"), []);
```

Joe That's a good start!

Theo I thought I was done. What did I miss?

Joe You forgot to test cases where the query string is all lowercase.

Theo You're right! Let me quickly add one more test case.

In less than a minute, Theo creates an additional test case and shows it to Joe. What a disappointment when Theo discovers that the test case with `"watchmen"` in lowercase fails!

Listing 6.18 Additional test case for `Catalog.searchBooksByTitle`

```
_.isEqual(Catalog.searchBooksByTitle(catalogData, "watchmen"),
  [bookInfo]);
```

Joe Don't be too upset, my friend. After all, the purpose of unit tests is to find bugs in the code so that you can fix them. Can you fix the code of `CatalogData.searchBooksByTitle`?

Theo Sure. All I need to do is to lowercase both the query string and the book title before comparing them. I'd probably do something like this.

Listing 6.19 Fixed code of `Catalog.searchBooksByTitle`

```
Catalog.searchBooksByTitle = function(catalogData, query) {
  var allBooks = _.get(catalogData, "booksByIsbn");
  var queryLowerCased = query.toLowerCase();          <-- Converts the query to lowercase
  var matchingBooks = _.filter(allBooks, function(book) {
    return _.get(book, "title")
      .toLowerCase()                  <-- Converts the book title to lowercase
      .includes(queryLowerCased);
  });
  var bookInfos = _.map(matchingBooks, function(book) {
    return Catalog.bookInfo(catalogData, book);
  });
  return bookInfos;
};
```

After fixing the code of `Catalog.searchBooksByTitle`, Theo runs all the test cases again. This time, all of them pass—what a relief!

Listing 6.20 Additional test case for `Catalog.searchBooksByTitle`

```
_.isEqual(Catalog.searchBooksByTitle(catalogData, "watchmen"),
  [bookInfo]);
```

Joe It's such good feeling when all the test cases pass.

Theo Sure is.

Joe I think we've written unit tests for all the search query code, so now we're ready to write unit tests for mutations. Thank goodness the waiter just brought our coffee orders.

6.4 Unit tests for mutations

Joe Before writing unit tests for the add member mutation, let's draw the tree of function calls for `System.addMember`.

Theo I can do that.

Theo takes a look at the code for the functions involved in the add member mutation. He notices the code is spread over three classes: `System`, `Library`, and `UserManagement`.

Listing 6.21 The functions involved in the add member mutation

```
System.addMember = function(systemState, member) {
  var previous = systemState.get();
  var next = Library.addMember(previous, member);
  systemState.commit(previous, next);
};

Library.addMember = function(library, member) {
  var currentUserManagement = _.get(library, "userManagement");
  var nextUserManagement = UserManagement.addMember(
    currentUserManagement, member);
  var nextLibrary = _.set(library, "userManagement", nextUserManagement);
  return nextLibrary;
};

UserManagement.addMember = function(userManagement, member) {
  var email = _.get(member, "email");
  var infoPath = ["membersByEmail", email];
  if(_.has(userManagement, infoPath)) {
    throw "Member already exists.";
  }
  var nextUserManagement =  _.set(userManagement,
    infoPath,
    member);
  return nextUserManagement;
};
```

Theo grabs another napkin. Drawing the tree of function calls for `System.addMember` is now quite easy (see figure 6.5).

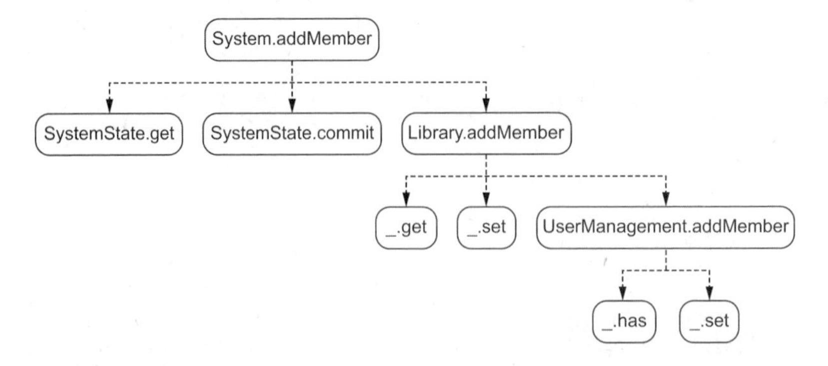

Figure 6.5 The tree of function calls for `System.addMember`

Joe Excellent! So which functions of the tree should be unit tested for the add member mutation?

Theo I think the functions we need to test are `System.addMember`, `SystemState.get`, `SystemState.commit`, `Library.addMember`, and `UserManagement.addMember`. That right?

Joe You're totally right. Let's defer writing unit tests for functions that belong to `SystemState` until later. Those are generic functions that should be tested outside the context of a specific mutation. Let's assume for now that we've already written unit tests for the `SystemState` class. We're left with three functions: `System.addMember`, `Library.addMember`, and `UserManagement.addMember`.

Theo In what order should we write the unit tests, bottom up or top down?

Joe Let's start where the real meat is—in `UserManagement.addMember`. The two other functions are just wrappers.

Theo OK.

Joe Writing a unit test for the main function of a mutation requires more effort than writing the test for a query. The reason is that a query returns a response based on the system data, whereas a mutation computes a new state of the system based on the current state of the system and some arguments (see figure 6.6).

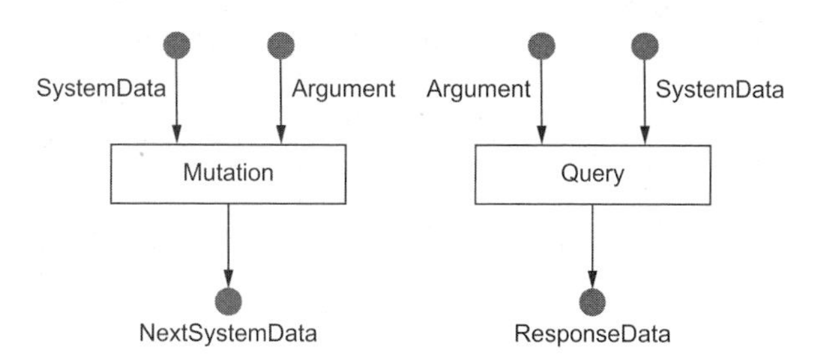

Figure 6.6 The output of a mutation is more complex than the output of a query.

TIP Writing a unit test for the main function of a mutation requires more effort than for a query.

Theo It means that in the test cases of `UserManagement.addMember`, both the input and the expected output are maps that describe the state of the system.

Joe Exactly. Let's start with the simplest case, where the initial state of the system is empty.

Theo You mean that `userManagementData` passed to `UserManagement.addMember` is an empty map?

Joe Yes.

Once again, Theo places his hands over his laptop keyboard, thinks for a moment, and begins typing. He reminds himself that the code needs to add a member to an empty user management map and to check that the resulting map is as expected. When he's finished, he shows his code to Joe.

Listing 6.22 Test case for `Catalog.addMember` without members

```
var member = {
  "email": "jessie@gmail.com",
  "password": "my-secret"
};

var userManagementStateBefore = {};

var expectedUserManagementStateAfter = {
  "membersByEmail": {
    "jessie@gmail.com": {
      "email": "jessie@gmail.com",
      "password": "my-secret"
    }
  }
};

var result = UserManagement.addMember(userManagementStateBefore, member);
_.isEqual(result, expectedUserManagementStateAfter);
```

Joe Very nice! Keep going and write a test case when the initial state is not empty.

Theo knows this requires a few more lines of code but nothing complicated. When he finishes, he once again shows the code to Joe.

Listing 6.23 Test case for `Catalog.addMember` with existing members

```
var jessie = {
  "email": "jessie@gmail.com",
  "password": "my-secret"
};

var franck = {
  "email": "franck@gmail.com",
  "password": "my-top-secret"
};

var userManagementStateBefore = {
  "membersByEmail": {
    "franck@gmail.com": {
      "email": "franck@gmail.com",
      "password": "my-top-secret"
    }
  }
};

var expectedUserManagementStateAfter = {
  "membersByEmail": {
    "jessie@gmail.com": {
      "email": "jessie@gmail.com",
```

```
        "password": "my-secret"
      },
      "franck@gmail.com": {
        "email": "franck@gmail.com",
        "password": "my-top-secret"
      }
    }
};

var result = UserManagement.addMember(userManagementStateBefore, jessie);
_.isEqual(result, expectedUserManagementStateAfter);
```

Joe Awesome! Can you think of other test cases for `UserManagement.addMember`?

Theo No.

Joe What about cases where the mutation fails?

Theo Right! I always forget to think about negative test cases. I assume that relates to the fact that I'm an optimistic person.

TIP Don't forget to include negative test cases in your unit tests.

Joe Me too. The more I meditate, the more I'm able to focus on the positive side of life. Anyway, how would you write a test case where the mutation fails?

Theo I would pass to `UserManagement.addMember` a member that already exists in `userManagementStateBefore`.

Joe And how would you check that the code behaves as expected in case of a failure?

Theo Let me see. When a member already exists, `UserManagement.addMember` throws an exception. Therefore, what I need to do in my test case is to wrap the code in a `try/catch` block.

Joe Sounds good to me.

Once again, it doesn't require too much of an effort for Theo to create a new test case. When he's finished, he eagerly turns his laptop to Joe.

Listing 6.24 Test case for `UserManagement.addMember` if it's expected to fail

```
var jessie = {
  "email": "jessie@gmail.com",
  "password": "my-secret"
};

var userManagementStateBefore = {
  "membersByEmail": {
    "jessie@gmail.com": {
      "email": "jessie@gmail.com",
      "password": "my-secret"
    }
  }
};
```

```
var expectedException = "Member already exists.";
var exceptionInMutation;

try {
  UserManagement.addMember(userManagementStateBefore, jessie);
} catch (e) {
  exceptionInMutation = e;
}

_.isEqual(exceptionInMutation, expectedException);
```

Theo Now, I think I'm ready to move forward and write unit tests for `Library.addMember` and `System.addMember`.

Joe I agree with you. Please start with `Library.addMember`.

Theo `Library.addMember` is quite similar to `UserManagement.addMember`. So I guess I'll write similar test cases.

Joe In fact, that won't be required. As I told you when we wrote unit tests for a query, when you write a unit test for a function, you can assume that the functions down the tree work as expected.

Theo Right. So I'll just write the test case for existing members.

Joe Go for it!

Theo starts with a copy-and-paste of the code from the `UserManagement.addMember` test case with the existing members in listing 6.23. After a few modifications, the unit test for `Library.addMember` is ready.

Listing 6.25 Unit test for `Library.addMember`

```
var jessie = {
  "email": "jessie@gmail.com",
  "password": "my-secret"
};

var franck = {
  "email": "franck@gmail.com",
  "password": "my-top-secret"
};

var libraryStateBefore = {
  "userManagement": {
    "membersByEmail": {
      "franck@gmail.com": {
        "email": "franck@gmail.com",
        "password": "my-top-secret"
      }
    }
  }
};

var expectedLibraryStateAfter = {
  "userManagement": {
    "membersByEmail": {
```

```
      "jessie@gmail.com": {
        "email": "jessie@gmail.com",
        "password": "my-secret"
      },
      "franck@gmail.com": {
        "email": "franck@gmail.com",
        "password": "my-top-secret"
      }
    }
  }
};

var result = Library.addMember(libraryStateBefore, jessie);
_.isEqual(result, expectedLibraryStateAfter);
```

Joe Beautiful! Now, we're ready for the last piece. Write a unit test for `System.addMember`. Before you start, could you please describe the input and the output of `System.addMember`?

Theo takes another look at the code for `System.addMember` and hesitates; he's a bit confused. The function doesn't seem to return anything!

Listing 6.26 The code of `System.addMember`

```
System.addMember = function(systemState, member) {
  var previous = systemState.get();
  var next = Library.addMember(previous, member);
  systemState.commit(previous, next);
};
```

Theo The input of `System.addMember` is a system state instance and a member. But, I'm not sure what the output of `System.addMember` is.

Joe In fact, `System.addMember` doesn't have any output. It belongs to this stateful part of our code that doesn't deal with data manipulation. Although DOP allows us to reduce the size of the stateful part of our code, it still exists. Here is how I visualize it.

Joe calls the waiter to see if he can get more napkins. With that problem resolved, he draws the diagram in figure 6.7.

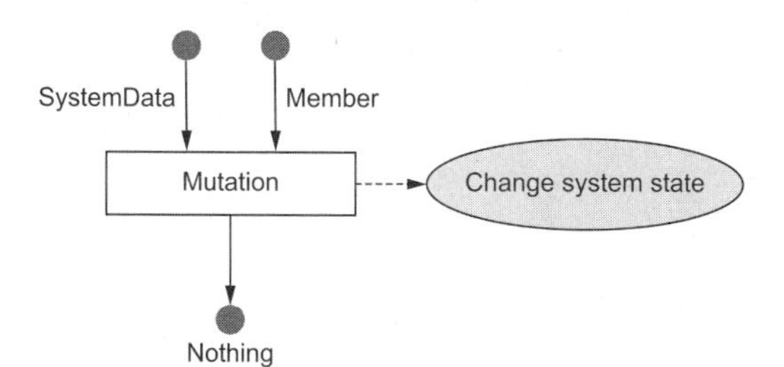

Figure 6.7 `System.addMember` doesn't return data—it changes the system state!

Theo Then how do we validate that the code works as expected?

Joe We'll retrieve the system state after the code is executed and compare it to the expected value of the state.

Theo OK. I'll try to write the unit test.

Joe Writing unit tests for stateful code is more complicated than for data manipulation code. It requires the calm of the office.

Theo Then let's go back to the office. Waiter! Check, please.

Theo picks up the tab, and he and Joe take the cable car back to Albatross. When they're back at the office, Theo starts coding the unit test for `Library.addMember`.

Theo Can we use `_.isEqual` with system state?

Joe Definitely. The system state is a map like any other map.

TIP The system state is a map. Therefore, in the context of a test case, we can compare the system state after a mutation is executed to the expected system state using `_.isEqual`

Theo copies and pastes the code for `Library.addMember` (listing 6.21), which initializes the data for the test. Then, he passes a `SystemState` object that is initialized with `libraryStateBefore` to `System.addMember`. Finally, to complete the test, he compares the system state after the mutation is executed with the expected value of the state.

```
class SystemState {
  systemState;

  get() {
    return this.systemState;
  }

  commit(previous, next) {
    this.systemState = next;
  }
}
window.SystemState = SystemState;
```

Listing 6.27 Unit test for `System.addMember`

```
var jessie = {
  "email": "jessie@gmail.com",
  "password": "my-secret"
};

var franck = {
  "email": "franck@gmail.com",
  "password": "my-top-secret"
};

var libraryStateBefore = {
  "userManagement": {
    "membersByEmail": {
```

```
      "franck@gmail.com": {
        "email": "franck@gmail.com",
        "password": "my-top-secret"
      }
    }
  }
};

var expectedLibraryStateAfter = {
  "userManagement": {
    "membersByEmail": {
      "jessie@gmail.com": {
        "email": "jessie@gmail.com",
        "password": "my-secret"
      },
      "franck@gmail.com": {
        "email": "franck@gmail.com",
        "password": "my-top-secret"
      }
    }
  }
};

var systemState = new SystemState();                    ◁ Creates an empty SystemState object (see chapter 4)
systemState.commit(null, libraryStateBefore);          ◁ Initializes the system state with the library data before the mutation
System.addMember(systemState, jessie);                 ◁ Executes the mutation on the SystemState object

_.isEqual(systemState.get(),
  expectedLibraryStateAfter);                          ◁ Validates the state after the mutation is executed
```

Joe Wow, I'm impressed; you did it! Congratulations!

Theo Thank you. I'm so glad that in DOP most of our code deals with data manipulation. It's definitely more pleasant to write unit tests for stateless code that only deals with data manipulation.

Joe Now that you know the basics of DOP, would you like to refactor the code of your Klafim prototype according to DOP principles?

Theo Definitely. Nancy told me yesterday that Klafim is getting nice market traction. I'm supposed to have a meeting with her in a week or so about the next steps. Hopefully, she'll be willing to work with Albatross for the long term.

Joe Exciting! Do you know what might influence Nancy's decision?

Theo Our cost estimate, certainly, but I know she's in touch with other software companies. If we come up with a competitive proposal, I think we'll get the deal.

Joe I'm quite sure that after refactoring to DOP, features will take much less time to implement. That means you should be able to quote Nancy a lower total cost than the competition, right?

Theo I'll keep my fingers crossed!

Moving forward

The meeting with Nancy went well. Albatross got the deal, Monica (Theo's boss) is pleased, and it's going to be a long-term project with a nice budget. They'll need to hire a team of developers in order to meet the tough deadlines. While driving back to the office, Theo gets a phone call from Joe.

Joe How was your meeting with Nancy?

Theo We got the deal!

Joe Awesome! I told you that with DOP the cost estimation would be lower.

Theo In fact, we are not going to use DOP for this project.

Joe Why?

Theo After refactoring the Library Management System prototype to DOP, I did a deep analysis with my engineers. We came to the conclusion that DOP might be a good fit for the prototype phase, but it won't work well at scale.

Joe Could you share the details of your analysis?

Theo I can't right now. I'm driving.

Joe Could we meet in your office later today?

Theo I'm quite busy with the new project and the tough deadlines.

Joe Let's meet at least in order to have a proper farewell.

Theo OK. Let's meet at 4 PM, then.

▶ **NOTE** The story continues in the opener of part 2.

Summary

- Most of the code in a data-oriented system deals with data manipulation.
- It's straightforward to write unit tests for code that deals with data manipulation.
- Test cases follow the same simple general pattern:
  a. Generate data input
  b. Generate expected data output
  c. Compare the output of the function with the expected data output
- In order to compare the output of a function with the expected data output, we need to recursively compare the two pieces of data.
- The *recursive comparison* of two pieces of data is implemented via a generic function.
- When a function returns a JSON string, we parse the string back to data so that we deal with data comparison instead of string comparison.
- A *tree of function calls* for a function `f` is a tree where the root is `f`, and the children of a node `g` in the tree are the functions called by `g`.
- The leaves of the tree are functions that are not part of the code base of the application and are functions that don't call any other functions.
- The tree of function calls visualization guides us regarding the quality and quantity of the test cases in a unit test.

- Functions that appear in a lower level in the tree of function calls tend to involve less complex data than functions that appear in a higher level in the tree.
- Functions that appear in a lower level in the tree of function calls usually need to be covered with more test cases than functions that appear in a higher level in the tree.
- Unit tests for mutations focus on the calculation phase of the mutation.
- The validity of the data depends on the context.
- The smaller the data, the easier it is to manipulate.
- We compare the output and the expected output of our functions with a generic function that recursively compares two pieces of data (e.g., `_.isEqual`).
- When we write a unit test for a function, we assume that the functions called by this function are covered by the unit tests and work as expected. This significantly reduces the quantity of test cases in our unit tests.
- We avoid using string comparison in unit tests for functions that deal with data.
- Writing a unit test for the main function of a mutation requires more effort than for a query.
- Remember to include negative test cases in your unit tests.
- The system state is a map. Therefore, in the context of a test case, we can compare the system state after a mutation is executed to the expected system state using a generic function like `_.isEqual`.

Part 2

Scalability

Theo feels a bit uncomfortable about the meeting with Joe. He was so enthusiastic about DOP, and he was very good at teaching it. Every meeting with him was an opportunity to learn new things. Theo feels lot of gratitude for the time Joe spent with him. He doesn't want to hurt him in any fashion. Surprisingly, Joe enters the office with the same relaxed attitude as usual, and he is even smiling.

Joe I'm really glad that you got the deal with Nancy.

Theo Yeah. There's lot of excitement about it here in the office, and a bit of stress too.

Joe What kind of stress?

Theo You know. . . . We need to hire a team of developers, and the deadlines are quite tight.

Joe But you told me that you won't use DOP. I assume that you gave regular deadlines?

Theo No, my boss Monica really wanted to close the deal. She feels that success with this project is strategically important for Albatross, so it's worthwhile to accept some risk by giving what she calls an "optimistic" time estimation. I told her that it was really an unrealistic time estimation, but Monica insists that if we make smart decisions and bring in more developers, we can do it.

Joe I see. Now I understand why you told me over the phone that you were very busy. Anyway, would you please share the reasons that made you think DOP wouldn't be a good fit at scale?

Theo First of all, let me tell you that I feel lot of gratitude for all the teaching you shared with me. Reimplementing the Klafim prototype with DOP was really fun and productive due to the flexibility this paradigm offers.

Joe I'm happy that you found it valuable.

Theo But, as I told you over the phone, now we're scaling up into a long-term project with several developers working on a large code base. We came to the conclusion that DOP will not be a good fit at scale.

Joe Could you share the reasons behind your conclusion?

Theo There are many of them. First of all, as DOP deals only with generic data structures, it's hard to know what kind of data we have in hand, while in OOP, we know the type of every piece of data. For the prototype, it was kind of OK. But as the code base grows and more developers are involved in the project, it would be too painful.

Joe I hear you. What else, my friend?

Theo Our system is going to run on a multi-threaded environment. I reviewed the concurrency control strategy that you presented, and it's not thread-safe.

Joe I hear you. What else, my friend?

Theo I have been doing a bit of research about implementing immutable data structures with structural sharing. I discovered that when the size of the data structures grows, there is a significant performance hit.

Joe I hear you. What else?

Theo As our system grows, we will use a database to store the application data and external services to enrich book information, and in what you have showed me so far, data lives in memory.

Joe I hear you. What else, my friend?

Theo Don't you think I have shared enough reasons to abandon DOP?

Joe I think that your concerns about DOP at scale totally make sense. However, it doesn't mean that you should abandon DOP.

Theo What do you mean?

Joe With the help of meditation, I learned not be attached to the objections that flow in my mind while I'm practicing. Sometimes all that is needed to quiet our minds is to keep breathing; sometimes, a deeper level of practice is needed.

Theo I don't see how breathing would convince me to give DOP a second chance.

Joe Breathing might not be enough in this case, but a deeper knowledge of DOP could be helpful. Until now, I have shared with you only the material that was needed in order to refactor your prototype. In order to use DOP in a big project, a few more lessons are necessary.

Theo But I don't have time for more lessons. I need to work.

Joe Have you heard the story about the young woodcutter and the old man?

Theo No.

Joe It goes like this.

The young woodcutter and the old man

A young woodcutter strained to saw down a tree. An old man who was watching nearby asked, "What are you doing?"

"Are you blind?" the woodcutter replied. "I'm cutting down this tree."

The old man replied, "You look exhausted! Take a break. Sharpen your saw."

The young woodcutter explained to the old man that he had been sawing for hours and did not have time to take a break.

The old man pushed back, "If you sharpen the saw, you would cut down the tree much faster."

The woodcutter said, "I don't have time to sharpen the saw. Don't you see, I'm too busy!"

Theo takes a moment to meditate on the story. He wonders if he needs to take the time to sharpen his saw and commit to a deeper level of practice.

Theo Do you really think that with DOP, it will take much less time to deliver the project?

Joe I know so!

Theo But if we miss the deadline, I will probably get fired. I'm the one that needs to take the risk, not you.

Joe Let's make a deal. If you miss the deadline and get fired, I will hire you at my company for double the salary you make at Albatross.

Theo And what if we meet the deadline?

Joe If you meet the deadline, you will probably get promoted. In that case, I will ask you to buy a gift for my son Neriah and my daughter Aurelia.

Theo Deal! When will I get my first lesson about going deeper into DOP?

Joe Why not start right now?

Theo Let me reschedule my meetings.

7 Basic data validation

A solemn gift

This chapter covers

- The importance of validating data at system boundaries
- Validating data using the JSON Schema language
- Integrating data validation into an existing code base
- Getting detailed information about data validation failures

At first glance, it may seem that embracing DOP means accessing data without validating it and engaging in wishful thinking, where data is always valid. In fact, data validation is not only possible but recommended when we follow data-oriented principles.

This chapter illustrates how to validate data when data is represented with generic data structures. It focuses on data validation occurring at the boundaries of the system, while in part 3, we will deal with validating data as it flows through the system. This chapter is a deep dive into the fourth principle of DOP.

PRINCIPLE #4 Separate data schema from data representation.

7.1 Data validation in DOP

Theo has rescheduled his meetings. With such an imposing deadline, he's still not sure if he's made a big mistake giving DOP a second chance.

▶ **NOTE** The reason why Theo rescheduled his meetings is explained in the opener for part 2. Take a moment to read the opener if you missed it.

Joe What aspect of OOP do you think you will miss the most in your big project?

Theo Data validation.

Joe Can you elaborate a bit?

Theo In OOP, I have this strong guarantee that when a class is instantiated, its member fields have the proper names and proper types. But with DOP, it's so easy to have small mistakes in field names and field types.

Joe Well, I have good news for you! There is a way to validate data in DOP.

Theo How does it work? I thought DOP and data validation were two contradictory concepts!

Joe Not at all. It's true that DOP doesn't force you to validate data, but it doesn't prevent you from doing so. In DOP, the data schema is separate from the data representation.

Theo I don't get how that would eliminate data consistency issues.

Joe According to DOP, the most important data to validate is data that crosses the boundaries of the system.

Theo Which boundaries are you referring to?

Joe In the case of a web server, it would be the areas where the web server communicates with its clients and with its data sources.

Theo A diagram might help me see it better.

Joe goes to the whiteboard and picks up the pen. He then draws a diagram like the one in figure 7.1.

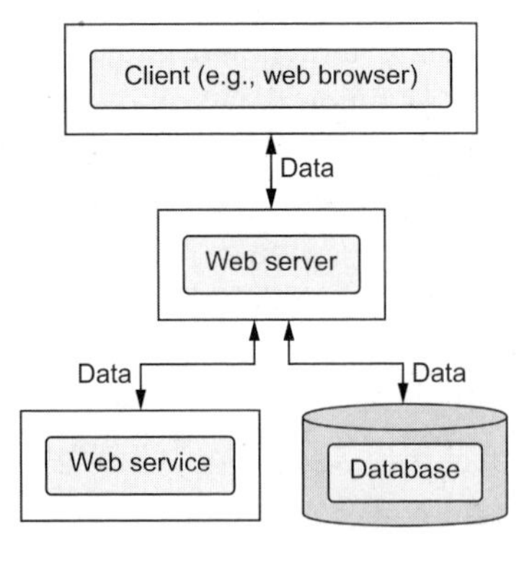

Figure 7.1 High-level architecture of a modern web server

Joe This architectural diagram defines what we call the boundaries of the system in terms of data exchange. Can you tell me what the three boundaries of the system are?

▶ **NOTE** The *boundaries* of a system are defined as the areas where the system exchanges data.

Theo Let me see. The first one is the client boundary, then we have the database boundary, and finally, the web service boundary.

Joe Exactly! It's important to identify the boundaries of a system because, in DOP, we differentiate between two kinds of data validation: validation that occurs at the boundaries of the system and validation that occurs inside the system. Today, we're going to focus on validation that occurs at the boundaries of the system.

Theo Does that mean data validation at the boundaries of the system is more important?

Joe Absolutely! Once you've ensured that data going into and out of the system is valid, the odds for an unexpected piece of data inside the system are pretty low.

TIP When data at system boundaries is validated, it's not critical to validate data again inside the system.

Theo Why do we need data validation inside the system then?

Joe It has to do with making it easier to code your system as your code base grows.

Theo And, what's the main purpose of data validation at the boundaries?

Joe To prevent invalid data from going in and out of the system, and to display informative errors when we encounter invalid data. Let me draw a table on the whiteboard so you can see the distinction (table 7.1).

Table 7.1 Two kinds of data validation

Kind of data validation	Purpose	Environment
Boundaries	Guardian	Production
Inside	Ease of development	Dev

Theo When will you teach me about data validation inside the system?

Joe Later, when the code base is bigger.

7.2 JSON Schema in a nutshell

Theo For now, the Library Management System is an application that runs in memory, with no database and no HTTP clients connected to it. But Nancy will probably want me to make the system into a real web server with clients, database, and external services.

Joe OK. Let's imagine how a client request for searching books would look.

Theo Basically, a search request is made of a string and the fields you'd like to retrieve for the books whose title contains the string. So the request has two fields: `title`, which is a string, and `fields`, which is an array of strings.

Theo quickly writes on the whiteboard. When he finishes, he steps aside to let Joe view his code for a search request.

Listing 7.1 An example of a search request

```
{
  "title": "habit",
  "fields": ["title", "weight", "number_of_pages"]
}
```

Joe I see. Let me show you how to express the schema of a search request separately from the representation of the search request data.

Theo What do you mean exactly by "separately?"

Joe Data representation stands on its own, and the data schema stands on its own. You are free to validate that a piece of data conforms with a data schema as you will and when you will.

TIP In DOP, the data schema is separate from the data representation.

Theo It's a bit abstract for me.

Joe I know. It will become much clearer in a moment. For now, I am going to show you how to build the data schema for the search request in a schema language called JSON Schema.

Theo I love JSON!

▶ **NOTE** Information on the JSON Schema language can be found at https://json-schema.org. The schemas in this book use JSON Schema version 2020-12.

Joe First, we have to express the data type of the request. What's the data type in the case of a book search request?

Theo It's a map.

Joe In JSON Schema, the data type for maps is called `object`. Look at this basic skeleton of a map. It's a map with two fields: `type` and `properties`.

Joe goes to the whiteboard. He quickly writes the code for the map with its two fields.

Listing 7.2 Basic schema skeleton of a map

```
{
  "type": "object",
  "properties": {...}
}
```

Joe The value of `type` is `"object"`, and the value of `properties` is a map with the schema for the map fields.

Theo I assume that, inside properties, we are going to express the schema of the map fields as JSON Schema.

Joe Correct.

Theo I am starting to feel the dizziness of recursion.

Joe In JSON Schema, a schema is usually a JSON object with a field called `type`, which specifies the data type. For example, the type for the `title` field is `string` and . . .

Theo . . . the type for the `fields` field is `array`.

Joe Yes!

Now it's Theo's turn to go to the whiteboard. He fills the holes in the search request schema with the information about the fields.

Listing 7.3 Schema skeleton for search request

```
{
  "type": "object",
  "properties": {
    "title": {"type": "string"},
    "fields": {"type": "array"}
  }
}
```

On Theo's way back from the whiteboard to his desk, Joe makes a sign with his right hand that says, "Stay near the whiteboard, please." Theo turns and goes back to the whiteboard.

Joe We can be a little more precise about the `fields` property by providing information about the type of the elements in the array. In JSON Schema, an array schema has a property called `items`, whose value is the schema for the array elements.

Without any hesitation, Theo adds this information on the whiteboard. Stepping aside, he shows Joe the result.

Listing 7.4 Schema for search request with information about array elements

```
{
  "type": "object",
  "properties": {
    "title": {"type": "string"},
    "fields": {
      "type": "array",
      "items": {"type": "string"}
    }
  }
}
```

Before going back to his desk, Theo asks Joe:

Theo Are we done now?

Joe Not yet. We can be more precise about the `fields` field in the search request. I assume that the fields in the request should be part of a closed list of fields. Therefore, instead of allowing any string, we could have a list of allowed values.

Theo Like an enumeration value?

Joe Exactly! In fact, JSON Schema supports enumeration values with the `enum` keyword. Instead of `{"type": "string"}`, you need to have `{"enum": [...]}` and replace the dots with the supported fields.

Once again, Theo turns to the whiteboard. He replaces the dots with the information Joe requests.

Listing 7.5 Schema for the search request with enumeration values

```
{
  "type": "object",
  "properties": {
    "title": {"type": "string"},
    "fields": {
      "type": "array",
      "items": {
        "enum": [
          "publishers",
          "number_of_pages",
          "weight",
          "physical_format",
          "subjects",
          "publish_date",
          "physical_dimensions"
        ]
      }
    }
  }
}
```

Theo Are we done, now?

Joe Almost. We need to decide whether the fields of our search request are optional or required. In our case, both `title` and `fields` are required.

Theo How do we express this information in JSON Schema?

Joe There is a field called `required` whose value is an array made of the names of the required fields in the map.

After adding the `required` field, Theo looks at Joe. This time he makes a move with his right hand that says, "Now you can go back to your desk."

Listing 7.6 Schema of a search request

```
var searchBooksRequestSchema = {
  "type": "object",
```

```
  "properties": {
    "title": {"type": "string"},
    "fields": {
      "type": "array",
      "items": {
        "enum": [
          "publishers",
          "number_of_pages",
          "weight",
          "physical_format",
          "subjects",
          "publish_date",
          "physical_dimensions"
        ]
      }
    }
  },
  "required": ["title", "fields"]
};
```

Joe Now I'll show you how to validate a piece of data according to a schema.

Theo What do you mean, validate?

Joe Validating data according to a schema means checking whether data conforms to the schema. In our case, it means checking whether a piece of data is a valid search books request.

TIP Data validation in DOP means checking whether a piece of data conforms to a schema.

Theo I see.

Joe There are a couple of libraries that provide JSON Schema validation. They have a `validate` function that receives a schema and a piece of data and returns `true` when the data is valid and `false` when the data is not valid. I just happen to have a file in my laptop that provides a table with a list of schema validation libraries (table 7.2). We can print it out if you like.

Theo turns on the printer as Joe scans through his laptop for the table. When he has it up, he checks with Theo and presses Print.

Table 7.2 Libraries for JSON Schema validation

Language	Library	URL
JavaScript	Ajv	https://github.com/ajv-validator/ajv
Java	Snow	https://github.com/ssilverman/snowy-json
C#	JSON.net Schema	https://www.newtonsoft.com/jsonschema
Python	jschon	https://github.com/marksparkza/jschon
Ruby	JSONSchemer	https://github.com/davishmcclurg/json_schemer

Theo So, if I call validate with this search request and that schema, it will return true?

Theo indicates the search request example from listing 7.7 and the schema from listing 7.6.

Listing 7.7 An example of a search request

```
{
  "title": "habit",
  "fields": ["title", "weight", "number_of_pages"]
}
```

Joe Give it a try, and you'll see.

Indeed! When Theo executes the code to validate the search request, it returns true.

Listing 7.8 Validating the search request

```
var searchBooksRequestSchema = {
  "type": "object",
  "properties": {
    "title": {"type": "string"},
    "fields": {
      "type": "array",
      "items": {"type": "string"}
    }
  },
  "required": ["title", "fields"]
};

var searchBooksRequest = {
  "title": "habit",
  "fields": ["title", "weight", "number_of_pages"]
};

validate(searchBooksRequestSchema, searchBooksRequest);
// → true
```

Joe Now, please try an invalid request.

Theo Let me think about what kind of invalidity to try. I know, I'll make a typo in the title field and call it tilte with the *l* before the *t*.

As expected, the code with the type returns false. Theo is not surprised, and Joe is smiling from ear to ear.

Listing 7.9 Validating an invalid search request

```
var invalidSearchBooksRequest = {
  "tilte": "habit",
  "fields": ["title", "weight", "number_of_pages"]
};
```

```
validate(searchBooksRequestSchema, invalidSearchBooksRequest);
// → false
```

Theo The syntax of JSON Schema is much more verbose than the syntax for declaring the members in a class. Why is that so?

Joe For two reasons. First, because JSON Schema is language independent, it can be used in any programming language. As I told you, there are JSON Schema validators available in most programming languages.

Theo I see.

Joe Second, JSON Schema allows you to express validation conditions that are much harder, if not impossible, to express when data is represented with classes.

TIP The expressive power of JSON Schema is high!

Theo Now you have triggered my curiosity. Can you give me some examples?

Joe In a moment, we'll talk about schema composition. Someday I'll show you some examples of advanced validation.

▶ **NOTE** Advanced validation is covered in chapter 12.

Theo What kind of advanced validation?

Joe What I mean by advanced validation is, for instance, validating that a number falls within a given range or validating that a string matches a regular expression.

Theo Is there a way to get details about why the request is invalid?

Joe Absolutely! I'll show you later. For now, let me show you how to make sure the response the server sends back to the client is valid.

Theo It sounds much more complicated than a search book request!

Joe Why?

Theo Because a search response is made of multiple book results, and in each book result, some of the fields are optional!

7.3 Schema flexibility and strictness

Joe Can you give me an example of what a book search response would look like?

Theo Take a look at this example. It's a search response with information about two books: *7 Habits of Highly Effective People* and *The Power of Habit.*

Listing 7.10 An example of a search response

```
[
  {
    "title": "7 Habits of Highly Effective People",
    "available": true,
    "isbn": "978-0812981605",
    "subtitle": "Powerful Lessons in Personal Change",
    "number_of_pages": 432
  },
```

```
  {
    "title": "The Power of Habit",
    "available": false,
    "isbn_13": "978-1982137274",
    "subtitle": "Why We Do What We Do in Life and Business",
    "subjects": [
      "Social aspects",
      "Habit",
      "Change (Psychology)"
    ]
  }
]
```

Joe It's funny that you mention *The Power of Habit.* I'm reading this book in order to get rid of my habit of biting my nails. Anyway, what fields are required and what fields are optional in a book search response?

Theo In book information, the `title` and `available` fields are required. The other fields are optional.

Joe As I told you when we built the schema for the book search request, fields in a map are optional by default. In order to make a field mandatory, we have to include it in the `required` array. I'd probably implement it with something like this.

Listing 7.11 Schema of a search response

```
var searchBooksResponseSchema = {
  "type": "array",
  "items": {
    "type": "object",
    "required": ["title", "available"],
    "properties": {
      "title": {"type": "string"},
      "available": {"type": "boolean"},
      "subtitle": {"type": "string"},
      "number_of_pages": {"type": "integer"},
      "subjects": {
        "type": "array",
        "items": {"type": "string"}
      },
      "isbn": {"type": "string"},
      "isbn_13": {"type": "string"}
    }
  }
};
```

TIP In JSON Schema, map fields are optional by default.

Theo I must admit that specifying a list of required fields is much simpler than having to specify that a member in a class in nullable!

Joe Agreed!

Theo On the other hand, I find the nesting of the book information schema in the search response schema a bit hard to read.

Joe Nothing prevents you from separating the book information schema from the search response schema.

Theo How?

Joe It's just JSON, my friend. It means, you are free to manipulate the schema as any other map in your program. For instance, you could have the book information schema in a variable named `bookInfoSchema` and use it in the search books response schema. Let me refactor the schema to show you what I mean.

Listing 7.12 Schema of a search response refactored

```
var bookInfoSchema = {
  "type": "object",
  "required": ["title", "available"],
  "properties": {
    "title": {"type": "string"},
    "available": {"type": "boolean"},
    "subtitle": {"type": "string"},
    "number_of_pages": {"type": "integer"},
    "subjects": {
      "type": "array",
      "items": {"type": "string"}
    },
    "isbn": {"type": "string"},
    "isbn_13": {"type": "string"}
  }
};

var searchBooksResponseSchema = {
  "type": "array",
  "items": bookInfoSchema
};
```

Theo Once again, I have to admit that JSON Schemas are more composable than class definitions.

TIP JSON Schemas are just maps. We are free to compose and manipulate them like any other map.

Joe Let's move on to validating data received from external data sources.

Theo Is that different?

Joe Not really, but I'll take it as an opportunity to show you some other features of JSON Schema.

Theo I'm curious to learn how data validation is used when we access data from the database.

Joe Each time we access data from the outside, it's a good practice to validate it. Can you show me an example of how a database response for a search query would look?

TIP It's a good practice to validate data that comes from an external data source.

Theo When we query books from the database, we expect to receive an array of books with three fields: `title`, `isbn`, and `available`. The first two values should be strings, and the third one should be a Boolean.

Joe Are those fields optional or required?

Theo What do you mean?

Joe Could there be books for which some of the fields are not defined?

Theo No.

Joe In that case, the schema is quite simple. Would you like to try writing the schema for the database response?

Theo Let me see. It's an array of objects where each object has three properties, so something like this?

Listing 7.13 Schema of a database response

```
{
  "type": "array",
  "items": {
    "type": "object",
    "required": ["title", "isbn", "available"],
    "properties": {
      "title": {"type": "string"},
      "available": {"type": "boolean"},
      "isbn": {"type": "string"}
    }
  }
}
```

Joe Well done, my friend! Now, I want to tell you about the `additionalProperties` field in JSON Schema.

Theo What's that?

Joe Take a look at this array.

Listing 7.14 A book array with an additional property

```
[
  {
    "title": "7 Habits of Highly Effective People",
    "available": true,
    "isbn": "978-0812981605",
    "dummy_property": 42
  },
  {
    "title": "The Power of Habit",
    "available": false,
    "isbn": "978-1982137274",
    "dummy_property": 45
  }
]
```

Joe Is it a valid database response?

Theo No. A database response should not have a `dummy_property` field. It should have only the three required fields specified in the schema.

Joe It might be surprising but, by default, fields not specified in the schema of an object are allowed in JSON Schema. In order to disallow them, one has to set `additionalProperties` to `false` like this.

Listing 7.15 Disallowing properties not mentioned in the schema

```
var booksFromDBSchema = {
  "type": "array",
  "items": {
    "type": "object",
    "required": ["title", "isbn", "available"],
    "additionalProperties": false,
    "properties": {
      "title": {"type": "string"},
      "available": {"type": "boolean"},
      "isbn": {"type": "string"}
    }
  }
};
```

TIP In JSON Schema, by default, fields not specified in the schema of a map are allowed.

Theo Why is that?

Joe The reason is that usually having additional fields in a map doesn't cause trouble. If your code doesn't care about a field, it simply ignores it. But sometimes we want to be as strict as possible, and we set `additionalProperties` to `false`.

Theo What about the search request and response schema from the previous discussions? Should we set `additionalProperties` to `false`?

Joe That's an excellent question. I'd say it's a matter of taste. Personally, I like to allow additional fields in requests and disallow them in responses.

Theo What's the advantage?

Joe Well, the web server is responsible for the responses it sends to its clients. It makes sense then to be as strict as possible. However, the requests are created by the clients, and I prefer to do my best to serve my clients even when they are not as strict as they should be.

Theo Naturally. "The client is always right."

Joe Actually, I prefer the way Jon Postel formulated his robustness principle: "Be conservative in what you send, be liberal in what you accept."

TIP It's a good practice to be strict with the data that you send and to be flexible with the data that you receive.

7.4 Schema composition

Theo What about validating data that comes from an external web service?

Joe Can you give me an example?

Theo In the near future, we'll have to integrate with a service called Open Library Books API that provides detailed information about books.

▶ **NOTE** For information on the Open Library Books API, see https://openlibrary.org/dev/docs/api/books.

Joe Can you show me, for instance, the service response for *Watchmen*?

Theo Sure. Here you go.

Theo taps a few keys on his keyboard and brings up the response. Joe looks at the JSON for a long time.

Listing 7.16 An Open Library Books API response example

```
{
  "publishers": [
    "DC Comics"
  ],
  "number_of_pages": 334,
  "weight": "1.4 pounds",
  "physical_format": "Paperback",
  "subjects": [
    "Graphic Novels",
    "Comics & Graphic Novels",
    "Fiction",
    "Fantastic fiction"
  ],
  "isbn_13": [
    "9780930289232"
  ],
  "title": "Watchmen",
  "isbn_10": [
    "0930289234"
  ],
  "publish_date": "April 1, 1995",
  "physical_dimensions": "10.1 x 6.6 x 0.8 inches"
}
```

Theo asks himself, "What could be so special in this JSON?" While Joe is meditating about this piece of JSON, Theo writes the JSON Schema for the Books API response. It doesn't seem to be more complicated than any of the previous schemas. When Theo is done, he asks Joe to take a look at the schema.

Listing 7.17 Schema of the Open Library Books API response

```
{
  "type": "object",
  "required": ["title"],
```

```
  "properties": {
    "title": {"type": "string"},
    "publishers": {
      "type": "array",
      "items": {"type": "string"}
    },
    "number_of_pages": {"type": "integer"},
    "weight": {"type": "string"},
    "physical_format": {"type": "string"},
    "subjects": {
      "type": "array",
      "items": {"type": "string"}
    },
    "isbn_13": {
      "type": "array",
      "items": {"type": "string"}
    },
    "isbn_10": {
      "type": "array",
      "items": {"type": "string"}
    },
    "publish_date": {"type": "string"},
    "physical_dimensions": {"type": "string"}
  }
}
```

Joe Good job!

Theo That wasn't so hard. I really don't see why you looked at this JSON response for such a long time.

Joe Well, it has to do with the `isbn_10` and `isbn_13` fields. I assume that they're not both mandatory.

Theo Right! That's why I didn't include them in the `required` field of my schema.

Joe But one of them should always be there. Right?

Theo Sometimes one of them and sometimes both of them, like for *Watchmen.* It depends on the publication year of the book. Books published before 2007 have `isbn_10`, and books published after 2007 have `isbn_13`.

Joe Oh, I see. And *Watchmen* has both because it was originally published in 1986 but published again after 2007.

Theo Correct.

Joe Then, you need your schema to indicate that one of the `isbn` fields is mandatory. That's a good opportunity for me to tell you about JSON Schema composition.

Theo What's that?

Joe It's a way to combine schemas, similarly to how we combine logical conditions with `AND`, `OR`, and `NOT`.

Theo I'd like to see that.

Joe Sure. How would you express the schema for the Books API response as a composition of three schemas: `basicBookInfoSchema`, the schema that you wrote where only `title` is required; `mandatoryIsbn13`, a schema where only isbn_13 is required; and mandatoryIsb10, a schema where only isbn_10 is required?

Theo I think it should be basicBookInfoSchema AND (mandatoryIsbn13 OR mandatoryIsbn10).

Joe Exactly! The only thing is that in JSON Schema, we use allOf instead of AND, and anyOf instead of OR.

Joe shows Theo the result in listing 7.18 and an example of its usage in listing 7.19.

Listing 7.18 Schema of an external API response

```
var basicBookInfoSchema = {
  "type": "object",
  "required": ["title"],
  "properties": {
    "title": {"type": "string"},
    "publishers": {
      "type": "array",
      "items": {"type": "string"}
    },
    "number_of_pages": {"type": "integer"},
    "weight": {"type": "string"},
    "physical_format": {"type": "string"},
    "subjects": {
      "type": "array",
      "items": {"type": "string"}
    },
    "isbn_13": {
      "type": "array",
      "items": {"type": "string"}
    },
    "isbn_10": {
      "type": "array",
      "items": {"type": "string"}
    },
    "publish_date": {"type": "string"},
    "physical_dimensions": {"type": "string"}
  }
};

var mandatoryIsbn13 = {
  "type": "object",
  "required": ["isbn_13"]
};

var mandatoryIsbn10 = {
  "type": "object",
  "required": ["isbn_10"]
};

var bookInfoSchema = {
  "allOf": [
    basicBookInfoSchema,
    {
```

```
      "anyOf": [mandatoryIsbn13, mandatoryIsbn10]
    }
  ]
};
```

Listing 7.19 Validating an external API response

```
var bookInfo = {
  "publishers": [
    "DC Comics"
  ],
  "number_of_pages": 334,
  "weight": "1.4 pounds",
  "physical_format": "Paperback",
  "subjects": [
    "Graphic Novels",
    "Comics & Graphic Novels",
    "Fiction",
    "Fantastic fiction"
  ],
  "isbn_13": [
    "9780930289232"
  ],
  "title": "Watchmen",
  "isbn_10": [
    "0930289234"
  ],
  "publish_date": "April 1, 1995",
  "physical_dimensions": "10.1 x 6.6 x 0.8 inches"
};

validate(bookInfoSchema, bookInfo);
// → true
```

Theo I see why they call it `allOf` and `anyOf`. The first one means that data must conform to all the schemas, and the second one means that data must conform to any of the schemas.

Joe Yup.

▶ **NOTE** JSON Schema also supports `oneOf` for cases where data must be valid against exactly one schema.

Theo Nice. With schema composition, JSON Schema seems to have more expressive power than what I was used to when representing data with classes.

Joe That's only the beginning. I'll show you more data validation conditions that can't be expressed when data is represented with classes some other time.

▶ **NOTE** Advanced data validation is covered in chapter 12.

Theo Something still bothers me, though. When data isn't valid, you don't know what went wrong.

7.5 Details about data validation failures

Joe So far, we've treated JSON Schema validation as though it were binary: either a piece of data is valid or it isn't.

Theo Right . . .

Joe But, in fact, when a piece of data is not valid, we can get details about the reason of the invalidity.

Theo Like when a required field is missing, can we get the name of the missing field?

Joe Yes. When a piece of data is not of the expected type, we can get information about that also.

Theo That sounds very useful!

Joe Indeed. Let me show you how it works. Until now, we used a generic `validate` function, but when we deal with validation failures, we need to be more specific.

Theo Why?

Joe Because each data validator library has its own way of exposing the details of a data validation failure. For instance, in JavaScript `Ajv`, the errors from the last data validation are stored as an array inside the validator instance.

Theo Why an array?

Joe Because there could be several failures. But let's start with the case of a single failure. Imagine we encounter a search book request where the title field is named `myTitle` instead of `title`. Take a look at this example. As you can see, we first instantiate a validator instance.

Listing 7.20 Accessing validation errors in `Ajv`

```
var searchBooksRequestSchema = {
  "type": "object",
  "properties": {
    "title": {"type": "string"},
    "fields": {
      "type": "array",
      "items": {"type": "string"}
    }
  },
  "required": ["title", "fields"]
};

var invalidSearchBooksRequest = {
  "myTitle": "habit",
  "fields": ["title", "weight", "number_of_pages"]
};

var ajv = new Ajv();        <-- Instantiates a validator instance

ajv.validate(searchBooksRequestSchema, invalidSearchBooksRequest);

ajv.errors        <-- Displays the validation errors
```

Theo And what does the information inside the errors array look like?

Joe Execute the code snippet. You'll see.

When Theo executes the code snippets from listing 7.20, he can hardly believe his eyes. He looks at the details, finding the results hard to digest.

Listing 7.21 Details for a single data validation failure in an array format

```
[
  {
    "instancePath": "",
    "schemaPath": "#/required",
    "keyword": "required",
    "params": {
      "missingProperty":"title"
    },
    "message": "must have required property 'title'"
  }
]
```

Theo I find the contents of the errors array a bit hard to understand.

Joe Me too. Fortunately, Ajv provides a errorsText utility function to convert the errors array in a human readable format. See, for instance, what is returned when you call errorsText.

Listing 7.22 Displaying the errors in human readable format

```
ajv.errorsText(ajv.errors);
// → "data must have required property 'title'"
```

Theo Let me see what happens when there are more than one validation failure in the data.

Joe By default, Ajv catches only one validation error.

TIP By default, Ajv catches only the first validation failure.

Theo I guess that's for performance reasons. Once the validator encounters an error, it doesn't continue the data parsing.

Joe Probably. Anyway, in order to catch more than one validation failure, you need to pass the allErrors options to the Ajv constructor. Check out this code.

Listing 7.23 Catching multiple validation failures

```
var searchBooksRequestSchema = {
  "type": "object",
  "properties": {
    "title": {"type": "string"},
    "fields": {
      "type": "array",
      "items": {"type": "string"}
```

```
    }
  },
  "required": ["title", "fields"]
};

var invalidSearchBooksRequest = {      ◁ A request with three failures
  "myTitle": "habit",
  "fields": [1, 2]
};

var ajv = new Ajv({allErrors: true});      ◁ Instantiates the Ajv constructor with allErrors: true in order to catch more than one failure

ajv.validate(searchBooksRequestSchema,
  invalidSearchBooksRequest);

ajv.errorsText(ajv.errors);      ◁ Converts the errors to a human readable format
// → "data must have required property 'title',
// →  data/fields/0 must be string,
// →  data/fields/1 must be string"
```

Joe We validate a search request with `myTitle` instead of `title` and numbers instead of strings in the `fields` array. As you can see in the output of the code snippet, three errors are returned.

Theo Great! I think I have all that I need in order to add data validation to the boundaries of my system when Nancy asks me to make the Library Management System into a web server.

Joe Would you allow me to give you a small gift as a token of our friendship?

Theo I'd be honored.

Joe takes a small package out of his bag, wrapped in a light-green ribbon. He hands Theo the package with a solemn gesture.

When Theo undoes the ribbon, he discovers an elegant piece of paper decorated with pretty little designs. In the center of the paper, Theo manages to read the inscription "JSON Schema cheat sheet." He smiles while browsing the cheat sheet. It's exactly what he needs.

Listing 7.24 JSON Schema cheat sheet

```
{
  "type": "array",      ◁ At the root level, data is an array.
  "items": {
    "type": "object",      ◁ Each element of the array is a map.
    "properties": {      ◁ The properties of each field in the map
      "myNumber": {"type": "number"},      ◁ myNumber is a number.
      "myString": {"type": "string"},      ◁ myString is a string.
      "myEnum": {"enum": ["myVal", "yourVal"]},      ◁ myEnum is a enumeration value with two possibilities: "myVal" and "yourVal".
      "myBool": {"type": "boolean"}      ◁ myBool is a boolean.
    },
    "required": ["myNumber", "myString"],      ◁ The mandatory fields in the map are myNumber and myString; other fields are optional.
```

```
    "additionalProperties": false       <-- We don't allow fields that
  }                                          are not explicitly mentioned
}                                            in the schema.
```

Then, Theo turns the paper over to find that the back is also filled with drawings. In the center of the paper, he reads the inscription, "An example of valid data."

Listing 7.25 An example of valid data

```
[
  {                                  <-- This map is valid
    "myNumber": 42,                      because all its
    "myString": "Hello",                 fields are valid.
    "myEnum": "myVal",
    "myBool": true
  },
  {                                  <-- This map is valid
    "myNumber": 54,                      because it contains all
    "myString": "Happy"                  the required fields.
  }
]
```

Summary

- DOP Principle #4 is to separate data schema and data representation.
- The *boundaries* of a system are defined to be the areas where the system exchanges data.
- Some examples of data validation at the boundaries of the system are validation of client requests and responses, and validation of data that comes from external sources.
- *Data validation* in DOP means checking whether a piece of data conforms to a schema.
- When a piece of data is not valid, we get information about the validation failures and send this information back to the client in a human readable format.
- When data at system boundaries is valid, it's not critical to validate data again inside the system.
- JSON Schema is a language that allows us to separate data validation from data representation.
- JSON Schema syntax is a bit verbose.
- The expressive power of JSON Schema is high.
- JSON Schemas are just maps and, as so, we are free to manipulate them like any other maps in our programs.
- We can store a schema definition in a variable and use this variable in another schema.
- In JSON Schema, map fields are optional by default.
- It's good practice to validate data that comes from an external data source.

- It's good practice to be strict regarding data that you send and to be flexible regarding data that you receive.
- Ajv is a JSON Schema library in JavaScript.
- By default, Ajv catches only the first validation failure.
- Advanced validation is covered in chapter 12.

8 Advanced concurrency control

No more deadlocks!

This chapter covers

- Atoms as an alternative to locks
- Managing a thread-safe counter and a thread-safe in-memory cache with atoms
- Managing the whole system state in a thread-safe way with atoms

The traditional way to manage concurrency in a multi-threaded environment involves lock mechanisms like *mutexes*. Lock mechanisms tend to increase the complexity of the system because it's not trivial to make sure the system is free of deadlocks. In DOP, we leverage the fact that data is immutable, and we use a lock-free mechanism, called an *atom*, to manage concurrency. Atoms are simpler to manage than locks because they are lock-free. As a consequence, the usual complexity of locks that are required to avoid deadlocks don't apply to atoms.

▶ **NOTE** This chapter is mostly relevant to multi-threaded environments like Java, C#, Python, and Ruby. It is less relevant to single-threaded environments like JavaScript. The JavaScript code snippets in this chapter are written as though JavaScript were multi-threaded.

8.1 The complexity of locks

This Sunday afternoon, while riding his bike across the Golden Gate Bridge, Theo thinks about the Klafim project with concern, not yet sure that betting on DOP was a good choice. Suddenly, Theo realizes that he hasn't yet scheduled the next session with Joe. He gets off his bike to call Joe. Bad luck, the line is busy.

When Theo gets home, he tries to call Joe again, but once again the phone is busy. After dinner, Theo tries to call Joe one more time, with the same result—a busy signal. "Obviously, Joe is very busy today," Theo tells himself. Exhausted by his 50-mile bike ride at an average of 17 miles per hour, he falls asleep on the sofa. When Theo wakes up, he's elated to see a text message from Joe, "See you Monday morning at 11 AM?" Theo answers with a thumbs up and prepares for another week of work.

When Joe arrives at the office, Theo asks him why his phone was constantly busy the day before. Joe answers that he was about to ask Theo the same question. They look at each other, puzzled, and then simultaneously break into laughter as they realize what happened: in an amazing coincidence, they'd tried to phone each other at exactly the same times. They both say at once:

"A deadlock!"

They both head for Theo's office. When they get to Theo's desk, Joe tells him that today's session is going to be about concurrency management in multi-threaded environments.

Joe How do you usually manage concurrency in a multi-threaded environment?

Theo I protect access to critical sections with a lock mechanism, a *mutex*, for instance.

Joe When you say access, do you mean write access or also read access?

Theo Both!

Joe Why do you need to protect read access with a lock?

Theo Because, without a lock protection, in the middle of a read, a write could happen in another thread. It would make my read logically inconsistent.

Joe Another option would be to clone the data before processing it in a read.

Theo Sometimes I would clone the data; but in many cases, when it's large, it's too expensive to clone.

TIP Cloning data to avoid read locks doesn't scale.

Joe In DOP, we don't need to clone or to protect read access.

Theo Because data is immutable?

Joe Right. When data is immutable, even if a write happens in another thread during a read, it won't make the read inconsistent because the write never mutates the data that is read.

Theo In a sense, a read always works on a data snapshot.

Joe Exactly!

TIP When data is immutable, a read is always safe.

Theo But what about write access? Don't you need to protect that with locks?

Joe Nope.

Theo Why not?

Joe We have a simpler mechanism—it's called an atom.

Theo I am glad to hear there is a something simpler than locks. I really struggle each time I have to integrate locks into a multi-threaded system.

Joe Me too! I remember a bug we had in production 10 years ago. We forgot to release a lock when an exception was thrown in a critical section. It caused a terrible deadlock.

Theo Deadlocks are really hard to avoid. Last year, we had a deadlock issue when two locks were not released in the proper order.

Joe I have great news for you. With atoms, deadlocks never happen!

TIP With atoms, deadlocks never happen.

Theo That sounds great. Tell me more!

TIP Atoms provide a way to manage concurrency without locks.

8.2 Thread-safe counter with atoms

Joe Let's start with a simple case: a counter shared between threads.

Theo What do you mean by a counter?

Joe Imagine that we'd like to count the number of database accesses and write the total number of accesses to a log every minute.

Theo OK.

Joe Could you write JavaScript code for this multi-threaded counter using locks?

Theo But JavaScript is single-threaded!

Joe I know, but it's just for the sake of illustration. Imagine that JavaScript were multi-threaded and that it provided a `Mutex` object that you could lock and unlock.

Theo It's a bit awkward. I guess it would look like this.

Theo goes to the whiteboard. He writes what he imagines to be JavaScript code for a multi-threaded counter with locks.

Listing 8.1 A thread-safe counter protected by a mutex

```
var mutex = new Mutex();
var counter = 0;


function dbAccess() {
  mutex.lock();
  counter = counter + 1;
  mutex.unlock();
  // access the database
}

function logCounter() {
  mutex.lock();
```

```
  console.log('Number of database accesses: ' + counter);
  mutex.unlock();
}
```

Joe Excellent. Now, I am going to show you how to write the same code with atoms. An atom provides three methods:

- `get` returns the current value of the atom.
- `set` overwrites the current value of the atom.
- `swap` receives a function and updates the value of the atom with the result of the function called on the current value of the atom.

Joe unzips a pocket in his laptop case and takes out a piece of paper. He hands it to Theo. Theo is pleasantly surprised as the sheet of paper succinctly describes the methods (table 8.1).

Table 8.1 The three methods of an atom

Method	Description
`get`	Returns the current value
`set`	Overwrites the current value
`swap`	Updates the current value with a function

Theo How would it look like to implement a thread-safe counter with an atom?

Joe It's quite simple, actually.

Joe pulls out his laptop, fires it up, and begins to type. When he's done, he turns the laptop around so that Theo can see the code to implement a thread-safe counter in an atom.

Listing 8.2 A thread-safe counter stored in an atom

```
var counter = new Atom();
counter.set(0);

function dbAccess() {
  counter.swap(function(x) {
    return x + 1;
  });
  // access the database
}

function logCounter() {
  console.log('Number of database accesses: ' + counter.get());
}
```

The argument x is the current value of the atom, same as counter.get().

Theo Could you tell me what's going on here?

Joe Sure! First, we create an empty atom. Then, we initialize the value of the atom with `counter.set(0)`. In the logger thread, we read the current value of the atom with `counter.get()`.

Theo And how do you increment the counter in the threads that access the database?

Joe We call swap with a function that receives x and returns x + 1.

Theo I don't understand how swap could be thread-safe without using any locks.

Joe quickly goes to the whiteboard. He sketches the diagram in figure 8.1.

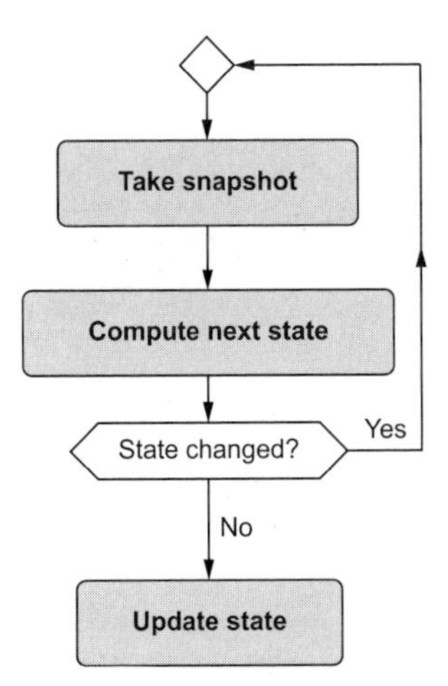

Figure 8.1 High-level flow of swap

Joe You see, swap computes the next value of the atom, and before modifying the current value of the atom, it checks whether the value of the atom has changed during the computation. If so, swap tries again, until no changes occur during the computation.

Theo Is swap easy to implement?

Joe Let me show you the implementation of the Atom class and you'll see.

Listing 8.3 Implementation of the Atom class

```
class Atom {
  state;

  constructor() {}

  get() {
    return this.state;
  }

  set(state) {
    this.state = state;
  }

  swap(f) {
    while(true) {
      var stateSnapshot = this.state;
      var nextState = f(stateSnapshot);
      if (!atomicCompareAndSet(this.state,
```

```
          stateSnapshot,
          nextState)) {
          continue;
        }
        return nextState;
      }
    }
  }
```

Uses a special thread-safe comparison operation as this.state might have changed in another thread during execution of the function f.

Theo comes closer to the whiteboard. He modifies Joe's diagram a bit to make the flow of the swap operation more detailed. The resulting diagram is in figure 8.2. Theo still has a few questions, though.

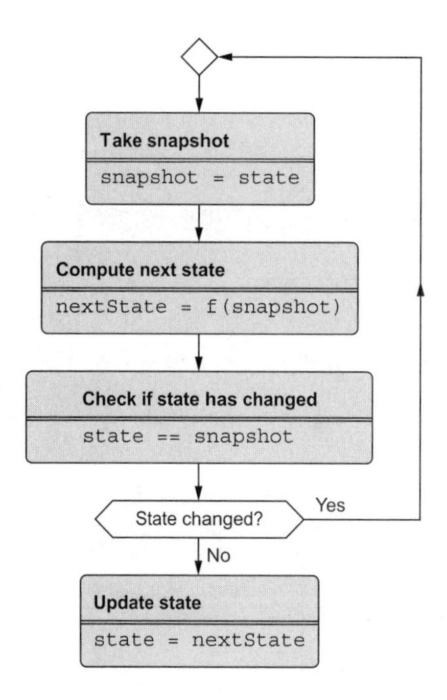

Figure 8.2 Detailed flow of `swap`

Theo What is `atomicCompareAndSet`?

Joe It's the core operation of an atom. `atomicCompareAndSet` atomically sets the state to a new value if, and only if, the state equals the provided old value. It returns `true` upon success and `false` upon failure.

Theo How could it be atomic without using locks?

Joe That's a great question! In fact, `atomicCompareAndSet` is a compare-and-swap operation, provided by the language that relies on a functionality of the CPU itself. For example, in Java the `java.util.concurrent.atomic` package has an `AtomicReference` generic class that provides a `compareAndSet()` method.

▶ **NOTE** See http://tutorials.jenkov.com/java-concurrency/compare-and-swap.html for general information about compare-and-swap operations. Implementations for multi-threaded languages appear in table 8.2.

Table 8.2 Implementation of an atomic compare and set in various languages

Language	Link
Java	http://mng.bz/mxOW
JavaScript	Not relevant (single-threaded language)
Ruby	http://mng.bz/5KG8
Python	https://github.com/maxcountryman/atomos
C#	http://mng.bz/6Zzp

Theo Apropos Java, how would the implementation of an atom look?

Joe It's quite the same, besides the fact that `Atom` has to use generics, and the inner state has to be stored in an `AtomicReference`.

Joe brings up a Java implementation of `Atom` on his laptop. Theo looks over the code.

Listing 8.4 Implementation of the `Atom` class in Java

```
class Atom<ValueType> {
  private AtomicReference<ValueType> state;

  public Atom() {}

  ValueType get() {
    return this.state.get();
  }

  void set(ValueType state) {
    this.state.set(state);
  }

  ValueType swap(UnaryOPerator<ValueType> f) {
    while(true) {
      ValueType stateSnapshot = this.state.get();
      ValueType nextState = f(stateSnapshot);
      if (!this.state.compareAndSet(stateSnapshot,
        nextState)) {
        continue;
      }
    }
    return nextState;
  }
}
```

this.state might have changed in another thread during the execution of f.

Theo What about using an atom in Java?

Joe Here, take a look. It's quite simple.

Listing 8.5 Using an `Atom` in Java

```
Atom<Integer> counter = new Atom<Integer>();

counter.set(0);

counter.swap(x -> x + 1);

counter.get();
```

Theo takes a couple of minutes to meditate about this atom stuff and to digest what he's just learned. Then, he asks Joe:

Theo What if `swap` never succeeds? I mean, could the `while` loop inside the code of `swap` turn out to be an infinite loop?

Joe No! By definition, when `atomicCompareAndSet` fails on a thread, it means that the same atom was changed on another thread during the execution of `swap`. In this race between threads, there is always a winner.

Theo But isn't it possible that some thread never succeeds because it always loses the race against other threads?

Joe In theory, yes, but I've never encountered such a situation. If you have thousands of threads that do nothing besides swapping an atom, it could happen I suppose. But, in practice, once the atom is swapped, the threads do some real work, for example, database access or I/O. This gives other threads the opportunity to swap the atom successfully.

▶ **NOTE** *In theory*, atoms could create starvation in a system with thousands of threads that do nothing beside swapping an atom. *In practice*, once an atom is swapped, the threads do some real work (e.g., database access), which creates an opportunity for other threads to swap the atom successfully.

Theo Interesting. . . . Indeed, atoms look much easier to manage than locks.

Joe Now let me show you how to use atoms with composite data.

Theo Why would that be different?

Joe Usually, dealing with composite data is more difficult than dealing with primitive types.

Theo When you sold me on DOP, you told me that we are able to manage data with the same simplicity as we manage numbers.

TIP In DOP, data is managed with the same simplicity as numbers.

Joe That's exactly what I am about to show you.

8.3 Thread-safe cache with atoms

Joe Are you familiar with the notion of in-memory cache?

Theo You mean memoization?

Joe Kind of. Imagine that database queries don't vary too much in your application. It makes sense in that case to store the results of previous queries in memory in order to improve the response time.

Theo Yes, of course!

Joe What data structure would you use to store the in-memory cache?

Theo Probably a string map, where the keys are the queries, and the values are the results from the database.

TIP It's quite common to represent an in-memory cache as a string map.

Joe Excellent! Now can you write the code to cache database queries in a thread-safe way using a lock?

Theo Let me see: I'm going to use an immutable string map. Therefore, I don't need to protect read access with a lock. Only the cache update needs to be protected.

Joe You're getting the hang of this!

Theo The code should be something like this.

Listing 8.6 Thread-safe cache with locks

```
var mutex = new Mutex();
var cache = {};

function dbAccessCached(query) {
  var resultFromCache = _.get(cache, query);
  if (resultFromCache != nil) {
    return resultFromCache;
  }
  var result = dbAccess(query);
  mutex.lock();
  cache = _.set(cache, query, result);
  mutex.unlock();
  return result;
}
```

Joe Nice! Now, let me show you how to write the same code using an atom instead of a lock. Take a look at this code and let me know if it's clear to you.

Listing 8.7 Thread-safe cache with atoms

```
var cache = new Atom();
cache.set({});

function dbAccessCached(query) {
  var resultFromCache = _.get(cache.get(), query);
  if (resultFromCache != nil) {
    return resultFromCache;
  }
  var result = dbAccess(query);
  cache.swap(function(oldCache) {
```

```
    return _.set(oldCache, query, result);
  });
  return result;
}
```

Theo I don't understand the function you're passing to the swap method.

Joe The function passed to swap receives the current value of the cache, which is a string map, and returns a new version of the string map with an additional key-value pair.

Theo I see. But something bothers me with the performance of the swap method in the case of a string map. How does the comparison work? I mean, comparing two string maps might take some time.

Joe Not if you compare them by reference. As we discussed in the past, when data is immutable, it is safe to compare by reference, and it's super fast.

TIP When data is immutable, it is safe (and fast) to compare it by reference.

Theo Cool. So atoms play well with immutable data.

Joe Exactly!

8.4 State management with atoms

Joe Do you remember a couple of weeks ago when I showed you how we resolve potential conflicts between mutations? You told me that the code was not thread-safe.

Theo Let me look again at the code.

Theo takes a look at the code for the SystemData class that he wrote some time ago (repeated in listing 8.8). Without the validation logic, it makes the code easier to grasp.

Listing 8.8 SystemData class from part 1

```
class SystemState {
  systemData;

  get() {
    return this.systemData;
  }

  set(_systemData) {
    this.systemData = _systemData;
  }

  commit(previous, next) {
    this.systemData = SystemConsistency.reconcile(this.systemData,
      previous,
      next);
  }
}
```

It takes him a few minutes to remember how the `commit` method works. Suddenly, he has an *Aha!* moment.

Theo This code is not thread-safe because the `SystemConsistency.reconcile` code inside the `commit` method is not protected. Nothing prevents the two threads from executing this code concurrently.

Joe Right! Now, can you tell me how to make it thread-safe?

Theo With locks?

Joe Come on . . .

Theo I was kidding, of course. We make the code thread-safe not with a lock but with an atom.

Joe Nice joke!

Theo Let me see. I'd need to store the system data inside an atom. The `get` and `set` method of `SystemData` would simply call the `get` and `set` methods of the atom. How does this look?

Listing 8.9 `SystemData` class with atom (without the `commit` method)

```
class SystemState {
  systemData;

  constructor() {
    this.systemData = new Atom();
  }

  get() {
    return this.systemData.get();
  }

  commit(prev, next) {
    this.systemData.set(next);
  }
}
```

Joe Excellent. Now for the fun part. Implement the `commit` method by calling the `swap` method of the atom.

Theo Instead of calling `SystemConsistency.reconcile()` directly, I need to wrap it into a call to `swap`. So, something like this?

Listing 8.10 Implementation of `SystemData.commit` with atom

```
SystemData.commit = function(previous, next) {
  this.systemData.swap(function(current) {
    return SystemConsistency.reconcile(current,
      previous,
      next);
  });
};
```

Joe Perfect.

Theo This atom stuff makes me think about what happened to us yesterday, when we tried to call each other at the exact same time.

Joe What do you mean?

Theo I don't know, but I am under the impression that mutexes are like phone calls, and atoms are like text messages.

Joe smiles at Theo but doesn't reveal the meaning of his smile. After the phone deadlock yesterday, Theo's pretty sure that he and Joe are on the same page.

Summary

- Managing concurrency with atoms is much simpler than managing concurrency with locks because we don't have to deal with the risk of deadlocks.
- Cloning data to avoid read locks doesn't scale.
- When data is immutable, reads are always safe.
- *Atoms* provide a way to manage concurrency without locks.
- With atoms, deadlocks never happen.
- Using atoms for a thread-safe counter is trivial because the state of the counter is represented with a primitive type (an integer).
- We can manage composite data in a thread-safe way with atoms.
- We make the highly scalable state management approach from part 1 thread-safe by keeping the whole system state inside an atom.
- It's quite common to represent an in-memory cache as a string map.
- When data is immutable, it is safe (and fast) to compare by reference.
- In theory, atoms could create starvation in a system with thousands of threads that do nothing besides swapping an atom.
- In practice, once an atom is swapped, the threads do some real work (e.g., database access) to provide an opportunity for other threads to swap the atom successfully.

9 Persistent data structures

Standing on the shoulders of giants

This chapter covers

- The internal details of persistent data structures
- The time and memory efficiency of persistent data structures
- Using persistent data structures in an application

In part 1, we illustrated how to manage the state of a system without mutating data, where immutability is maintained by constraining ourselves to manipulate the state only with immutable functions using structural sharing. In this chapter, we present a safer and more scalable way to preserve data immutability—representing data with so-called persistent data structures. Efficient implementations of persistent data structures exist for most programming languages via third-party libraries.

9.1 The need for persistent data structures

It's at the university where Theo meets Joe this time. When Theo asks Joe if today's topic is academic in nature, Joe tells him that the use of persistent data structures only became possible in programming languages following a discovery in 2001 by a computer researcher named Phil Bagwell.[1] In 2007, Rich Hickey, the creator of Clojure, used this discovery as the foundation of persistent data structures in Clojure. Unveiling the secrets of these data structures to Theo in a university classroom is a way for Joe to honor the memory of Phil Bagwell, who unfortunately passed away in 2012. When they get to the university classroom, Joe starts the conversation with a question.

Joe Are you getting used to DOP's prohibition against mutating data in place and creating new versions instead?

Theo I think so, but two things bother me about the idea of structural sharing that you showed me.

Joe What bothers you, my friend?

Theo Safety and performance.

Joe What do you mean by safety?

Theo I mean that using immutable functions to manipulate data doesn't prevent it from being modified accidentally.

Joe Right! Would you like me to show you the naive way to handle immutability or the real way?

Theo What are the pros and cons of each way?

Joe The naive way is easy but not efficient, although the real way is efficient but not easy.

Theo Let's start with the naive way then.

Joe Each programming language provides its own way to protect data from being mutated.

Theo How would I do that in Java, for instance?

Joe Java provides immutable collections, and there is a way to convert a list or a map to an immutable list or an immutable map.

▶ **NOTE** Immutable collections are not the same as persistent data structures.

Joe opens his laptop and fires it up. He brings up two code examples, one for immutable lists and one for immutable maps.

Listing 9.1 Converting a mutable list to an immutable list in Java

```
var myList = new ArrayList<Integer>();
myList.add(1);
myList.add(2);
myList.add(3);

var myImmutableList = List.of(myList.toArray());
```

[1] P. Bagwell, "Ideal hash trees" (No. REP_WORK), 2001. [Online]. Available: https://lampwww.epfl.ch/papers/idealhashtrees.pdf.

Listing 9.2 Converting a mutable map to an immutable map in Java

```
var myMap = new HashMap<String, Object>();
myMap.put("name", "Isaac");
myMap.put("age", 42);

var myImmutableMap = Collections.unmodifiableMap(myMap);
```

Theo What happens when you try to modify an immutable collection?

Joe Java throws an `UnsupportedOperationException`.

Theo And in JavaScript?

Joe JavaScript provides an `Object.freeze()` function that prevents data from being mutated. It works both with JavaScript arrays and objects.

Joe takes a minute to scroll through his laptop. When he finds what he's looking for, he shows Theo the code.

Listing 9.3 Making an object immutable in JavaScript

```
var a = [1, 2, 3];
Object.freeze(a);

var b = {foo: 1};
Object.freeze(b);
```

Theo What happens when you try to modify a frozen object?

Joe It depends. In JavaScript strict mode, a `TypeError` exception is thrown, and in nonstrict mode, it fails silently.

▶ **NOTE** JavaScript's *strict mode* is a way to opt in to a restricted variant of JavaScript that changes some silent errors to throw errors.

Theo In case of a nested collection, are the nested collections also frozen?

Joe No, but in JavaScript, one can write a `deepFreeze()` function that freezes an object recursively. Here's another example.

Listing 9.4 Freezing an object recursively in JavaScript

```
function deepFreeze(object) {
  // Retrieve the property names defined on object
  const propNames = Object.getOwnPropertyNames(object);

  // Freeze properties before freezing self

  for (const name of propNames) {
    const value = object[name];

    if (value && typeof value === "object") {
      deepFreeze(value);
    }
  }
```

```
  return Object.freeze(object);
}
```

Theo I see that it's possible to ensure that data is never mutated, which answers my concerns about safety. Now, let me share my concerns about performance.

TIP It's possible to manually ensure that our data isn't mutated, but it's cumbersome.

Joe Sure.

Theo If I understand correctly, the main idea behind structural sharing is that most data is usually shared between two versions.

Joe Correct.

Theo This insight allows us to create new versions of our collections using a shallow copy instead of a deep copy, and you claimed that it was efficient.

Joe Exactly!

Theo Now, here is my concern. In the case of a collection with many entries, a shallow copy might be expensive.

Joe Could you give me an example of a collection with many entries?

Theo A catalog with 100,000 books, for instance.

Joe On my machine, making a shallow copy of a collection with 100,000 entries doesn't take more than 50 milliseconds.

Theo Sometimes, even 50 milliseconds per update isn't acceptable.

Joe I totally agree with you. When one needs data immutability at scale, naive structural sharing is not appropriate.

Theo Also, shallow copying an array of 100,000 elements on each update would increase the program memory by 100 KB.

Joe Indeed, at scale, we have a problem both with memory and computation.

TIP At scale, naive structural sharing causes a performance hit, both in terms of memory and computation.

Theo Is there a better solution?

Joe Yes! For that, you'll need to learn the real way to handle immutability. It's called persistent data structures.

9.2 The efficiency of persistent data structures

Theo In what sense are those data structures persistent?

Joe Persistent data structures are so named because they always preserve their previous versions.

TIP Persistent data structures always preserve the previous version of themselves when they are modified.

Joe Persistent data structures address the two main limitations of naive structural sharing: safety and performance.

Theo Let's start with safety. How do persistent data structures prevent data from being mutated accidentally?

Joe In a language like Java, they implement the mutation methods of the collection interfaces by throwing the run-time exception `UnsupportedOperationException`.

Theo And, in a language like JavaScript?

Joe In JavaScript, persistent data structures provide their own methods to access data, and none of those methods mutate data.

Theo Does that mean that we can't use the dot notation to access fields?

Joe Correct. Fields of persistent data structures are accessed via a specific API.

Theo What about efficiency? How do persistent data structures make it possible to create a new version of a huge collection in an efficient way?

Joe Persistent data structures organize data in such a way that we can use structural sharing at the level of the data structure.

Theo Could you explain?

Joe Certainly. Let's start with the simplest data structure: a linked list. Imagine that you have a linked list with 100,000 elements.

Theo OK.

Joe What would it take to prepend an element to the head of the list?

Theo You mean to create a new version of the list with an additional element?

Joe Exactly!

Theo Well, we could copy the list and then prepend an element to the list, but it would be quite expensive.

Joe What if I tell you that the original linked list is guaranteed to be immutable?

Theo In that case, I could create a new list with a new head that points to the head of the original list.

Theo goes to the classroom blackboard. He picks up a piece of chalk and draws the diagram shown in figure 9.1.

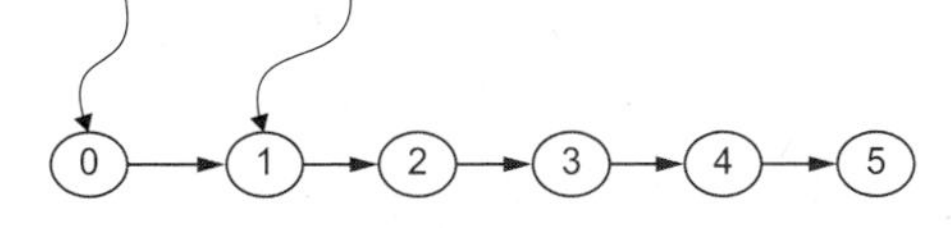

Figure 9.1 Structural sharing with linked lists

Joe Would the efficiency of this operation depend on the size of the list?

Theo No, it would be efficient, no matter the size of the list.

Joe That's what I mean by structural sharing at the level of the data structure itself. It relies on a simple but powerful insight—when data is immutable, it is safe to share it.

TIP When data is immutable, it is safe to share it.

Theo I understand how to use structural sharing at the level of the data structure for linked lists and prepend operations, but how would it work with operations like appending or modifying an element in a list?

Joe For that purpose, we need to be smarter and represent our list as a tree.

Theo How does that help?

Joe It helps because when a list is represented as a tree, most of the nodes in the tree can be shared between two versions of the list.

Theo I am totally confused.

Joe Imagine that you take a list with 100,000 elements and split it into two lists of 50,000 elements each: elements 0 to 49,999 in list 1, and elements 50,000 to 99,999 in list 2. How many operations would you need to create a new version of the list where a single element—let's say, element at index 75,100—is modified?

It's hard for Theo to visualize this kind of stuff mentally. He goes back to the blackboard and draws a diagram (see figure 9.2). Once Theo looks at the diagram, it's easy for him to answer Joe's question.

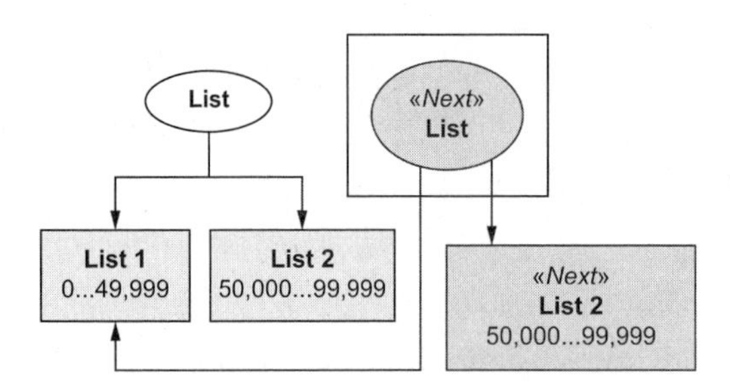

Figure 9.2 Structural sharing when a list of 100,000 elements is split

Theo List 1 could be shared with one operation. I'd need to create a new version of list 2, where element 75,100 is modified. It would take 50,000 operations, so it's one operation of sharing and one operation of copying 50,000 elements. Overall, it's 50,001 operations.

Joe Correct. You see that by splitting our original list into two lists, we can create a new version of the list with a number of operations in the order of the size of the list divided by 2.

Theo I agree, but 50,000 is still a big number.

Joe Indeed, but nobody prevents us from applying the same trick again, splitting list 1 and list 2 in two lists each.

Theo How exactly?

Joe We can make list 1.1 with elements 0 to 24,999, then list 1.2 with elements 25,000 to 49,999, list 2.1 with elements 50,000 to 74,999, and list 2.2 with elements 75,000 to 99,999.

Theo Can you draw that on the blackboard?

Joe Sure.

Now, it's Joe that goes to the blackboard. He draws the diagram in figure 9.3.

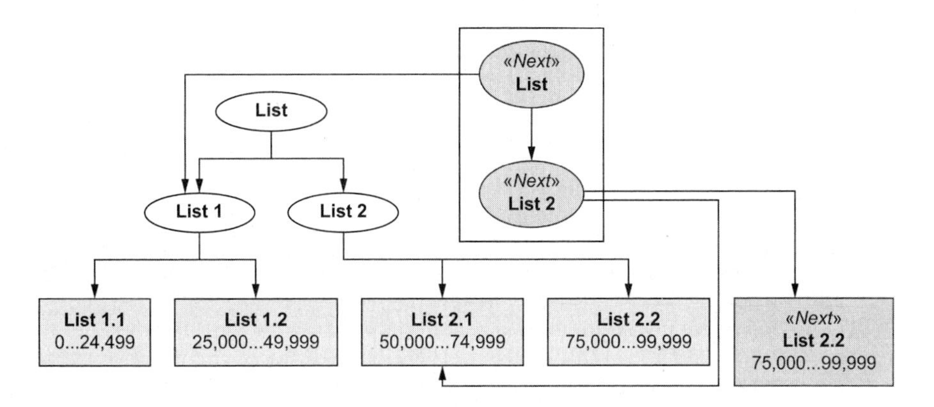

Figure 9.3 Structural sharing when a list of 100,000 elements is split twice

Theo Let me count the number of operations for updating a single element. It takes 2 operations of sharing and 1 operation of copying 25,000 elements. Overall, it takes 25,002 operations to create a new version of the list.

Joe Correct!

Theo Let's split the list again then!

Joe Absolutely. In fact, we can split the list again and again until the size of the lists is at most 2. Can you guess what is the complexity of creating a new version then?

Theo I'd say around log2 *N* operations.

Joe I see that you remember well your material from school. Do you have a gut feeling about what is log2 *N* when *N* is 100,000?

Theo Let me see . . . 2 to the power of 10 is around 1,000, and 2 to the power of 7 is 128. So, it should be a bit less than 17.

Joe It's 16.6 to be precise. It means that in order to update an element in a persistent list of 100,000 elements, we need around 17 operations. The same goes for accessing elements.

Theo Nice, but 17 is still not negligible.

Joe I agree. We can easily improve the performance of accessing elements by using a higher branching factor in our tree.

Theo What do you mean?

Joe Instead of splitting by 2 at each level, we could split by 32.

Theo But the running time of our algorithm would still grow with log *N*.

Joe You're right. From a theoretical perspective, it's the same. From a practical perspective, however, it makes a big difference.

Theo Why?

Joe Because log32 *N* is 5 times lower than log2 *N*.

Theo That's true: 2 to the power of 5 is 32.

Joe Back to our list of 100,000 elements, can you tell me how many operations are required to access an element if the branching factor is 32?

Theo With a branching factor of 2, it was 16.6. If I divide 16.6 by 5, I get 3.3.

Joe Correct!

TIP By using a branching factor of 32, we make elements accessed in persistent lists more efficient.

Theo Does this trick also improve the performance of updating an element in a list?

Joe Yes, indeed, it does.

Theo How? We'd have to copy 32 elements at each level instead of 2 elements. It's a 16× performance hit that's not compensated for by the fact that the tree depth is reduced by 5×!

Joe I see that you are quite sharp with numbers. There is another thing to take into consideration in our practical analysis of the performance: modern CPU architecture.

Theo Interesting. The more you tell me about persistent data structures, the more I understand why you wanted to have this session at a university: it's because we're dealing with all this academic stuff.

Joe Yep. So, to continue, modern CPUs read and write data from and to the main memory in units of cache lines, often 32 or 64 bytes long.

Theo What difference does that make?

Joe A nice consequence of this data access pattern is that copying an array of size 32 is much faster than copying 16 arrays of size 2 that belong to different levels of the tree.

Theo Why is that?

Joe The reason is that copying an array of size 32 can be done in a single pair of cache accesses: one for read and one for write. Although for arrays that belong to different tree levels, each array requires its own pair of cache accesses, even if there are only 2 elements in the array.

Theo In other words, the performance of updating a persistent list is dominated by the depth of the tree.

TIP In modern CPU architectures, the performance of updating a persistent list is dominated much more by the depth of the tree than by the number of nodes at each level of the tree.

Joe That's correct, up to a certain point. With today's CPUs, using a branching factor of 64 would, in fact, decrease the performance of update operations.

Theo I see.

Joe Now, I am going to make another interesting claim that is not accurate from a theoretical perspective but accurate in practice.

Theo What is it?

Joe The number of operations it takes to get or update an element in a persistent list with branching factor 32 is constant.

Theo How can that be? You just made the point that the number of operations is log32 *N*.

Joe Be patient, my friend. What is the highest number of elements that you can have in a list, in practice?

Theo I don't know. I never thought about that.

Joe Let's assume that it takes 4 bytes to store an element in a list.

Theo OK.

Joe Now, can you tell me how much memory it would take to hold a list with 10 billion elements?

Theo You mean 1 with 10 zeros?

Joe Yes.

Theo Each element take 4 bytes, so it would be around 40 GB!

Joe Correct. Do you agree that it doesn't make sense to hold a list that takes 40 GB of memory?

Theo I agree.

Joe So let's take 10 billion as an upper bound to the number of elements in a list. What is log32 of 10 billion?

Once again, Theo uses the blackboard to clarify his thoughts. With that, he quickly finds the answer.

Theo 1 billion is approximately 2^30. Therefore, 10 billion is around 2^33. That means that log2 of 10 billion is 33, so log32 of 10 billion should be around 33/5, which is a bit less than 7.

Joe I am impressed again by your sharpness with numbers. To be precise, log32 of 10 billion is 6.64.

Theo (smiling) I didn't get that far.

Joe Did I convince you that, in practice, accessing or updating an element in a persistent list is essentially constant?

Theo Yes, and I find it quite amazing!

 **TIP** Persistent lists can be manipulated in near constant time.

Joe Me too.

Theo What about persistent maps?

Joe It's quite similar, but I don't think we have time to discuss it now.

Startled, Theo looks at his watch. This morning's session has gone by so quickly. He notices that it's time to get back to the office and have lunch.

9.3 Persistent data structures libraries

On their way back to the office, Theo and Joe don't talk too much. Theo's thoughts take him back to what he learned in the university classroom. He feels a lot of respect for Phil Bagwell, who discovered how to manipulate persistent data structures efficiently, and for Rich Hickey, who created a programming language incorporating that discovery as a core feature and making it available to the world. Immediately after lunch, Theo asks Joe to show him what it looks like to manipulate persistent data structures for real in a programming language.

Theo Are persistent data structures available in all programming languages?

Joe A few programming languages like Clojure, Scala, and C# provide them as part of the language. In most programming languages, though, you need a third-party library.

Theo Could you give me a few references?

Joe Sure.

Using Theo's laptop, Joe bookmarks some sites. He knows exactly which URLs to look for. Then, while Theo is looking over the bookmarked sites, Joe goes to the whiteboard and jots down the specific libraries in table 9.1.

- Immutable.js for JavaScript at https://immutable-js.com/
- Paguro for Java at https://github.com/GlenKPeterson/Paguro
- Immutable Collections for C# at http://mng.bz/QW51
- Pyrsistent for Python at https://github.com/tobgu/pyrsistent
- Hamster for Ruby at https://github.com/hamstergem/hamster

Table 9.1 Persistent data structure libraries

Language	Library
JavaScript	Immutable.js
Java	Paguro
C#	Provided by the language
Python	Pyrsistent
Ruby	Hamster

Theo What does it take to integrate persistent data structures provided by a third-party library into your code?

9.3.1 Persistent data structures in Java

Joe In an object-oriented language like Java, it's quite straightforward to integrate persistent data structures in a program because persistent data structures implement collection interfaces, besides the parts of the interface that mutate in place.

Theo What do you mean?

Joe Take for instance, Paguro for Java. Paguro persistent maps implement the read-only methods of java.util.Map like `get()` and `containsKey()`, but not methods like `put()` and `remove()`. On the other hand, Paguro vectors implement the read-only methods of java.util.List like `get()` and `size()`, but not methods like `set()`.

Theo What happens when we call `put()` or `remove()` on a Paguro map?

Joe It throws an `UnSupportedOperationException` exception.

Theo What about iterating over the elements of a Paguro collection with a `forEach()`?

Joe That works like it would in any Java collection. Here, let me show you an example.

Listing 9.5 Iterating over a Paguro vector

```
var myVec = PersistentVector.ofIter(
  List.of(10, 2, 3));          <-- Creates a Paguro
                                   vector from a
for (Integer i : myVec) {          Java list
  System.out.println(i);
}
```

Theo What about Java streams?

Joe Paguro collections are Java collections, so they support the Java stream interface. Take a look at this code.

Listing 9.6 Streaming a Paguro vector

```
var myVec = PersistentVector.ofIter(List.of(10, 2, 3));

vec1.stream().sorted().map(x -> x + 1);
```

TIP Paguro collections implement the read-only parts of Java collection interfaces. Therefore, they can be passed to any methods that expect to receive a Java collection without mutating it.

Theo So far, you told me how do use Paguro collections as Java read-only collections. How do I make modifications to Paguro persistent data structures?

Joe In a way similar to the `_.set()` function of Lodash FP that we talked about earlier. Instead of mutating in place, you create a new version.

Theo What methods does Paguro expose for creating new versions of a data structure?

Joe For vectors, you use `replace()`, and for maps, you use `assoc()`.

Listing 9.7 Creating a modified version of a Paguro vector

```
var myVec = PersistentVector.ofIter(List.of(10, 2, 3));

var myNextVec = myVec.replace(0, 42);
```

Listing 9.8 Creating a modified version of a Paguro map

```
var myMap = PersistentHashMap.of(Map.of("aa", 1, "bb", 2)
.entrySet());

var myNextMap = myMap.assoc("aa", 42);
```

Creates a Paguro map from a Java map entry set

Theo Yes! Now I see how to use persistent data structures in Java, but what about JavaScript?

9.3.2 Persistent data structures in JavaScript

Joe In a language like JavaScript, it's a bit more cumbersome to integrate persistent data structures.

Theo How so?

Joe Because JavaScript objects and arrays don't expose any interface.

Theo Bummer.

Joe It's not as terrible as it sounds because Immutable.js exposes its own set of functions to manipulate its data structures.

Theo What do you mean?

Joe I'll show you in a moment. But first, let me show you how to initiate Immutable.js persistent data structures.

Theo OK!

Joe Immutable.js provides a handy function that recursively converts a native data object to an immutable one. It's called `Immutable.fromJS()`.

Theo What do you mean by recursively?

Joe Consider the map that holds library data from our Library Management System: it has values that are themselves maps. `Immutable.fromJS()` converts the nested maps into immutable maps.

Theo Could you show me some code?

Joe Absolutely. Take a look at this JavaScript code for library data.

Listing 9.9 Conversion to immutable data

```
var libraryData = Immutable.fromJS({
  "catalog": {
    "booksByIsbn": {
      "978-1779501127": {
        "isbn": "978-1779501127",
        "title": "Watchmen",
        "publicationYear": 1987,
        "authorIds": ["alan-moore",
          "dave-gibbons"]
      }
    },
    "authorsById": {
      "alan-moore": {
        "name": "Alan Moore",
```

```
        "bookIsbns": ["978-1779501127"]
      },
      "dave-gibbons": {
        "name": "Dave Gibbons",
        "bookIsbns": ["978-1779501127"]
      }
    }
  }
});
```

Theo Do you mean that the `catalog` value in `libraryData` map is itself an immutable map?

Joe Yes, and the same for `booksByIsbn`, `authorIds`, and so forth.

Theo Cool! So how do I access a field inside an immutable map?

Joe As I told you, Immutable.js provides its own API for data access. For instance, in order to access a field inside an immutable map, you use `Immutable.get()` or `Immutable.getIn()` like the following.

Listing 9.10 Accessing a field and a nested field in an immutable map

```
Immutable.get(libraryData, "catalog");
Immutable.getIn(libraryData,
  ["catalog", "booksByIsbn", "978-1779501127", "title"]);
// → "Watchmen"
```

Theo How do I make a modification to a map?

Joe Similar to what we did with Lodash FP, you use an `Immutable.set()` or `Immutable.setIn()` map to create a new version of the map where a field is modified. Here's how.

Listing 9.11 Creating a new version of a map where a field is modified

```
Immutable.setIn(libraryData,
  ["catalog", "booksByIsbn",
    "978-1779501127", "publicationYear"],
  1988);
```

Theo What happens when I try to access a field in the map using JavaScript's dot or bracket notation?

Joe You access the internal representation of the map instead of accessing a map field.

Theo Does that mean that we can't pass data from Immutable.js to Lodash for data manipulation?

Joe Yes, but it's quite easy to convert any immutable collection into a native JavaScript object back and forth.

Theo How?

Joe Immutable.js provides a `toJS()` method to convert an arbitrary deeply nested immutable collection into a JavaScript object.

Theo But if I have a huge collection, it could take lots of time to convert it, right?

Joe True. We need a better solution. Hopefully, Immutable.js provides its own set of data manipulation functions like `map()`, `filter()`, and `reduce()`.

Theo What if I need more data manipulation like Lodash's `_.groupBy()`?

Joe You could write your own data manipulation functions that work with the Immutable.js collections or use a library like mudash, which provides a port of Lodash to Immutable.js.

▶ **NOTE** You can access the mudash library at https://github.com/brianneisler/mudash.

Theo What would you advise?

Joe A cup of coffee, then I'll show you how to port functions from Lodash to Immutable.js and how to adapt the code from your Library Management System. You can decide on whichever approach works best for your current project.

9.4 Persistent data structures in action

Joe Let's start with our search query. Can you look at the current code and tell me the Lodash functions that we used to implement the search query?

Theo Including the code for the unit tests?

Joe Of course!

▶ **NOTE** See chapter 6 for the unit test of the search query.

9.4.1 Writing queries with persistent data structures

Theo The Lodash functions we used were `get`, `map`, `filter`, and `isEqual`.

Joe Here's the port of those four functions from Lodash to Immutable.js.

Listing 9.12 Porting some functions from Lodash to Immutable.js

```
Immutable.map = function(coll, f) {
  return coll.map(f);
};

Immutable.filter = function(coll, f) {
  if(Immutable.isMap(coll)) {
    return coll.valueSeq().filter(f);
  }
  return coll.filter(f);
};

Immutable.isEqual = Immutable.is;
```

Theo The code seems quite simple. But can you explain it to me, function by function?

Joe Sure. Let's start with `get`. For accessing a field in a map, Immutable.js provides two functions: `get` for direct fields and `getIn` for nested fields. It's different from Lodash, where `_.get` works both on direct and nested fields.

Theo What about map?

Joe Immutable.js provides its own map function. The only difference is that it is a method of the collection, but it is something that we can easily adapt.

Theo What about filter? How would you make it work both for arrays and maps like Lodash's filter?

Joe Immutable.js provides a valueSeq method that returns the values of a map.

Theo Cool. And what about isEqual to compare two collections?

Joe That's easy. Immutable.js provides a function named is that works exactly as isEqual.

Theo So far, so good. What do I need to do now to make the code of the search query work with Immutable.js?

Joe You simply replace each occurrence of an _ with Immutable; _.map becomes Immutable.map, _.filter becomes Immutable.filter, and _.isEqual becomes Immutable.isEqual.

Theo I can't believe it's so easy!

Joe Try it yourself; you'll see. Sometimes, it's a bit more cumbersome because you need to convert the JavaScript objects to Immutable.js objects using Immutable.fromJS.

Theo copies and pastes the snippets for the code and the unit tests of the search query. Then, he uses his IDE to replace the _ with Immutable. When Theo executes the tests and they pass, he is surprised but satisfied. Joe smiles.

Listing 9.13 Implementing book search with persistent data structures

```
class Catalog {
  static authorNames(catalogData, authorIds) {
    return Immutable.map(authorIds, function(authorId) {
      return Immutable.getIn(
        catalogData,
        ["authorsById", authorId, "name"]);
    });
  }

  static bookInfo(catalogData, book) {
    var bookInfo =  Immutable.Map({
      "title": Immutable.get(book, "title"),
      "isbn": Immutable.get(book, "isbn"),
      "authorNames": Catalog.authorNames(
        catalogData,
        Immutable.get(book, "authorIds"))
    });
    return bookInfo;
  }

  static searchBooksByTitle(catalogData, query) {
    var allBooks = Immutable.get(catalogData, "booksByIsbn");
    var queryLowerCased = query.toLowerCase();
    var matchingBooks = Immutable.filter(allBooks, function(book) {
```

```
      return Immutable.get(book, "title").
        toLowerCase().
        includes(queryLowerCased);
    });
    var bookInfos = Immutable.map(matchingBooks, function(book) {
      return Catalog.bookInfo(catalogData, book);
    });
    return bookInfos;
  }
}
```

Listing 9.14 Testing book search with persistent data structures

```
var catalogData = Immutable.fromJS({
  "booksByIsbn": {
    "978-1779501127": {
      "isbn": "978-1779501127",
      "title": "Watchmen",
      "publicationYear": 1987,
      "authorIds": ["alan-moore",
        "dave-gibbons"]
    }
  },
  "authorsById": {
    "alan-moore": {
      "name": "Alan Moore",
      "bookIsbns": ["978-1779501127"]
    },
    "dave-gibbons": {
      "name": "Dave Gibbons",
      "bookIsbns": ["978-1779501127"]
    }
  }
});

var bookInfo = Immutable.fromJS({
  "isbn": "978-1779501127",
  "title": "Watchmen",
  "authorNames": ["Alan Moore",
    "Dave Gibbons"]
});

Immutable.isEqual(
  Catalog.searchBooksByTitle(catalogData, "Watchmen"),
  Immutable.fromJS([bookInfo]));
// → true

Immutable.isEqual(
  Catalog.searchBooksByTitle(catalogData, "Batman"),
  Immutable.fromJS([]));
// → true
```

9.4.2 Writing mutations with persistent data structures

Theo Shall we move forward and port the add member mutation?

Joe Sure. Porting the add member mutation from Lodash to Immutable.js only requires you to again replace the underscore (_) with `Immutable`. Let's look at some code.

Listing 9.15 Implementing member addition with persistent data structures

```
UserManagement.addMember = function(userManagement, member) {
  var email = Immutable.get(member, "email");
  var infoPath = ["membersByEmail", email];
  if(Immutable.hasIn(userManagement, infoPath)) {
    throw "Member already exists.";
  }
  var nextUserManagement =  Immutable.setIn(userManagement,
    infoPath,
    member);
  return nextUserManagement;
};
```

Theo So, for the tests, I'd convert the JavaScript objects to Immutable.js objects with `Immutable.fromJS()`. How does this look?

Listing 9.16 Testing member addition with persistent data structures

```
var jessie = Immutable.fromJS({
  "email": "jessie@gmail.com",
  "password": "my-secret"
});

var franck = Immutable.fromJS({
  "email": "franck@gmail.com",
  "password": "my-top-secret"
});

var userManagementStateBefore = Immutable.fromJS({
  "membersByEmail": {
    "franck@gmail.com": {
      "email": "franck@gmail.com",
      "password": "my-top-secret"
    }
  }
});

var expectedUserManagementStateAfter = Immutable.fromJS({
  "membersByEmail": {
    "jessie@gmail.com": {
      "email": "jessie@gmail.com",
      "password": "my-secret"
    },
    "franck@gmail.com": {
      "email": "franck@gmail.com",
      "password": "my-top-secret"
```

```
    }
  }
});

var result = UserManagement.addMember(userManagementStateBefore, jessie);
Immutable.isEqual(result, expectedUserManagementStateAfter);
// → true
```

Joe Great!

9.4.3 *Serialization and deserialization*

Theo Does Immutable.js also support JSON serialization and deserialization?

Joe It supports serialization out of the box. As for deserialization, we need to write our own function.

Theo Does Immutable.js provide an `Immutable.stringify()` function?

Joe That's not necessary because the native `JSON.stringify()` function works with Immutable.js objects. Here's another example.

Listing 9.17 JSON serialization of an Immutable.js collection

```
var bookInfo = Immutable.fromJS({
  "isbn": "978-1779501127",
  "title": "Watchmen",
  "authorNames": ["Alan Moore",
    "Dave Gibbons"]
});

JSON.stringify(bookInfo);
// → {\"isbn\":\"978-1779501127\",\"title\":\"Watchmen\",
// → \"authorNames\":[\"Alan Moore\",\"Dave Gibbons\"]}
```

Theo How does `JSON.stringify()` know how to handle an Immutable.js collection?

Joe As an OOP developer, you shouldn't be surprised by that.

Theo Hmm . . . let me think a minute. OK, here's my guess. Is that because `JSON.stringify()` calls some method on its argument?

Joe Exactly! If the object passed to `JSON.stringify()` has a `.toJSON()` method, it's called by `JSON.stringify()`.

Theo Nice. What about JSON deserialization?

Joe That needs to be done in two steps. You first convert the JSON string to a JavaScript object and then to an immutable collection.

Theo Something like this piece of code?

Listing 9.18 Converting a JSON string into an immutable collection

```
Immutable.parseJSON = function(jsonString) {
  return Immutable.fromJS(JSON.parse(jsonString));
};
```

Joe Exactly.

9.4.4 Structural diff

Theo So far, we have ported pieces of code that dealt with simple data manipulations. I'm curious to see how it goes with complex data manipulations such as the code that computes the structural diff between two maps.

▶ **NOTE** Chapter 5 introduces structural diff.

Joe That also works smoothly, but we need to port another eight functions.

Listing 9.19 Porting Lodash functions involved in structural diff computation

```
Immutable.reduce = function(coll, reducer, initialReduction) {
  return coll.reduce(reducer, initialReduction);
};

Immutable.isEmpty = function(coll) {
  return coll.isEmpty();
};

Immutable.keys = function(coll) {
  return coll.keySeq();
};

Immutable.isObject = function(coll) {
  return Immutable.Map.isMap(coll);
};

Immutable.isArray = Immutable.isIndexed;

Immutable.union = function() {
  return Immutable.Set.union(arguments);
};
```

Theo Everything looks trivial with one exception: the use of `arguments` in `Immutable.union`.

Joe In JavaScript, `arguments` is an implicit array-like object that contains the values of the function arguments.

Theo I see. It's one of those pieces of JavaScript magic!

Joe Yep. We need to use `arguments` because Lodash and Immutable.js differ slightly in the signature of the `union` function. `Immutable.Set.union` receives an array of lists, whereas a Lodash `_.union` receives several arrays.

Theo Makes sense. Let me give it a try.

Blowing on his fingers like a seasoned safecracker, first one hand and then the next, Theo begins typing. Once again, Theo is surprised to discover that after replacing the `_` with `Immutable` in listing 9.20, the tests pass with the code in listing 9.21.

Listing 9.20 Implementing structural diff with persistent data structures

```
function diffObjects(data1, data2) {
  var emptyObject = Immutable.isArray(data1) ?
    Immutable.fromJS([]) :
```

```
    Immutable.fromJS({});
  if(data1 == data2) {
    return emptyObject;
  }
  var keys = Immutable.union(Immutable.keys(data1), Immutable.keys(data2));
  return Immutable.reduce(keys,
    function (acc, k) {
      var res = diff(Immutable.get(data1, k),
        Immutable.get(data2, k));
      if((Immutable.isObject(res) && Immutable.isEmpty(res)) ||
        (res == "data-diff:no-diff")) {
        return acc;
      }
      return Immutable.set(acc, k, res);
    },
    emptyObject);
}

function diff(data1, data2) {
  if(Immutable.isObject(data1) && Immutable.isObject(data2)) {
    return diffObjects(data1, data2);
  }
  if(data1 !== data2) {
    return data2;
  }
  return "data-diff:no-diff";
}
```

Listing 9.21 Testing structural diff with persistent data structures

```
var data1 = Immutable.fromJS({
  g: {
    c: 3
  },
  x: 2,
  y: {
    z: 1
  },
  w: [5]
});

var data2 = Immutable.fromJS({
  g: {
    c:3
  },
  x: 2,
  y: {
    z: 2
  },
  w: [4]
});

Immutable.isEqual(diff(data1, data2),
  Immutable.fromJS({
```

```
  "w": [
    4
  ],
  "y": {
    "z": 2
  }
}));
```

Joe What do you think of all this, my friend?

Theo I think that using persistent data collections with a library like Immutable.js is much easier than understanding the internals of persistent data structures. But I'm also glad that I know how it works under the hood.

After accompanying Joe to the office door, Theo meets Dave. Dave had been peering through the window in Theo's office, looking at the whiteboard, anxious to catch a glimpse of today's topic on DOP.

Dave What did Joe teach you today?

Theo He took me to the university and taught me the foundations of persistent data structures for dealing with immutability at scale.

Dave What's wrong with the structural sharing that I implemented a couple of months ago?

Theo When the number of elements in the collection is big enough, naive structural sharing has performance issues.

Dave I see. Could you tell me more about that?

Theo I'd love to, but my brain isn't functioning properly after this interesting but exhausting day. We'll do it soon, promise.

Dave No worries. Have a nice evening, Theo.

Theo You too, Dave.

Summary

- It's possible to manually ensure that our data isn't mutated, but it's cumbersome.
- At scale, *naive* structural sharing causes a performance hit, both in terms of memory and computation.
- Naive structural sharing doesn't prevent data structures from being accidentally mutated.
- *Immutable collections* are not the same as persistent data structures.
- Immutable collections don't provide an efficient way to create new versions of the collections.
- *Persistent data structures* protect data from mutation.
- Persistent data structures provide an efficient way to create new versions of the collections.
- Persistent data structures always preserve the previous version of themselves when they are modified.

- Persistent data structures represent data internally in such a way that structural sharing scales well, both in terms of memory and computation.
- When data is immutable, it is safe to share it.
- Internally, persistence uses a branching factor of 32.
- In practice, manipulation of persistent data structures is efficient even for collections with 10 billion entries!
- Due to modern architecture considerations, the performance of updating a persistent list is dominated much more by the depth of the tree than by the number of nodes at each level of the tree.
- Persistent lists can be manipulated in near constant time.
- In most languages, third-party libraries provide an implementation of persistent data structures.
- Paguro collections implement the read-only parts of Java collection interfaces.
- Paguro collections can be passed to any methods that expect to receive a Java collection without mutating them.

10 Database operations

A cloud is a cloud

This chapter covers

- Fetching data from the database
- Storing data in the database
- Manipulating data fetched from the database

Traditionally in OOP, we use design patterns and complex layers of objects to structure access to the database. In DOP, we prefer to represent data fetched from the database with generic data collections, namely, lists of maps, where fields in the maps correspond to database column values. As we'll see throughout the chapter, the fact that fields inside a map are accessible dynamically via their names allows us to use the same generic code for different data entities.

TIP The best way to manipulate data is to represent data as data.

In this chapter, we'll illustrate the application of data-oriented principles when accessing data from a relational database. Basic knowledge of relational database and SQL query syntax (like `SELECT`, `AS`, `WHERE`, and `INNER JOIN`) is assumed. This approach can be easily adapted to NoSQL databases.

Applications that run on the server usually store data in a database. In DOP, we represent data retrieved from the database the same way we represent any other data in our application—with generic data collections. This leads to

- Reduced system complexity.
- Increased genericity.

10.1 Fetching data from the database

Theo and Joe go for a walk in a park near the office. They sit on a bench close to a beautiful lake and gaze at the clouds in the sky. After a couple of minutes of meditative silence, Joe asks Theo, "What do you see?" Theo tells him that this cloud looks to him like a horse, and that one looks like a car. On their way back to the office, Theo asks Joe for an explanation about the clouds. Joe answers with a mysterious smile on his lips, "A cloud is a cloud."

Theo So far you've shown me how DOP represents data that lives in the memory of the application. What about data that comes from the outside?

Joe What do you mean by outside?

Theo Data that comes from the database.

Joe I'll return the question to you. How do you think that we should represent data that comes from the database in DOP?

Theo As generic data collections, I guess.

Joe Exactly! In DOP, we always represent data with generic data collections.

Theo Does that mean that we can manipulate data from the database with the same flexibility as we manipulate in-memory data?

Joe Definitely.

TIP In DOP, we represent data from the database with generic data collections, and we manipulate it with generic functions.

Theo Would you show me how to retrieve book search results when the catalog data is stored in an SQL database?

Joe I'll show you in a moment. First, tell me how you would design the tables that store catalog data.

Theo Do you mean the exact table schemas with the information about primary keys and nullability of each and every column?

Joe No, I only need a rough overview of the tables, their columns, and the relationships between the tables.

Theo goes to the whiteboard. Figure 10.1 shows the diagram he draws as he explains his thinking to Joe.

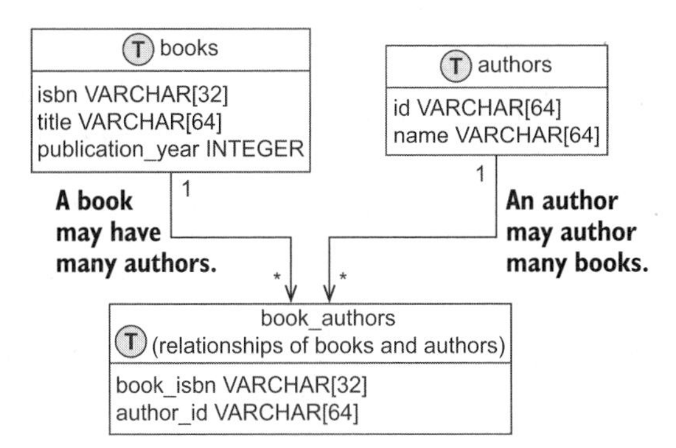

Figure 10.1 The database model for books and authors

Theo I have a `books` table with three columns: `title`, `isbn`, and `publication_year`. I also have an `authors` table with two columns: for `id` and `name`. Here, let me draw these tables on the whiteboard to give you a visual (see tables 10.1 and 10.2).

Table 10.1 The `books` table filled with two books

title	isbn	publication_year
The Power of Habit	978-0812981605	2012
7 Habits of Highly Effective People	978-1982137274	1989

Table 10.2 The `authors` table filled with three authors

id	name
sean-covey	Sean Covey
stephen-covey	Stephen Covey
charles-duhigg	Charles Duhigg

Joe What about the connection between books and authors?

Theo Let's see, a book could be written by multiple authors, and an author could write multiple books. Therefore, I need a many-to-many `book_authors` table that connects authors and books with two columns, `book_isbn` and `author_id`.

Theo once again turns to the whiteboard. He pens the `book_authors` table 10.3 to show Joe.

Table 10.3 The `book_authors` table with rows connecting books with their authors

book_isbn	author_id
978-1982137274	sean-covey
978-1982137274	stephen-covey
978-0812981605	charles-duhigg

Joe Great! Let's start with the simplest case. We're going to write code that searches for books matching a title and that returns basic information about the books. By basic information, I mean title, ISBN, and publication year.

Theo What about the book authors?

Joe We'll deal with that later, as it's a bit more complicated. Can you write an SQL query for retrieving books that contain he word *habit* in their title?

Theo Sure.

This assignment is quite easy for Theo. First, he jots down the SQL query, then he displays the results in table 10.4.

Listing 10.1 SQL query to retrieve books whose title contains `habit`

```
SELECT
title,
isbn,
publication_year
FROM
books
WHERE title LIKE '%habit%';
```

Table 10.4 Results of the SQL query for books whose title contains the word *habit*

title	isbn	publication_year
The Power of Habit	978-0812981605	2012
7 Habits of Highly Effective People	978-1982137274	1989

Joe How would you describe these results as a data collection?

Theo I would say it's a list of maps.

TIP In DOP, accessing data from a NoSQL database is similar to the way we access data from a relational database.

Joe Right! Now, can you write the search results as a list of maps?

Theo It doesn't sound too complicated. How about this?

Listing 10.2 Search results as a list of maps

```
[
  {
    "title": "7 Habits of Highly Effective People",
    "isbn": "978-1982137274",
    "publication_year": 1989
  },
  {
    "title": "The Power of Habit",
    "isbn": "978-0812981605",
    "publication_year": 2012
  }
]
```

Joe What about the JSON schema for the search results?

Theo It shouldn't be too difficult if you allow me to take a look at the JSON schema cheat sheet you kindly offered me the other day.

Joe Of course. The purpose of a gift is to be used by the one who receives it.

Theo takes a look at the JSON Schema cheat sheet to refresh his memory about the JSON Schema syntax. After a few minutes, Theo comes up with a schema for the search results. He certainly is putting Joe's gift to good use.

Listing 10.3 JSON schema cheat sheet

```
{
  "type": "array",
  "items": {
    "type": "object",
    "properties": {
      "myNumber": {"type": "number"},
      "myString": {"type": "string"},
      "myEnum": {"enum": ["myVal", "yourVal"]},
      "myBool": {"type": "boolean"}
    },
    "required": ["myNumber", "myString"],
    "additionalProperties": false
  }
}
```

Listing 10.4 The JSON schema for search results from the database

```
var dbSearchResultSchema = {
  "type": "array",
  "items": {
    "type": "object",
    "required": ["title", "isbn", "publication_year"],
    "properties": {
      "title": {"type": "string"},
      "isbn": {"type": "string"},
      "publication_year": {"type": "integer"}
    }
  }
};
```

Joe Excellent. Now I'm going to show you how to implement `searchBooks` in a way that fetches data from the database and returns a JSON string with the results. The cool thing is that we're only going to use generic data collections from the database layer down to the JSON serialization.

Theo Will it be similar to the implementation of `searchBooks` that we wrote when you taught me the basis of DOP?

Joe Absolutely. The only difference is that then the state of the system was stored locally, and we queried it with a function like `_.filter`. Now, we use SQL queries to fetch the state from the database. In terms of data representation and manipulation, it's exactly the same.

Joe goes to the whiteboard and sketches out the data flow in figure 10.2. Theo studies the diagram.

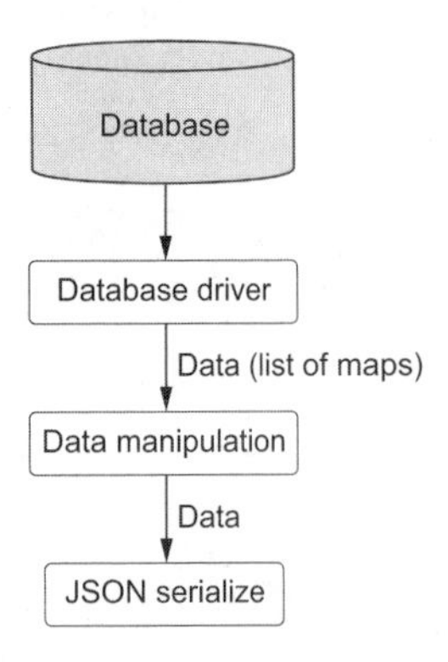

Figure 10.2 Data flow for serving a request that fetches data from the database

Joe The data manipulation step in the diagram is implemented via generic functions that manipulate data collections. As our examples get more elaborate, I think you'll see the benefits of being able to manipulate data collections with generic functions.

Theo Sounds intriguing . . .

Joe For the communication with the database, we use a driver that returns a list of maps. In JavaScript, you could use an SQL driver like node-postgres.

▶ **NOTE** See https://node-postgres.com for more information about this collection of node.js modules for interfacing with PostgreSQL databases.

Theo And in Java?

Joe In Java, you could use JDBC (Java database connectivity) in addition to a small utility function that converts a JDBC result set into a list of maps. If I can use your laptop, I'll show you what I mean.

Joe pulls a piece of code from one of his personal GitHub repositories. He then shows the code for the JDBC conversion to Theo, who seems a bit surprised.

Listing 10.5 Converting a JDBC result set into a list of hash maps

```
List<Map<String, Object>> convertJDBCResultSetToListOfMaps(ResultSet rs) {
  List<Map<String, Object>> listOfMaps =
    new ArrayList<Map<String, Object>>();
  ResultSetMetaData meta = rs.getMetaData();
  while (rs.next()) {
    Map map = new HashMap();
    for (int i = 1; i <= meta.getColumnCount(); i++) {
      String key = meta.getColumnLabel(i);
      Object value = rs.getObject(i);
```

```
      map.put(key, value);
    }
    listOfMaps.add(map);
  }
  return listOfMaps;
}
```

TIP Converting a JDBC result set into a list of hash maps is quite straightforward.

Theo I expected it to be much more complicated to convert a JDBC result set into a list of hash maps.

Joe It's straightforward because, in a sense, JDBC is data-oriented.

Theo What about the field types?

Joe When we convert a JDBC result set into a list of maps, each value is considered an `Object`.

Theo That's annoying because it means that in order to access the value, we need to cast it to its type.

Joe Yes and no. Look at our book search use case. We pass all the values along without really looking at their type. The concrete value type only matters when we serialize the result into JSON and that's handled by the JSON serialization library. It's called late binding.

▶ **NOTE** With *late binding*, we defer dealing with data types as long as possible.

Theo Does that mean in my application that I'm allowed to manipulate data without dealing with concrete types?

TIP In DOP, flexibility is increased as many parts of the system are free to manipulate data without dealing with concrete types.

Joe Exactly. You'll see late binding in action in a moment. That's one of the greatest benefits of DOP.

Theo Interesting, I can't wait to see that!

Joe One last thing before I show you the code for retrieving search results from the database. In order to make it easier to read, I'm going to write JavaScript code as if JavaScript were dealing with I/O is a synchronous way.

Theo What do you mean?

Joe In JavaScript, an I/O operation like sending a query to the database is done asynchronously. In real life, it means using either callback functions or using `async` and `await` keywords.

Theo Oh yeah, that's because JavaScript is single-threaded.

▶ **NOTE** For sake of simplicity, the JavaScript snippets in this chapter are written as if JavaScript were dealing with I/O in a synchronous way. In real-life JavaScript, we need to use `async` and `await` around I/O calls.

Joe Indeed, so I'll be writing the code that communicates with the database as though JavaScript were dealing with I/O synchronously. Here's an example.

Listing 10.6 Searching books in the database, returning the results in JSON

```
var dbClient;                                  ◁ dbClient holds the DB connection.
var ajv = new Ajv({allErrors: true});          ◁ Initializes Ajv (a JSON schema validation
                                                 library) with allErrors: true to catch all
                                                 the data validation errors

var title = "habit";
var matchingBooksQuery = `SELECT title, isbn
                          FROM books
                          WHERE title LIKE '%$1%'`;   ◁ Uses a parameterized
                                                        SQL query as a security
                                                        best practice
var books = dbClient.query(matchingBooksQuery,
  [title]);                                    ◁ Passes the parameters to the SQL
                                                 query as a list of values (in our
                                                 case, a list with a single value)
if(!ajv.validate(dbSearchResultSchema, books)) {
  var errors = ajv.errorsText(ajv.errors);
  throw "Internal error: Unexpected result from the database: " + errors;
}

JSON.stringify(books);
```

Theo In a dynamically-typed language like JavaScript, I understand that the types of the values in the list of maps returned by `dbClient.query` are determined at run time. How does it work in a statically-typed language like Java, and what are the types of the data fields in `books`?

Joe The function `convertJDBCResultSetToListOfMaps` we created earlier (see listing 10.5) returns a list of `Map<String, Object>`. But JSON serialization libraries like Gson know how to detect at run time the concrete type of the values in a map and serialize the values according to their type.

▶ **NOTE** See https://github.com/google/gson for information about Gson's Java serialization/deserialization library.

Theo What do you mean by *serializing a value according to its type?*

Joe For instance, the value of the field `publication_year` is a number; therefore, it is not wrapped with quotes. However, the value of the field `title` is a string; therefore, it is wrapped with quotes.

Theo Nice! Now, I understand what you mean by late binding.

Joe Cool! Now, let me show you how we store data in the database.

10.2 Storing data in the database

In the previous section, we saw how to retrieve data from the database as a list of maps. Next, we'll see how to store data in the database when data is represented with a map.

Theo I guess that storing data in the database is quite similar to fetching data from the database.

Joe It's similar in the sense that we deal only with generic data collections. Can you write a parameterized SQL query that inserts a row with user info using only `email` and `encrypted_password`, please?

Theo OK.

Theo takes a moment to think about the code and writes a few lines of SQL as Joe requested. He shows it to Joe.

Listing 10.7 SQL statement to add a member

```
INSERT
INTO members
(email, encrypted_password)
VALUES ($1, $2)
```

Joe Great! And here's how to integrate your SQL query in our application code.

Listing 10.8 Adding a member from inside the application

```
var addMemberQuery =
  "INSERT INTO members (email, password) VALUES ($1, $2)";
dbClient.query(addMemberQuery,
  [_.get(member, "email"),                          <-- Passes the two parameters to
    _.get(member, "encryptedPassword")]);                 the SQL query as an array
```

Theo Your code is very clear, but something still bothers me.

Joe What is that?

Theo I find it cumbersome that you use `_.get(user, "email")` instead of `user.email`, like I would if the data were represented with a class.

Joe In JavaScript, you are allowed to use the dot notation `user.email` instead of `_.get(user, "email")`.

Theo Then why don't you use the dot notation?

Joe Because I wanted to show you how you can apply DOP principles even in languages like Java, where the dot notation is not available for hash maps.

▶ **NOTE** In this book, we avoid using the JavaScript dot notation to access a field in a hash map in order to illustrate how to apply DOP in languages that don't support dot notation on hash maps.

Theo That's exactly my point. I find it cumbersome in a language like Java to use `_.get(user, "email")` instead of `user.email` like I would if the data were represented with a class.

Joe On one hand, it's cumbersome. On the other hand, representing data with a hash map instead of a static class allows you to access fields in a flexible way.

Theo I know—you've told me so many times! But I can't get used to it.

Joe Let me give you another example of the benefits of the flexible access to data fields in the context of adding a member to the database. You said that writing `[_.get(member, "email"), _.get(member, "encryptedPassword")]` was less convenient than writing `[member.email, member.encryptedPassword]`. Right?

Theo Absolutely!

Joe Let me show you how to write the same code in a more succinct way, using a function from Lodash called `_.at`.

Theo What does this `_.at` function do?

Joe It receives a map `m`, a list `keyList`, and returns a list made of the values in `m` associated with the keys in `keyList`.

Theo How about an example?

Joe Sure. We create a list made of the fields `email` and `encryptedPassword` of a member.

Joe types for a bit. He shows this code to Theo.

Listing 10.9 Creating a list made of some values in a map with `_.at`

```
var member = {
  "email": "samantha@gmail.com",
  "encryptedPassword": "c2VjcmV0",
  "isBlocked": false
};

_.at(member,
  ["email", "encryptedPassword"]);
// ? ["samantha@gmail.com", "c2VjcmV0"]
```

Theo Do the values in the results appear in the same order as the keys in `keyList`?

Joe Yes!

Theo That's cool.

TIP Accessing a field in a hash map is more flexible than accessing a member in an object instantiated from a class.

Joe And here's the code for adding a member using `_.at`.

Listing 10.10 Using `_.at` to return multiple values from a map

```
class CatalogDB {
  static addMember(member) {
    var addMemberQuery = `INSERT
                          INTO members
                               (email, encrypted_password)
                          VALUES ($1, $2)`;
    dbClient.query(addMemberQuery,
      _.at(member, ["email",
        "encryptedPassword"]));
  }
}
```

Theo I can see how the `_.at` function becomes really beneficial when we need to pass a bigger number of field values.

Joe I'll be showing you more examples that use the flexible data access that we have in DOP.

10.3 Simple data manipulation

Quite often, in a production application, we need to reshape data fetched from the database. The simplest case is when we need to rename the columns from the database to those that are more appropriate for our application.

Joe Did you notice that the column names in our database follow the snake case convention?

Theo I'm so used to the convention, no. I didn't even think about that.

Joe Well, for instance, the column for the publication year of a book is called `publication_year`.

Theo Go on . . .

Joe Inside JSON, I like to use Pascal case, like `publicationYear`.

Theo And I'd prefer to have `bookTitle` instead of `title`.

Joe So we're both unhappy with the JSON string that `searchBooks` returns if we pass the data retrieved from the database as is.

Theo Indeed!

Joe How would you fix it?

Theo I would modify the SQL query so that it renames the columns in the results. Here, let me show you the query.

Listing 10.11 Renaming columns inside the SQL query

```
SELECT
title AS bookTitle,
isbn,
publication_year AS publicationYear
FROM
books
WHERE title LIKE '%habit%';
```

Joe That would work, but it seems a bit weird to modify an SQL query so that it fits the naming convention of the application.

Theo Yeah, I agree. I imagine a database like MongoDB doesn't make it easy to rename the fields inside a query.

Joe Yep. Sometimes it makes more sense to deal with field names in application code. How would you handle that?

Theo Well, in that case, for every map returned by the database query, I'd use a function to modify the field names.

Joe Could you show me what the code would look like?

Theo Sure. How about this?

Listing 10.12 Renaming specific keys in a list of maps

```
function renameBookInfoKeys(bookInfo) {
  return {
```

```
    "bookTitle": _.get(bookInfo, "title"),
    "isbn": _.get(bookInfo, "isbn"),
    "publicationYear": _.get(bookInfo, "publication_year")
  };
}

var bookResults = [
  {
    "title": "7 Habits of Highly Effective People",
    "isbn": "978-1982137274",
    "publication_year": 1989
  },
  {
    "title": "The Power of Habit",
    "isbn": "978-0812981605",
    "publication_year": 2012
  }
];

_.map(bookResults, renameBookInfoKeys);
```

Joe Would you write a similar piece of code for every query that you fetched from the database?

Theo What do you mean?

Joe Suppose you want to rename the fields returned by a query that retrieves the books a user has borrowed.

Theo I see. I'd write a similar piece of code for each case.

Joe In DOP, we can use the fact that a field name is just a string and write a generic function called `renameResultKeys` that works on every list of maps.

Theo Wow! How does `renameResultKeys` know what fields to rename?

Joe You pass the mapping between the old and the new names as a map.

TIP In DOP, field names are just strings. It allows us to write generic functions to manipulate a list of maps that represent data fetched from the database.

Theo Could you show me an example?

Joe Sure. A map like this can be passed to `renameResultKeys` to rename the fields in the book search results. So, for example, you could write `renameResultKeys` like this.

Listing 10.13 Renaming fields in SQL results

```
renameResultKeys(bookResults, {
  "title": "bookTitle",
  "publication_year": "publicationYear"
});
```

Theo What happened to the field that stores the `isbn`?

Joe When a field is not mentioned, `renameResultKeys` leaves it as-is.

Theo Awesome! Can you show me the implementation of `renameResultKeys`?

Joe Sure, it's only about `map` and `reduce`, so I'd do something like the following.

Listing 10.14 Renaming the keys in SQL results

```
function renameKeys(map, keyMap) {
  return _.reduce(keyMap,
    function(res, newKey, oldKey) {
      var value = _.get(map, oldKey);
      var resWithNewKey = _.set(res, newKey, value);
      var resWithoutOldKey = _.omit(resWithNewKey, oldKey);
      return resWithoutOldKey;
    },
    map);
}

function renameResultKeys(results, keyMap) {
  return _.map(results, function(result) {
    return renameKeys(result, keyMap);
  });
}
```

Theo That code isn't exactly easy to understand!

Joe Don't worry. The more you write data manipulation functions with `map`, `filter`, and `reduce`, the more you get used to it.

Theo I hope so!

Joe What's really important for now is that you understand what makes it possible in DOP to write a function like `renameResultKeys`.

Theo I would say it's because fields are accessible dynamically with strings.

Joe Exactly. You could say that fields are first-class citizens.

TIP In DOP, fields are first-class citizens.

Theo How would you write unit tests for a data manipulation function like `renameResultKeys`?

Joe It's similar to the unit tests we wrote earlier. You generate input and expected results, and you make sure that the actual results equal the expected results. Hang on; this may take a while.

While Joe is busy coding, Theo takes this opportunity to run to the kitchen and prepare two espressos. What luck! There's a box of Swiss chocolates on the counter. He grabs a couple of pieces and returns to his office just as Joe is finishing up the unit test.

Listing 10.15 Unit test for `renameResultKeys`

```
var listOfMaps = [
  {
    "title": "7 Habits of Highly Effective People",
    "isbn": "978-1982137274",
```

```
    "publication_year": 1989
  },
  {
    "title": "The Power of Habit",
    "isbn": "978-0812981605",
    "publication_year": 2012
  }
];

var expectedResults = [
  {
    "bookTitle": "7 Habits of Highly Effective People",
    "isbn": "978-1982137274",
    "publicationYear": 1989
  },
  {
    "bookTitle": "The Power of Habit",
    "isbn": "978-0812981605",
    "publicationYear": 2012
  }
];


var results = renameResultKeys(listOfMaps,
  {"title": "bookTitle",
    "publication_year": "publicationYear"});

_.isEqual(expectedResults, results);
```

Theo Nice!

Joe Do you see why you're free to use `renameResultKeys` with the results of any SQL query?

Theo Yes, because the code of `renameResultKeys` is decoupled from the internal details of the representation of data it operates on.

Joe Exactly! Now, suppose an SQL query returns user info in a table. How would you use `renameResultKeys` to rename `email` to `userEmail`? Assume the table looks like this (table 10.5).

Once again, the whiteboard comes in to play. When he's finished, Joe shows Theo the table.

Table 10.5 Results of an SQL query that returns `email` and `encrypted_password` of some users

email	encrypted_password
jennie@gmail.com	secret-pass
franck@hotmail.com	my-secret

Theo That's easy!

On his laptop, Theo writes the code to rename `email`. Satisfied, he turns the laptop to Joe.

Listing 10.16 Renaming `email` to `userEmail`

```
var listOfMaps = [
  {
    "email": "jennie@gmail.com",
    "encryptedPassword": "secret-pass"
  },
  {
    "email": "franck@hotmail.com",
    "encryptedPassword": "my-secret"
  }
];


renameResultKeys(listOfMaps,
  {"email": "userEmail"});
```

Joe Excellent! I think you're ready to move on to advanced data manipulation.

10.4 Advanced data manipulation

In some cases, we need to change the structure of the rows returned by an SQL query (for instance, aggregating fields from different rows into a single map). This could be done at the level of the SQL query, using advanced features like JSON aggregation in PostgreSQL. However, sometimes it makes more sense to reshape the data inside the application because it keeps the SQL queries simple. As with the simple data manipulation scenario of the previous section, once we write code that implements some data manipulation, we're free to use the same code for similar use cases, even if they involve data entities of different types.

Theo What kind of advanced data manipulation did you have in mind?

Joe You'll see in a minute, but first, an SQL task for you. Write an SQL query that returns books, including author names, that contain the word *habit* in their title.

Theo Let me give it a try.

After some trial and error, Theo is able to nail it down. He jots down an SQL query that joins the three tables: `books`, `book_authors`, and `authors`.

Listing 10.17 SQL query to retrieve books containing the word *habit*

```
SELECT
title,
isbn,
authors.name AS author_name
FROM
books
INNER JOIN
book_authors
```

```
ON books.isbn = book_authors.book_isbn
INNER JOIN
authors
ON book_authors.author_id = authors.id
WHERE books.title LIKE '%habit%';
```

Joe How many rows are in the results?

Theo goes to the whiteboard. He quickly sketches a table showing the results, then he answers Joe's question. Because *7 Habits of Highly Effective People* has two authors, Theo lists the book twice in table 10.6.

Table 10.6 Results of the SQL query that retrieves books whose title contain the word *habit*, including author names

title	isbn	author_name
7 Habits of Highly Effective People	978-1982137274	Sean Covey
7 Habits of Highly Effective People	978-1982137274	Stephen Covey
The Power of Habit	978-0812981605	Charles Duhigg

Theo Three rows.

Joe And how many books?

Theo Two books.

Joe Can you show me the results of the SQL query as a list of maps?

Theo Sure.

Listing 10.18 A list of maps with the results for listing 10.17

```
[
  {
    "title": "7 Habits of Highly Effective People",
    "isbn": "978-1982137274",
    "publication_year": "Sean Covey"
  },
  {
    "title": "7 Habits of Highly Effective People",
    "isbn": "978-1982137274",
    "author_name": "Stephen Covey"
  },
  {
    "title": "The Power of Habit",
    "isbn": "978-0812981605",
    "author_name": "Charles Duhigg"
  }
]
```

Joe And what does the list of maps that we need to return look like?

Theo It's a list with two maps, where the author names are aggregated in a list. Let me write the code for that.

Listing 10.19 Aggregating author names in a list

```
[
  {
    "isbn": "978-1982137274",
    "title": "7 Habits of Highly Effective People",
    "authorNames": [
      "Sean Covey",
      "Stephen Covey"
    ]
  },
  {
    "isbn": "978-0812981605",
    "title": "The Power of Habit",
    "authorNames": ["Charles Duhigg"]
  }
]
```

Joe Perfect! Now, let's take an example of an advanced data manipulation task, where we convert the list of maps as returned from the database to a list of maps where the author names are aggregated.

Theo Hmm . . . That sounds tough.

Joe Let me break the task in two steps. First, we group together rows that belong to the same book (with the same ISBN). Then, in each group, we aggregate author names in a list. Hold on, I'll diagram it as a data processing pipeline.

Joe goes the whiteboard. He draws the diagram in figure 10.3.

Joe Does it makes sense to you now?

Theo Yes, the data pipeline makes sense, but I have no idea how to write code that implements it!

Joe Let me guide you step by step. Let's start by grouping together books with the same ISBN using `_.groupBy`.

Listing 10.20 Grouping rows by ISBN

```
var sqlRows = [
  {
    "title": "7 Habits of Highly Effective People",
    "isbn": "978-1982137274",
    "author_name": "Sean Covey"
  },
  {
    "title": "7 Habits of Highly Effective People",
    "isbn": "978-1982137274",
    "author_name": "Stephen Covey"
  },
  {
    "title": "The Power of Habit",
    "isbn": "978-0812981605",
    "author_name": "Charles Duhigg"
  }
];

_.groupBy(sqlRows, "isbn");
```

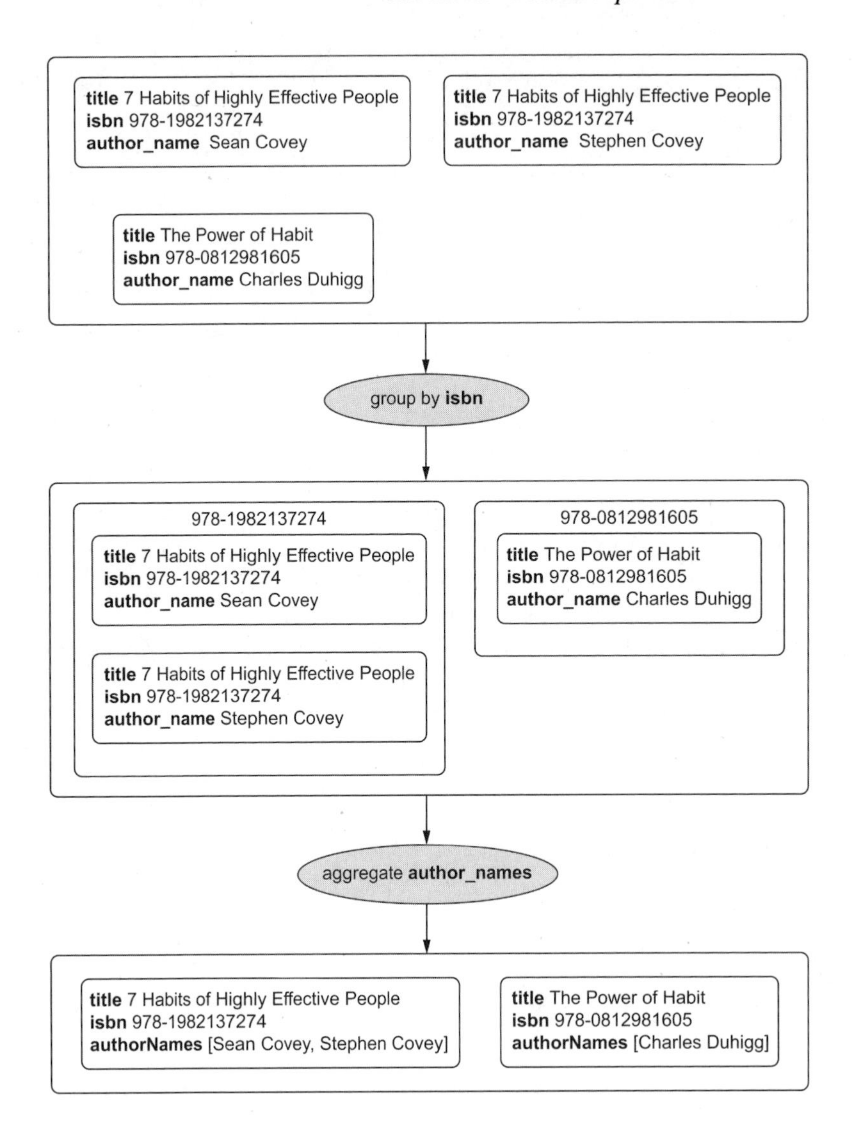

Figure 10.3 Data pipeline for aggregating author names

Theo What does `rowsByIsbn` look like?

Joe It's a map where the keys are `isbn`, and the values are lists of rows. Here's how that would look.

Listing 10.21 Rows grouped by ISBN

```
{
  "978-0812981605": [
    {
      "author_name": "Charles Duhigg",
      "isbn": "978-0812981605",
```

```
      "title": "The Power of Habit"
    }
  ],
  "978-1982137274": [
    {
      "author_name": "Sean Covey",
      "isbn": "978-1982137274",
      "title": "7 Habits of Highly Effective People"
    },
    {
      "author_name": "Stephen Covey",
      "isbn": "978-1982137274",
      "title": "7 Habits of Highly Effective People"
    }
  ]
}
```

Theo What's the next step?

Joe Now, we need to take each list of rows in `rowsByIsbn` and aggregate author names.

Theo And how do we do that?

Joe Let's do it on the list of two rows for *7 Habits of Highly Effective People.* The code looks like this.

Listing 10.22 Aggregating author names

```
var rows7Habits = [
  {
    "author_name": "Sean Covey",
    "isbn": "978-1982137274",
    "title": "7 Habits of Highly Effective People"
  },
  {
    "author_name": "Stephen Covey",
    "isbn": "978-1982137274",
    "title": "7 Habits of Highly Effective People"
  }
];

var authorNames = _.map(rows7Habits, "author_name");    // Takes the author names from all rows
var firstRow = _.nth(rows7Habits, 0);
var bookInfoWithAuthorNames = _.set(firstRow, "authorNames", authorNames);
_.omit(bookInfoWithAuthorNames, "author_name");    // Removes the author_name field
```

Joe First, we take the author names from all the rows. Then, we take the first row as a basis for the book info, we add a field `authorNames`, and remove the field `author_name`.

Theo Can we make a function of it?

Joe That's exactly what I was going to suggest!

Theo I'll call the function aggregateField. It will receive three arguments: the rows, the name of the field to aggregate, and the name of the field that holds the aggregation.

Theo turns to his laptop. After a couple of minutes, his screen displays the implementation for aggregateField.

Listing 10.23 Aggregating an arbitrary field

```
function aggregateField(rows, fieldName, aggregateFieldName) {
  var aggregatedValues = _.map(rows, fieldName);
  var firstRow = _.nth(rows, 0);
  var firstRowWithAggregatedValues = _.set(firstRow,
    aggregateFieldName,
    aggregatedValues);
  return _.omit(firstRowWithAggregatedValues, fieldName);
}
```

Joe Do you mind writing a test case to make sure your function works as expected?

Theo With pleasure! Take a look.

Listing 10.24 Test case for aggregateField

```
var expectedResults = {
  "isbn": "978-1982137274",
  "title": "7 Habits of Highly Effective People",
  "authorNames": [
    "Sean Covey",
    "Stephen Covey"
  ]
};

_.isEqual(expectedResults,
  aggregateField(rows7Habits,
    "author_name",
    "authorNames"));
```

Joe Excellent! Now that we have a function that aggregates a field from a list of rows, we only need to map the function over the values of our rowsByIsbn. Let me code that up for you.

Listing 10.25 Aggregating author names in rowsByIsbn

```
var rowsByIsbn = _.groupBy(sqlRows, "isbn");
var groupedRows = _.values(rowsByIsbn);

_.map(rowsByIsbn, function(groupedRows) {
  return aggregateField(groupedRows, "author_name", "authorNames");
})
```

Theo Why did you take the values of rowsByIsbn?

Joe Because we don't really care about the keys in rowsByIsbn. We only care about the grouping of the rows in the values of the hash map.

Theo Let me try to combine everything we've done and write a function that receives a list of rows and returns a list of book info with the author names aggregated in a list.

Joe Good luck, my friend!

To Theo, it's less complicated than it seems. After a couple of trials and errors, he arrives at the code and the test case.

Listing 10.26 Aggregating a field in a list of rows

```
function aggregateFields(rows, idFieldName,
  fieldName, aggregateFieldName) {
  var groupedRows = _.values(_.groupBy(rows, idFieldName));
  return _.map(groupedRows, function(groupedRows) {
    return aggregateField(groupedRows, fieldName, aggregateFieldName);
  });
}

var sqlRows = [
  {
    "title": "7 Habits of Highly Effective People",
    "isbn": "978-1982137274",
    "author_name": "Sean Covey"
  },
  {
    "title": "7 Habits of Highly Effective People",
    "isbn": "978-1982137274",
    "author_name": "Stephen Covey"
  },
  {
    "title": "The Power of Habit",
    "isbn": "978-0812981605",
    "author_name": "Charles Duhigg"
  }
];

var expectedResults =
[
  {
    "authorNames": [
      "Sean Covey",
      "Stephen Covey"
    ],
    "isbn": "978-1982137274",
    "title": "7 Habits of Highly Effective People"
  },
  {
    "authorNames": ["Charles Duhigg"],
    "isbn": "978-0812981605",
    "title": "The Power of Habit",
```

```
  }
];


_.isEqual(aggregateFields(sqlRows,
  "isbn",
  "author_name",
  "authorNames"),
  expectedResults);
```

Theo I think I've got it.

Joe Congratulations! I'm proud of you, Theo.

Now Theo understands what Joe meant when he told him "a cloud is cloud" when they were walking back from the park to the office. Instead of trapping data in the limits of our objects, DOP guides us to represent data as data.

Summary

- Inside our applications, we represent data fetched from the database, no matter if it is relational or nonrelational, as a *generic data structure.*
- In the case of a relational database, data is represented as a *list of maps.*
- Representing data from the database as data reduces system complexity because we don't need design patterns or complex class hierarchies to do it.
- We are free to manipulate data from the database with *generic functions,* such as returning a list made of the values of some data fields, creating a version of a map omitting a data field, or grouping maps in a list according to the value of a data field.
- We use generic functions for data manipulation with great flexibility, using the fact that inside a hash map, we access the value of a field via its name, represented as a string.
- When we package our data manipulation logic into custom functions that receive field names as arguments, we are able to use those functions on different data entities.
- The best way to manipulate data is to represent *data as data.*
- We represent data from the database with generic data collections, and we manipulate it with generic functions.
- Accessing data from a NoSQL database is done in a similar way to the approach presented in this chapter for accessing data from a relational database.
- With *late binding,* we care about data types as late as possible.
- Flexibility is increased as many parts of the system are free to manipulate data without dealing with concrete types.
- Accessing a field in a hash map is more flexible than accessing a member in an object instantiated from a class.

- In DOP, field names are just strings. It allows us to write generic functions to manipulate list of maps representing data fetched from the database.
- In DOP, fields are first-class citizens.
- We can implement renaming keys in a list of maps or aggregating rows returned by a database query via generic functions.
- JDBC stands for Java database connectivity.
- Converting a JDBC result set into a list of maps is quite straightforward.

Lodash functions introduced in this chapter

Function	Description
`at(map, [paths])`	Creates an array of values corresponding to `paths` of `map`
`omit(map, [paths])`	Creates a map composed of the fields of `map` not in `paths`
`nth(arr, n)`	Gets the element at index `n` in `arr`
`groupBy(coll, f)`	Creates a map composed of keys generated from the results of running each element of `coll` through `f`. The corresponding value for each key is an array of elements responsible for generating the key.

11 Web services
A faithful messenger

This chapter covers

- Representing a client request as a map
- Representing a server response as a map
- Passing data forward
- Combining data from different sources

The architecture of modern information systems is made of software components written in various programming languages like JSON, which communicate over the wire by sending and receiving data represented in a language-independent data exchange format. DOP applies the same principle to the communication between inner parts of a program.

▶ **NOTE** When a web browser sends a request to a web service, it's quite common that the web service itself sends requests to other web services in order to fulfill the web browser request. One popular data exchange format is JSON.

Inside a program, components communicate by sending and receiving data represented in a component independent format—namely, immutable data collections. In the context of a web service that fulfills a client request by fetching data from a database and other web services, representing data, as with immutable data collections, leads to these benefits:

- Using generic data manipulation functions to manipulate data from multiple data sources
- Passing data forward freely with no additional complexity

11.1 Another feature request

After having delivered the database milestone on time, Theo calls Nancy to share the good news. Instead of celebrating Theo's success, Nancy asks him about the ETA for the next milestone, Book Information Enrichment with the Open Library Books API. Theo tells her that he'll get back to her with an ETA by the end of the day. When Joe arrives at the office, Theo tells him about the discussion with Nancy.

Theo I just got a phone call from Nancy, and she is stressed about the next milestone.

Joe What's in the next milestone?

Theo Do you remember the Open Library Books API that I told you about a few weeks ago?

▶ **NOTE** You can find the Open Library Books API at https://openlibrary.org/dev/docs/api/books.

Joe No.

Theo It's a web service that provides detailed information about books.

Joe Cool!

Theo Nancy wants to enrich the book search results. Instead of fetching book information from the database, we need to retrieve extended book information from the Open Library Books API.

Joe What kind of book information?

Theo Everything! Number of pages, weight, physical format, topics, etc. . . .

Joe What about the information from the database?

Theo Besides the information about the availability of the books, we don't need it anymore.

Joe Have you already looked at the Open Library Books API?

Theo It's a nightmare! For some books, the information contains dozen of fields, and for other books, it has only two or three fields.

Joe What's the problem then?

Theo I have no idea how to represent data that is so sparse and unpredictable.

Joe When we represent data as data, that's not an issue. Let's have a coffee and I'll show you.

11.2 Building the insides like the outsides

While Theo drinks his macchiato, Joe draws a diagram on a whiteboard. Figure 11.1 shows Joe's diagram.

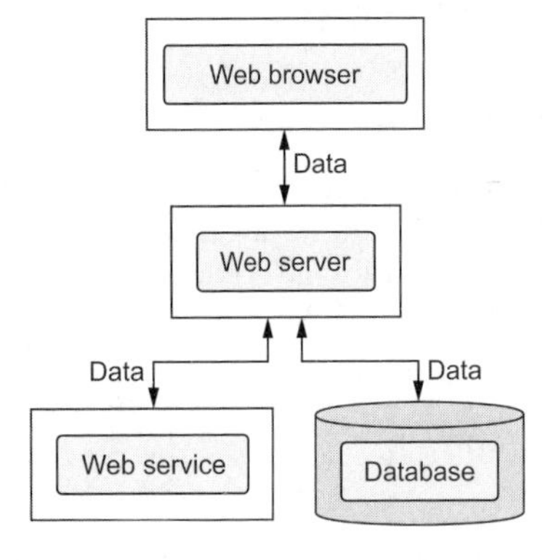

Figure 11.1 The high-level architecture of a modern information system

Joe Before we dive into the details of the implementation of the book search result enrichment, let me give you a brief intro.

Theo Sure.

Joe takes a sip of his espresso. He then points to the diagram (figure 11.1) on the whiteboard.

Joe Does this look familiar to you?

Theo Of course!

Joe Can you show me, roughly, the steps in the data flow of a web service?

Theo Sure.

Theo moves closer to the whiteboard. He writes a list of steps (see the sidebar) near the architecture diagram.

The steps of the data flow inside a web service

1. Receive a request from a client.
2. Apply business logic to the request.
3. Fetch data from external sources (e.g., database and other web services).
4. Apply business logic to the responses from external sources.
5. Send the response to the client.

Joe Excellent! Now comes an important insight about DOP.

Theo I'm all ears.

Joe We should build the insides of our systems like we build the outsides.

Theo What do you mean?

Joe How do components of a system communicate over the wire?

Theo By sending data.

Joe Does the data format depend on the programming language of the components?

Theo No, quite often it's JSON, for which we have parsers in all programming languages.

Joe What the idiom says is that, inside our program, the inner components of a program should communicate in a way that doesn't depend on the components.

Theo I don't get that.

Joe Let me explain why traditional OOP breaks this idiom. Perhaps it will be clearer then. When data is represented with classes, the inner components of a program need to know the internals of the class definitions in order to communicate.

Theo What do you mean?

Joe In order to be able to access a member in a class, a component needs to import the class definition.

Theo How could it be different?

Joe In DOP, as we have seen so far, the inner components of a program communicate via generic data collections. It's similar to how components of a system communicate over the wire.

TIP We should build the insides of our systems like we build the outsides.

Theo Why is that so important?

Joe From a design perspective, it's important because it means that the inner components of a program are loosely coupled.

Theo What do you mean by loosely coupled?

Joe I mean that components need no knowledge about the internals of other components. The only knowledge required is the names of the fields.

TIP In DOP, the inner components of a program are loosely coupled.

Theo And from an implementation perspective?

Joe As you'll see in a moment, implementing the steps of the data flow that you just wrote on the whiteboard is easy. It comes down to expressing the business logic in terms of generic data manipulation functions. Here, let me show you a diagram.

Joe steps up to the whiteboard and sketches the drawing in figure 11.2. As Joe finishes, his cell phone rings. He excuses himself and steps outside to take the call.

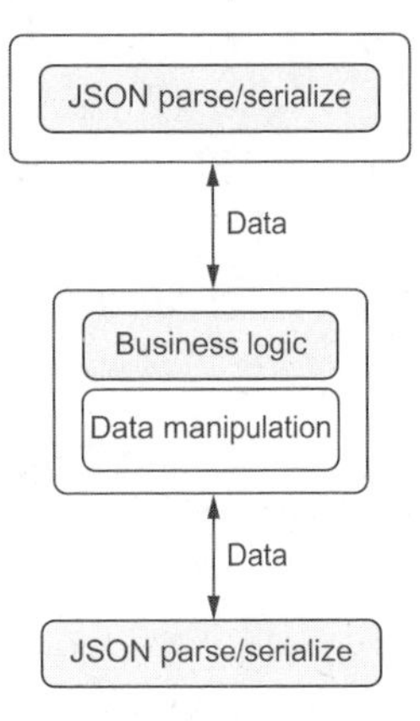

Figure 11.2 The internals of a data-oriented web service

Theo stands alone for a few minutes in front of the whiteboard, meditating about "building the insides of our systems like we build the outsides." Without really noticing it, he takes a marker and starts drawing a new diagram (see figure 11.3), which summarizes the insights that Joe just shared with him.

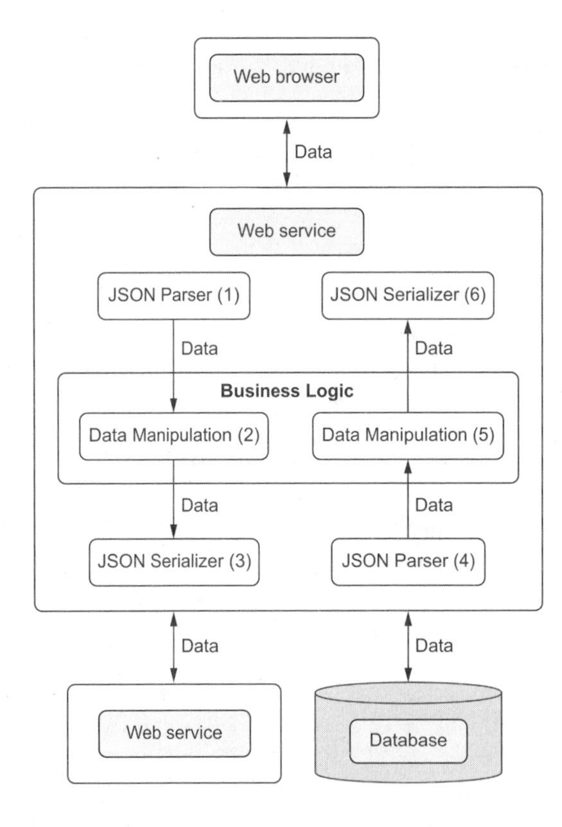

Figure 11.3 Building the insides of our systems like building the outsides. The inner components of a web service communicate with data. As an example, here is a typical flow of a web service handling a client request: (1) Parse the client JSON request into data. (2) Manipulate data according to business logic. (3) Serialize data into a JSON request to a database and another Web service. (4) Parse JSON responses into data. (5) Manipulate data according to business logic. (6) Serialize data into a JSON response to the client.

11.3 Representing a client request as a map

After a few minutes, Joe comes back. When he looks at Theo's new drawing in figure 11.3, he seems satisfied.

Joe Sorry for the interruption. Let's start from the beginning—parsing a client request. How do you usually receive the parameters of a client request?

Theo It depends. The parameters could be sent as URL query parameters in a GET request or as a JSON payload in the body of a POST request.

Joe Let's suppose we receive a JSON payload inside a web request. Can you give me an example of a JSON payload for an advanced search request?

Theo It would contain the text that the book title should match.

Joe And what are the details about the fields to retrieve from the Open Library Books API?

Theo They won't be passed as part of the JSON payload because they're the same for all search requests.

Joe I can imagine a scenario where you want the client to decide what fields to retrieve. For instance, a mobile client would prefer to retrieve only the most important fields and save network bandwidth.

Theo Well, in that case, I would have two different search endpoints: one for mobile and one for desktop.

Joe What about situations where the client wants to display different pieces of information, depending on the application screen. For instance, in an extended search result screen, we display all the fields. In a basic search result screen, we display only the most important fields. Now you have four different use cases: desktop extended, desktop basic, mobile extended, and mobile basic. Would you create four different endpoints?

Theo OK, you've convinced me. Let's have a single search endpoint and let the client decide what fields to retrieve.

Joe Can you show me an example of a JSON payload for a search request?

Theo Sure.

Because there's not much code, Theo writes the search request on the whiteboard. It takes very little time to show how the clients would decide on what fields to retrieve for each search result.

Listing 11.1 Example of the search request payload

```
{
  "title": "habit",
  "fields": ["title", "weight", "number_of_pages"]
}
```

Joe Excellent! Now, the first step is to parse the JSON string into a data structure.

Theo Let me guess, it's going to be a generic data structure.

Joe Of course! In that case, we'll have a map. Usually, JSON parsing is handled by the web server framework, but I'm going to show you how to do it manually.

Theo Wait! What do you mean by the web server framework?

Joe Stuff like Express in Node.js, Spring in Java, Django in Python, Ruby on Rails, ASP.net in C#, and so forth.

Theo Oh, I see. So, how do you manually parse a JSON string into a map?

Joe In JavaScript, we use `JSON.parse`. In Java, we use a third-party library like Gson (https://github.com/google/gson), maintained by Google.

Joe opens his laptop and writes two code fragments, one in JavaScript and the other in Java with Gson. When he's done, he shows the code to Theo.

Listing 11.2 Parsing a JSON string in JavaScript

```
var jsonString =
  '{"title":"habit","fields":["title","weight","number_of_pages"]}';
JSON.parse(jsonString);
```

Listing 11.3 Parsing a JSON string in Java with Gson

```
var jsonString =
  '{"title":"habit","fields":["title","weight","number_of_pages"]}';
gson.fromJson(jsonString, Map.class);
```

Joe Can you write the JSON schema for the payload of a search request?

Theo Sure. It would look something like this.

Listing 11.4 The JSON schema for a search request

```
var searchBooksRequestSchema = {
  "type": "object",
  "properties": {
    "title": {"type": "string"},
    "fields": {
      "type": "array",
      "items": {
        "enum": [
          "title",
          "full_title",
          "subtitle",
          "publisher",
          "publish_date",
          "weight",
          "physical_dimensions",
          "number_of_pages",
          "subjects",
          "publishers",
          "genre"
        ]
      }
    }
  },
  "required": ["title", "fields"]
};
```

Joe Nice! You marked the elements in the `fields` array as enums and not as strings. Where did you get the list of allowed values?

Theo Nancy gave me the list of the fields that she wants to expose to the users. Here, let me show you her list.

Listing 11.5 The important fields from the Open Library Books API

```
- title
- full_title
- subtitle
- publisher
- publish_date
- weight
- physical_dimensions
- number_of_pages
- subjects
- publishers
- genre
```

11.4 Representing a server response as a map

Joe What does the Open Library Books API look like?

Theo It's quite straightforward. We create a GET request with the book ISBN, and it gives us a JSON string with extended information about the book. Take a look at this.

When Theo executes the code snippet, it displays a JSON string with the extended information about *7 Habits of Highly Effective People.*

Listing 11.6 Fetching data from the Open Library Books API

```
fetchAndLog(
  "https://openlibrary.org/isbn/978-1982137274.json"
);
//{
//  "authors": [
//    {
//      "key": "/authors/OL383159A",
//    },
//    {
//      "key": "/authors/OL30179A",
//    },
//    {
//      "key": "/authors/OL1802361A",
//    },
//  ],
//  "created": {
//    "type": "/type/datetime",
//    "value": "2020-08-17T14:26:27.274890",
//  },
//  "full_title": "7 Habits of Highly Effective
//  People : Revised and Updated Powerful
//  Lessons in Personal Change",
```

A utility function that fetches JSON and displays it to the console

```
//   "isbn_13": [
//     "9781982137274",
//   ],
//   "key": "/books/OL28896586M",
//   "languages": [
//     {
//       "key": "/languages/eng",
//     },
//   ],
//   "last_modified": {
//     "type": "/type/datetime",
//     "value": "2021-09-08T19:07:57.049009",
//   },
//   "latest_revision": 3,
//   "lc_classifications": [
//     "",
//   ],
//   "number_of_pages": 432,
//   "publish_date": "2020",
//   "publishers": [
//     "Simon & Schuster, Incorporated",
//   ],
//   "revision": 3,
//   "source_records": [
//     "bwb:9781982137274",
//   ],
//   "subtitle": "Powerful Lessons in Personal Change",
//   "title": "7 Habits of Highly Effective
//   People : Revised and Updated",
//   "type": {
//     "key": "/type/edition",
//   },
//   "works": [
//     {
//       "key": "/works/OL2629977W",
//     },
//   ],
//}
```

Joe Did Nancy ask for any special treatment of the fields returned by the API?

Theo Nothing special besides keeping only the fields I showed you.

Joe That's it?

Theo Yes. For example, here's the JSON string returned by the Open Library Books API for *7 Habits of Highly Effective People* after having kept only the necessary fields.

Listing 11.7 Open Library response for *7 Habits of Highly Effective People*

```
{
  "title":"7 Habits of Highly Effective People : Revised and Updated",
  "subtitle":"Powerful Lessons in Personal Change",
  "number_of_pages":432,
  "full_title":"7 Habits of Highly Effective People : Revised and Updated
```

```
  Powerful Lessons in Personal Change",
  "publish_date":"2020",
  "publishers":["Simon & Schuster, Incorporated"]
}
```

Theo Also, Nancy wants us to keep only the fields that appear in the client request.

Joe Do you know how to implement the double field filtering?

Theo Yeah, I'll parse the JSON string from the API into a hash map, like we parsed a client request, and then I'll use `_.pick` twice to keep only the required fields.

Joe It sounds like a great plan to me. Can you code it, including validating the data that is returned by the Open Library API?

Theo Sure! Let me first write the JSON schema for the Open Library API response.

Theo needs to refresh his memory with the materials about schema composition in order to express the fact that either `isbn_10` or `isbn_13` are mandatory. After a few moments, he shows the JSON schema to Joe.

Listing 11.8 The JSON schema for the Open Library Books API response

```
var basicBookInfoSchema = {
  "type": "object",
  "required": ["title"],
  "properties": {
    "title": {"type": "string"},
    "publishers": {
      "type": "array",
      "items": {"type": "string"}
    },
    "number_of_pages": {"type": "integer"},
    "weight": {"type": "string"},
    "physical_format": {"type": "string"},
    "subjects": {
      "type": "array",
      "items": {"type": "string"}
    },
    "isbn_13": {
      "type": "array",
      "items": {"type": "string"}
    },
    "isbn_10": {
      "type": "array",
      "items": {"type": "string"}
    },
    "publish_date": {"type": "string"},
    "physical_dimensions": {"type": "string"}
  }
};

var mandatoryIsbn13 = {
  "type": "object",
  "required": ["isbn_13"]
};
```

```
var mandatoryIsbn10 = {
  "type": "object",
  "required": ["isbn_10"]
};

var bookInfoSchema = {
  "allOf": [
    basicBookInfoSchema,
    {
      "anyOf": [mandatoryIsbn13, mandatoryIsbn10]
    }
  ]
};
```

Theo Now, assuming that I have a `fetchResponseBody` function that sends a request and retrieves the body of the response as a string, let me code up the how to do the retrieval. Give me a sec.

Theo types away in his IDE for several minutes. He shows the result to Joe.

Listing 11.9 Retrieving book information from the Open Library Books API

```
var ajv = new Ajv({allErrors: true});
class OpenLibraryDataSource {
  static rawBookInfo(isbn) {
    var url = `https://openlibrary.org/isbn/${isbn}.json`;
    var jsonString = fetchResponseBody(url);      <-- Fetches JSON in the body of a response
    return JSON.parse(jsonString);
  }

  static bookInfo(isbn, requestedFields) {
    var relevantFields = ["title", "full_title",
      "subtitle", "publisher",
      "publish_date", "weight",
      "physical_dimensions", "genre",
      "subjects", "number_of_pages"];
    var rawInfo = rawBookInfo(isbn);
    if(!ajv.validate(bookInfoSchema, rawInfo)) {
      var errors = ajv.errorsText(ajv.errors);
      throw "Internal error: Unexpected result from Open Books API: " +
        errors;
    }
    var relevantInfo =
      _.pick(_.pick(rawInfo, relevantFields), requestedFields);
    return  _.set(relevantInfo, "isbn", isbn);
  }
}
```

▶ **NOTE** The JavaScript snippets of this chapter are written as if JavaScript were dealing with I/O in a synchronous way. In real life, we need to use `async` and `await` around I/O calls.

Joe Looks good! But why did you add the `isbn` field to the map returned by `bookInfo`?

Theo It will allow me to combine information from two sources about the same book.

Joe I like it!

11.5 Passing information forward

Joe If I understand it correctly, the program needs to combine two kinds of data: basic book information from the database and extended book information from the Open Library API. How are you going to combine them into a single piece of data in the response to the client?

Theo In traditional OOP, I would create a specific class for each type of book information.

Joe What to you mean?

Theo You know, I'd have classes like `DBBook`, `OpenLibraryBook`, and `CombinedBook`.

Joe Hmm . . .

Theo But that won't work because we decided to go with a dynamic approach, where the client decides what fields should appear in the response.

Joe True, and classes don't bring any added value because we need to pass data forward. Do you know the story of the guy who asked his friend to bring flowers to his fiancée?

Theo No.

Joe takes a solemn position as if to speak before a gathering of peers. With a deep breath, he tells Theo the following story. Entranced, Theo listens carefully.

The story of the guy who asked his friend to bring flowers to his fiancée

A few weeks before their wedding, Hugo wanted to send flowers to Iris, his fiancée, who was on vacation with her family in a neighboring town. Unable to travel because he's needed at work to fix a critical error in a security app, Hugo asks his friend Willy to make the trip and to take the bouquet of flowers to his beloved, accompanied by an envelope containing a love letter that Hugo had written for his fiancée. Willy, having to make the trip anyway, kindly accepts.

Before giving the flowers to Iris, Willy phoned his friend Hugo to let him know that he was about to complete his mission. Hugo's joy was beyond belief until Willy told Hugo how much he admired the quality of his writing style.

Hugo was disappointed. "What! Did you read the letter I wrote to my fiancée?"

"Of course!" answered Willy. "It was necessary to do so in order to fulfill my duty faithfully."

Theo That doesn't make any sense! Why would Willy have to read the letter in order to fulfill his duty?

Joe That's exactly the point of the story! In a sense, traditional OOP is like Hugo's friend, Willy. In order to pass information forward, OOP developers think they need to "open the letter" and represent information with specific classes.

Theo Oh, I see. And DOP developers emulate the spirit of what Hugo expected from a delivery person; they just pass information forward as generic data structures.

Joe Exactly.

Theo That's a subtle but funny analogy.

Joe Let's get back to the question of combining data from the database with data from the Books API. There are two ways to do this—nesting and merging.

Joe goes to the whiteboard. He finds an area to draw table 11.1 for Theo.

Table 11.1 Two ways to combine hash maps

	Advantages	Disadvantages
Nesting	No need to handle conflicts.	Result is not flat.
Merging	Result is flat.	Need to handle conflicts.

Theo How does nesting work?

Joe In nesting, we add a field named `extendedInfo` to the information fetched from the Open Library API.

Theo I see. And what about merging?

Joe In merging, we combine the fields of both maps into a single map.

Theo If there are fields with the same name in both maps, what then?

Joe Then you have a merge conflict, and you need to decide how to handle the conflict. That's the drawback of merging.

▶ **NOTE** When merging maps, we need to think about the occurrences of conflicting fields.

Theo Hopefully, in the context of extended search results, the maps don't have any fields in common.

Joe Then let's merge them!

Theo Would I need to write custom code for merging two maps?

Joe No! As you might remember from one of our previous sessions, Lodash provides a handy `_.merge` function.

▶ **NOTE** `_.merge` was introduced in chapter 5.

Theo Could you refresh my memory?

Joe Sure. Show me an example of maps with data from the database and data from the Open Library Books API, and I'll show you how to merge them.

Theo From the database, we get only two fields: `isbn` and `available`. From the Open Library API, we get six fields. Here's what they look like.

Listing 11.10 A map with book information from the database

```
var dataFromDb = {
  "available": true,
  "isbn": "978-1982137274"
};
```

Listing 11.11 A map with book information from the Open Library Books API

```
var dataFromOpenLib = {
  "title":"7 Habits of Highly Effective People : Revised and Updated",
  "subtitle":"Powerful Lessons in Personal Change",
  "number_of_pages":432,
  "full_title":"7 Habits of Highly Effective People : \
  Revised and Updated Powerful Lessons in Personal Change",
  "publish_date":"2020",
  "publishers":["Simon & Schuster, Incorporated"]
};
```

Joe After calling `_.merge`, the result is a map with fields from both maps.

Listing 11.12 Merging two maps

```
_.merge(dataFromDb, dataFromOpenLib);
//{
//  "available": true,
//  "full_title": "7 Habits of Highly Effective People :\
//  Revised and Updated Powerful Lessons in Personal Change",
//  "isbn": "978-1982137274",
//  "number_of_pages": 432,
//  "publish_date": "2020",
//  "publishers": [ "Simon & Schuster, Incorporated"],
//  "subtitle": "Powerful Lessons in Personal Change",
//  "title": "7 Habits of Highly Effective People : Revised and Updated"
//}
```

Theo Let me code the JSON schema for the search books response. Here's how that would look.

Listing 11.13 JSON schema for search books response

```
var searchBooksResponseSchema = {
  "type": "object",
  "required": ["title", "isbn", "available"],
  "properties": {
    "title": {"type": "string"},
    "available": {"type": "boolean"},
    "publishers": {
      "type": "array",
      "items": {"type": "string"}
    },
    "number_of_pages": {"type": "integer"},
    "weight": {"type": "string"},
```

```
    "physical_format": {"type": "string"},
    "subjects": {
      "type": "array",
      "items": {"type": "string"}
    },
    "isbn": {"type": "string"},
    "publish_date": {"type": "string"},
    "physical_dimensions": {"type": "string"}
  }
};
```

Theo Yes! I think we now have all the pieces to enrich our search results.

11.6 Search result enrichment in action

Joe Can you write the steps of the enrichment data flow?

Theo Sure.

Theo goes to the whiteboard. He takes a moment to gather his thoughts, and then erases enough space so there's room to list the steps.

The steps for the search result enrichment data flow

1. Receive a request from a client.
2. Extract from the client's request the query and the fields to fetch from Open Library.
3. Retrieve from the database the books that match the query.
4. Fetch information from Open Library for each ISBN that match the query.
5. Extract from Open Library responses for the required fields.
6. Combine book information from the database with information from Open Library.
7. Send the response to the client.

Joe Perfect! Would you like to try to implement it?

Theo I think I'll start with the implementation of the book retrieval from the database. It's quite similar to what we did last month.

▶ **NOTE** See chapter 10 for last month's lesson.

Joe Actually, it's even simpler because you don't need to join tables.

Theo That's right, I need values only for the `isbn` and `available` columns.

Theo works for a bit in his IDE. He begins with the book retrieval from the database.

Listing 11.14 Retrieving books whose title matches a query

```
var dbSearchResultSchema = {
  "type": "array",
  "items": {
```

```
    "type": "object",
    "required": ["isbn", "available"],
    "properties": {
      "isbn": {"type": "string"},
      "available": {"type": "boolean"}
    }
  }
};

class CatalogDB {
  static matchingBooks(title)  {
    var matchingBooksQuery = `
SELECT isbn, available
 FROM books
 WHERE title = like '%$1%';
`;
    var books = dbClient.query(catalogDB, matchingBooksQuery, [title]);
    if(!ajv.validate(dbSearchResultSchema, books)) {
      var errors = ajv.errorsText(ajv.errors);
      throw "Internal error: Unexpected result from the database: " +
        errors;
    }
    return books;
  }
}
```

Joe So far, so good . . .

Theo Next, I'll go with the implementation of the retrieval of book information from Open Library for several books. Unfortunately, the Open Library Books API doesn't support querying several books at once. I'll need to send one request per book.

Joe That's a bit annoying. Let's make our life easier and pretend that `_.map` works with asynchronous functions. In real life, you'd need something like `Promise.all` in order to send the requests in parallel and combine the responses.

Theo OK, then it's quite straightforward. I'll take the book retrieval code and add a `multipleBookInfo` function that maps over `bookInfo`.

Theo looks over the book retrieval code in listing 11.9 and then concentrates as he types into his IDE. When he's done, he shows the result in listing 11.15 to Joe.

Listing 11.15 Retrieving book information from Open Library for several books

```
class OpenLibraryDataSource {
  static rawBookInfo(isbn) {
    var url = `https://openlibrary.org/isbn/${isbn}.json`;
    var jsonString = fetchResponseBody(url);
    return JSON.parse(jsonString);
  }

  static bookInfo(isbn, requestedFields) {
    var relevantFields = ["title", "full_title",
      "subtitle", "publisher",
      "publish_date", "weight",
```

```
      "physical_dimensions", "genre",
      "subjects", "number_of_pages"];
    var rawInfo = rawBookInfo(isbn);
    if(!ajv.validate(dbSearchResultSchema, bookInfoSchema)) {
      var errors = ajv.errorsText(ajv.errors);
      throw "Internal error: Unexpected result from Open Books API: " +
        errors;
    }
    var relevantInfo =
      _.pick(_.pick(rawInfo, relevantFields), requestedFields);
    return  _.set(relevantInfo, "isbn", isbn);
  }

  static multipleBookInfo(isbns, fields) {
    return _.map(function(isbn) {
      return bookInfo(isbn, fields);
    }, isbns);
  }
}
```

Joe Nice! Now comes the fun part: combining information from several data sources.

Theo Yeah. I have two arrays in my hands: one with book information from the database and one with book information from Open Library. I somehow need to join the arrays, but I'm not sure I can assume that the positions of the book information are the same in both arrays.

Joe What would you like to have in your hands?

Theo I wish I had two hash maps.

Joe And what would the keys in the hash maps be?

Theo Book ISBNs.

Joe Well, I have good news for you: your wish is granted!

Theo How?

Joe Lodash provides a function named `_.keyBy` that transforms an array into a map.

Theo I can't believe it. Can you show me an example?

Joe Sure. Let's call `_.keyBy` on an array with two books.

Listing 11.16 Transforming an array into a map with `_.keyBy`

```
var books = [
  {
    "title": "7 Habits of Highly Effective People",
    "isbn": "978-1982137274",
    "available": true
  },
  {
    "title": "The Power of Habit",
    "isbn": "978-0812981605",
    "available": false
  }
];

_.keyBy(books, "isbn");
```

Joe And here's the result.

Listing 11.17 The result of keyBy

```
{
  "978-0812981605": {
    "available": false,
    "isbn": "978-0812981605",
    "title": "The Power of Habit"
  },
  "978-1982137274": {
    "available": true,
    "isbn": "978-1982137274",
    "title": "7 Habits of Highly Effective People"
  }
}
```

Theo keyBy is awesome!

Joe Don't exaggerate, my friend; _.keyBy is quite similar to _.groupBy. The only difference is that _.keyBy assumes that there's only one element in each group.

Theo I think that, with _.keyBy, I'll be able to write a generic joinArrays function.

Joe I'm glad to see you thinking in terms of implementing business logic through generic data manipulation functions.

TIP Many parts of the business logic can be implemented through generic data manipulation functions.

Theo The joinArrays function needs to receive the arrays and the field name for which we decide the two elements that need to be combined, for instance, isbn.

Joe Remember, in general, it's not necessarily the same field name for both arrays.

Theo Right, so joinArrays needs to receive four arguments: two arrays and two field names.

Joe Go for it! And, please, write a unit test for joinArrays.

Theo Of course . . .

Theo works for a while and produces the code in listing 11.18. He then types the unit test in listing 11.19.

Listing 11.18 A generic function for joining arrays

```
function joinArrays(a, b, keyA, keyB) {
  var mapA = _.keyBy(a, keyA);
  var mapB = _.keyBy(b, keyB);
  var mapsMerged = _.merge(mapA, mapB);
  return _.values(mapsMerged);
}
```

Listing 11.19 A unit test for `joinArrays`

```
var dbBookInfos = [
  {
    "isbn": "978-1982137274",
    "title": "7 Habits of Highly Effective People",
    "available": true
  },
  {
    "isbn": "978-0812981605",
    "title": "The Power of Habit",
    "available": false
  }
];

var openLibBookInfos = [
  {
    "isbn": "978-0812981605",
    "title": "7 Habits of Highly Effective People",
    "subtitle": "Powerful Lessons in Personal Change",
    "number_of_pages": 432,
  },
  {
    "isbn": "978-1982137274",
    "title": "The Power of Habit",
    "subtitle": "Why We Do What We Do in Life and Business",
    "subjects": [
      "Social aspects",
      "Habit",
      "Change (Psychology)"
    ],
  }
];

var joinedArrays =  [
  {
    "available": true,
    "isbn": "978-1982137274",
    "subjects":  [
      "Social aspects",
      "Habit",
      "Change (Psychology)",
    ],
    "subtitle": "Why We Do What We Do in Life and Business",
    "title": "The Power of Habit",
  },
  {
    "available": false,
    "isbn": "978-0812981605",
    "number_of_pages": 432,
    "subtitle": "Powerful Lessons in Personal Change",
    "title": "7 Habits of Highly Effective People",
  },
]
```

```
_.isEqual(joinedArrays,
  joinArrays(dbBookInfos, openLibBookInfos, "isbn", "isbn"));
```

Joe Excellent! Now, you are ready to adjust the last piece of the extended search result endpoint.

Theo That's quite easy. We fetch data from the database and from Open Library and join them.

Theo works quite rapidly. He then shows Joe the code.

Listing 11.20 Search books and enriched book information

```
class Catalog {
  static enrichedSearchBooksByTitle(searchPayload) {
    if(!ajv.validate(searchBooksRequestSchema, searchPayload)) {
      var errors = ajv.errorsText(ajv.errors);
      throw "Invalid request:" + errors;
    }
    var title = _.get(searchPayload, "title");
    var fields = _.get(searchPayload, "fields");

    var dbBookInfos = CatalogDataSource.matchingBooks(title);
    var isbns = _.map(dbBookInfos, "isbn");

    var openLibBookInfos =
      OpenLibraryDataSource.multipleBookInfo(isbns, fields);

    var res = joinArrays(dbBookInfos, openLibBookInfos);
    if(!ajv.validate(searchBooksResponseSchema, request)) {
      var errors = ajv.errorsText(ajv.errors);
      throw "Invalid response:" + errors;
    }

    return res;
  }
}
```

Now comes the tricky part. Theo takes a few moments to meditate about the simplicity of the code that implements the extended search endpoint. He thinks about how classes are much less complex when we use them only to aggregate stateless functions that operate on similar domain entities and then goes to work plotting the code.

Listing 11.21 Schema for the extended search endpoint (Open Books API part)

```
var basicBookInfoSchema = {
  "type": "object",
  "required": ["title"],
  "properties": {
    "title": {"type": "string"},
    "publishers": {
      "type": "array",
      "items": {"type": "string"}
    },
```

```
    "number_of_pages": {"type": "integer"},
    "weight": {"type": "string"},
    "physical_format": {"type": "string"},
    "subjects": {
      "type": "array",
      "items": {"type": "string"}
    },
    "isbn_13": {
      "type": "array",
      "items": {"type": "string"}
    },
    "isbn_10": {
      "type": "array",
      "items": {"type": "string"}
    },
    "publish_date": {"type": "string"},
    "physical_dimensions": {"type": "string"}
  }
};

var mandatoryIsbn13 = {
  "type": "object",
  "required": ["isbn_13"]
};

var mandatoryIsbn10 = {
  "type": "object",
  "required": ["isbn_10"]
};

var bookInfoSchema = {
  "allOf": [
    basicBookInfoSchema,
    {
      "anyOf": [mandatoryIsbn13, mandatoryIsbn10]
    }
  ]
};
```

Listing 11.22 Extended search endpoint (Open Books API part)

```
var ajv = new Ajv({allErrors: true});

class OpenLibraryDataSource {
  static rawBookInfo(isbn) {
    var url = `https://openlibrary.org/isbn/${isbn}.json`;
    var jsonString = fetchResponseBody(url);
    return JSON.parse(jsonString);
  }

  static bookInfo(isbn, requestedFields) {
    var relevantFields = ["title", "full_title",
      "subtitle", "publisher",
      "publish_date", "weight",
```

```
        "physical_dimensions", "genre",
        "subjects", "number_of_pages"];
    var rawInfo = rawBookInfo(isbn);
    if(!ajv.validate(bookInfoSchema, rawInfo)) {
      var errors = ajv.errorsText(ajv.errors);
      throw "Internal error: Unexpected result from Open Books API: " +
        errors;
    }
    var relevantInfo = _.pick(
      _.pick(rawInfo, relevantFields),
      requestedFields);
    return  _.set(relevantInfo, "isbn", isbn);
  }

  static multipleBookInfo(isbns, fields) {
    return _.map(function(isbn) {
      return bookInfo(isbn, fields);
    }, isbns);
  }
}
```

Listing 11.23 Extended search endpoint (database part)

```
var dbClient;
var dbSearchResultSchema = {
  "type": "array",
  "items": {
    "type": "object",
    "required": ["isbn", "available"],
    "properties": {
      "isbn": {"type": "string"},
      "available": {"type": "boolean"}
    }
  }
};

class CatalogDB {
  static matchingBooks(title)  {
    var matchingBooksQuery = `
SELECT isbn, available
 FROM books
 WHERE title = like '%$1%';
`;
    var books = dbClient.query(catalogDB, matchingBooksQuery, [title]);
    if(!ajv.validate(dbSearchResultSchema, books)) {
      var errors = ajv.errorsText(ajv.errors);
      throw "Internal error: Unexpected result from the database: "
        + errors;
    }

    return books;
  }
}
```

Listing 11.24 Schema for the implementation of the extended search endpoint

```
var searchBooksRequestSchema = {
  "type": "object",
  "properties": {
    "title": {"type": "string"},
    "fields": {
      "type": "array",
      "items": {
        "type": [
          "title",
          "full_title",
          "subtitle",
          "publisher",
          "publish_date",
          "weight",
          "physical_dimensions",
          "number_of_pages",
          "subjects",
          "publishers",
          "genre"
        ]
      }
    }
  },
  "required": ["title", "fields"]
};

var searchBooksResponseSchema = {
  "type": "object",
  "required": ["title", "isbn", "available"],
  "properties": {
    "title": {"type": "string"},
    "available": {"type": "boolean"},
    "publishers": {
      "type": "array",
      "items": {"type": "string"}
    },
    "number_of_pages": {"type": "integer"},
    "weight": {"type": "string"},
    "physical_format": {"type": "string"},
    "subjects": {
      "type": "array",
      "items": {"type": "string"}
    },
    "isbn": {"type": "string"},
    "publish_date": {"type": "string"},
    "physical_dimensions": {"type": "string"}
  }
};
```

Listing 11.25 Schema for the extended search endpoint (combines the pieces)

```
class Catalog {
  static enrichedSearchBooksByTitle(request) {
```

```
    if(!ajv.validate(searchBooksRequestSchema, request)) {
      var errors = ajv.errorsText(ajv.errors);
      throw "Invalid request:" + errors;
    }

    var title = _.get(request, "title");
    var fields = _.get(request, "fields");

    var dbBookInfos = CatalogDataSource.matchingBooks(title);
    var isbns = _.map(dbBookInfos, "isbn");

    var openLibBookInfos =
      OpenLibraryDataSource.multipleBookInfo(isbns, fields);

    var response = joinArrays(dbBookInfos, openLibBookInfos);
    if(!ajv.validate(searchBooksResponseSchema, request)) {
      var errors = ajv.errorsText(ajv.errors);
      throw "Invalid response:" + errors;
    }
    return response;
  }
}

class Library {
  static searchBooksByTitle(payloadBody) {
    var payloadData = JSON.parse(payloadBody);
    var results = Catalog.searchBooksByTitle(payloadData);
    return JSON.stringify(results);
  }
}
```

TIP Classes are much less complex when we use them as a means to aggregate stateless functions that operate on similar domain entities.

Joe interrupts Theo's meditation moment. After looking over the code in the previous listings, he congratulates Theo.

Joe Excellent job, my friend! By the way, after reading *The Power of Habit,* I quit chewing my nails.

Theo Wow! That's terrific! Maybe I should read that book to overcome my habit of drinking too much coffee.

Joe Thanks, and good luck with the coffee habit.

Theo I was supposed to call Nancy later today with an ETA for the Open Library Book milestone. I wonder what her reaction will be when I tell her the feature is ready.

Joe Maybe you should tell her it'll be ready in a week, which would give you time to begin work on the next milestone.

Delivering on time

Joe was right! Theo recalls Joe's story about the young woodcutter and the old man. Theo was able to learn DOP and deliver the project on time! He's pleased that he took the time "to sharpen his saw and commit to a deeper level of practice."

▶ **NOTE** If you are unable to recall the story or if you missed it, check out the opener to part 2.

The Klafim project is a success. Nancy is pleased. Theo's boss is satisfied. Theo got promoted. What more can a person ask for?

Theo remembers his deal with Joe. As he strolls through the stores of the Westfield San Francisco Center to look for a gift for each of Joe's children, Neriah and Aurelia, he is filled with a sense of purpose and great pleasure. He buys a DJI Mavic Air 2 drone for Neriah, and the latest Apple Airpod Pros for Aurelia. He also takes this opportunity to buy a necklace and a pair of earrings for his wife, Jane. It's a way for him to thank her for having endured his long days at work since the beginning of the Klafim project.

▶ **NOTE** The story continues in the opener of part 3.

Summary

- We build the insides of our systems like we build the outsides.
- Components inside a program communicate via data that is represented as immutable data collections in the same way as components communicate via data over the wire.
- In DOP, the inner components of a program are loosely coupled.
- Many parts of business logic can be implemented through *generic* data manipulation functions. We use generic functions to
  - Implement each step of the data flow inside a web service.
  - Parse a request from a client.
  - Apply business logic to the request.
  - Fetch data from external sources (e.g., database and other web services).
  - Apply business logic to the responses from external sources.
  - Serialize response to the client.
- Classes are much less complex when we use them as a means to aggregate together stateless functions that operate on similar domain entities.

Lodash functions introduced in this chapter

Function	Description
`keyBy(coll, f)`	Creates a map composed of keys generated from the results of running each element of `coll` through `f`; the corresponding value for each key is the last element responsible for generating the key.

Part 3

Maintainability

After a month, the Klafim project enters what Alabatross calls the maintenance phase. Small new features need to be added on a weekly basis. Bugs need to be fixed; nothing dramatic. . . .

Monica, Theo's boss, decides to allocate Dave to the maintenance of the Klafim project. It makes sense. Over the last few months, Dave has demonstrated a great attitude of curiosity and interest, and he has solid programming skills. Theo sets up a meeting with Joe and Dave, hoping that Joe will be willing to teach DOP to Dave so that he can continue to advance the good work he's already done on Klafim. Theo and Dave place a conference call to Joe.

Theo Hi, Joe. Will you have time over the next few weeks to teach Dave the principles of DOP?

Joe Yes, but I prefer not to.

Dave Why? Is it because I don't have enough experience in software development? I can guarantee you that I'm a fast learner.

Joe It has nothing to do with your experience, Dave.

Theo Why not then?

Joe Theo, I think that you could be a great mentor for Dave.

Theo But, I don't even know all the parts of DOP!

Dave Come on! No false modesty between us, my friend.

Joe Knowledge is never complete. As the great Socrates used to say, "The more I know, the more I realize I know nothing." I'm confident you will be able to learn the missing parts by yourself and maybe even invent some.

Theo How will I be able to invent missing parts?

Joe You see, DOP is such a simple paradigm that it's fertile material for innovation. Part of the material I taught you I learned from others, and part of it was an invention of mine. If you keep practicing DOP, I'm quite sure you, too, will come up with some inventions of your own.

Theo What do you say Dave? Are you willing to learn DOP from me?

Dave Definitely!

Theo Joe, will you be continue to be available if we need your help from time to time?

Joe Of course!

12 Advanced data validation

A self-made gift

This chapter covers

- Validating function arguments
- Validating function return values
- Data validation beyond static types
- Automatic generation of data model diagrams
- Automatic generation of schema-based unit tests

As the size of a code base grows in a project that follows DOP principles, it becomes harder to manipulate functions that receive and return only generic data. It is hard to figure out the expected shape of the function arguments, and when we pass invalid data, we don't get meaningful errors.

Until now, we have illustrated how to validate data at system boundaries. In this chapter, we will illustrate how to validate data when it flows inside the system by defining data schemas for function arguments and their return values. This allows us to make explicit the expected shape of function arguments, and it eases development. We gain some additional benefits from this endeavor, such as automatic generation of data model diagrams and schema-based unit tests.

12.1 Function arguments validation

Dave's first task is to implement a couple of new HTTP endpoints to download the catalog as a CSV file, search books by author, and rate the books. Once he is done with the tasks, Dave calls Theo for a code review.

▶ **NOTE** The involvement of Dave in the Klafim project is explained in the opener for part 3. Please take a moment to read the opener if you missed it.

Theo Was it difficult to get your head around the DOP code?

Dave Not so much. I read your notes of the meetings with Joe, and I must admit, the code is quite simple to grasp.

Theo Cool!

Dave But there is something that I can't get used to.

Theo What's that?

Dave I'm struggling with the fact that all the functions receive and return generic data. In OOP, I know the expected shape of the arguments for each and every function.

Theo Did you validate data at system boundaries, like I have done?

Dave Absolutely. I defined a data schema for every additional user request, database query, and external service response.

Theo Nice!

Dave Indeed, when the system runs in production, it works well. When data is valid, the data flows through the system, and when data is invalid, we are able to display a meaningful error message to the user.

Theo What's the problem then?

Dave The problem is that during development, it's hard to figure out the expected shape of the function arguments. And when I pass invalid data by mistake, I don't get clear error messages.

Theo I see. I remember that when Joe showed me how to validate data at system boundaries, I raised this concern about the development phase. Joe told me then that we validate data as it flows inside the system exactly like we validate data at system boundaries: we separate between data schema and data representation.

Dave Are we going to use JSON Schema also?

Theo Yes.

Dave Cool. . . . I like JSON Schema.

Theo The main purpose of data validation at system boundaries is to prevent invalid data from getting into the system, whereas the main purpose of data validation inside the system is to make it easier to develop the system. Here, let me draw a table on the whiteboard for you to visualize this (table 12.1).

Table 12.1 Two kinds of data validation

Kind of data validation	Purpose	Environment
Boundaries	Guardian	Production
Inside	Ease of development	Dev

Dave By making it easier to develop the system, do you mean to help the developers understand the expected shape of function arguments as in OOP?

Theo Exactly.

Dave But I'm impatient. . . . Will you help me figure out how to validate the arguments of the function that implements a book search?

Theo Let me see the code of the implementation, and I'll do my best.

Dave We have two implementations of a book search: one where library data lives in memory from the prototype phase and one where library data lives in the database.

Theo I think that the schema for library data in memory is going to be more interesting than the schema for library data in the database, as the book search function receives catalog data in addition to the query.

Dave When you say more interesting data schema, you mean more difficult to write?

Theo More difficult to write, but it's also more insightful.

Dave Then let's go with library data in memory. The code for `Catalog.searchBooksByTitle` from the prototype phase would look like this.

Dave pulls up some code on his laptop. He shows it to Theo.

Listing 12.1 The implementation of search without data validation

```
class Catalog {
  static authorNames(catalogData, book) {
    var authorIds = _.get(book, "authorIds");
    var names = _.map(authorIds, function(authorId) {
      return _.get(catalogData, ["authorsById", authorId, "name"]);
    });
    return names;
  }

  static bookInfo(catalogData, book) {
    var bookInfo = {
      "title": _.get(book, "title"),
      "isbn": _.get(book, "isbn"),
      "authorNames": Catalog.authorNames(catalogData, book)
    };
    return bookInfo;
  }

  static searchBooksByTitle(catalogData, query) {
    var allBooks = _.get(catalogData, "booksByIsbn");
    var matchingBooks = _.filter(allBooks, function(book) {
      return _.get(book, "title").includes(query);
    });
    var bookInfos = _.map(matchingBooks, function(book) {
      return Catalog.bookInfo(catalogData, book);
    });
    return bookInfos;
  }
}
```

Theo Dave, please remind me of the expected shapes for `catalogData` and `query`.

Dave Sure. `query` should be a string, and `catalogData` should be a map that conforms to the catalog data model.

Theo What is the catalog data model?

Dave Let me see. I have seen a diagram of it somewhere.

Dave rummages around a bit in his folder for Klafim's Library Management System. Finding what he's looking for, he draws the diagram in figure 12.1 on the whiteboard.

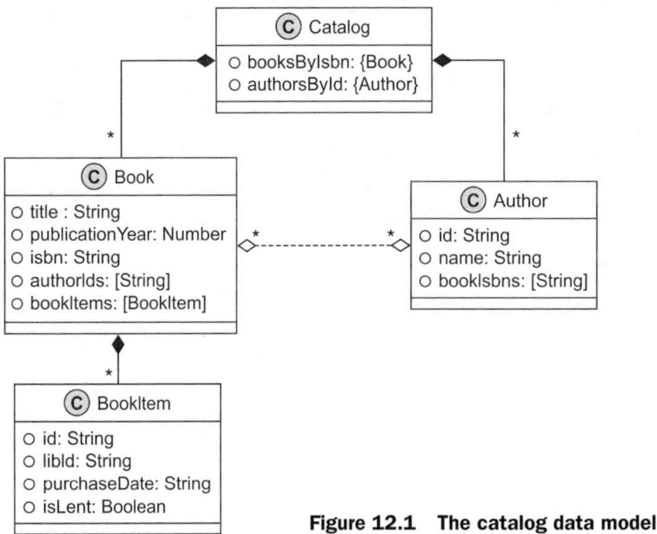

Figure 12.1 The catalog data model

▶ **NOTE** The schemas for this book use JSON Schema version 2020-12.

Theo Can you write a JSON Schema for the catalog data model?

Dave Am I allowed to use internal variables for book and author schemas, or do I have to nest all the schemas inside the catalog schema?

Theo JSON Schema is part of the code. If you feel that using internal variables would make the code more readable, go for it.

Dave OK. Now I need the JSON Schema gift that Joe gave you.

Theo picks up a well-worn piece of paper that is a bit torn and quite wrinkled. He gives Dave the JSON Schema cheat sheet.

Listing 12.2 JSON Schema cheat sheet

```
{
  "type": "array",                 // At the root level, data is an array.
  "items": {
    "type": "object",              // Each element of the array is a map.
    "properties": {                // The properties of each field in the map
```

```
      "myNumber": {"type": "number"},     ◁ myNumber is a number.
      "myString": {"type": "string"},     ◁ myString is a string.
      "myEnum": {"enum": ["myVal", "yourVal"]},     ◁ myEnum is an enumeration value with two possibilities, "myVal" and "yourVal".
      "myBool": {"type": "boolean"}     ◁ myBool is a boolean.
    },
    "required": ["myNumber", "myString"],     ◁ The mandatory fields in the map are myNumber and myString. Other fields are optional.
    "additionalProperties": false     ◁ We don't allow fields that are not explicitly mentioned in the schema.
  }
}
```

Dave I think I'll start with the author schema. It seems simpler than the book schema.

Quickly composing the code, Dave shows Theo the author schema. Dave, still new to DOP, looks for Theo's reaction.

Listing 12.3 The author schema

```
var authorSchema = {
  "type": "object",
  "required": ["id", "name", "bookIsbns"],
  "properties": {
    "id": {"type": "string"},
    "name": {"type": "string"},
    "bookIsbns": {
      "type": "array",
      "items": {"type": "string"}
    }
  }
};
```

Theo Well done! Let's move on to the book schema now.

Dave I think I am going to store the book item schema in a variable.

Listing 12.4 The book item schema

```
var bookItemSchema = {
  "type": "object",
  "properties":{
    "id": {"type": "string"},
    "libId": {"type": "string"},
    "purchaseDate": {"type": "string"},
    "isLent": {"type": "boolean"}
  },
  "required": ["id", "libId", "purchaseDate", "isLent"]
};

var bookSchema = {
  "type": "object",
  "required": ["title", "isbn", "authorIds", "bookItems"],
  "properties": {
    "title": {"type": "string"},
    "publicationYear": {"type": "integer"},
```

```
    "isbn": {"type": "string"},
    "authorIds": {
      "type": "array",
      "items": {"type": "string"}
    },
    "bookItems": {
      "type": "array",
      "items": bookItemSchema
    }
  }
};
```

TIP When you define a complex data schema, it is advisable to store nested schemas in variables to make the schemas easier to read.

Theo Why didn't you include `publicationYear` in the list of required fields in the book schema?

Dave Because, for some books, the publication year is missing. Unlike in OOP, it will then be easy to deal with nullable fields.

Theo Excellent! And now, please tackle the final piece, the catalog schema.

Dave Here I have a problem. The catalog should be a map with two fields, `booksByIsbn` and `authorsById`. Both values should be indexes, represented in the model diagram with curly braces. I have no idea how to define the schema for an index.

Theo Do you remember how we represent indexes in DOP?

Dave Yes, indexes are represented as maps.

Theo Right, and what's the difference between those maps and the maps that we use for records?

Dave For records, we use maps where the names of the fields are known and the values can have different shapes. For indexes, we use maps where the names of the fields are unknown and the values have a common shape.

Theo Right. We call the maps for records heterogeneous maps and the maps for indexes homogeneous maps.

TIP In DOP, records are represented as *heterogeneous maps*, whereas indexes are represented as *homogeneous maps*.

Dave Then how do we define the schema of an homogeneous map in JSON Schema?

Theo I don't know. Let's check the JSON Schema online documentation.

▶ **NOTE** See https://json-schema.org/ to access the online documentation for JSON Schema version 2020-12.

After a couple of minutes of digging into the JSON Schema online documentation, Theo finds a piece about `additionalProperties`. He studies the information for a while before making up his mind.

Theo I think we could use `additionalProperties`. Here's the JSON Schema for an homogeneous map where the values are numbers.

Listing 12.5 The JSON Schema for an homogeneous map with values as numbers

```
{
  "type": "object",
  "additionalProperties": {"type": "number"}
}
```

Dave I thought that `additionalProperties` was supposed to be a boolean and that it was used to allow or forbid properties not mentioned in the schema.

Theo That's correct. Usually `additionalProperties` is a boolean, but the documentation says it could also be a map that defines a schema. In that case, it means properties not mentioned in the schema should have the value of the schema associated with `additionalProperties`.

Dave I see. But what does that have to do with homogeneous maps?

Theo Well, a homogeneous map could be seen as a map with no predefined properties, where all the additional properties are of an expected type.

Dave Tricky!

TIP In JSON Schema, homogeneous string maps have `type: object` with no `properties` and `additionalProperties` associated to a schema.

Theo Indeed. Now, let me show you what the catalog schema looks like.

Theo types briefly on his laptop. He shows Dave the catalog schema.

Listing 12.6 The schema for catalog data

```
var catalogSchema = {
  "type": "object",
  "properties": {
    "booksByIsbn": {
      "type": "object",
      "additionalProperties": bookSchema
    },
    "authorsById": {
      "type": "object",
      "additionalProperties": authorSchema
    }
  },
  "required": ["booksByIsbn", "authorsById"]
};
```

Dave Are we ready to plug the catalog and the query schema into the `Catalog.searchBooksByTitle` implementation?

Theo We could, but I think we can do better by defining a single schema that combines both the catalog and query schemas.

Dave How would we combine two schemas into a single schema?

Theo Do you know what a tuple is?

Dave I think I know, but I can't define it formally.

Theo A tuple is an array where the size is fixed, and the elements can be of different shapes.

Dave OK. So, how do we define tuples in JSON Schema?

Once again, Theo explores the JSON Schema online documentation. Fortunately, he has bookmarked the page, and in no time at all, finds the information he needs.

Theo I found it! We use `prefixItems` in the definition of a tuple made of a string and a number, for instance.

Theo types more code on his laptop. When he finishes, he shows Dave the schema for a tuple.

Listing 12.7 The schema for a tuple made of a string and a number

```
{
  "type": "array",
  "prefixItems": [
    { "type": "string" },
    { "type": "number" }
  ]
}
```

Dave I see. And how would you define the schema for the arguments of `Catalog.searchBooksByTitle`?

Theo Well, it's a tuple of size 2, where the first element is a catalog and the second element is a string.

Dave Something like this schema?

Listing 12.8 The schema for the arguments of `Catalog.searchBooksByTitle`

```
var searchBooksArgsSchema = {
  "type": "array",
  "prefixItems": [
    catalogSchema,
    { "type": "string" },
  ]
};
```

Theo Exactly!

Dave Now that we have the schema for the arguments, how do we plug it into the implementation of search books?

Theo That's similar to the way we validate data at system boundaries. The main difference is that the data validation for data that flows inside the system should run only at development time, and it should be disabled when the code runs in production.

Dave Why?

Theo Because that data has been already validated up front at a system boundary. Validating it again on a function call is superfluous, and it would impact performance.

Dave When you say development time, does that include testing and staging environments?

Theo Yes, all the environments besides production.

Dave I see. It's like assertions in Java. They are disabled in production code.

TIP Data validation inside the system should be disabled in production.

Theo Exactly. For now, I am going to assume that we have a `dev` function that returns `true` when the code runs in the development environment and `false` when it runs in production. Having said that, take a look at this code.

Listing 12.9 Implementation of search with validation of function arguments

```
Catalog.searchBooksByTitle = function(catalogData, query) {
  if(dev()) {
    var args = [catalogData, query];
    if(!ajv.validate(searchBooksArgsSchema, args)) {
      var errors = ajv.errorsText(ajv.errors);
      throw ("searchBooksByTitle called with invalid arguments: " +
        errors);
    }
  }

  var allBooks = _.get(catalogData, "booksByIsbn");
  var matchingBooks = _.filter(allBooks, function(book) {
    return _.get(book, "title").includes(query);
  });
  var bookInfos = _.map(matchingBooks, function(book) {
    return Catalog.bookInfo(catalogData, book);
  });

  return bookInfos;
};
```

The implementation of dev() depends on the run-time environment: it returns true when the code runs in dev environments and false when it runs in production.

Dave Do you think we should validate the arguments of all the functions?

Theo No. I think we should treat data validation like we treat unit tests. We should validate function arguments only for functions for whom we would write unit tests.

TIP Treat data validation like unit tests.

12.2 Return value validation

Dave Do you think it would make sense to also validate the return value of functions?

Theo Absolutely.

Dave Cool. Let me try to write the JSON Schema for the return value of `Catalog.searchBooksByTitle`.

After a few minutes, Dave comes up with the schema. Taking a deep breath, then releasing it, he shows the code to Theo.

Listing 12.10 The schema for the return value of `Catalog.searchBooksByTitle`

```
var searchBooksResponseSchema = {
  "type": "array",
  "items": {
    "type": "object",
    "required": ["title", "isbn", "authorNames"],
    "properties": {
      "title": {"type": "string"},
      "isbn": {"type": "string"},
      "authorNames": {
        "type": "array",
        "items": {"type": "string"}
      }
    }
  }
};
```

Theo Well done! Now, would you like to try adding return value validation to the code of `Catalog.searchBooksByTitle`?

Dave Sure.

Dave works for a bit in his IDE. A bit more confident this time, he shows the result to Theo.

Listing 12.11 Search with data validation for both input and output

```
Catalog.searchBooksByTitle = function(catalogData, query) {
  if(dev()) {
    if(!ajv.validate(searchBooksArgsSchema, [catalogData, query])) {
      var errors = ajv.errorsText(ajv.errors);
      throw ("searchBooksByTitle called with invalid arguments: " +
        errors);
    }
  }

  var allBooks = _.get(catalogData, "booksByIsbn");
  var matchingBooks = _.filter(allBooks, function(book) {
    return _.get(book, "title").includes(query);
  });
  var bookInfos = _.map(matchingBooks, function(book) {
    return Catalog.bookInfo(catalogData, book);
  });

  if(dev()) {
    if(!ajv.validate(searchBooksResponseSchema, bookInfos)) {
      var errors = ajv.errorsText(ajv.errors);
      throw ("searchBooksByTitle returned an invalid value: " +
        errors);
    }
  }
```

```
  return bookInfos;
};
```

Theo Excellent! Now we need to figure out how to deal with advanced data validation.

12.3 Advanced data validation

Dave What do you mean by advanced data validation?

Theo I mean going beyond static types.

Dave Could you give me an example?

Theo Sure. Take, for instance, the publication year of a book. It's an integer, but what else could you say about this number?

Dave It has to be positive. It would say it's a positive integer.

Theo Come on, Dave! Be courageous, go beyond types.

Dave I don't know. I would say it's a number that should be higher than 1900. I don't think it makes sense to have a book that is published before 1900.

Theo Exactly. And what about the higher limit?

Dave I'd say that the publication year should be less than the current year.

Theo Very good! I see that JSON Schema supports number ranges. Here is how we can write the schema for an integer that represents a year and should be between 1900 and 2021.

Listing 12.12 The schema for an integer between 1900 and 2021

```
var publicationYearSchema = {
  "type": "integer",
  "minimum": 1900,
  "maximum": 2021
};
```

Dave Why isn't this kind of data validation possible in OOP?

Theo I'll let you think about that for a moment.

Dave I think have it! In DOP, data validation is executed at run time, while static type validation in OOP is executed at compile time. At compile time, we only have information about static types; at run time, we have the data itself. That's why in DOP data validation, it's possible to go beyond types.

▶ **NOTE** Of course, it's also possible in traditional OOP to write custom run-time data validation. Here, though, we are comparing data schema with static types.

Theo You got it! Now, let me show you how to write the schema for a string that should match a regular expression.

▶ **NOTE** See http://mng.bz/OGNP for the JavaScript Guide to regular expressions.

Theo Let's take for example the book ID. I am assuming it must be a UUID.

Dave Right.

Theo Can you write the regular expression for a valid UUID?

Dave googles "UUID regex" and finds something he thinks just might work. He shows the regular expression to Theo.

Listing 12.13 The regular expression for a valid UUID

```
[0-9a-fA-F]{8}-[0-9a-fA-F]{4}-[0-9a-fA-F]{4}-[0-9a-fA-F]{4}-[0-9a-fA-F]{12}
```

Dave Now, how do we plug a regular expression into a JSON Schema?

Theo While you were looking for the UUID regular expression, I read about the `pattern` field. Here's how we can plug the UUID regular expression into a JSON Schema.

Listing 12.14 The schema for a UUID

```
var uuidSchema = {
  "type": "string",
  "pattern": "[0-9a-fA-F]{8}-[0-9a-fA-F]{4}-[0-9a-fA-F]{4}" +
    "-[0-9a-fA-F]{4}-[0-9a-fA-F]{12}"
};
```

Dave Nice! Let me improve the catalog schema and refine the schema for `purchaseDate`, `isbn`, `libId`, and `authorId` with regular expressions.

Theo Before you do that, though, let me tell you something I read about regular expressions: some of them are predefined. For example, there is a predefined regular expression for dates.

Dave How does it work?

Theo With the help of the `format` field.

▶ **NOTE** According to JSON Schema specification, `format` is just for annotation and doesn't affect validation. But in practice, JSON Schema validation libraries use `format` also for validation.

Theo moves to his laptop. He inputs the schema for a date and shows it to Dave.

Listing 12.15 The schema for a date

```
{
  "type": "string",
  "format": "date"
}
```

TIP In DOP, data validation goes beyond static types (e.g., number ranges, regular expressions, and so on).

Dave Very cool! Do I have all the information I need in order to refine the catalog schema?

Theo Yes, go for it!

It takes Dave a bit of time to write the regular expressions for `isbn`, `authorId`, and `libId`. But with the help of Google (again) and a bit of simplification, Dave comes up with the schema in listings 12.16 and 12.17.

Listing 12.16 The refined schema of the catalog data (Part 1)

```
var isbnSchema = {
  "type": "string",
  "pattern": "^[0-9-]{10,20}$"
};

var libIdSchema = {
  "type": "string",
  "pattern": "^[a-z0-9-]{3,20}$"
};

var authorIdSchema ={
  "type": "string",
  "pattern": "[a-z-]{2,50}"
};

var bookItemSchema = {
  "type": "object",
  "additionalProperties": {
    "id": uuidSchema,
    "libId": libIdSchema,
    "purchaseDate": {
      "type": "string",
      "format": "date"
    },
    "isLent": {"type": "boolean"}
  }
};
```

Listing 12.17 The refined schema of the catalog data (Part 2)

```
var bookSchema = {
  "type": "object",
  "required": ["title", "isbn", "authorIds", "bookItems"],
  "properties": {
    "title": {"type": "string"},
    "publicationYear": publicationYearSchema,
    "isbn": isbnSchema,
    "publisher": {"type": "string"},
    "authorIds": {
      "type": "array",
      "items": authorIdSchema
    },
    "bookItems": bookItemSchema
  }
};

var authorSchema = {
  "type": "object",
  "required": ["id", "name", "bookIsbns"],
  "properties": {
    "id": {"type": "string"},
    "name": {"type": "string"},
```

```
      "bookIsbns": {
        "items": isbnSchema
      }
    }
};

var catalogSchema = {
  "type": "object",
  "properties": {
    "booksByIsbn": {
      "type": "object",
      "additionalProperties": bookSchema
    },
    "authorsById": {
      "type": "object",
      "additionalProperties": authorSchema
    }
  },
  "required": ["booksByIsbn", "authorsById"]
};
```

12.4 Automatic generation of data model diagrams

Before going home, Theo phones Joe to tell him about how he and Dave used data validation inside the system. Joe tells Theo that that's exactly how he recommends doing it and suggests he come and visit Theo and Dave at the office tomorrow. He wants to show them some cool advanced stuff related to data validation. The next day, with coffee in hand, Joe starts the discussion.

Joe Are you guys starting to feel the power of data validation à la DOP?

Dave Yes, it's a bit less convenient to validate a JSON Schema than it is to write the class of function arguments, but this drawback is compensated by the fact that JSON Schema supports conditions that go beyond static types.

Theo We also realized that we don't have to validate data for each and every function.

Joe Correct. Now, let me show you another cool thing that we can do with JSON Schema.

Dave What's that?

Joe Generate a data model diagram.

Dave Wow! How does that work?

Joe There are tools that receive a JSON Schema as input and produce a diagram in a data model format.

Dave What is a data model format?

Joe It's a format that allows you to define a data model in plain text. After that, you can generate an image from the text. My favorite data format is PlantUML.

▶ **NOTE** For more on PlantUML, see https://plantuml.com/.

Dave Do you know of other tools that generate data model diagrams?

Joe I have used JSON Schema Viewer and Malli.

▶ **NOTE** You can find information on the JSON Schema Viewer at https://navneethg.github.io/jsonschemaviewer/ and on Malli at https://github.com/metosin/malli.

Joe shows Dave and Theo the PlantUML diagram that Malli generated (listing 12.18) from the catalog schema in listings 12.16 and 12.17.

Listing 12.18 A PlantUML diagram generated from the catalog data schema

```
@startuml

Entity1     *--  Entity2
Entity1     *--  Entity4

Entity2        *-- Entity3


class Entity1 {
  + booksByIsbn: {Entity2}
  + authorsById: {Entity4}
}

class Entity2 {
  + title : String
    + publicationYear: Number
    + isbn: String
    + authorIds: [String]
    + bookItems: [Entity3]
}

class Entity3 {
  + id: String
    + libId: String
    + purchaseDate: String
    + isLent: Boolean
}

class Entity4 {
  + id: String
    + name: String
    + bookIsbns: [String]
}

@enduml
```

Dave Is it possible to visualize this diagram?

Joe Absolutely. Let me copy and paste the diagram text into the PlantText online tool.

▶ **NOTE** See https://www.planttext.com/ for more on the PlantText online tool.

Dave opens his web browser and types the URL for PlantText. After copying and pasting the text, he steps aside so that Theo and Dave can view the diagram that looks like the image in figure 12.2.

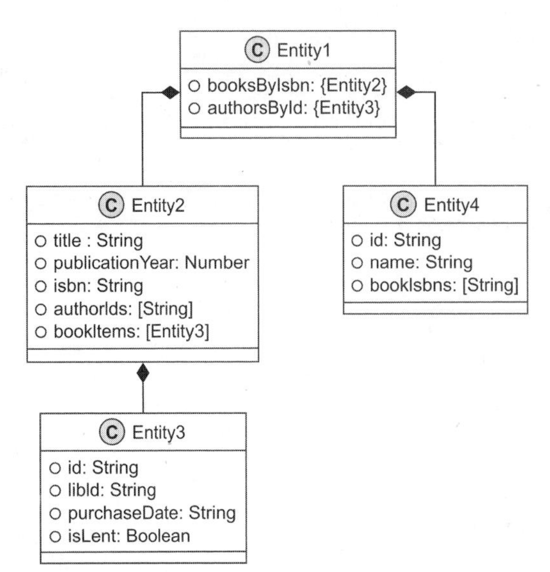

Figure 12.2 A visualization of the PlantUML diagram generated from the catalog data schema

Dave That's cool! But why are the diagram entities named `Entity1`, `Entity2`, and so on?

Joe Because in JSON Schema, there's no way to give a name to a schema. Malli has to autogenerate random names for you.

Theo Also, I see that the extra information we have in the schema, like the number range for `publicationYear` and string regular expression for `isbn`, is missing from the diagram.

Joe Right, that extra information is not part of the data model. That's why it's not included in the generated data model diagram.

Dave Anyway, it's very cool!

Joe If you guys like the data model generation feature, I'm sure you're going to like the next feature.

Dave What's it about?

Joe Automatic generation of unit tests.

Theo Wow, sounds exciting!

12.5 Automatic generation of schema-based unit tests

Joe Once you've defined a data schema for function arguments and for its return value, it's quite simple to generate a unit test for this function.

Dave How?

Joe Well, think about it. What's the essence of a unit test for a function?

Dave A unit test calls a function with some arguments and checks whether the function returns the expected value.

Joe Exactly! Now, let's adapt it to the context of data schema and DOP. Let's say you have a function with a schema for their arguments and for their return value.

Dave OK.

Joe Here's the flow of a schema-based unit test. We call the function with random arguments that conform to the schema of the function arguments. Then, we check whether the function returns a value that conforms to the schema of the return value. Here, let me diagram it.

Joe goes to the whiteboard. He draws the diagram in figure 12.3.

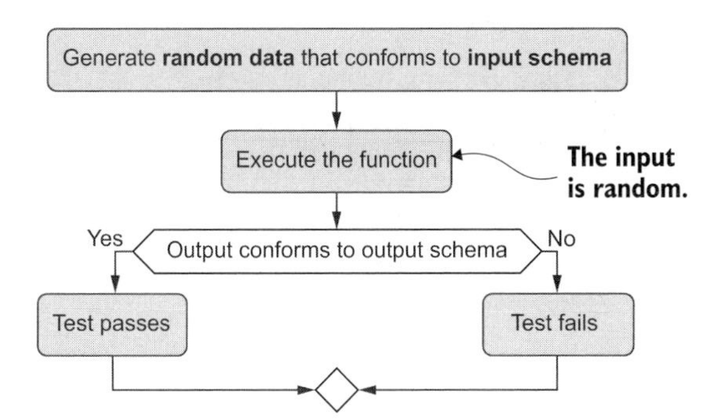

Figure 12.3 The flow of a schema-based unit test

Dave How do you generate random data that conforms to a schema?

Joe Using a tool like JSON Schema Faker. For example, let's start with a simple schema: the schema for a UUID. Let me show you how to generate random data that conforms to the schema.

▶ **NOTE** You'll find more information about JSON Schema Faker at https://github.com/json-schema-faker/json-schema-faker.

Joe types on the keyboard for a bit. He then shows the code to generate random data to Dave and Theo.

Listing 12.19 Generating random data that conforms to a UUID schema

```
var uuidSchema = {
  "type": "string",
  "pattern": "[0-9a-fA-F]{8}-[0-9a-fA-F]{4}-[0-9a-fA-F]{4}" +
    "-[0-9a-fA-F]{4}-[0-9a-fA-F]{12}"
};

JSONSchemaFaker.generate(uuidSchema);
// → "7aA8CdF3-14DF-9EF5-1A19-47dacdB16Fa9"
```

Dave executes the code snippet a couple of times, and indeed, on each evaluation, it returns a different UUID.

Dave Very cool! Let me see how it works with more complex schemas like the catalog schema.

When Dave calls `JSONSchemaFaker.generate` with the catalog schema, he gets some quite long random data. He's a bit surprised by the results.

Listing 12.20 Generating random data that conforms to the catalog schema

```
{
  "booksByIsbn": {
    "Excepteur7": {
      "title": "elit veniam anim",
      "isbn": "5419903-3563-7",
      "authorIds": [
        "vfbzqahmuemgdegkzntfhzcjhjrbgfoljfzogfuqweggchum",
        "inxmqh-",
      ],
      "bookItems": {
        "ullamco5": {
          "id": "f7dac8c3-E59D-bc2E-7B33-C27F3794E2d6",
          "libId": "4jtbj7q7nrylfu114m",
          "purchaseDate": "2001-08-01",
          "isLent": false
        },
        "culpa_3e": {
          "id": "423DCdDF-CDAe-2CAa-f956-C6cd9dA8054b",
          "libId": "6wcxbh",
          "purchaseDate": "1970-06-24",
          "isLent": true
        }
      },
      "publicationYear": 1930,
      "publisher": "sunt do nisi"
    },
    "aliquip_d7": {
      "title": "aute",
      "isbn": "348782167518177",
      "authorIds": ["owfgtdxjbiidsobfgvjpjlxuabqpjhdcqmmmrjb-ezrsz-u"],
      "bookItems": {
        "ipsum__0b": {
          "id": "6DfE93ca-DB23-5856-56Fd-82Ab8CffEFF5",
          "libId": "bvjh0p2p2666vs7dd",
          "purchaseDate": "2018-03-30",
          "isLent": false
        }
      },
      "publisher": "ea anim ut ex id",
      "publicationYear": 1928
    }
  },
  "authorsById": {
    "labore_b88": {
      "id": "adipisicing nulla proident",
      "name": "culpa in minim",
      "bookIsbns": [
        "6243029--7",
        "5557199424742986"
      ]
```

```
    },
    "ut_dee": {
      "id": "Lorem officia culpa qui in",
      "name": "aliquip eiusmod",
      "bookIsbns": [
        "0661-8-5772"
      ]
    }
  }
}
```

Joe I see that you have some bugs in your regular expressions.

Theo How can you see that?

Joe Some of the generated ISBNs don't seem to be valid ISBNs.

Dave You're right. I hate regular expressions!

Joe Dave, I don't think you're the only one with that sentiment. Let me show you how to implement the flow of a schema-based unit test for `Catalog.searchBooksByTitle`.

Listing 12.21 Implementation of the flow of a schema-based unit test

```
function searchBooksTest () {
  var catalogRandom = JSONSchemaFaker.generate(catalogSchema);
  var queryRandom = JSONSchemaFaker.generate({ "type": "string" });
  Catalog.searchBooksByTitle(catalogRandom, queryRandom);
}
```

Dave Wait a moment. I can't see where you check that `Catalog.searchBooksByTitle` returns a value that conforms to the return value schema.

Theo If you look closer at the code, you'll see it.

Dave takes a closer look at the code for `Catalog.searchBooksByTitle`. Now he sees it.

Listing 12.22 The implementation of `Catalog.searchBooksByTitle`

```
Catalog.searchBooksByTitle = function(catalogData, query) {
  if(dev()) {
    if(!ajv.validate(searchBooksArgsSchema, [catalogData, query])) {
      var errors = ajv.errorsText(ajv.errors);
      throw ("searchBooksByTitle called with invalid arguments: " +
        errors);
    }
  }

  var allBooks = _.get(catalogData, "booksByIsbn");
  var matchingBooks = _.filter(allBooks, function(book) {
    return _.get(book, "title").includes(query);
  });
  var bookInfos = _.map(matchingBooks, function(book) {
    return Catalog.bookInfo(catalogData, book);
  });
```

```
  if(dev()) {
    if(!ajv.validate(searchBooksResponseSchema, bookInfos)) {
      var errors = ajv.errorsText(ajv.errors);
      throw ("searchBooksByTitle returned an invalid value: " +
        errors);
    }
  }
  return bookInfos;
};
```

Dave Of course! It's in the code of `Catalog.searchBooksByTitle`. If the return value doesn't conform to the schema, it throws an exception, and the test fails.

Joe Correct. Now, let's improve the code of our unit test and return `false` when an exception occurs inside `Catalog.searchBooksByTitle`.

Joe edits the test code. He shows his changes to Theo and Dave.

Listing 12.23 A complete data schema-based unit test for search books

```
function searchBooksTest () {
  var catalogRandom = JSONSchemaFaker.generate(catalogSchema);
  var queryRandom = JSONSchemaFaker.generate({ "type": "string" });
  try {
    Catalog.searchBooksByTitle(catalogRandom, queryRandom);
    return true;
  } catch (error) {
    return false;
  }
}
```

Dave Let me see what happens when I run the test.

Joe Before we run it, we need to fix something in your unit test.

Dave What?

Joe The catalog data and the query are random. There's a good chance that no books will match the query. We need to create a query that matches at least one book.

Dave How are we going to find a query that's guaranteed to match at least one book?

Joe Our query will be the first letter of the first book from the catalog data that is generated.

Joe types for a bit and shows Theo and Dave his refined test. They are delighted that Joe is taking the time to fix their unit test.

Listing 12.24 A refined data schema-based unit test for search books

```
function searchBooksTest () {
  var catalogRandom = JSONSchemaFaker.generate(catalogSchema);
  var queryRandom = JSONSchemaFaker.generate({ "type": "string" });
  try {
    var firstBook = _.values(_.get(catalogRandom, "booksByIsbn"))[0];
```

```
    var query = _.get(firstBook, "title").substring(0,1);
    Catalog.searchBooksByTitle(catalogRandom, query);
    return true;
  } catch (error) {
    return false;
  }
}
```

Dave I see. It's less complicated than what I thought. Does it happen often that you need to tweak the random data?

Joe No, usually the random data is just fine.

Dave OK, now I'm curious to see what happens when I execute the unit test.

When Dave executes the unit test, it fails. His expression is one of bewilderment. Theo is just astonished.

Listing 12.25 Running the schema-based unit test

```
searchBooksTest();
// → false
```

Dave I think something's wrong in the code of the unit test.

Theo Maybe the unit test caught a bug in the implementation of `Catalog.searchBooksByTitle`.

Dave Let's check it out. Is there a way to have the unit test display the return value of the function?

Joe Yes, here it is.

Joe once again turns to his laptop to update the code. He shows the others his new unit test that includes the return value for `Catalog.searchBooksByTitle`.

Listing 12.26 Including the return value in the unit test output

```
function searchBooksTest () {
  var catalogRandom = JSONSchemaFaker.generate(catalogSchema);
  var queryRandom = JSONSchemaFaker.generate({ "type": "string" });
  try {
    var firstBook = _.values(_.get(catalogRandom, "booksByIsbn"))[0];
    var query = _.get(firstBook, "title").substring(0,1);
    Catalog.searchBooksByTitle(catalogRandom, query);
    return true;
  } catch (error) {
    console.log(error);
    return false;
  }
}
```

Dave Now, let's see what's displayed when I again run the unit test.

Listing 12.27 Running the schema-based unit test again

```
searchBooksTest();
// → searchBooksByTitle returned a value that doesn\'t conform to schema:
//   data[0].authorNames[0] should be string,
//   data[0].authorNames[1] should be string,
//   data[1].authorNames[0] should be string
```

Dave I think I understand what happened. In our random catalog data, the authors of the books are not present in the `authorByIds` index. That's why we have all those `undefined`s in the values returned by `Catalog.searchBooksByTitle`, whereas in the schema, we expect a string.

Theo How do we fix that?

Dave Simple. Have `Catalog.authorNames` return the string `Not available` when an author doesn't exist in the catalog. Maybe something like this.

Listing 12.28 Fixing a bug in the search books implementation

```
Catalog.authorNames = function(catalogData, book) {
  var authorIds = _.get(book, "authorIds");
  var names = _.map(authorIds, function(authorId) {
    return _.get(catalogData,
      ["authorsById", authorId, "name"],
      "Not available");
  });
  return names;
};
```

When no value is associated with the key ["authorsById", authorId, "name"], we return "Not available".

Dave executes the unit test again. Thankfully, this time it passes.

Listing 12.29 Running the schema-based unit test again

```
searchBooksTest();
// → true
```

Joe Well done, Dave!

Dave You were right. The automatically generated unit tests were able to catch a bug in the implementation of `Catalog.searchBooksByTitle`.

Joe Don't worry. The same thing has happened to me so many times.

Dave Data validation à la DOP is really cool!

Joe That's just the beginning, my friend. The more you use it, the more you love it!

Dave I must admit, I still miss one cool IDE feature from OOP.

Joe Which one?

Dave The autocompletion of field names in a class.

Joe For the moment, field name autocompletion for data is only available in Clojure via clj-kondo and the integration it provides with Malli.

▶ **NOTE** See https://github.com/clj-kondo/clj-kondo and https://github.com/metosin/malli for the autocompletion feature provided by clj-kondo and its integration with Malli.

Dave Do you think that someday this functionality will be available in other programming languages?

Joe Absolutely. IDEs like IntelliJ and Visual Studio Code already support JSON Schema validation for JSON files. It's only a matter of time before they support JSON Schema validation for function arguments and provide autocompletion of the field names in a map.

Dave I hope it won't take them too much time.

12.6 A new gift

When Joe leaves the office, Dave gets an interesting idea. He shares it with Theo.

Dave Do you think we could make our own JSON Schema cheat sheet with the advanced JSON schema features that we discovered today?

Theo Excellent idea! But you'll have to do it on your own. I have to run to a meeting!

After his meeting, Theo comes back to Dave's desk. When he sees Theo, Dave takes a small package like the one Joe gave Theo a few weeks ago from the top of his desk. This one, however, is wrapped in a light blue ribbon. With a solemn demeanor, Dave hands Theo the gift.

When Theo undoes the ribbon, he discovers an stylish piece of paper decorated with little computers in different colors. In the center of the paper, he reads the inscription, "Advanced JSON Schema cheat sheet." Theo smiles while browsing the JSON schema (see listing 12.30). Then, he turns the paper over to find that the back is also filled with drawings, this time keyboards and mice. In the center of the paper, Theo reads the inscription, "Example of valid data" (see listing 12.31).

Listing 12.30 Advanced JSON Schema cheat sheet

```
{
  "type": "array",                                 // At the root level, data is an array.
  "items": {
    "type": "object",                              // Each element of the array is a map.
    "properties": {                                // The properties of each field in the map
      "myNumber": {"type": "number"},              // myNumber is a number.
      "myString": {"type": "string"},              // myString is a string.
      "myEnum": {"enum": ["myVal", "yourVal"]},    // myEnum is an enumeration value with two possibilities, "myVal" and "yourVal".
      "myBool": {"type": "boolean"}                // myBool is a boolean.
      "myAge": {                                   // myAge is an integer between 0 and 120.
      "type": "integer",
      "minimum": 0,
      "maximum": 120
    },
    "myBirthday": {                                // myBirthday is a string conforming to the date format.
      "type": "string",
      "format": "date"
    },
```

```
      "myLetters": {                    <-- myLetters is a string with
        "type": "string",                   letters only (lowercase or
        "pattern": "[a-zA-Z]*"              uppercase).
      }
      "myNumberMap": {                  <-- myNumberMap is an homogeneous
      "type": "object",                     string map where all the values are
      "additionalProperties": {"type": "number"}   numbers.
    },
    "myTuple": {                        <-- myTuple is a tuple where the first
      "type": "array",                      element is a string and the second
      "prefixItems": [                      element is a number.
        { "type": "string" },
        { "type": "number" }
      ]
    }
  },                                        The mandatory fields in the map
                                            are myNumber and myString.
                                            Other fields are optional.
  "required": ["myNumber", "myString"],  <--
  "additionalProperties": false         <-- We don't allow fields that
  }                                         are not explicitly mentioned
  }                                         in the schema.
```

Listing 12.31 An example of valid data

```
[
  {
    "myNumber": 42,
    "myString": "I-love-you",
    "myEnum": "myVal",
    "myBool": true,
    "myTuple": ["Hello", 42]
  },
  {
    "myNumber": 54,
    "myString": "Happy",
    "myAge": 42,
    "myBirthday": "1978-11-23",
    "myLetters": "Hello",
    "myNumberMap": {
      "banana": 23,
      "apple": 34
    }
  }
]
```

Summary

- We define data schemas using a language like JSON Schema for function arguments and return values.
- *Function argument schemas* allow developers to figure out the expected shape of the function arguments they want to call.
- When invalid data is passed, data validation third-party libraries give meaningful errors with detailed information about the data parts that are not valid.

- Unlike data validation at system boundaries, data validation inside the system is supposed to run only at development time and should be disabled in production.
- We visualize a *data schema* by generating a data model diagram out of a JSON Schema.
- For functions that have data schemas for their arguments and return values, we can automatically generate schema-based unit tests.
- *Data validation* is executed at run time.
- We can define advanced data validation conditions that go beyond static types, like checking whether a number is within a range or if a string matches a regular expression.
- Data validation inside the system should be disabled in production.
- *Records* are represented as heterogeneous maps, and *indexes* are represented as homogeneous maps.
- When you define a complex data schema, it is advised to store nested schemas in variables to make the schemas easier to read.
- We treat data validation like unit tests.

13 Polymorphism

Playing with the animals in the countryside

This chapter covers

- Mimicking objects with multimethods (single dispatch)
- Implementing multimethod on several argument types (multiple dispatch)
- Implementing multimethods dynamically on several arguments (dynamic dispatch)

OOP is well-known for allowing different classes to be called with the same interface via a mechanism called *polymorphism*. It may seem that the only way to have polymorphism in a program is with objects. In fact, in this chapter, we are going to see that it is possible to have polymorphism without objects, thanks to multimethods. Moreover, multimethods provide a more advanced polymorphism than OOP polymorphism because they support cases where the chosen implementation depends on several argument types (multiple dispatch) and even on the dynamic value of the arguments (dynamic dispatch).

13.1 The essence of polymorphism

For today's session, Dave has invited Theo to come and visit him at his parents' house in the countryside. As Theo's drive across the Golden Gate Bridge takes him from the freeway to increasingly rural country roads, he lets himself be carried away by the beauty of the landscape, the smell of fresh earth, and the sounds of animals in nature. This "nature bath" puts him in an excellent mood. What a way to start the week!

Dave receives Theo in jeans and a T-shirt, a marked contrast with the elegant clothes he wears at the office. A straw hat completes his country look. Theo says hello to Dave's parents, now retired. Dave suggests that they go pick a few oranges in the field to squeeze for juice. After drinking a much more flavorful orange juice than they are used to in San Francisco, Theo and Dave get to work.

Dave When I was waiting for you this morning, I thought of another thing I miss from OOP.

Theo What's that?

Dave Polymorphism.

Theo What kind of polymorphism?

Dave You know, you define an interface, and different classes implement the same interface in different ways.

Theo I see. And why do you think polymorphism is valuable?

Dave Because it allows us to decouple an interface from its implementations.

Theo Would you mind illustrating that with a concrete example?

Dave Sure. Because we're in the country, I'll use the classic OOP polymorphism example with animals.

Theo Good idea!

Dave Let's say that each animal has its own greeting by making a sound and saying its name.

Theo Oh cool, like in anthropomorphic comics books.

Dave *Anthro* what?

Theo You know, comics books where animals can walk, speak, and so forth—like Mickey Mouse.

Dave Of course, but I don't know that term. Where does it come from?

Theo Anthropomorphism comes from the Greek *ánthrōpos*, which means *human*, and *morphē*, which means *form*.

Dave I see. So an anthropomorphic book is a book where animals have human traits. The word sounds related to polymorphism.

Theo Absolutely. Polymorphism comes from the Greek *polús*, which means *many*, and *morphē*, which, again, means *form*.

Dave That makes sense. Polymorphism is the ability of different objects to implement the same method in different ways. That brings me back to my animal example. In OOP, I'd define an `IAnimal` interface with a `greet` method, and each animal class would implement `greet` in its own way. Here, I happen to have an example.

Listing 13.1 OOP polymorphism illustrated with animals

```
interface IAnimal {
public void greet();
}

class Dog implements IAnimal {
  private String name;
  public void greet() {
    System.out.println("Woof woof! My name is " + animal.name);
  }
}

class Cat implements IAnimal {
  private String name;
  public void greet() {
    System.out.println("Meow! I am " + animal.name);
  }
}


class Cow implements IAnimal {
  private String name;
  public void greet() {
    System.out.println("Moo! Call me " + animal.name);
  }
}
```

Theo Let me challenge you a bit. What is the fundamental difference between OOP polymorphism and a switch statement?

Dave What do you mean?

Theo I could, for instance, represent an animal with a map having two fields, `name` and `type`, and call a different piece of code, depending on the value of `type`.

Theo pulls his laptop from its bag and fires it up. While the laptop is booting up, he enjoys another taste of that wonderful orange juice. When the laptop is ready, he quickly types in the example switch case. Meanwhile, Dave has finished his glass of orange juice.

Listing 13.2 A switch case where behavior depends on type

```
function greet(animal) {
  switch (animal.type) {
    case "dog":
      console.log("Woof Woof! My name is: " + animal.name);
      break;
    case "cat":
      console.log("Meow! I am: " + animal.name);
      break;
    case "cow":
      console.log("Moo! Call me " + animal.name);
      break;
  };
}
```

Dave How would `animal` look, exactly?

Theo Like I just said, a map with two fields: `name` and `type`. Let me input that for you.

Listing 13.3 Representing animals with maps

```
var myDog = {
  "type": "dog",
  "name": "Fido"
};


var myCat = {
  "type": "cat",
  "name": "Milo"
};


var myCow = {
  "type": "cow",
  "name": "Clarabelle"
};
```

Dave Could you have given another name to the field that holds the animal type?

Theo Absolutely. It could be anything.

Dave I see. You're asking me the fundamental difference between your code with a switch statement and my code with an interface and three classes?

Theo Exactly.

Dave First of all, if you pass an invalid map to your `greet` function, bad things will happen.

Theo You're right. Let me fix that and validate input data.

Listing 13.4 Data validation

```
var animalSchema = {
  "type": "object",
  "properties": {
    "name": {"type": "string"},
    "type": {"type": "string"}
  },
  "required": ["name", "type"],
};

function greet(animal) {
  if(dev()) {                     <-- See chapter 12 about data validation for details.
    if(!ajv.validate(animalSchema, animal)) {
      var errors = ajv.errorsText(ajv.errors);
      throw ("greet called with invalid arguments: " + errors);
    }
  }
  switch (animal.type) {
    case "dog":
```

```
      console.log("Woof Woof! My name is: " + animal.name);
      break;
    case "cat":
      console.log("Meow! I am: " + animal.name);
      break;
    case "cow":
      console.log("Moo! Call me " + animal.name);
      break;
  };
}
```

▶ **NOTE** You should not use switch statements like this in your production code. We use them here for didactic purposes only as a step towards distilling the essence of polymorphism.

Dave Another drawback of your approach is that when you want to modify the implementation of greet for a specific animal, you have to change the code that deals with all the animals, while in my approach, you would change only a specific animal class.

Theo I agree, and I could also fix that by having a separate function for each animal, something like this.

Listing 13.5 Different implementations in different functions

```
function greetDog(animal) {
  console.log("Woof Woof! My name is: " + animal.name);
}

function greetCat(animal) {
  console.log("Meow! I am: " + animal.name);
}

function greetCow(animal) {
  console.log("Moo! Call me " + animal.name);
}

function greet(animal) {
  if(dev()) {
    if(!ajv.validate(animalSchema, animal)) {
      var errors = ajv.errorsText(ajv.errors);
      throw ("greet called with invalid arguments: " + errors);
    }
  }
  switch (animal.type) {
    case "dog":
      greetDog(animal);
      break;
    case "cat":
      greetCat(animal);
      break;
    case "cow":
      greetCow(animal);
```

```
        break;
    };
}
```

Dave But what if you want to extend the functionality of `greet` and add a new animal?

Theo Now you got me. I admit that with a switch statement, I can't add a new animal without modifying the original code, whereas in OOP, I can add a new class without having to modify the original code.

Dave Yeah, but you helped me to realize that the main benefit of polymorphism is that it makes the code easily extensible.

TIP The main benefit of polymorphism is extensibility.

Theo I'm going to ask Joe if there's a way to benefit from polymorphism without objects.

Theo sends a message to Joe and asks him about polymorphism in DOP. Joe answers that he doesn't have time to get into a deep response because he is in a tech conference where he is about to give a talk about DOP. The only thing he has time to tell Theo is that he should take a look at multimethods.

Theo and Dave read some online material about multimethods. It doesn't look too complicated. They decide that after lunch they will give multimethods a try.

13.2 Multimethods with single dispatch

During lunch, Theo asks Dave how it feels to have grown up in the country. Dave starts with an enthusiastic description about being in direct contact with nature and living a simpler life than in the city. He's grateful for the experience, but he admits that country life can sometimes be hard without the conveniences of the city. But who said simple was easy?

After lunch, they decide to have coffee. Dave asks Theo if he'd like to grind the coffee beans himself. Theo accepts with joy. Next, Dave explains how to use a French press coffee maker to get the ideal tradeoff between bitterness and rich taste. While savoring their French press coffee in the garden, Theo and Dave continue their exploration of polymorphism à la DOP.

Theo From what I read before lunch, it seems that multimethods are a software construct that provide polymorphism without the need for objects.

Dave I don't get how that's possible.

Theo Multimethods have two parts: a dispatch function and a set of methods that provide an implementation for each dispatched value.

Dave I'm not sure I'm clear on that. Is a dispatch function like an interface?

Theo It's like an interface in the sense that it defines the way the function needs to be called, but it goes beyond that. It also dispatches a value that differentiates between the different implementations.

Dave That's a bit abstract for me.

Theo I think I understand how to implement the animal greeting capabilities. If we use a multimethod called `greet`, we need a dispatch function and three methods. Let's call the dispatch function `greetDispatch`. It dispatches the animal type, either `"dog"`, `"cat"`, or `"cow"`. Then, each dispatch value is handled by a specific method: `"dog"` by `greetDog`, `"cat"` by `greetCat`, and `"cow"` by `greetCow`.

Theo takes out his notebook and opens it to a blank piece of paper. He draws a diagram like the one in figure 13.1.

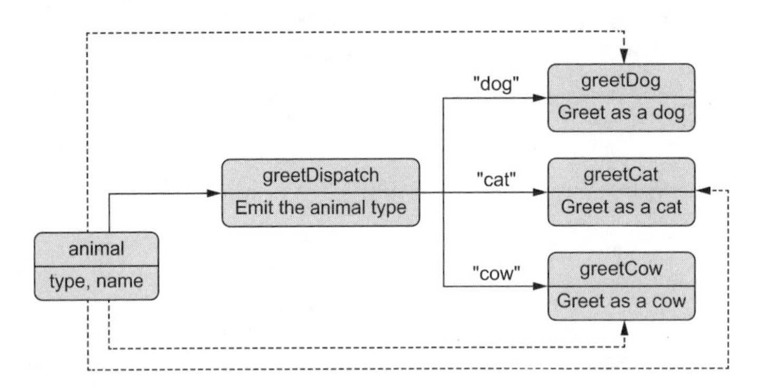

Figure 13.1 The logic flow of the `greet` multimethod

Dave Why is there an arrow between `animal` and the methods, in addition to the arrows between `animal` and the dispatch functions?

Theo Because the arguments of a multimethod are passed to the dispatch function and to the methods.

TIP The arguments of a multimethod are passed to the dispatch function and to the methods.

Dave Arguments plural? . . . I see only a single argument.

Theo You're right. Right now our multimethod only receives a single argument, but soon it will receive several arguments.

Dave I see. Could you show me how to write the code for the `greet` multimethod?

Theo For that, we need a library. For instance, in JavaScript, the `arrows/multi-method` library provides an implementation of multimethods. Basically, we call `multi` to create a multimethod called `method` to add a method.

NOTE See http://mng.bz/nY9v for examples and documentation about this library.

Dave Where should we start?

Theo We'll start with multimethod initialization by creating a dispatch function `greetDispatch` that defines the signature of the multimethod, validates the arguments, and emits the type of the animal. Then we'll pass `greetDispatch` to `multi` in order to create the `greet` multimethod. Our dispatch function would then look like this.

Listing 13.6 The dispatch function for `greet` multimethod

```
function greetDispatch(animal) {      <-- Signature definition
  if(dev()) {
```

```
    if(!ajv.validate(animalSchema, animal)) {            <-- Argument validation
      var errors = ajv.errorsText(ajv.errors);
      throw ("greet called with invalid arguments: " + errors);
    }
  }

  return animal.type;          <-- Dispatch value
}
                                            Multimethod
var greet = multi(greetDispatch);      <-- initialization
```

TIP A multimethod dispatch function is responsible for three things: it defines the signature of the multimethod, it validates the arguments, and it emits a dispatch value.

Dave What's next?

Theo Now we need to implement a method for each dispatched value. Let's start with the method that deals with dogs. We create a `greetDog` function that receives an `animal` and then add a `dog` method to the `greet` multimethod using the `method` function from the `arrows/multimethod` library. The `method` function receives two arguments: the dispatched value and a function that corresponds to the dispatch value.

Listing 13.7 Implementation of `greet` method for dogs

```
function greetDog(animal) {                                 <-- Method
  console.log("Woof woof! My name is " + animal.name);          implementation
}
greet = method("dog", greetDog)(greet);          <-- Method declaration
```

Dave Does the method implementation have to be in the same module as the multimethod initialization?

Theo No, not at all! Method declarations are decoupled from multimethod initialization exactly like class definitions are decoupled from the interface definition. That's what make multimethods extensible.

TIP Multimethods provides extensibility by decoupling between multimethod initialization and method implementations.

Dave What about cats and cows?

Theo We add their method implementations like we did for dogs.

Theo takes a moment to envision the implementation. Then he codes up two more `greet` methods for cats and cows.

Listing 13.8 Implementation of `greet` method for cats

```
function greetCat(animal) {
  console.log("Meow! I am " + animal.name);
}

greet = method("cat", greetCat)(greet);
```

Listing 13.9 Implementation of `greet` method for cows

```
function greetCow(animal) {
  console.log("Moo! Call me " + animal.name);
}

greet = method("cow", greetCow)(greet);
```

TIP In the context of multimethods, a method is a function that provides an implementation for a dispatch value.

Dave Are the names of dispatch functions and methods important?

Theo According to what I read, not really, but I like to follow a simple naming convention: use the name of the multimethod (for example, `greet`) as a prefix for the dispatch function (for example, `greetDispatch`) and the methods. Then I'd have the `Dispatch` suffix for the dispatch function and a specific suffix for each method (for example, `greetDog`, `greetCat`, and `greetCow`).

Dave How does the multimethod mechanism work under the hood?

Theo Internally, a multimethod maintains a hash map where the keys are the dispatched values, and the values are the methods. When we add a method, an entry is added to the hash map, and when we call the multimethod, we query the hash map to find the implementation that corresponds to the dispatched value.

Dave I don't think you've told me yet how to call a multimethod.

Theo We call it as a regular function. Give me a minute, and I'll show you an example that calls a multimethod.

Listing 13.10 Calling a multimethod like a regular function

```
greet(myDog);
// → "Woof woof! My name is Fido"

greet(myCat);
// → "Meow! I am Milo"

greet(myCow);
// → "Moo! Call me Clarabelle"
```

TIP Multimethods are called like regular functions.

Dave You told me earlier that in the dispatch function, we should validate the arguments. Is that mandatory or is it a best practice?

Theo It's a best practice.

Dave What happens if the dispatch function doesn't validate the arguments, and we pass an invalid argument?

Theo Like when an animal has no corresponding method?

Dave Exactly!

Theo In that case, you'll get an error. For instance, the `arrows/multimethods` library throws a `NoMethodError` exception.

Dave That's annoying. Is there a way to provide a default implementation?

Theo Absolutely! In order to define a default implementation, you pass to `method`—as a single argument—the function that provides the default implementation.

Theo writes the code and shows it to Dave. Dave then tests Theo's code and seems satisfied with the result.

Listing 13.11 Defining a default implementation

```
function greetDefault(animal) {
  console.log("My name is " + animal.name);
}
greet = method(greetDefault)(greet);
```

Listing 13.12 Calling a multimethod when no method fits the dispatch value

```
var myHorse = {
  "type": "horse",
  "name": "Horace"
};
greet(myHorse);
// → "My name is Horace"
```

TIP Multimethods support default implementations that are called when no method corresponds to the dispatch value.

Dave Cool!

13.3 Multimethods with multiple dispatch

Theo So far, we've mimicked OOP by having the type of the multimethod argument as a dispatch value. But if you think again about the flow of a multimethod, you'll discover something interesting. Would you like to try and draw a diagram that describes the flow of a multimethod in general?

Dave Let me get a fresh napkin. The one under my glass is a bit wet.

Theo Uh, Dave, you can use my notebook.

It takes Dave a few minutes to draw a diagram like the one in figure 13.2. He pushes the notebook back to Theo.

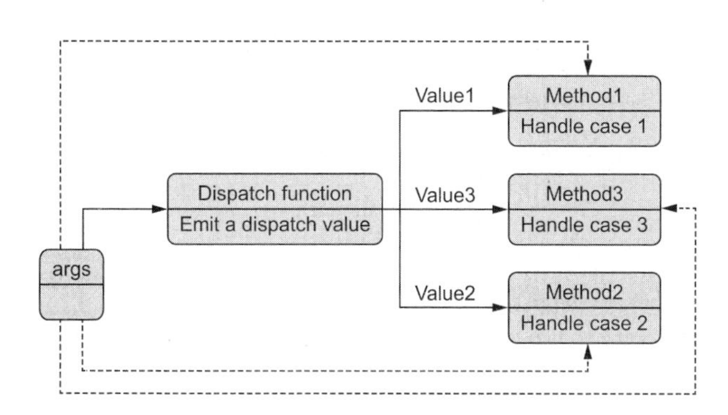

Figure 13.2 The logic flow of multimethods

Theo Excellent! I hope you see that the dispatch function can emit any value.

Dave Like what?

Theo Like emitting the type of two arguments!

Dave What do you mean?

Theo Imagine that our animals are polyglot.

Dave Poly what?

Theo Polyglot comes from the Greek *polús*, meaning *much*, and from *glôssa*, meaning *language*. A polyglot is a person who can speak many languages.

Dave What languages would our animals speak?

Theo I don't know. Let's say English and French.

Dave OK, and how would we represent a language in our program?

Theo With a map, of course!

Dave What fields would we have in a language map?

Theo Let's keep things simple and have two fields: `type` and `name`.

Dave Like an animal map?

Theo Not exactly. In a language map, the `type` field must be either `fr` for French or `en` for English, whereas in the animal map, the type field is either `dog`, `cat`, or `cow`.

Dave Let me try to write the language map schema and the two language maps.

Theo gladly consents; his French press coffee is getting cold! Dave writes his implementation of the code and shows Theo.

Listing 13.13 The schema of a language map

```
var languageSchema = {
  "type": "object",
  "properties": {
    "name": {"type": "string"},
    "type": {"type": "string"}
  },
  "required": ["name", "type"],
};
```

Listing 13.14 Two language maps

```
var french = {
  "type": "fr",
  "name": "Français"
};

var english = {
  "type": "en",
  "name": "English"
};
```

Theo Excellent! Now, let's write the code for the dispatch function and the methods for our polyglot animals. Let's call our multimethod, `greetLang`. We have one dispatch function and six methods.

Dave Right, three animals (dog, cat, and cow) times two languages (en and fr). Before the implementation, I'd like to draw a flow diagram. It will help me to make things crystal clear.

Theo You need my notebook again?

Not waiting for Dave to respond, Theo pushes his notebook across the table to Dave. Dave draws a diagram like the one in figure 13.3 and slides the notebook back to Theo.

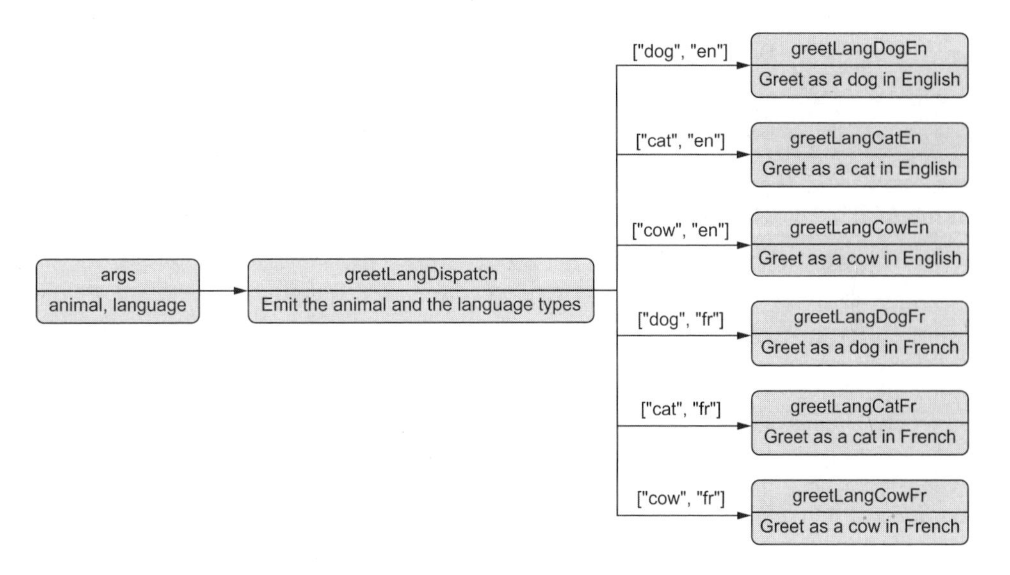

Figure 13.3 The logic flow of the `greetLang` multimethod

Theo Why did you omit the arrow between the arguments and the methods?

Dave In order to keep the diagram readable. Otherwise, there would be too many arrows.

Theo OK, I see. Are you ready for coding?

Dave Yes!

Theo The dispatch function needs to validate its arguments and return an array with two elements: the type of animal and the type of language.

Dave types for a bit on his laptop. He initializes the multimethod with a dispatch function that returns the type of its arguments and then shows the code to Theo.

Listing 13.15 Initializing a multimethod with a dispatch function

```
var greetLangArgsSchema = {
  "type": "array",
  "prefixItems": [animalSchema, languageSchema]
};

function greetLangDispatch(animal, language) {
  if(dev()) {
```

```
    if(!ajv.validate(greetLangArgsSchema, [animal, language])) {
      throw ("greetLang called with invalid arguments: " +
        ajv.errorsText(ajv.errors));
    }
  }
  return [animal.type, language.type];
};

var greetLang = multi(greetLangDispatch);
```

Dave Does the order of the elements in the array matter?

Theo It doesn't matter, but it needs to be consistent with the wiring of the methods. The implementation of greetLang would therefore look like this.

Listing 13.16 The implementation of `greetLang` methods

```
function greetLangDogEn(animal, language) {
  console.log("Woof woof! My name is " +
    animal.name +
    " and I speak " +
    language.name);
}

greetLang = method(["dog", "en"], greetLangDogEn)(greetLang);

function greetLangDogFr(animal, language) {
  console.log("Ouaf Ouaf! Je m'appelle " +
    animal.name +
    " et je parle " +
    language.name);
}

greetLang = method(["dog", "fr"], greetLangDogFr)(greetLang);

function greetLangCatEn(animal, language) {
  console.log("Meow! I am " +
    animal.name +
    " and I speak " +
    language.name);
}
greetLang = method(["cat", "en"], greetLangCatEn)(greetLang);

function greetLangCatFr(animal, language) {
  console.log("Miaou! Je m'appelle " +
    animal.name +
    " et je parle " +
    language.name);
}
greetLang = method(["cat", "fr"], greetLangCatFr)(greetLang);

function greetLangCowEn(animal, language) {
  console.log("Moo! Call me " +
    animal.name +
    " and I speak " +
```

```
    language.name);
}
greetLang = method(["cow", "en"], greetLangCowEn)(greetLang);

function greetLangCowFr(animal, language) {
  console.log("Meuh! Appelle moi " +
    animal.name +
    " et je parle " +
    language.name);
}
greetLang = method(["cow", "fr"], greetLangCowFr)(greetLang);
```

Dave looks at the code for the methods that deal with French. He is surprised to see `Ouaf Ouaf` instead of `Woof Woof` for dogs, `Miaou` instead of `Meow` for cats, and `Meuh` instead of `Moo` for cows.

Dave I didn't know that animal onomatopoeia were different in French than in English!

Theo Ono what?

Dave Onomatopoeia, from the Greek *ónoma* that means *name* and *poiéō* that means *to produce*. It is the property of words that sound like what they represent; for instance, *Woof*, *Meow*, and *Moo*.

Theo Yeah, for some reason in French, dogs *Ouaf*, cats *Miaou*, and cows *Meuh*.

Dave I see that in the array the animal type is always before the language type.

Theo Right! As I told you before, in a multimethod that features multiple dispatch, the order doesn't really matter, but it has to be consistent.

TIP *Multiple dispatch* is when a dispatch function emits a value that depends on more than one argument. In a multimethod that features multiple dispatch, the order of the elements in the array emitted by the dispatch function has to be consistent with the order of the elements in the wiring of the methods.

Dave Now let me see if I can figure out how to use a multimethod that features multiple dispatch.

Dave remembers that Theo told him earlier that multimethods are used like regular functions. With that in mind, he comes up with the code for a multimethod that features multiple dispatch.

Listing 13.17 Calling a multimethod that features multiple dispatch

```
greetLang(myDog, french);
// → "Ouaf Ouaf! Je m\'appelle Fido et je parle Français"

greetLang(myDog, english);
// → "Woof woof! My name is Fido and I speak English"

greetLang(myCat, french);
// → "Miaou! Je m\'appelle Milo et je parle Français"
```

```
greetLang(myCat, english);
// → "Meow! I am Milo and I speak English"

greetLang(myCow, french);
// → "Meuh! Appelle moi Clarabelle et je parle Français"

greetLang(myCow, english);
// → "Moo! Call me Clarabelle and I speak English"
```

Theo Now do you agree that multimethods with multiple dispatch offer a more powerful polymorphism that OOP polymorphism?

Dave Indeed, I do.

Theo Let me show you an even more powerful polymorphism called dynamic dispatch. But first, let's get some more of that wonderful French press coffee.

Dave Great idea! While we're in the kitchen, I think my mom made an orange Bundt cake using the oranges from the grove.

13.4 Multimethods with dynamic dispatch

Dave refills their coffee cups as Theo takes two slices from the cake and dishes them up. They take their coffee and cake outside to enjoy more of the fresh country air before resuming their conversation.

Dave What is dynamic dispatch?

Theo It's when the dispatch function of a multimethod returns a value that goes beyond the static type of its arguments.

Dave Like what, for example?

Theo Like a number or a Boolean, for instance.

Dave Why would such a thing be useful?

Theo Imagine that instead of being polyglot, our animals would suffer from dysmakrylexia.

Dave Suffering from what?

Theo Dysmakrylexia. It comes from the Greek *dus*, expressing the idea of *difficulty*, *makrýs* meaning *long*, and *léxis* meaning *diction*. Therefore, dysmakrylexia is difficulty pronouncing long words.

Dave I've never heard of that.

Theo That's because I just invented it.

Dave Funny. What's considered a long word for our animals?

Theo Let's say that when their name has more than five letters, they're not able to say it.

Dave A bit weird, but OK.

Theo Let's call our multimethod `dysGreet`. Its dispatch function returns an array with two elements: the animal type and a Boolean about whether the name is long or not. Take a look at this multimethod initialization.

Listing 13.18 A multimethod using a dispatch function with dynamic dispatch

```
function dysGreetDispatch(animal) {
  if(dev()) {
    if(!ajv.validate(animalSchema, animal)) {
      var errors = ajv.errorsText(ajv.errors);
      throw ("dysGreet called with invalid arguments: " + errors);
    }
  }
  var hasLongName = animal.name.length > 5;

  return [animal.type, hasLongName];
};

var dysGreet = multi(dysGreetDispatch);
```

Dave Writing the dysGreet methods doesn't seem too complicated.

As Theo reaches over to pass Dave his notebook, he accidently hits his coffee cup. Now Theo's notebook is completely wet, and all the diagrams are soggy! Fortunately, Dave brought an extra napkin from the kitchen, and it's still clean. He draws a flow diagram as in figure 13.4 and then grabs his laptop and writes the implementation of the dysGreet methods.

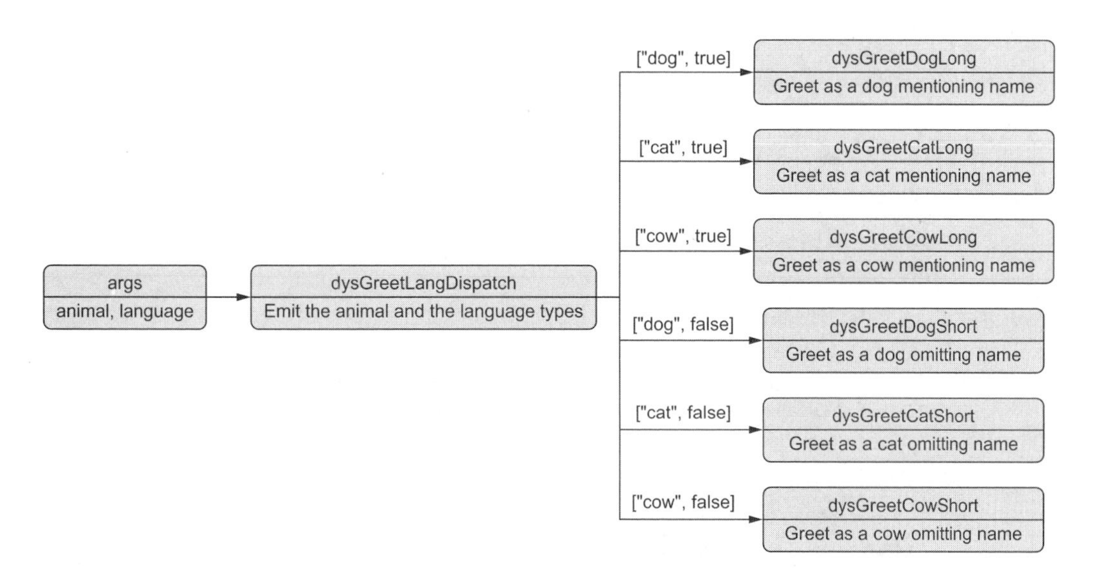

Figure 13.4 The logic flow of the `dysGreet` multimethod

Listing 13.19 The `dysGreet` methods

```
function dysGreetDogLong(animal) {
  console.log("Woof woof! My name is " + animal.name);
}
dysGreet = method(["dog", true], dysGreetDogLong)(dysGreet);
```

```
function dysGreetDogShort(animal) {
  console.log("Woof woof!");
}
dysGreet = method(["dog", false], dysGreetDogShort)(dysGreet);

function dysGreetCatLong(animal) {
  console.log("Meow! I am " + animal.name);
}
dysGreet = method(["cat", true], dysGreetCatLong)(dysGreet);

function dysGreetCatShort(animal) {
  console.log("Meow!");
}
dysGreet = method(["cat", false], dysGreetCatShort)(dysGreet);

function dysGreetCowLong(animal) {
  console.log("Moo! Call me " + animal.name);
}
dysGreet = method(["cow", true], dysGreetCowLong)(dysGreet);

function dysGreetCowShort(animal) {
  console.log("Moo!");
}
dysGreet = method(["cow", false], dysGreetCowShort)(dysGreet);
```

Theo checks that the code works as expected. He compliments Dave, not only on the method implementation but also for having the foresight to grab an extra napkin.

Listing 13.20 Testing `dysGreet`

```
dysGreet(myDog);
dysGreet(myCow);
dysGreet(myCat);
//"Woof woof!"
//"Moo! Call me Clarabelle"
//"Meow!"
```

Theo Well done, my friend! Our exploration of multimethods has come to an end. I think it's time for me to drive back if I want to get home before dark and beat the rush hour traffic.

Dave Before you leave, let's check if multimethods are available in programming languages other than JavaScript.

Theo That's a question for Joe.

Dave Do you think it's OK if I call him now?

Theo I think it's probably better if you send him an email. He's in a tech conference, and I'm not sure if it's all day. Thank you for this beautiful day in the country and the wonderful refreshments.

Dave I enjoyed it, also, especially our discussions about etymology. I think there are some oranges for you to take home and enjoy later.

Theo Great! I can't wait until my wife tries one.

After Theo leaves, Dave sends Joe an email. A few minutes later, Dave receives an email from Joe with the subject, "Support for multimethods in different languages."

Support for multimethods in different languages

Python has a library called multimethods (https://github.com/weissjeffm/multimethods), and Ruby has one called Ruby multimethods (https://github.com/psantacl/ruby-multimethods). Both seem to work quite like the JavaScript `arrows/multimethod` library.

In Java, there is the Java Multimethod Framework (http://igm.univ-mlv.fr/~forax/works/jmmf/), and C# supports multimethods natively via the `dynamic` keyword. However, in both Java and C#, multimethods work only with static data types and not with generic data structures.

Language	URL	Generic data structure support
JavaScript	https://github.com/caderek/arrows/tree/master/packages/multimethod	Yes
Java	http://igm.univ-mlv.fr/~forax/works/jmmf/	No
C#	Native support	No
Python	https://github.com/weissjeffm/multimethods	Yes
Ruby	https://github.com/psantacl/ruby-multimethods	Yes

13.5 Integrating multimethods in a production system

While Theo is driving back home, his thoughts take him back to the fresh air of the country. This pleasant moment is interrupted by a phone call from Nancy at Klafim.

Nancy How are you doing?

Theo Fine. I'm driving back from the countryside.

Nancy Cool. Are you available to talk about work?

Theo Sure.

Nancy I'd like to add a tiny feature to the catalog.

In the past, when Nancy qualified a feature as *tiny*, it scared Theo because tiny turned into huge. What seemed easy to her always took him a surprising amount of time to develop. But after refactoring the system according to DOP principles, now what seems tiny to Nancy is usually quite easy to implement.

Theo What feature?

Nancy I'd like to allow librarians to view the list of authors, ordered by last name, in two formats: HTML and Markdown.

Theo It doesn't sound too complicated.

Nancy Also, I need a bit of text formatting.

Theo What kind of text formatting?

Nancy Depending on the number of books an author has written, their name should be in bold and italic fonts.

Theo Could you send me an email with all the details. I'll take a look at it tomorrow morning.

Nancy Perfect. Have a safe drive!

Before going to bed, Theo reflects about today's etymology lessons. He realizes that he never looked for the etymology of the word *etymology* itself! He searches for the term *etymology* online and learns that the word *etymology* derives from the Greek *étumon*, meaning *true sense*, and the suffix *logia*, denoting *the study of*. During the night, Theo dreams of dogs, cats, and cows programming on their laptops in a field of grass.

When Theo arrives at the office the next day, he opens Nancy's email with the details about the text formatting feature. The details are summarized in table 13.1.

Table 13.1 Text formatting for author names according to the number of books they have written

Number of books	Italic	Bold
10 or fewer	Yes	No
Between 11 and 50	No	Yes
51 or more	Yes	Yes

Theo forwards Nancy's email to Dave and asks him to take care of this task. Delegating responsibility, after all, is the trait of a great manager.

Dave thinks the most difficult part of the feature lies in implementing an `Author.myName(author, format)` function that receives two arguments: the author data and the text format. He asks himself whether he can implement this function as a multimethod and use what he learned yesterday with Theo at his parents' home in the country. It seems that this feature is quite similar to the one that dealt with dysmakrylexia. Instead of checking the length of a string, he needs to check the length of an array.

First, Dave needs a data schema for the text format. He could represent a format as a map with a `type` field like Theo did yesterday for languages, but at the moment, it seems simpler to represent a format as a string that could be either `markdown` or `html`. He comes up with the text format schema in listing 13.21. He already wrote the author schema with Theo last week. It's in listing 13.22.

Listing 13.21 The text format schema

```
var textFormatSchema = {
  "name": {"type": "string"},
  "type": {"enum": ["markdown", "html"]}
};
```

Listing 13.22 The author schema

```
var authorSchema = {
  "type": "object",
  "required": ["name", "bookIsbns"],
  "properties": {
    "name": {"type": "string"},
    "bookIsbns": {
      "type": "array",
      "items": {"type": "string"}
    }
  }
};
```

Now, Dave needs to write a dispatch function and initialize the multimethod. Remembering that Theo had no qualms about creating the word *dysmakrylexia*, he decides that he prefers his own neologism, *prolificity*, over the existing nominal form *prolificness*. He finds it useful to have an `Author.prolificityLevel` helper function that returns the level of prolificity of the author: either `low`, `medium`, or `high`. Now he's ready to code the `authorNameDispatch` function.

Listing 13.23 `Author.myName` multimethod initialization

```
Author.prolificityLevel = function(author) {
  var books = _.size(_.get(author, "bookIsbns"));
  if (books <= 10) {
    return "low";
  };
  if (books >= 51) {
    return "high";
  }
  return "medium";
};

var authorNameArgsSchema = {
  "type": "array",
  "prefixItems": [
    authorSchema,
    {"enum": ["markdown", "html"]}
  ]
};

function authorNameDispatch(author, format) {
  if(dev()) {
    if(!ajv.validate(authorNameArgsSchema, [author, format])) {
      throw ("Author.myName called with invalid arguments: " +
        ajv.errorsText(ajv.errors));
    }
  }

  return [Author.prolificityLevel(author), format];
};

Author.myName = multi(authorNameDispatch);
```

Then Dave works on the methods: first, the HTML format methods. In HTML, bold text is wrapped inside a <b> tag, and italic text is wrapped in a <i> tag. For instance, in HTML, three authors with different levels of prolificity would be written like this.

Listing 13.24 Examples of bold and italic in HTML

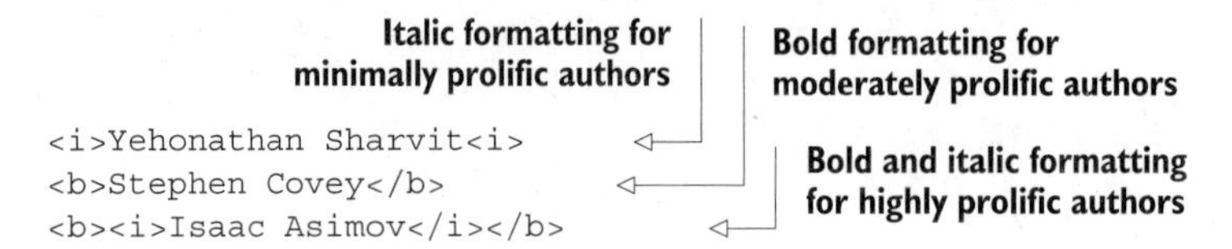

With this information in hand, Dave writes the three methods that deal with HTML formatting. Easy!

Listing 13.25 The methods that deal with HTML formatting

```
function authorNameLowHtml(author, format) {
  return "<i>" + _.get(author, "name") + "</i>";
}

Author.myName = method(["low", "html"], authorNameLowHtml)(Author.myName);

function authorNameMediumHtml(author, format) {
  return "<b>" + _.get(author, "name") + "</b>";
}

Author.myName =
  method(["medium", "html"], authorNameMediumHtml)(Author.myName);

function authorNameHighHtml(author, format) {
  return "<b><i>" + _.get(author, "name") + "</i></b>";
}

Author.myName =
  method(["high", "html"], authorNameHighHtml)(Author.myName);
```

Then, Dave moves on to the three methods that deal with Markdown formatting. In Markdown, bold text is wrapped in two asterisks, and italic text is wrapped in a single asterisk. For instance, in Markdown, three authors with different levels of prolificity would be written like the code in listing 13.26. The code for the Markdown methods is in listing 13.27.

Listing 13.26 Examples of bold and italic in Markdown

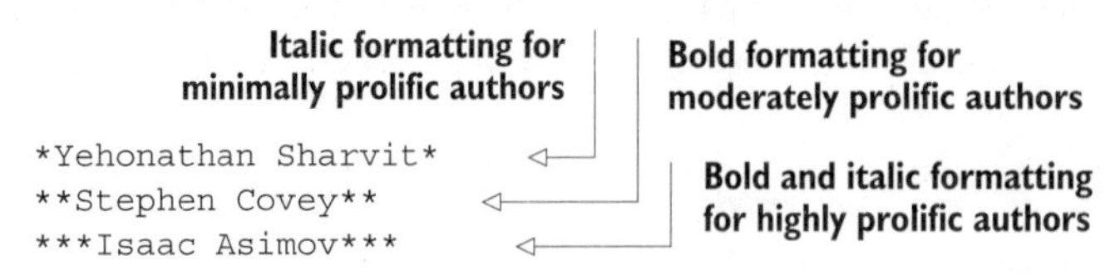

Listing 13.27 The methods that deal with Markdown formatting

```
function authorNameLowMarkdown(author, format) {
  return "*" + _.get(author, "name") + "*";
}

Author.myName =
  method(["low", "markdown"], authorNameLowMarkdown)(Author.myName);

function authorNameMediumMarkdown(author, format) {
  return "**" + _.get(author, "name") + "**";
}

Author.myName =
  method(["medium", "markdown"], authorNameMediumMarkdown)(Author.myName);

function authorNameHighMarkdown(author, format) {
  return "***" + _.get(author, "name") + "***";
}

Author.myName =
  method(["high", "markdown"], authorNameHighMarkdown)(Author.myName);
```

Dave decides to test his code by involving a *mysterious* author. Listing 13.28 and listing 13.29 show the tests.

Listing 13.28 Testing HTML formatting

```
var yehonathan = {
  "name": "Yehonathan Sharvit",
  "bookIsbns": ["9781617298578"]
};

Author.myName(yehonathan, "html");
// → "<i>Yehonathan Sharvit</i>"
```

Listing 13.29 Testing Markdown formatting

```
Author.myName(yehonathan, "markdown");
// → "*Yehonathan Sharvit*"
```

Theo shows up at Dave's desk and asks to review Dave's implementation of the list of authors feature. Curious, Theo asks Dave about the author that appears in the test of `Author.myName`.

Theo Who is Yehonathan Sharvit?

Dave I don't really know. The name appeared when I googled "data-oriented programming" yesterday. He wrote a book on the topic. I thought it would be cool to use its ISBN in my test.

Summary

- The main benefit of polymorphism is *extensibility*.
- *Multimethods* make it possible to benefit from polymorphism when data is represented with generic maps.
- A multimethod is made of a dispatch function and multiple methods.
- The dispatch function of a multimethod emits a dispatch value.
- Each of the methods used in a multimethod provides an implementation for a specific dispatch value.
- Multimethods can mimic OOP class inheritance via single dispatch.
- In *single dispatch*, a multimethod receives a single map that contains a `type` field, and the dispatch function of the multimethod emits the value of the `type` field.
- In addition to single dispatch, multimethods provide two kinds of advanced polymorphisms: multiple dispatch and dynamic dispatch.
- *Multiple dispatch* is used when the behavior of the multimethod depends on multiple arguments.
- *Dynamic dispatch* is used when the behavior of the multimethod depends on runtime arguments.
- The arguments of a multimethod are passed to the dispatch function and to the methods.
- A multimethod dispatch function is responsible for
  - Defining the signature.
  - Validating the arguments.
  - Emitting a dispatch value.
- Multimethods provides extensibility by decoupling between multimethod initialization and method implementations.
- Multimethods are called like regular functions.
- Multimethods support default implementations that are called when no method corresponds to the dispatch value.
- In a multimethod that features multiple dispatch, the order of the elements in the array emitted by the dispatch function has to be consistent with the order of the elements in the wiring of the methods.

Lodash functions introduced in this chapter

Function	Description
`size(coll)`	Gets the size of `coll`

14 Advanced data manipulation

Whatever is well-conceived is clearly said

This chapter covers

- Manipulating nested data
- Writing clear and concise code for business logic
- Separating business logic and generic data manipulation
- Building custom data manipulation tools
- Using the best tool for the job

When our business logic involves advanced data processing, the generic data manipulation functions provided by the language run time and by third-party libraries might not be sufficient. Instead of mixing the details of data manipulation with business logic, we can write our own generic data manipulation functions and implement our custom business logic using them. Separating business logic from the internal details of data manipulation makes the business logic code concise and easy to read for other developers.

14.1 Updating a value in a map with eloquence

Dave is more and more autonomous on the Klafim project. He can implement most features on his own, typically turning to Theo only for code reviews. Dave's code quality standards are quite high. Even when his code is functionally solid, he tends to be unsatisfied with its readability. Today, he asks for Theo's help in improving the readability of the code that fixes a bug Theo introduced a long time ago.

Dave I think I have a found a bug in the code that returns book information from the Open Library API.

Theo What bug?

Dave Sometimes, the API returns duplicate author names, and we pass the duplicates through to the client.

Theo It doesn't sound like a complicated bug to fix.

Dave Right, I fixed it, but I'm not satisfied with the readability of the code I wrote.

Theo Being critical of our own code is an important quality for a developer to progress. What is it exactly that you don't like?

Dave Take a look at this code.

Listing 14.1 Removing duplicates in a straightforward but tedious way

```
function removeAuthorDuplicates(book) {
  var authors = _.get(book, "authors");
  var uniqAuthors = _.uniq(authors);
  return _.set(book,"authors", uniqAuthors);
}
```

Dave I'm using `_.get` to retrieve the array with the author names, then `_.uniq` to create a duplicate-free version of the array, and finally, `_.set` to create a new version of the book with no duplicate author names.

Theo The code is tedious because the next value of `authorNames` needs to be based on its current value.

Dave But it's a common use case! Isn't there a simpler way to write this kind of code?

Theo Your astonishment definitely honors you as a developer, Dave. I agree with you that there must be a simpler way. Let me phone Joe and see if he's available for a conference call.

Joe How's it going, Theo?

Theo Great! Are you back from your tech conference?

Joe I just landed. I'm on my way home now in a taxi.

Theo How was your talk about DOP?

Joe Pretty good. At the beginning people were a bit suspicious, but when I told them the story of Albatross and Klafim, it was quite convincing.

Theo Yeah, adults are like children in that way; they love stories.

Joe What about you? Did you manage to achieve polymorphism with multimethods?

Theo Yes! Dave even managed to implement a feature in Klafim with multimethods.

Joe Cool!

Theo Do you have time to help Dave with a question about programming?

Joe Sure.

Dave Hi Joe. How are you doing?

Joe Hello Dave. Not bad. What kind of help do you need?

Dave I'm wondering if there's a simpler way to remove duplicates inside an array value in a map. Using `_.get`, `_.uniq`, and `_.set` looks quite tedious.

Joe You should build your own data manipulation tools.

Dave What do you mean?

Joe You should write a generic `update` function that updates a value in a map, applying a calculation based on its current value.[1]

Dave What would the arguments of `update` be in your opinion?

Joe Put the cart before the horse.

Dave What?!

Joe Rewrite your business logic as if `update` were already implemented, and you'll discover what the arguments of `update` should be.

Dave I see what you mean: the *horse* is the implementation of `update`, and the *cart* is the usage of `update`.

Joe Exactly. But remember, it's better if you keep your `update` function generic.

Dave How?

Joe By not limiting it to your specific use case.

Dave I see. The implementation of `update` should not deal with removing duplicate elements. Instead, it should receive the updating function—in my case, `_.uniq`—as an argument.

Joe Exactly! Uh, sorry Dave, I gotta go, I just got home. Good luck!

Dave Take care, Joe, and thanks!

Dave ends the conference call. Looking at Theo, he reiterates the conversation with Joe.

Dave Joe advised me to write my own `update` function. For that purpose, he told me to start by rewriting `removeAuthorDuplicates` as if `update` were already implemented. That will allow us to make sure we get the signature of `update` right.

Theo Sounds like a plan.

Dave Joe called it "putting the cart before the horse."

Theo Joe and his funny analogies . . .

TIP The best way to find the signature of a custom data manipulation function is to think about the most convenient way to use it.

Dave Anyway, the way I'd like to use `update` inside `removeAuthorDuplicates` is like this.

[1] Lodash provides an implementation of `update`, but for the sake of teaching, we are writing our own implementation.

Listing 14.2 The code that removes duplicates in an elegant way

```
function removeAuthorDuplicates(book) {
  return update(book, "authors", _.uniq);
}
```

Theo Looks good to me!

Dave Wow! Now the code with `update` is much more elegant than the code with `_.get` and `_.set`!

Theo Before you implement `update`, I suggest that you write down in plain English exactly what the function does.

Dave It's quite easy: `update` receives a map called `map`, a path called `path`, and a function called `fun`. It returns a new version of `map`, where `path` is associated with `fun(currentValue)`, and `currentValue` is the value associated with `path` in `map`.

Thinking out loud, Dave simultaneously draws a diagram like that in figure 14.1. Theo is becoming more and more impressed with his young protegé as he studies the figure.

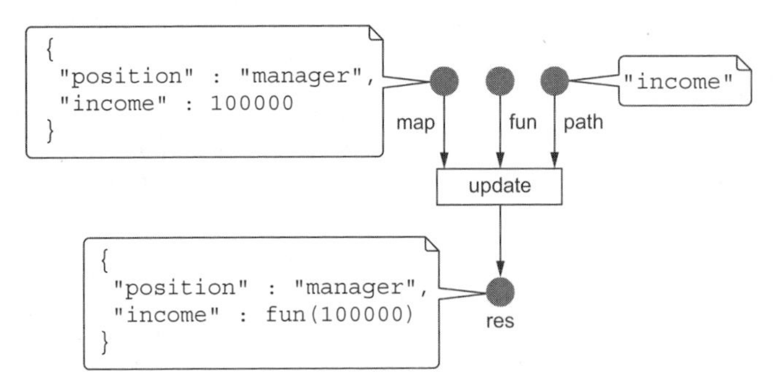

Figure 14.1 The behavior of `update`

TIP Before implementing a custom data manipulation function, formulate in plain English exactly what the function does.

Theo With such a clear definition, it's going to be a piece of cake to implement `update`!

After a few minutes, Dave comes up with the code. It doesn't take long because the plain-English diagram helps him to organize the code.

Listing 14.3 A generic `update` function

```
function update(map, path, fun) {
  var currentValue = _.get(map, path);
  var nextValue = fun(currentValue);
  return _.set(map, path, nextValue);
}
```

Theo Why don't you see if it works with a simple case such as incrementing a number in a map?

Dave Good idea! I'll try multiplying a value in a map by 2 with `update`. How's this look?

Listing 14.4 Multiplying a value in a map by 2

```
var m = {
  "position": "manager",
  "income": 100000
};
update(m, "income", function(x) {
  return x * 2;
});
// → {"position": "manager", "income": 200000}
```

Theo Great! It seems to work.

14.2 Manipulating nested data

The next Monday, during Theo and Dave's weekly sync meeting, they discuss the upcoming features for Klafim. Theo fondly remembers another Monday where they met at Dave's family home in the country. Coming back to the present moment, Theo begins.

Theo Recently, Nancy has been asking for more and more administrative features.

Dave Like what?

Theo I'll give you a few examples. . . . Let me find the email I got from Nancy yesterday.

Dave OK.

Theo Here it is. There are three feature requests for now: listing all the book author IDs, calculating the book lending ratio, and grouping books by a physical library.

Dave What feature should I tackle first?

Theo It doesn't matter, but you should deliver the three of these before the end of the week. Good luck, and don't hesitate to call me if you need help.

On Tuesday, Dave asks for Theo's help. Dave is not pleased with how his code looks.

Dave I started to work on the three admin features, but I don't like the code I wrote. Let me show you the code for retrieving the list of author IDs from the list of books returned from the database.

Theo Can you remind me what an element in a book list returned from the database looks like?

Dave Each book is a `map` with an `authorIds` array field.

Theo OK, so it sounds like a `map` over the books should do it.

Dave This is what I did, but it doesn't work as expected. Here's my code for listing the book author IDs.

Listing 14.5 Retrieving the author IDs in books as an array of arrays

```
function authorIdsInBooks(books) {
  return _.map(books, "authorIds");
}
```

Theo What's the problem?

Dave The problem is that it returns an array of arrays of author IDs instead of an array of author IDs. For instance, when I run `authorIdsInBooks` on a catalog with two books, I get this result.

Listing 14.6 The author IDs in an array of arrays

```
[
  ["sean-covey", "stephen-covey"],
  ["alan-moore", "dave-gibbons"]
]
```

Theo That's not a big problem. You can flatten an array of arrays with `_.flatten`, and you should get the result you expect.

Dave Nice! This is exactly what I need! Give me a moment to fix the code of `authorIdsInBooks`. . . here you go.

Listing 14.7 Retrieving the author IDs in books as an array of strings

```
function authorIdsInBooks(books) {
  return _.flatten(_.map(books, "authorIds"));
}
```

Theo Don't you think that mapping and then flattening deserves a function of its own?

Dave Maybe. It's quite easy to implement a `flatMap` function.[2] How about this?

Listing 14.8 The implementation of flatMap

```
function flatMap(coll, f) {
  return _.flatten(_.map(coll,f));
}
```

Theo Nice!

Dave I don't know. . . . It's kind of weird to have such a small function.

Theo I don't think that code size is what matters here.

Dave What do you mean?

Theo See what happens when you rewrite `authorIdsInBooks` using `flatMap`.

Dave OK, here's how I'd use `flatMap` to list the author IDs.

---

[2] Lodash provides an implementation of `flatMap`, but for the sake of teaching, we are writing our own implementation.

Listing 14.9 Retrieving the author IDs as an array of strings using `flatMap`

```
function authorIdsInBooks(books) {
  return flatMap(books, "authorIds");
}
```

Theo What implementation do you prefer, the one with `flatten` and `map` (in listing 14.7) or the one with `flatMap` (in listing 14.9)?

Dave I don't know. To me, they look quite similar.

Theo Right, but which implementation is more readable?

Dave Well, assuming I know what `flatMap` does, I would say the implementation with `flatMap`. Because it's more concise, it is a bit more readable.

Theo Again, it's not about the *size* of the code. It's about the clarity of intent and the power of naming things.

Dave I don't get that.

Theo Let me give you an example from our day-to-day language.

Dave OK.

Theo Could you pass me that thing on your desk that's used for writing?

It takes Dave a few seconds to get that Theo has asked him to pass the pen on the desk. After he passes Theo the pen, he asks:

Dave Why didn't you simply ask for the pen?

Theo I wanted you to experience how it feels when we use descriptions instead of names to convey our intent.

Dave Oh, I see. You mean that once we use a name for the operation that maps and flattens, the code becomes clearer.

Theo Exactly.

Dave Let's move on to the second admin feature: calculating the book lending ratio.

Theo Before that, I think we deserve a short period for rest and refreshments, where we drink a beverage made by percolation from roasted and ground seeds.

Dave A coffee break!

14.3 Using the best tool for the job

After the coffee break, Dave shows Theo his implementation of the book lending ratio calculation. This time, he seems to like the code he wrote.

Dave I'm quite proud of the code I wrote to calculate the book lending ratio.

Theo Show me the money!

Dave My function receives a list of books from the database like this.

Listing 14.10 A list of two books with `bookItems`

```
[
  {
    "isbn": "978-1779501127",
```

```
      "title": "Watchmen",
      "bookItems": [
        {
          "id": "book-item-1",
          "libId": "nyc-central-lib",
          "isLent": true
        }
      ]
    },
    {
      "isbn":  "978-1982137274",
      "title": "7 Habits of Highly Effective People",
      "bookItems": [
        {
          "id": "book-item-123",
          "libId": "hudson-park-lib",
          "isLent": true
        },
        {
          "id": "book-item-17",
          "libId": "nyc-central-lib",
          "isLent": false
        }
      ]
    }
]
```

Theo Quite a nested piece of data!

Dave Yeah, but now that I'm using `flatMap`, calculating the lending ratio is quite easy. I'm going over all the book items with `forEach` and incrementing either the `lent` or the `notLent` counter. At the end, I return the ratio between `lent` and `(lent + notLent)`. Here's how I do that.

Listing 14.11 Calculating the book lending ratio using `forEach`

```
function lendingRatio(books) {
  var bookItems = flatMap(books, "bookItems");
  var lent = 0;
  var notLent = 0;
  _.forEach(bookItems, function(item) {
    if(_.get(item, "isLent")) {
      lent = lent + 1;
    } else {
      notLent = notLent + 1;
    }
  });
  return lent/(lent + notLent);
}
```

Theo Would you allow me to tell you frankly what I think of your code?

Dave If you are asking this question, it means that you don't like it. Right?

Theo It's nothing against you; I don't like any piece of code with `forEach`.

Dave What's wrong with `forEach`?

Theo It's too generic!

Dave I thought that genericity was a positive thing in programming.

Theo It is when we *build* a utility function, but when we *use* a utility function, we should use the least generic function that solves our problem.

Dave Why?

Theo Because we ought to choose the right tool for the job, like in the real life.

Dave What do you mean?

Theo Let me give you an example. Yesterday, I had to clean my drone from the inside. Do you think that I used a screwdriver or a Swiss army knife to unscrew the drone cover?

Dave A screwdriver, of course! It's much more convenient to manipulate.

Theo Right. Also, imagine that someone looks at me using a screwdriver. It's quite clear to them that I am turning a screw. It conveys my intent clearly.

Dave Are you saying that `forEach` is like the Swiss army knife of data manipulation?

Theo That's a good way to put it.

TIP Pick the least generic utility function that solves your problem.

Dave What function should I use then, to iterate over the book item collection?

Theo You could use `_.reduce`.

Dave I thought `reduce` was about returning data from a collection. Here, I don't need to return data; I need to update two variables, `lent` and `notLent`.

Theo You could represent those two values in a map with two keys.

Dave Can you show me how to rewrite my `lendingRatio` function using `reduce`?

Theo Sure. The initial value passed to `reduce` is the map, `{"lent": 0, "notLent": 0}`, and inside each iteration, we update one of the two keys, like this.

Listing 14.12 Calculating the book lending ratio using `reduce`

```
function lendingRatio(books) {
  var bookItems = flatMap(books, "bookItems");
  var stats = _.reduce(bookItems, function(res, item) {
    if(_.get(item, "isLent")) {
      res.lent = res.lent + 1;
    } else {
      res.notLent = res.notLent + 1;
    }
    return res;
  }, {notLent: 0, lent:0});
  return stats.lent/(stats.lent + stats.notLent);
}
```

Dave Instead of updating the variables `lent` and `notLent`, now we are updating `lent` and `notLent` map fields. What's the difference?

Theo Dealing with map fields instead of variables allows us to get rid of `reduce` in our business logic code.

Dave How could you iterate over a collection without `forEach` and without `reduce`?

Theo I can't avoid the iteration over a collection, but I can hide `reduce` behind a utility function. Take a look at the way `reduce` is used inside the code of `lendingRatio`. What is the meaning of the `reduce` call?

Dave looks at the code in listing 14.12. He thinks for a long moment before he answers.

Dave I think it's counting the number of times `isLent` is `true` and `false`.

Theo Right. Now, let's use Joe's advice about building our own data manipulation tool.

Dave How exactly?

Theo I suggest that you write a `countByBoolField` utility function that counts the number of times a field is `true` and `false`.

Dave OK, but before implementing this function, let me first rewrite the code of `lendingRatio`, assuming this function already exists.

Theo You are definitely a fast learner, Dave!

Dave Thanks! I think that by using `countByBoolField`, the code for calculating the lending ratio using a custom utility function would be something like this.

Listing 14.13 Calculating the book lending ratio

```
function lendingRatio(books) {
  var bookItems = flatMap(books, "bookItems");
  var stats = countByBoolField(bookItems, "isLent", "lent", "notLent");
  return stats.lent/(stats.lent + stats.notLent);
}
```

TIP Don't use `_.reduce` or any other low-level data manipulation function inside code that deals with business logic. Instead, write a utility function—with a proper name—that hides `_.reduce`.

Theo Perfect. Don't you think that this code is clearer than the code using `_.reduce`?

Dave I do! The code is both more concise and the intent is clearer. Let me see if I can implement `countByBoolField` now.

Theo I suggest that you write a unit test first.

Dave Good idea.

Dave types for a bit. When he's satisfied, he shows Theo the result.

Listing 14.14 A unit test for `countByBoolField`

```
var input = [
  {"a": true},
  {"a": false},
  {"a": true},
```

```
  {"a": true}
];

var expectedRes = {
  "aTrue": 3,
  "aFalse": 1
};

_.isEqual(countByBoolField(input, "a", "aTrue", "aFalse"), expectedRes);
```

Theo Looks good to me. Now, for the implementation of `countByBoolField`, I think you are going to need our `update` function.

Dave I think you're right. On each iteration, I need to increment the value of either `aTrue` or `aFalse` using `update` and a function that increments a number by 1.

After a few minutes of trial and error, Dave comes up with the piece of code that uses `reduce`, `update`, and `inc`. He shows Theo the code for `countByBoolField`.

Listing 14.15 The implementation of `countByBoolField`

```
function inc (n) {
  return n + 1;
}

function countByBoolField(coll, field, keyTrue, keyFalse) {
  return _.reduce(coll, function(res, item) {
    if (_.get(item, field)) {
      return update(res, keyTrue, inc);
    }
    return update(res, keyFalse, inc);
  }, {[keyTrue]: 0,              <-- Creates a map with
      [keyFalse]: 0});               keyTrue and keyFalse
}                                    associated to 0
```

Theo Well done! Shall we move on and review the third admin feature?

Dave The third feature is more complicated. I would like to use the teachings from the first two features for the implementation of the third feature.

Theo OK. Call me when you're ready for the code review.

14.4 Unwinding at ease

Dave really struggled with the implementation of the last admin feature, grouping books by a physical library. After a couple of hours of frustration, Dave calls Theo for a rescue.

Dave I really had a hard time implementing the grouping by library feature.

Theo I only have a couple of minutes before my next meeting, but I can try to help you. What's the exact definition of grouping by library?

Dave Let me show you the unit test I wrote.

Listing 14.16 Unit test for grouping books by a library

```
var books = [
  {
    "isbn": "978-1779501127",
    "title": "Watchmen",
    "bookItems": [
      {
        "id": "book-item-1",
        "libId": "nyc-central-lib",
        "isLent": true
      }
    ]
  },
  {
    "isbn":  "978-1982137274",
    "title": "7 Habits of Highly Effective People",
    "bookItems": [
      {
        "id": "book-item-123",
        "libId": "hudson-park-lib",
        "isLent": true
      },
      {
        "id": "book-item-17",
        "libId": "nyc-central-lib",
        "isLent": false
      }
    ]
  }
];

var expectedRes =
{
  "hudson-park-lib": [
    {
      "bookItems": {
        "id": "book-item-123",
        "isLent": true,
        "libId": "hudson-park-lib",
      },
      "isbn": "978-1982137274",
      "title": "7 Habits of Highly Effective People",
    },
  ],
  "nyc-central-lib": [
    {
      "bookItems":  {
        "id": "book-item-1",
        "isLent": true,
        "libId": "nyc-central-lib",
      },
      "isbn": "978-1779501127",
      "title": "Watchmen",
    },
```

```
    {
      "bookItems":  {
        "id": "book-item-17",
        "isLent": false,
        "libId": "nyc-central-lib",
      },
      "isbn": "978-1982137274",
      "title": "7 Habits of Highly Effective People",
    },
  ],
};
_.isEqual(booksByRack(books) , expectedRes);
```

Theo Cool. . . . Writing unit tests before implementing complicated functions was also helpful for me when I refactored Klafim from OOP to DOP.

Dave Writing unit tests for functions that receive and return data is much more fun than writing unit tests for the methods of stateful objects.

TIP Before implementing a complicated function, write a unit test for it.

Theo What was difficult about the implementation of `booksByLib`?

Dave I started with a complicated implementation involving `merge` and `reduce` before I remembered that you advised me to hide `reduce` behind a generic function. But I couldn't figure out what kind of generic function I needed.

Theo Indeed, it's not easy to implement.

Dave I'm glad to hear that. I thought I was doing something wrong.

Theo The challenge here is that you need to work with book items, but the book title and ISBN are not present in the book item map.

Dave Exactly!

Theo It reminds me a query I had to write a year ago on MongoDB, where data was laid out in a similar way.

Dave And what did your query look like?

Theo I used MongoDB's `$unwind` operator. Given a map `m` with a field `<arr, myArray>`, it returns an array where each element is a map corresponding to `m` without `arr` and with `item` associated to an element of `myArray`.

Dave That's a bit abstract for me. Could you give me an example?

Theo moves to the whiteboard. He draws a diagram like the one in figure 14.2.

Theo In my case, I was dealing with an online store, where a customer cart was represented as a map with a `customer-id` field and an `items` array field. Each element in the array represented an item in the cart. I wrote a query with `unwind` that retrieved the cart items with the `customer-id` field.

Dave Amazing! That's exactly what we need. Let's write our own `unwind` function!

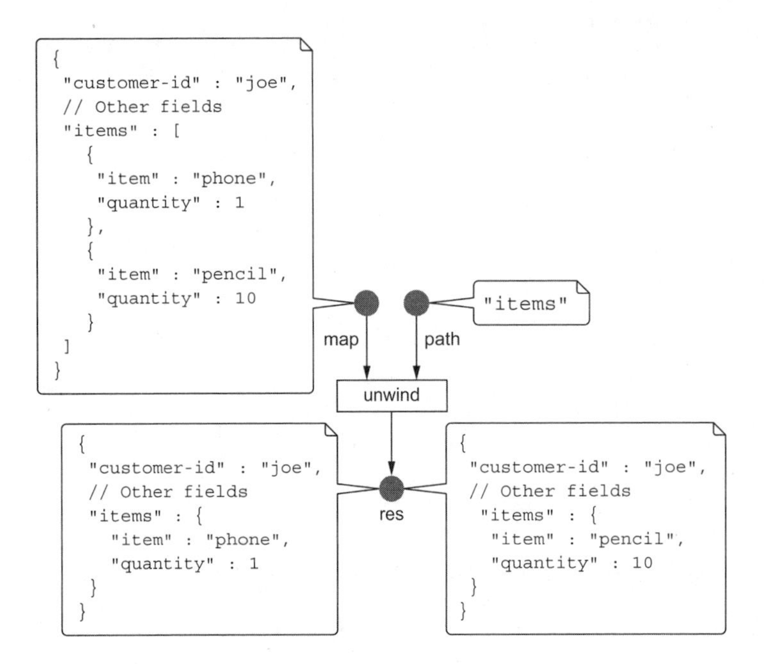

Figure 14.2 The behavior of `unwind`

Theo I'd be happy to pair program with you on this cool stuff, but I'm already running late for another meeting.

Dave I'm glad I'm not a manager!

When Theo leaves for his meeting, Dave goes to the kitchen and prepares himself a long espresso as a reward for all that he's accomplished today. He thoroughly enjoys it as he works on the implementation of `unwind`.

As Joe advised, Dave starts by writing the code for `booksByLib` as if `unwind` were already implemented. He needs to go over each book and unwind its book items using `flatMap` and `unwind`. He then groups the book items by their `libId` using `_.groupBy`. Satisfied with the resulting code, he finishes his espresso.

Listing 14.17 Grouping books by a library using `unwind`

```
function booksByRack(books) {
  var bookItems =  flatMap(books, function(book) {
    return unwind(book, "bookItems");
  });
  return _.groupBy(bookItems, "bookItems.libId")
}
```

Dave cannot believe that such a complicated function could be implemented so clearly and compactly. Dave says to himself that the complexity must reside in the implementation of `unwind`—but he soon finds out that he's wrong; it is not going to be as complicated as he thought! He starts by writing a unit test for `unwind`, similar to Theo's MongoDB customer cart scenario.

Listing 14.18 A unit test for `unwind`

```
var customer = {
  "customer-id": "joe",
  "items": [
    {
      "item": "phone",
      "quantity": 1
    },
    {
      "item": "pencil",
      "quantity": 10
    }
  ]
};

var expectedRes = [
  {
    "customer-id": "joe",
    "items": {
      "item": "phone",
      "quantity": 1
    }
  },
  {
    "customer-id": "joe",
    "items": {
      "item": "pencil",
      "quantity": 10
    }
  }
]

_.isEqual(unwind(customer, "items"), expectedRes)
```

The implementation of `unwind` is definitely not as complicated as Dave thought. It retrieves the array `arr` associated with `f` in `m` and creates, for each element of `arr`, a version of `m`, where `f` is associated with `elem`. Dave is happy to remember that data being immutable, there is no need to clone `m`.

Listing 14.19 The implementation of `unwind`

```
function unwind(map, field) {
  var arr = _.get(map, field);
  return _.map(arr, function(elem) {
    return _.set(map, field, elem);
  });
}
```

After a few moments of contemplating his beautiful code, Dave sends Theo a message with a link to the pull request that implements grouping books by a library with `unwind`. After that he leaves the office to go home, by bike, tired but satisfied.

Summary

- Maintain a clear separation between the code that deals with business logic and the implementation of the data manipulation.
- Separating business logic from data manipulation makes our code not only concise, but also easy to read because it conveys the intent in a clear manner.
- We design and implement custom data manipulation functions in a four-step process:
  - **a** Discover the function signature by using it before it is implemented.
  - **b** Write a unit test for the function.
  - **c** Formulate the behavior of the function in plain English.
  - **d** Implement the function.
- The best way to find the signature of a custom data manipulation function is to think about the most convenient way to use it.
- Before implementing a custom data manipulation function, formulate in plain English exactly what the function does.
- Pick the least generic utility function that solves your problem.
- Don't use `_.reduce` or any other low-level data manipulation function inside code that deals with business logic. Instead, write a utility function—with a proper name—that hides `_.reduce`.
- Before implementing a complicated function, write a unit test for it.

Lodash functions introduced in this chapter

Function	Description
`flatten(arr)`	Flattens `arr` a single level deep
`sum(arr)`	Computes the sum of the values in `arr`
`uniq(arr)`	Creates an array of unique values from `arr`
`every(coll, pred)`	Checks if `pred` returns `true` for all elements of `coll`
`forEach(coll, f)`	Iterates over elements of `coll` and invokes `f` for each element
`sortBy(coll, f)`	Creates an array of elements, sorted in ascending order, by the results of running each element in `coll` through `f`

15 Debugging

Innovation at the museum

This chapter covers

- Reproducing a bug in code that involves primitive data types
- Reproducing a bug in code that involves aggregated data
- Replaying a scenario in the REPL
- Creating unit tests from bugs

When our programs don't behave as expected, we need to investigate the source code. The traditional tool for code investigation is the debugger. The debugger allows us to run the code, step by step, until we find the line that causes the bug. However, a debugger doesn't allow us to reproduce the scenario that causes the problem.

In DOP, we can capture the context of a scenario that causes a bug and replay it in a separate process like a REPL or a unit test. This allows us to benefit from a short feedback loop between our attempt to fix the code and the results of our attempt.

15.1 Determinism in programming

After a few months, Theo calls Dave to tell him that he's leaving Albatross. After Dave recovers from this first surprise, he's given another, more pleasant one. Theo informs Dave that after consulting with the management team, they have decided that Dave will be in charge of DOP at Albatross. In addition to the farewell at the office next week, Theo invites Dave for a last one-on-one work session at the Exploratorium Museum of Science.

During their visit, Dave particularly enjoys the Cells to Self exhibit in the Living Systems gallery; meanwhile, Theo is having fun with the Colored Shadows exhibit in the Reflections gallery. After the visit, Theo and Dave settle in the back row of the museum's auditorium and open their laptops.

Dave Why did you want our last meeting to happen here at the Museum of Science?

Theo Remember when Joe told us that someday we'd be able to innovate in DOP?

Dave Yes.

Theo Well, that day may have come. I think I have discovered an interesting connection between DOP and science, and it has implications in the way we debug a program.

Dave I'm curious.

Theo Do you believe in determinism?

Dave You mean that everything that happens in the universe is predestined and that free will is an illusion?

Theo No, I don't want to get into a philosophy. This is more of a scientific question. Do you think that the same causes always produce the same effects?

Dave I think so. Otherwise, each time I use an elevator, I'd be scared to death that the laws of physics have changed, and the elevator might go down instead of up, or even crash!

Theo What about determinism in programming?

Dave How would you define causes and effects in programming?

Theo Let's say, for the sake of simplicity, that in the context of programming, causes are function arguments and effects are return values.

Dave What about side effects?

Theo Let's leave them aside for now.

Dave What about the program state? I mean, a function could return a different value for the same arguments if the program state changes.

Theo That's why we should avoid state as much as possible.

Dave But you can't avoid state in real-life applications!

Theo Right, but we can minimize the number of modules that deal with state. In fact, that's exactly what DOP has encouraged us to do: only the `SystemState` module deals with state, and all other modules deal with immutable data.

Dave Then, I think that in modules that deal with immutable data, determinism as you defined it holds. For the same arguments, a function will always return the same value.

TIP In modules that deal with immutable data, function behavior is deterministic—the same arguments always lead to the same return values.

Theo Perfect. Let's give a name to the values of the function arguments that a function is called with: the function run-time context or, in short, the function context.

Dave I think I see what you mean. In general, the function context should involve both the function arguments and the program state. But in DOP, because we deal with immutable data, a function context is made only of the values of the function arguments.

TIP In DOP, the *function context* is made of the values of the function arguments.

Theo Exactly! Now, let's talk about reproducibility. Let's say that you want to capture a function context and reproduce it in another environment.

Dave Could you be a bit more concrete about reproducing a function context in another environment?

Theo Take, for example, a web service endpoint. You trigger the endpoint with some parameters. Inside the program, down the stack, a function `foo` is called. Now, you want to capture the context in which `foo` is called in order to reproduce later the same behavior of `foo`.

Dave We deal with immutable data. So, if we call `foo` again with the same arguments, it will behave the same.

Theo The problem is how do you know the values of the function arguments? Remember that we didn't trigger `foo` directly. We triggered the endpoint.

Dave That's not a problem. You use a debugger and set a breakpoint inside the code of `foo`, and you inspect the arguments when the program stops at the breakpoint.

Theo Let's say `foo` receives three arguments: a number, a string, and a huge nested map. How do you capture the arguments and replay `foo` with the same arguments?

Dave I am not sure what you mean exactly by replaying `foo`?

Theo I mean executing `foo` in the REPL.

▶ **NOTE** The REPL (Read Eval Print Loop), sometimes called language shell, is a programming environment that takes pieces of code, executes them, and displays the result. See table 15.1 for a list of REPLs for different programming languages.

Table 15.1 REPLs per programming language

JavaScript (Browser)	Browser console
Node.js	Node CLI
Java	JShell
C#	C# REPL
Python	Python interpreter
Ruby	Interactive Ruby

Dave Does the REPL have to be part of the process that I'm debugging?

Theo It doesn't have to be. Think of the REPL as a scientific lab, where developers perform experiments. Let's say you're using a separate process for the REPL.

Dave OK. For the number and the string, I can simply copy their values to the clipboard, paste them to the REPL, and execute `foo` in the REPL with the same arguments.

Theo That's the easy part. What about the nested map?

Dave I don't know. I don't think I can copy a nested map from a debugger to the clipboard!

Theo In fact, JavaScript debuggers can. For instance, in Chrome, there is a Copy option that appears when you right-click on data that is displayed in the browser console.

Dave I never noticed it.

Theo Even without that, you could serialize the nested map to a JSON string, copy the string to the clipboard, and then paste the JSON string to the REPL. Finally, you could deserialize the string into a hash map and call `foo` with it.

Dave Nice trick!

Theo I don't think of it as a trick, but rather as a fundamental aspect of DOP: data is represented with generic data structures.

Dave I see. It's easy to serialize a generic data structure.

TIP In order to copy and paste a generic data structure, we serialize and deserialize it.

Theo You just discovered the two conditions for reproducibility in programming.

Dave The first one is that data should be immutable.

Theo Right, and the second one?

Dave It should be easy to serialize and deserialize any data.

TIP The two conditions for reproducibility in programming are immutability and ease of (de)serialization.

15.2 Reproducibility with numbers and strings

Theo In fact, we don't even need a debugger in order to capture a function context.

Dave But the function context is basically made of its arguments. How can you inspect the arguments of a function without a debugger?

Theo By modifying the code of the function under investigation and printing the serialization of the arguments to the console.

Dave I don't get that.

Theo Let me show you what I mean with a function that deals with numbers.

Dave OK.

Theo Take for instance a function that returns the nth digit of a number.

Dave Oh no, I hate digit arithmetic!

Theo Don't worry, we'll find some code for it on the web.

Theo googles "nth digit of a number in JavaScript" and takes a piece of code from StackOverflow that seems to work.

Listing 15.1 Calculate the nth digit of a number

```
function nthDigit(a, n) {
  return Math.floor((a / (Math.pow(10, n - 1)))) % 10;
}
```

Dave Do you understand how it works?

Theo Let's see, dividing a by 10^{n-1} is like right-shifting it $n-1$ places. Then we need to get the rightmost digit.

Dave And the last digit of a number is obtained by the `modulo 10` operation?

Theo Right! Now, imagine that this function is called down the stack when some endpoint is triggered. I'm going to modify it by adding context-capturing code.

Dave What's that?

Theo Context-capturing code is code that we insert at the beginning of a function body to print the values of the arguments. Let me edit the `nthDigit` code to give you an example.

Listing 15.2 Capturing a context made of numbers

```
function nthDigit(a, n) {
  console.log(a);
  console.log(n);
  return Math.floor((a / (Math.pow(10, n - 1)))) % 10;
}
```

Dave It looks trivial.

Theo It is trivial for now, but it will get less trivial in a moment. Now, tell me what happens when I trigger the endpoint.

Dave When the endpoint is triggered, the program will display the two numbers, `a` and `n`, in the console.

Theo Exactly, and what would you have to do in order to replay the function in the same context as when the endpoint was triggered?

Dave I would need to copy the values of `a` and `n` from the console, paste them into the REPL, and call `nthDigit` with those two values.

Theo What makes you confident that when we run `nthDigit` in the REPL, it will reproduce exactly what happened when the endpoint was triggered? Remember, the REPL might run in a separate process.

Dave I know that `nthDigit` depends only on its arguments.

Theo Good. Now, how can you be sure that the arguments you pass are the same as the arguments that were passed?

Dave A number is a number!

Theo I agree with you. Let's move on and see what happens with strings.

Dave I expect it to be exactly the same.

Theo It's going to be almost the same. Let's write a function that receives a sentence and a prefix and returns `true` when the sentence contains a word that starts with the prefix.

Dave Why would anyone ever need such a weird function?

Theo It could be useful for the Library Management System when a user wants to find books whose title contains a prefix.

Dave Interesting. I'll talk about that with Nancy. Anyway, coding such a function seems quite obvious. I need to split the sentence string into an array of words and then check whether a word in the array starts with the prefix.

Theo How are you going to check whether any element of the array satisfies the condition?

Dave I think I'll use Lodash `filter` and check the length of the returned array.

Theo That would work but it might have a performance issue.

Dave Why?

Theo Think about it for a minute.

Dave I got it! `filter` processes all the elements in the array rather than stopping after the first match. Is there a function in Lodash that stops after the first match?

Theo Yes, it's called `find`.

Dave Cool. I'll use that. Hang on.

Dave reaches over for his laptop and write the code to check whether a sentence contains a word that starts with a prefix. After a brief period, he shows Theo his implementation of `hasWordStartingWith` using `_.find`.

Listing 15.3 Checking if a sentence contains a word starting with a prefix

```
function hasWordStartingWith(sentence, prefix) {
  var words = sentence.split(" ");
  return _.find(words, function(word) {
    return word.startsWith(prefix);
  }) != null;
}
```

Theo OK, now, please add the context-capturing code at the beginning of the function.

Dave Sure, let me edit this code a bit. Voilà!

Listing 15.4 Capturing a context made of strings

```
function hasWordStartingWith(sentence, prefix) {
  console.log(sentence);
  console.log(prefix);
  var words = sentence.split(" ");
  return _.find(words, function(word) {
    return word.startsWith(prefix);
  }) != null;
}
```

Theo Let me inspect your code for a minute. I want to see what happens when I check whether the sentence "I like the word *reproducibility*" contains a word that starts with *li*.

Theo uses Dave's laptop to examine Dave's code. It returns `true` as expected, but it doesn't display to the console the text that Dave expected. He shares his surprise with Theo.

Listing 15.5 Testing `hasWordStartingWith`

```
hasWordStartingWith("I like the word \"reproducibility\"", "li");
// It returns true
// It displays the following two lines:
// I like the word "reproducibility"
// li
```

Dave Where are the quotes around the strings? And where are the backslashes before the quotes surrounding the word *reproducibility*?

Theo They disappeared!

Dave Why?

Theo When you print a string to the console, the content of the string is displayed without quotes. It's more human-readable.

Dave Bummer! That's not good for reproducibility. So, after I copy and paste a string I have to manually wrap it with quotes and backslashes.

Theo Fortunately, there is a simpler solution. If you serialize your string to JSON, then it has the quotes and the backslashes. For instance, this code displays the string you expected.

Listing 15.6 Displaying to the console the serialization of a string

```
console.log(JSON.stringify(
  "I like the word \"reproducibility\""));
// → "I like the word \"reproducibility\""
```

Dave I didn't know that strings were considered valid JSON data. I thought only objects and arrays were valid.

Theo Both compound data types and primitive data types are valid JSON data.

Dave Cool! I'll fix the code in `hasWordStartingWith` that captures the string arguments. Here you go.

Listing 15.7 Capturing a context made of strings using JSON serialization

```
function hasWordStartingWith(sentence, prefix) {
  console.log(JSON.stringify(sentence));
  console.log(JSON.stringify(prefix));
  var words = sentence.split(" ");
  return _.find(words, function(word) {
    return word.startsWith(prefix);
  }) != null;
}
```

Theo Great! Capturing strings takes a bit more work than with numbers, but with JSON they're not too bad.

Dave Right. Now, I'm curious to see if using JSON serialization for context capturing works well with numbers.

Theo It works. In fact, it works well with any data, whether it's a primitive data type or a collection.

Dave Nice!

Theo Next, I'll show you how to use this approach to reproduce a real scenario that happens in the context of the Library Management System.

Dave No more digit arithmetic?

Theo No more!

15.3 Reproducibility with any data

The essence of DOP is that it treats data as a first-class citizen. As a consequence, we can reproduce any scenario that deals with data with the same simplicity as we reproduce a scenario that deals with numbers and strings.

Dave I just called Nancy to tell her about the improved version of the book search, where a prefix could match any word in the book title.

Theo And?

Dave She likes the idea.

Theo Great! Let's use this feature as an opportunity to exercise reproducibility with any data.

Dave Where should we start?

Theo First, we need to add context-capturing code inside the function that does the book matching.

Dave The function is `Catalog.searchBooksByTitle`.

Theo What are the arguments of `Catalog.searchBooksByTitle`?

Dave It has two arguments: `catalogData` is a big nested hash map, and `query` is a string.

Theo Can you edit the code and add the context-capturing piece?

Dave Sure. What about this code?

Listing 15.8 Capturing the arguments of `Catalog.searchBooksByTitle`

```
Catalog.searchBooksByTitle = function(catalogData, query) {
  console.log(JSON.stringify(catalogData));
  console.log(JSON.stringify(query));
  var allBooks = _.get(catalogData, "booksByIsbn");
  var queryLowerCased = query.toLowerCase();
  var matchingBooks = _.filter(allBooks, function(book) {
    return _.get(book, "title")
      .toLowerCase()
      .startsWith(queryLowerCased);
  });
  var bookInfos = _.map(matchingBooks, function(book) {
    return Catalog.bookInfo(catalogData, book);
  });
  return bookInfos;
};
```

Theo Perfect. Now let's trigger the search endpoint.

Theo triggers the search endpoint with the query "Watch," hoping to get details about *Watchmen*. When the endpoint returns, Theo opens the console and Dave can see two lines of output.

Listing 15.9 Console output when triggering the search endpoint

```
{"booksByIsbn":{"978-1982137274":{"isbn":"978-1982137274"\
 ,"title":"7 Habits of Highly Effective People","authorIds":\
 ["sean-covey","stephen-covey"]},"978-1779501127":{"isbn":\
 "978-1779501127","title":"Watchmen","publicationYear":\
 1987,"authorIds":["alan-moore", "dave-gibbons"]}},\
 "authorsById":{"stephen-covey":{"name":"Stephen Covey",\
 "bookIsbns":["978-1982137274"]},"sean-covey":{"name":"Sean Covey",\
 "bookIsbns":["978-1982137274"]},"dave-gibbons":{"name":"Dave Gibbons",\
 "bookIsbns":["978-1779501127"]},"alan-moore":{"name":"Alan Moore",\
 "bookIsbns":["978-1779501127"]}}}
   "Watch"
```

Dave I know that the first line contains the catalog data, but it's really hard to read.

Theo That doesn't matter too much. You only need to copy and paste it in order to reproduce the `Catalog.searchBooksByTitle` call.

Dave Let me do that. Here.

Listing 15.10 Reproducing a function call

```
var catalogData = {"booksByIsbn":{"978-1982137274":
  {"isbn":"978-1982137274","title":"7 Habits of Highly Effective People",
    "authorIds":["sean-covey","stephen-covey"]},"978-1779501127":
  {"isbn":"978-1779501127","title":"Watchmen","publicationYear":1987,
    "authorIds":["alan-moore","dave-gibbons"]}},"authorsById":
  {"stephen-covey":{"name":"Stephen Covey","bookIsbns":
    ["978-1982137274"]},"sean-covey":{"name":"Sean Covey","bookIsbns":
     ["978-1982137274"]},"dave-gibbons":{"name":"Dave Gibbons","bookIsbns":
     ["978-1779501127"]},"alan-moore":{"name":"Alan Moore","bookIsbns":
     ["978-1779501127"]}}};
var query = "Watch";

Catalog.searchBooksByTitle(catalogData, query);
```

Theo Now that we have real catalog data in hand, we can do some interesting things in the REPL.

Dave Like what?

Theo Like implementing the improved search feature without having to leave the REPL.

TIP Reproducibility allows us to reproduce a scenario in a pristine environment.

Dave Without triggering the search endpoint?

Theo Exactly! We are going to improve our code until it works as desired, using the short feedback loop that the console provides.

Dave Cool! In the catalog, we have the book, *7 Habits of Highly Effective People.* Let's see what happens when we search books that match the word *Habit.*

Theo replaces the value of the query in listing 15.10 with `"Habit"`. The code now returns an empty array as in listing 15.11. This is expected because the current implementation only searches for books whose title starts with the query, whereas the title starts with `7 Habits`.

Listing 15.11 Testing `searchBooksByTitle`

```
Catalog.searchBooksByTitle(catalogData, 'Habit');
// → []
```

Theo Would you like to implement the improved search?

Dave It's not too hard; we have already implemented `hasWordStartingWith`. Here's the improved search.

Listing 15.12 An improved version of book search

```
Catalog.searchBooksByTitle = function(catalogData, query) {
  console.log(JSON.stringify(catalogData));
  console.log(JSON.stringify(query));
  var allBooks = _.get(catalogData, "booksByIsbn");
  var matchingBooks = _.filter(allBooks, function(book) {
    return hasWordStartingWith(_.get(book, "title"), query);
  });
  var bookInfos = _.map(matchingBooks, function(book) {
    return Catalog.bookInfo(catalogData, book);
  });
  return bookInfos;
};
```

Theo I like it. Let's see if it works as expected.

Dave is about to trigger the search endpoint when suddenly Theo stops him. He says with an authoritative tone:

Theo Dave, don't do that!

Dave Don't do what?

Theo Don't trigger an endpoint to test your code.

Dave Why?

Theo Because the REPL environment gives you a much quicker feedback than triggering the endpoint. The main benefit of reproducibility is to be able to reproduce the real-life conditions in a more effective environment.

Dave executes the code from his improved search with the word *Habit.* This time, however, it returns the details about the book, *7 Habits of Highly Effective People.*

Listing 15.13 Testing `searchBooksByTitle` again

```
Catalog.searchBooksByTitle(catalogData, 'Habit');
// →  [ { "title": "7 Habits of Highly Effective People", …}]
```

Dave It works!

Theo Let's try more queries: `abit` and `bit` should not return any book, but `habit` and `7 Habits` should return only one book.

In the REPL, Dave tries the four queries that Theo suggested. For `abit` and `bit`, the code works as expected, but for `habit` and `7 Habits` it fails.

Dave Let me try to fix that code.

Theo I suggest that you instead write a couple of unit tests that check the various inputs.

Dave Good idea. Is there a way to use reproducibility in the context of unit tests?

Theo Absolutely!

15.4 Unit tests

Dave How do we use reproducibility in a unit test?

Theo As Joe told showed me so many times, in DOP, unit tests are really simple. They call a function with some data, and they check that the data returned by the function is the same as we expect.

Dave I remember that! I have written many unit tests for the Library Management System following this approach. But sometimes, I struggled to provide input data for the functions under test. For instance, building catalog data with all its nested fields was not a pleasure.

Theo Here's where reproducibility can help. Instead of building data manually, you put the system under the conditions you'd like to test, and then capture data inside the function under test. Once data is captured, you use it in your unit test.

Dave Nice! Let me write a unit test for `Catalog.searchBooksByTitle` following this approach.

Dave triggers the search endpoint once again. Then, he opens the console and copies the line with the captured catalog data to the clipboard. Finally, he pastes it inside the code of the unit test.

Listing 15.14 A unit test with captured data

```
var catalogData =
  {"booksByIsbn":{"978-1982137274":{"isbn":"978-1982137274",
  "title":"7 Habits of Highly Effective People","authorIds":["sean-covey",
    "stephen-covey"]},"978-1779501127":{"isbn":"978-1779501127","title":
    "Watchmen","publicationYear":1987,"authorIds":["alan-moore",
      "dave-gibbons"]}},"authorsById":{"stephen-covey":{"name":
    "Stephen Covey","bookIsbns":["978-1982137274"]},"sean-covey":
    {"name":"Sean Covey","bookIsbns":["978-1982137274"]},"dave-gibbons":
    {"name":"Dave Gibbons","bookIsbns":["978-1779501127"]},"alan-moore":
    {"name":"Alan Moore","bookIsbns":["978-1779501127"]}}};
var query = "Habit";
```

```
var result = Catalog.searchBooksByTitle(catalogData, query);
var expectedResult = [
  {
    "authorNames": [
      "Sean Covey",
      "Stephen Covey",
    ],
    "isbn": "978-1982137274",
    "title": "7 Habits of Highly Effective People",
  }
];

_.isEqual(result, expectedResult);
// → true
```

Theo Well done! Now, would you like me to show you how to do the same without copying and pasting?

Dave Definitely.

Theo Instead of displaying the captured data to the console, we're going to write it to a file and read data from that file inside the unit test.

Dave Where are you going to save the files that store captured data?

Theo Those files are part of the unit tests. They need to be under the same file tree as the unit tests.

Dave There are so many files! How do we make sure a file doesn't override an existing file?

Theo By following a simple file-naming convention. A name for a file that stores captured data is made of two parts: a context (for example, the name of the function where data was captured) and a universal unique identifier (a UUID).

Dave How do you generate a UUID?

Theo In some languages it's part of the language, but in other languages like JavaScript, you need a third-party library like `uuid`. Let me bookmark its site for you. I also happen to have a list of libraries for UUIDs. I'll send that table to you too.

Theo bookmarks the site for the third-party library `uuid` (https://github.com/uuidjs/uuid) on Dave's computer. Then, using his laptop, he finds his list and sends that to Dave. Dave receives the email, and he takes a moment to quickly glance through the table 15.2 before turning his attention back to Theo.

Table 15.2 Libraries for UUID generation

Language	UUID library
JavaScript	https://github.com/uuidjs/uuid
Java	`java.util.UUID`
C#	`Guid.NewGuid`
Python	`uuid`
Ruby	`SecureRandom`

Theo The code for the dataFilePath function that receives a context and returns a file path is fairly simple. Check this out.

Listing 15.15 Computing the file path for storing captured data

```
var capturedDataFolder = "test-data";        // The root folder for captured data
function dataFilePath(context) {
  var uuid = generateUUID();                 // UUID generation is language-dependent (see table 15.2).
  return capturedDataFolder
    + "/" + context
    + "-" + ".json";                         // Uses json as a file extension because we serialize data to JSON
}
```

Dave How do we store a piece of data in a JSON file?

Theo We serialize it and write it to disk.

Dave Synchronously or asynchronously?

Theo I prefer to write to the disk asynchronously or in a separate thread in run times that support multithreading to avoid slowing down the real work. Here's my implementation of dumpData.

Listing 15.16 Dumping data in JSON format

```
function dumpData(data, context) {
  var path = dataFilePath(context);
  var content = JSON.stringify(data);
  fs.writeFile(path, content, function () {   // Writes asynchronously to prevent blocking the real work
                                              // The third argument is a callback function, called when write completes.
    console.log("Data for " +
      context +
      "stored in: " +
      path);                                  // Displays a message once data is written to the file
  });
}
```

Dave Let me see if I can use dumpData inside Catalog.searchBooksByTitle and capture the context to a file. I think that something like this should work.

Listing 15.17 Capturing the context into a file

```
Catalog.searchBooksByTitle = function(catalogData, query) {
  dumpData([catalogData, query], 'searchBooksByTitle');
  var allBooks = _.get(catalogData, "booksByIsbn");
  var queryLowerCased = query.toLowerCase();
  var matchingBooks = _.filter(allBooks, function(book) {
    return _.get(book, "title")
      .toLowerCase()
      .startsWith(queryLowerCased);
  });
  var bookInfos = _.map(matchingBooks, function(book) {
    return Catalog.bookInfo(catalogData, book);
  });
```

```
  return bookInfos;
};
```

Theo Trigger the endpoint to see if it works.

Dave triggers the search endpoint once again and views the output in the console. When he opens the file mentioned in the log message, he sees a single line that is hard to decipher.

Listing 15.18 Console output when triggering the search endpoint

```
Data for searchBooksByTitle stored in
test-data/searchBooksByTitle-68e57c85-2213-471a-8442-c4516e83d786.json
```

Listing 15.19 The content of the JSON file that captured the context


```
[{"booksByIsbn":{"978-1982137274":{"isbn":"978-1982137274",
  "title":"7 Habits of Highly Effective People","authorIds":
  ["sean-covey","stephen-covey"]},"978-1779501127":{"isbn":
    "978-1779501127","title":"Watchmen","publicationYear":1987,
    "authorIds":["alan-moore","dave-gibbons"]}},"authorsById":
  {"stephen-covey":{"name":"Stephen Covey","bookIsbns":
    ["978-1982137274"]},"sean-covey":{"name":"Sean Covey",
      "bookIsbns":["978-1982137274"]},"dave-gibbons":
    {"name":"Dave Gibbons","bookIsbns":["978-1779501127"]},
    "alan-moore":{"name":"Alan Moore","bookIsbns":
      ["978-1779501127"]}}},"Habit"]
```


Dave Reading this JSON file is very difficult!

Theo We can beautify the JSON string if you want.

Dave How?

Theo By passing to `JSON.stringify` the number of space characters to use for indentation. How many characters would you like to use for indentation?

Dave Two.

After adding the number of indentation characters to the code of `dumpData`, Dave then opens the JSON file mentioned in the log message (it's a different file name!). He now sees a beautiful JSON array with two elements.

Listing 15.20 Dumping data in JSON format with indentation

```
function dumpData(data, context) {
  var path = dataFilePath(context);
  var content = JSON.stringify(data, null, 2);

  fs.writeFile(path, content, function () {
    console.log("Data for " + context + "stored in: " + path);
  });
}
```

The second argument to JSON.stringify is ignored. The third argument to JSON.stringify specifies the number of characters to use for indentation.

Listing 15.21 The captured context with indentation in the JSON file

```
[
  {
    "booksByIsbn": {
      "978-1982137274": {
        "isbn": "978-1982137274",
        "title": "7 Habits of Highly Effective People",
        "authorIds": [
          "sean-covey",
          "stephen-covey"
        ]
      },
      "978-1779501127": {
        "isbn": "978-1779501127",
        "title": "Watchmen",
        "publicationYear": 1987,
        "authorIds": [
          "alan-moore",
          "dave-gibbons"
        ]
      }
    },
    "authorsById": {
      "stephen-covey": {
        "name": "Stephen Covey",
        "bookIsbns": [
          "978-1982137274"
        ]
      },
      "sean-covey": {
        "name": "Sean Covey",
        "bookIsbns": [
          "978-1982137274"
        ]
      },
      "dave-gibbons": {
        "name": "Dave Gibbons",
        "bookIsbns": [
          "978-1779501127"
        ]
      },
      "alan-moore": {
        "name": "Alan Moore",
        "bookIsbns": [
          "978-1779501127"
        ]
      }
    }
  },
  "Habit"
]
```

Dave While looking at the contents of the JSON file, I thought about the fact that we write data to the file in an asynchronous way. It means that data is written concurrently to the execution of the function code, right?

Theo Right! As I told you, we don't want to slow down the real work.

Dave I get that. What happens if the code of the function modifies the data that we are writing? Will we write the original data to the file or the modified data?

Theo I'll let you think about that while I get a cup of tea at the museum coffee shop. Would you like some coffee?

Dave What, you're not having coffee?

Theo I finally found the time to read the book *The Power of Habit* by Charles Duhigg. Joe read the book and quit biting his fingernails, so I decided to read it to cut down on my habit of going for yet another cup of coffee.

Dave That's impressive, but I'd like an espresso, please.

While Theo goes to the coffee shop, Dave explores the Wind Arrows exhibit outside the auditorium. He's hoping that his mind will be inspired by the beauty of science. He takes a few breaths to relax, and after a couple of minutes, Dave has an *Aha!* moment. He knows the answer to his question about the function changing data.

Theo comes back, gingerly carrying the hot beverages, and finds Dave in the auditorium. Dave smiles at Theo and says:

Dave In DOP, we never mutate data. Therefore, my question is no longer a question: the code of the function cannot modify the data while we are writing it to the file.

Theo You've got it! Now, let me show you how to use data from the JSON file in a unit test. First, we need a function that reads data from a JSON file and deserializes it, probably something like `readData`.

Listing 15.22 Reading data from a JSON file

```
function readData(path) {
  return JSON.parse(fs.readFileSync(path));
}
```

Dave Why are you reading synchronously and not asynchronously like you did when we captured the data?

Theo Because `readData` is meant to be used inside a unit test, and we cannot run the test before the data is read from the file.

Dave That makes sense. Using `readData` inside a unit test seems straightforward. Let me use it to read our captured data.

Listing 15.23 A unit test that reads captured data from a file

```
var data = readData("test-data/" +
  "searchBooksByTitle-68e57c85-2213-471a-8442-c4516e83d786.json");
var catalogData = data[0];
var query = data[1];
```

```
var result = Catalog.searchBooksByTitle(catalogData, query);
var expectedResult = [
  {
    "authorNames": [
      "Sean Covey",
      "Stephen Covey",
    ],
    "isbn": "978-1982137274",
    "title": "7 Habits of Highly Effective People",
  }
];

_.isEqual(result, expectedResult);
// → false
```

Theo Do you prefer the version of the unit test with the inline data or with the data read from the file?

Dave It depends. When data is minimal, I prefer to have the data inline because it allows me to see the data. But when data is substantial, like the catalog data, having the data inline makes the code hard to read.

Theo OK. Let's fix the code of the improved search so that it works with the two queries that return an empty result.

Dave I completely forgot about that. Do you remember those two queries?

Theo Yes, it was `habit` and `7 Habits`.

Dave The first query doesn't work because the code leaves the strings in their original case. I can easily fix that by converting both the book title and the query to lowercase.

Theo And what about the second query?

Dave It's much harder to deal with because it's made of two words. I somehow need to check whether the title subsequently contains those two prefixes.

Theo Are you familiar with the `\b` regular expression metacharacter?

Dave No.

Theo `\b` matches a position that is called a *word boundary*. It allows us to perform prefix matching.

Dave Cool. Can you give me an example?

Theo Sure. For instance, `\bHabits` and `\b7 Habits` match `7 Habits of Highly Effective People`, but `abits` won't match.

Dave What about `\bHabits of`?

Theo It also matches.

Dave Excellent. This is exactly what I need! Let me fix the code of `hasWordStartingWith` so that it does a case-insensitive prefix match.

Listing 15.24 A revised version of hasWordStartingWith

```
function hasWordStartingWith(sentence, prefix) {
  var sentenceLowerCase = sentence.toLowerCase();
  var prefixLowerCase = prefix.toLowerCase();
```

```
  var prefixRegExp = new RegExp("\\b" +
    prefixLowerCase);
  return sentenceLowerCase.match(prefixRegExp) != null;
}
```

When passing \b to the RegExp constructor, we need an extra backslash.

Theo Now, let me write unit tests for all the cases.

Dave One test per query?

Theo You could, but it's more efficient to have a unit test for all the queries that should return a book and another one for all the queries that should return no books. Give me a minute.

Theo codes for a while and produces two unit tests. He then shows the tests to Dave and enjoys another sip of his tea.

Listing 15.25 A unit test for several queries that should return a book

```
var data =
readData("test-data/" +
  "searchBooksByTitle-68e57c85-2213-471a-8442-c4516e83d786.json");
var catalogData = data[0];
var queries = ["Habit", "habit", "7 Habit", "habits of"];
var expectedResult = [
  {
    "authorNames": [
      "Sean Covey",
      "Stephen Covey",
    ],
    "isbn": "978-1982137274",
    "title": "7 Habits of Highly Effective People",
  }
];

_.every(queries, function(query) {
  var result = Catalog.searchBooksByTitle(catalogData, query);
  return _.isEqual(result, expectedResult);
});
// → [true, true, true, true]
```

Listing 15.26 A unit test for several queries that should return no book

```
var data =
readData("test-data/" +
  "searchBooksByTitle-68e57c85-2213-471a-8442-c4516e83d786.json");
var catalogData = data[0];
var queries = ["abit", "bit", "7 abit", "habit of"];
var expectedResult = [ ];

_.every(queries, function(query) {
  var result = Catalog.searchBooksByTitle(catalogData, query);
  return _.isEqual(result, expectedResult);
});
// → [true, true, true, true]
```

Dave What is `_.every`?

Theo It's a Lodash function that receives a collection and a predicate and returns `true` if the predicate returns `true` for every element of the collection.

Dave Nice!

Dave runs the unit tests and they pass. He then enjoys a sip of his espresso.

Dave Now, am I allowed to trigger the search endpoint with `7 Habit` in order to confirm that the improved search works as expected?

Theo Of course. It's only during the multiple iterations of code improvements that I advise you *not* to trigger the system from the outside in order to benefit from a shorter feedback loop. Once you're done with the debugging and fixing, you must then test the system from end to end.

Dave triggers the search endpoint with `7 Habit`. It returns the details about `7 Habits of Highly Effective People` as expected.

15.5 Dealing with external data sources

Dave Can we also use reproducibility when the code involves fetching data from an external data source like a database or an external service?

Theo Why not?

Dave The function context might be exactly the same, but the behavior might be different if the function fetches data from a data source that returns a different response for the same query.

Theo Well, it depends on the data source. Some databases are immutable in the sense that the same query always returns the same response.

Dave I have never heard about immutable databases.

Theo Sometimes, they are called functional databases or append-only databases.

Dave Never heard about them either. Did you mean read-only databases?

Theo Read-only databases are immutable for sure, but they are not useful for storing the state of an application.

Dave How could a database be both writable and immutable?

Theo By embracing time.

Dave What does time have to do with immutability?

Theo In an immutable database, a record has an automatically generated timestamp, and instead of updating a record, we create a new version of it with a new timestamp. Moreover, a query always has a time range in addition to the query parameters.

Dave Why does that guarantee that the same query will always return the same response?

Theo In an immutable database, queries don't operate on the database itself. Instead, they operate on a database snapshot, which never changes. Therefore, queries with the same parameters are guaranteed to return the same response.

Dave Are there databases like that for real?

Theo Yes. For instance, the Datomic immutable database is used by some digital banks.

▶ **NOTE** See https://www.datomic.com for more information on the Datomic transactional database.

Dave But most databases don't provide such a guarantee!

Theo Right, but in practice, when we're debugging an issue in our local environment, data usually doesn't change.

Dave What do you mean?

Theo Take, for instance, Klafim's database. In theory, between the time you trigger the search endpoint and the time you replay the search code from the REPL with the same context, a book might have been borrowed, and its availability state in the database has changed. This leads to a difference response to the search query.

Dave Exactly.

Theo But in practice, you are the only one that interacts with the system in your local environment. Therefore, it should not happen.

Dave I see. Because we are at the Museum of Science, would you allow me an analogy with science?

Theo Of course!

Dave In a sense, external data sources are like hidden variables in quantum physics. In theory, they can alter the result of an experiment for no obvious reason. But in practice, our physical world looks stable at the macro level.

With today's discussion at an end, Theo searches his bag to find a parcel wrapped with gift wrap from the museum's souvenir shop, which he hands to Dave with a smile. Dave opens the gift to find a T-shirt. On one side there is an Albert Einstein avatar and his famous quote: "God does not play dice with the universe"; on the other side, an avatar of Alan Kay and his quote: "The last thing you want to do is to mess with internal state."

Dave thanks Theo for his gift. Theo can feel a touch of emotion at the back of his throat. He's really enjoyed playing the role of mentor with Dave, a rather skilled student.

Farewell

A week after the meeting with Dave at the museum, Theo invites Joe and Nancy for his farewell party at Albatross. This is the first time that Joe meets Nancy, and Theo takes the opportunity to tell Nancy that if the Klafim project met its deadlines, it was thanks to Joe. Everyone is curious about the name of the company Theo is going to work for, but no one dares to ask him. Finally, it's Dave who gets up the courage to ask.

Dave May I ask you what company are you going to work for?

Theo I'm going to take a break.

Dave Really?

Theo Yes. I'll be traveling around the world for a couple of months.

Dave And after that, will you go back to work in programming?

Theo I'm not sure.

Dave Do you have other projects in mind?

Theo I'm thinking of writing a book.

Dave A book?

Theo Yes. DOP has been a meaningful journey for me. I have learned some interesting lessons about reducing complexity in programming, and I would like to share my story with the community of developers.

Dave Well, if you are as good of a storyteller as you are as a teacher, I am sure your book will be a success.

Theo Thank you, Dave!

Monica, Dave, Nancy, Joe, and all the other Albatross employees raise their glasses to Theo's health and exclaim together, "Cheers! Here's to a successful book."

Summary

- We reproduce a scenario by capturing the context in which a function is called and replaying it either in the REPL or in a unit test. In this chapter, we call it *context capturing*.
- In DOP, a *function context* is made only of data.
- There are various locations to capture a function context—the clipboard, the console, a file.
- We are able to capture a function's context because data is represented with a generic data structure and, therefore, it is easily serializable.
- Replaying a scenario in the REPL provides a short feedback loop that allows us to be effective when we want to fix our code.
- When we execute a function with a captured context, the behavior of the function is guaranteed to be the same as long as it only manipulates immutable data as specified by DOP.
- In modules that deal with immutable data, function behavior is *deterministic*—the same arguments always lead to the same return values.
- The function context is made of the values of the function arguments.
- The REPL (Read Eval Print Loop), sometimes called language shell, is a programming environment that takes pieces of code, executes them, and displays the result.
- In order to copy and paste a generic data structure, we serialize and deserialize it.

- *Reproducibility* allows us to reproduce a scenario in a pristine environment.
- The two conditions for reproducibility in programming are immutability and ease of (de)serialization.

Lodash functions introduced in this chapter

Function	Description
`find(coll, pred)`	Iterates over elements of `coll`, returning the first element for which `pred` returns `true`

appendix A Principles of data-oriented programming

Data-oriented programming (DOP) is a programming paradigm aimed at simplifying the design and implementation of software systems, where information is at the center in systems such as frontend or backend web applications and web services, for example. Instead of designing information systems around software constructs that combine code and data (e.g., objects instantiated from classes), DOP encourages the *separation* of code from data. Moreover, DOP provides guidelines about how to represent and manipulate data.

TIP In DOP, data is treated as a first-class citizen.

The essence of DOP is that it treats data as a first-class citizen. It gives developers the ability to manipulate data inside a program with the same simplicity as they manipulate numbers or strings. Treating data as a first-class citizen is made possible by adhering to four core principles:

- Separating code (behavior) from data.
- Representing data with generic data structures.
- Treating data as immutable.
- Separating data schema from data representation.

When these four principles are combined, they form a cohesive whole as figure A.1 shows. Systems built using DOP are simpler and easier to understand, so the developer experience is significantly improved.

TIP In a data-oriented system, code is separated from data. Data is represented with generic data structures that are immutable and have a separate schema.

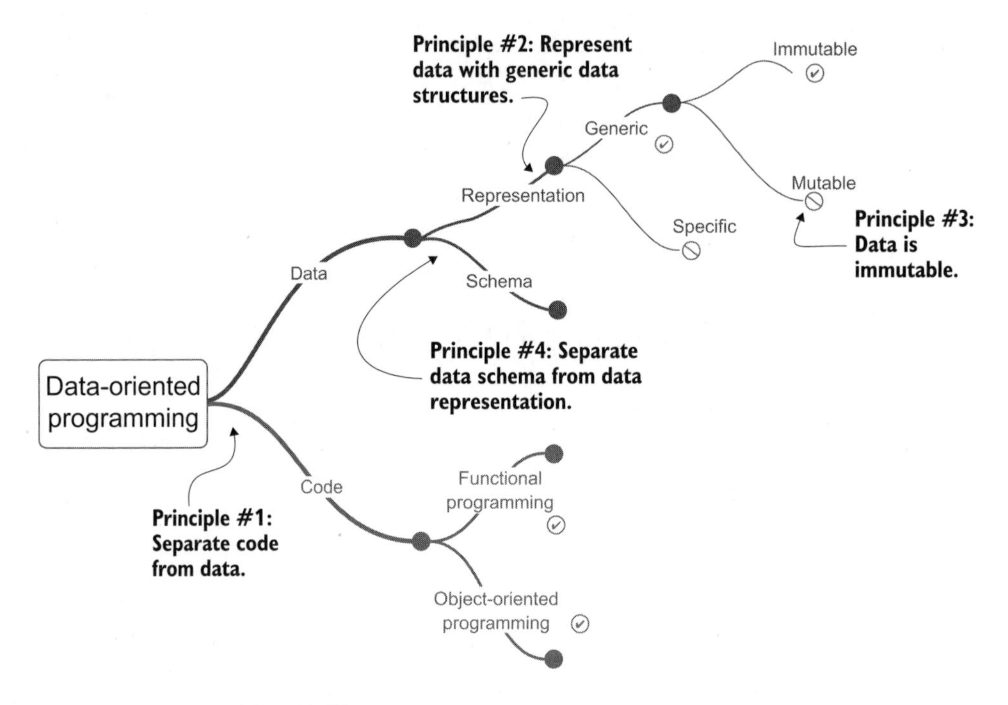

Figure A.1 The principles of DOP

Notice that DOP principles are language-agnostic. They can be adhered to (or broken) in

- Object-oriented programming (OOP) languages such as Java, C#, C++, etc.
- Functional programming (FP) languages such as Clojure, OCaml, Haskell, etc.
- Languages that support both OOP and FP such as JavaScript, Python, Ruby, Scala, etc.

TIP DOP principles are language-agnostic.

▶ **NOTE** For OOP developers, the transition to DOP might require more of a mind shift than for FP developers because DOP prohibits the encapsulation of data in stateful classes.

This appendix succinctly illustrates how these principles can be applied or broken in JavaScript. Mentioned briefly are the benefits of adherence to each principle, and the costs paid to enjoy those benefits. This appendix also illustrates the principles of DOP via simple code snippets. Throughout the book, the application of DOP principles to production information systems is explored in depth.

A.1 Principle #1: Separate code from data

Principle #1 is a design principle that recommends a clear separation between code (behavior) and data. This may appear to be a FP principle, but in fact, one can adhere to it or break it either in FP or in OOP:

- Adherence to this principle in OOP means aggregating the code as methods of a static class.
- Breaking this principle in FP means hiding state in the lexical scope of a function.

Also, this principle does not relate to the way data is represented. Data representation is addressed by Principle #2.

> PRINCIPLE #1 Separate code from data in a way that the code resides in functions whose behavior does not depend on data that is encapsulated in the function's context.

A.1.1 Illustration of Principle #1

Our exploration of Principle #1 begins by illustrating how it can be applied to OOP and FP. The following sections illustrate how this principle can be adhered to or broken in a simple program that deals with:

- An author entity with a `firstName`, a `lastName`, and the number of `books` they wrote.
- A piece of code that calculates the full name of the author.
- A piece of code that determines if an author is prolific, based on the number of books they wrote.

Breaking Principle #1 in OOP

Breaking Principle #1 in OOP happens when we write code that combines data and code together in an object. The following listing demonstrates what this looks like.

Listing A.1 Breaking Principle #1 in OOP

```
class Author {
  constructor(firstName, lastName, books) {
    this.firstName = firstName;
    this.lastName = lastName;
    this.books = books;
  }
  fullName() {
    return this.firstName + " " + this.lastName;
  }
  isProlific() {
    return this.books > 100;
  }
}
```

```
var obj = new Author("Isaac", "Asimov", 500);
obj.fullName();
// → "Isaac Asimov"
```

Isaac Asimov really wrote around 500 books!

BREAKING PRINCIPLE #1 IN FP

Breaking this principle without classes in FP means hiding data in the lexical scope of a function. The next listing provides an example of this.

Listing A.2 Breaking Principle #1 in FP

```
function createAuthorObject(firstName, lastName, books) {
  return {
    fullName: function() {
      return firstName + " " + lastName;
    },
    isProlific: function () {
      return books > 100;
    }
  };
}

var obj = createAuthorObject("Isaac", "Asimov", 500);
obj.fullName();
// → "Isaac Asimov"
```

ADHERING TO PRINCIPLE #1 IN OOP

Listing A.3 shows an example that adheres to Principle #1 in OOP. Compliance with this principle may be achieved even with classes by writing programs such that:

- The code consists of static methods.
- The data is encapsulated in data classes (classes that are merely containers of data).

Listing A.3 Following Principle #1 in OOP

```
class AuthorData {
  constructor(firstName, lastName, books) {
    this.firstName = firstName;
    this.lastName = lastName;
    this.books = books;
  }
}

class NameCalculation {
  static fullName(data) {
    return data.firstName + " " + data.lastName;
  }
}

class AuthorRating {
  static isProlific (data) {
    return data.books > 100;
  }
}
```

```
var data = new AuthorData("Isaac", "Asimov", 500);
NameCalculation.fullName(data);
// → "Isaac Asimov"
```

Adhering to Principle #1 in FP

Listing A.4 shows an example that adheres to Principle #1 in FP. Compliance with this principle means separating code from data.

Listing A.4 Following Principle #1 in FP

```
function createAuthorData(firstName, lastName, books) {
  return {
    firstName: firstName,
    lastName: lastName,
    books: books
  };
}

function fullName(data) {
  return data.firstName + " " + data.lastName;
}

function isProlific (data) {
  return data.books > 100;
}

var data = createAuthorData("Isaac", "Asimov", 500);
fullName(data);
// → "Isaac Asimov"
```

A.1.2 Benefits of Principle #1

Having illustrated how to follow or break Principle #1 both in OOP and FP, let's look at the benefits that Principle #1 brings to our programs. Careful separation of code from data benefits our programs in the following ways:

- Code can be reused in different contexts.
- Code can be tested in isolation.
- Systems tend to be less complex.

Benefit #1: Code can be reused in different contexts

Imagine that besides the author entity, there is a user entity that has nothing to do with authors but has two of the same data fields as the author entity: `firstName` and `lastName`. The logic of calculating the full name is the same for authors and users—retrieving the values of two fields with the same names. However, in traditional OOP as in the version with `createAuthorObject` in listing A.5, the code of `fullName` cannot be reused on a user in a *straightforward* way because it is locked inside the `Author` class.

Listing A.5 The code of `fullName` is locked in the `Author` class

```
class Author {
  constructor(firstName, lastName, books) {
```

```
    this.firstName = firstName;
    this.lastName = lastName;
    this.books = books;
  }
  fullName() {
    return this.firstName + " " + this.lastName;
  }
  isProlific() {
    return this.books > 100;
  }
}
```

One way to achieve code reusability when code and data are mixed is to use OOP mechanisms like inheritance or composition to let the `User` and `Author` classes use the same `fullName` method. These techniques are adequate for simple use cases, but in real-world systems, the abundance of classes (either base classes or composite classes) tends to increase complexity.

Listing A.6 shows a simple way to avoid inheritance. In this listing, we duplicate the code of `fullName` inside a `createUserObject` function.

Listing A.6 Duplicating code in OOP to avoid inheritance

```
function createAuthorObject(firstName, lastName, books) {
  var data = {firstName: firstName, lastName: lastName, books: books};

  return {
    fullName: function fullName() {
      return data.firstName + " " + data.lastName;
    }
  };
}

function createUserObject(firstName, lastName, email) {
  var data = {firstName: firstName, lastName: lastName, email: email};

  return {
    fullName: function fullName() {
      return data.firstName + " " + data.lastName;
    }
  };
}

var obj = createUserObject("John", "Doe", "john@doe.com");
obj.fullName();
// → "John Doe"
```

In DOP, no modification to the code that deals with author entities is necessary in order to make it available to user entities, because:

- The code that deals with full name calculation is separate from the code that deals with the creation of author data.
- The function that calculates the full name works with any hash map that has a `firstName` and a `lastName` field.

It is possible to leverage the fact that data relevant to the full name calculation for a user and an author has the same shape. With no modifications, the `fullName` function works properly both on author data and on user data as the following listing shows.

Listing A.7 The same code on data entities of different types (FP style)

```
function createAuthorData(firstName, lastName, books) {
  return {firstName: firstName, lastName: lastName, books: books};
}

function fullName(data) {
  return data.firstName + " " + data.lastName;
}

function createUserData(firstName, lastName, email) {
  return {firstName: firstName, lastName: lastName, email: email};
}

var authorData = createAuthorData("Isaac", "Asimov", 500);
fullName(authorData);

var userData = createUserData("John", "Doe", "john@doe.com");
fullName(userData);
// → "John Doe"
```

When Principle #1 is applied in OOP, code reuse is straightforward even when classes are used. In statically-typed OOP languages like Java or C, we would have to create a common interface for `AuthorData` and `UserData`. In a dynamically-typed language like JavaScript, however, that is not required. The code of `NameCalculation.fullName()` works both with author data and user data as the next listing demonstrates.

Listing A.8 The same code on data entities of different types (OOP style)

```
class AuthorData {
  constructor(firstName, lastName, books) {
    this.firstName = firstName;
    this.lastName = lastName;
    this.books = books;
  }
}

class NameCalculation {
  static fullName(data) {
    return data.firstName + " " + data.lastName;
  }
}

class UserData {
  constructor(firstName, lastName, email) {
    this.firstName = firstName;
    this.lastName = lastName;
    this.email = email;
```

```
  }
}

var userData = new UserData("John", "Doe", "john@doe.com");
NameCalculation.fullName(userData);

var authorData = new AuthorData("Isaac", "Asimov", 500);
NameCalculation.fullName(authorData);
// → "John Doe"
```

TIP When code is separate from data, it is straightforward to reuse code in different contexts. This benefit is achievable both in FP and in OOP.

Benefit #2: Code can be tested in isolation

A similar benefit is the ability to test code in an isolated context. When code is not separate from data, it is necessary to instantiate an object to test its methods. For instance, in order to test the `fullName` code that lives inside the `createAuthorObject` function, we need to instantiate an author object as the following listing shows.

Listing A.9 Testing code when code and data are mixed

```
var author =  createAuthorObject("Isaac", "Asimov", 500);
author.fullName() === "Isaac Asimov"
// → true
```

In this simple scenario, it is not overly burdensome. We only load (unnecessarily) the code for `isProlific`. Although in a real-world situation, instantiating an object might involve complex and tedious setup.

In the DOP version, where `createAuthorData` and `fullName` are separate, we can create the data to be passed to `fullName` in isolation, testing `fullName` in isolation as well. The following listing provides an example.

Listing A.10 Testing code in isolation (FP style)

```
var author =  {
  firstName: "Isaac",
  lastName: "Asimov"
};
fullName(author) === "Isaac Asimov"
// → true
```

If classes are used, it is only necessary to instantiate a data object. We do not need to load the code for `isProlific`, which lives in a separate class than `fullName`, in order to test `fullName`. The next listing lays out an example of this approach.

Listing A.11 Testing code in isolation (OOP style)

```
var data =  new AuthorData("Isaac", "Asimov");

NameCalculation.fullName(data) === "Isaac Asimov"
// → true
```

TIP Writing tests is easier when code is separated from data.

Benefit #3: Systems tend to be less complex

The third benefit of applying Principle #1 to our programs is that systems tend to be less complex. This benefit is the deepest one but also the one that is most subtle to explain.

The type of complexity I refer to is the one that makes systems hard to understand as defined in the paper, "Out of the Tar Pit," by Ben Moseley and Peter Marks (http://mng.bz/enzq). It has nothing to do with the complexity of the resources consumed by a program. Similarly, references to *simplicity* mean *not complex* (in other words, easy to understand).

▶ **NOTE** Complex in the context of this book means *hard to understand.*

Keep in mind that complexity and simplicity (like hard and easy) are not absolute but relative concepts. The complexity of two systems can be compared to determine whether system A is more complex (or simpler) than system B. When code and data are kept separate, the system tends to be easier to understand for two reasons:

- *The scope of a data entity or a code entity is smaller than the scope of an entity that combines code and data.* Each entity is therefore easier to understand.
- *Entities of the system are split into disjoint groups: code and data.* Entities therefore have fewer relations to other entities.

This insight is illustrated in a class diagram of our fictitious Library Management System, where code and data are mixed. It is not necessary to know the details of the classes of this system to see that the diagram in figure A.2 represents a complex system;

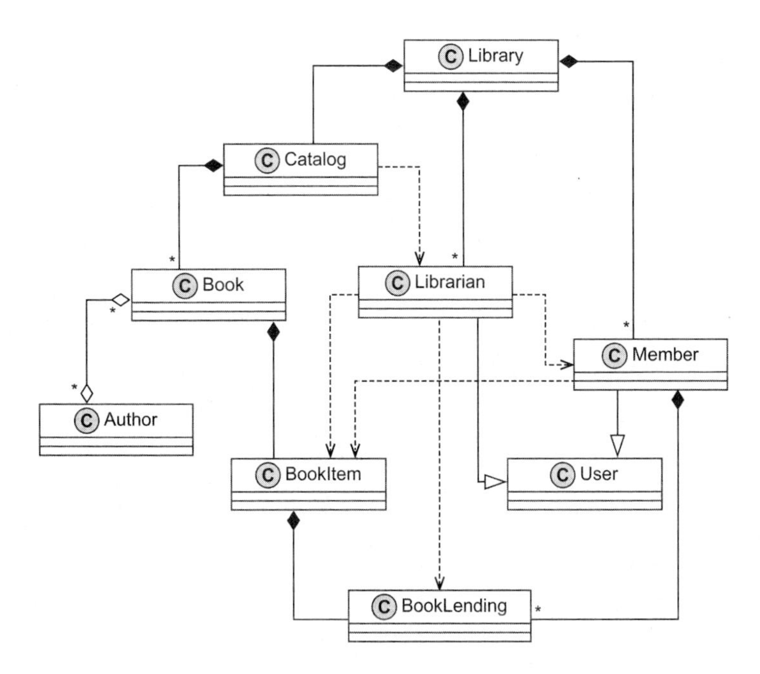

Figure A.2 A class diagram overview for the Library Management System

this in the sense that it is hard to understand. The system is hard to understand because there are many dependencies between the entities that compose the system.

The most complex entity of the system in figure A.2 is the `Librarian` entity, which is connected via six relations to other entities. Some relations are data relations (association and composition), and some relations are code relations (inheritance and dependency). But in this design, the `Librarian` entity mixes code and data, and therefore, it has to be involved in both data and code relations. If each entity of the system is split into a code entity and a data entity *without making any further modification to the system*, the result (see figure A.3) is made of two disconnected parts:

- The left part is made only of data entities and data relations: association and composition.
- The right part is made only of code entities and code relations: dependency and inheritance.

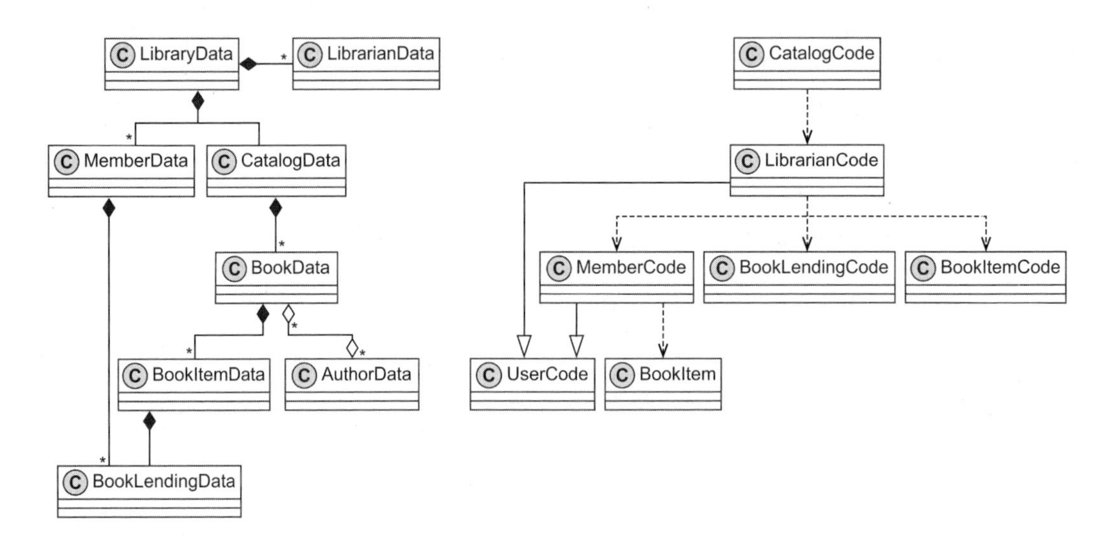

Figure A.3 A class diagram where every class is split into code and data entities

The new system, where code and data are separate, is easier to understand than the original system, where code and data are mixed. Thus, the data part of the system and the code part of the system can each be understood on its own.

TIP A system made of disconnected parts is less complex than a system made of a single part.

One could argue that the complexity of the original system, where code and data are mixed, is due to a bad design and that an experienced OOP developer would have designed a simpler system using smart design patterns. That is true, but in a sense, it is irrelevant. The point of Principle #1 is that a system made of entities that do not combine code and data tends to be simpler than a system made of entities that do combine code and data.

It has been said many times that *simplicity is hard*. According to the first principle of DOP, simplicity is easier to achieve when separating code and data.

TIP Simplicity is easier to achieve when code is separated from data.

A.1.3 Cost for Principle #1

This section looks at the cost involved when we implement Principle #1. The price we pay in order to benefit from the separation between code and data is threefold:

- There is no control on what code can access what data.
- There is no packaging.
- Our systems are made from more entities.

Cost #1: There is no control on what code can access what data

When code and data are mixed, it is easy to understand what pieces of code can access what kinds of data. For example, in OOP, the data is encapsulated in an object, which guarantees that the data is accessible only by the object's methods. In DOP, data stands on its own. It is transparent if you like, and as a consequence, it can be accessed by any piece of code.

When refactoring the shape of some data, *every* place in our code that accesses this kind of data must be known. Moreover, without the application of Principle #3 (enforcing data immutability), which we discuss later, accessing data by any piece of code is inherently unsafe. In that case, it would be hard to guarantee the validity of our data.

TIP Data safety is ensured by another principle (Principle #3) that enforces data immutability.

Cost #2: There is no packaging

One of the benefits of mixing code and data is that when you have an object in hand, it is a package that contains both the code (via methods) and the data (via members). As a consequence, it is easy to discover how to manipulate the data: you look at the methods of the class.

In DOP, the code that manipulates the data could be anywhere. For example, `createAuthorData` might be in one file and `fullName` in another file. This makes it difficult for developers to discover that the `fullName` function is available. In some situations, it could lead to wasted time and unnecessary code duplication.

Cost #3: Our systems are made from more entities

Let's do simple arithmetic. Imagine a system made of N classes that combine code and data. When you split the system into code entities and data entities, you get a system made of $2N$ entities. This calculation is not accurate, however, because usually when you separate code and data, the class hierarchy tends to get simpler as we need less class inheritance and composition. Therefore, the number of classes in the resulting system will probably be somewhere between *N* and 2*N*.

On one hand, when adhering to Principle #1, the entities of the system are simpler. On the other hand, there are more entities. This cost is mitigated by Principle #2, which guides us to represent our data with generic data structures.

TIP When adhering to Principle #1, systems are made of simpler entities, but there are more of them.

A.1.4 Summary of Principle #1

DOP requires the separation of code from data. In OOP languages, aggregate code in static methods and data in classes with no methods. In FP languages, avoid hiding data in the lexical scope of functions.

Separating code from data comes at a price. It reduces control over what pieces of code access our data and can cause our systems to be made of more entities. But it's worth paying the price because, when adhering to this principle, our code can be reused in different contexts in a straightforward way and tested in isolation. Moreover, a system made of separate entities for code and data tends to be easier to understand.

DOP Principle #1: Separate code from data

To follow this principle, we separate code from data in such a way that the code resides in functions whose behavior does not depend on data that is encapsulated in the function's context. The following diagram provides a visual representation of this.

DOP Principle #1: Separate code from data

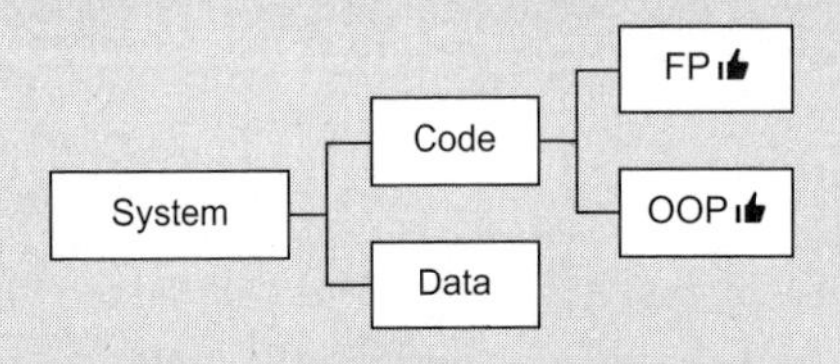

- Benefits include
  - Code can be reused in different contexts.
  - Code can be tested in isolation.
  - Systems tend to be less complex.
- The cost for implementing Principle #1 includes
  - No control on what code accesses which data.
  - No packaging.
  - More entities.

A.2 Principle #2: Represent data with generic data structures

When adhering to Principle #1, code is separated from data. DOP is not opinionated about the programming constructs to use for organizing the code, but it has a lot to say about how the data should be represented. This is the theme of Principle #2.

The most common generic data structures are maps (aka dictionaries) and arrays (or lists). But other generic data structures (e.g., sets, trees, and queues) can be used as well. Principle #2 does not deal with the mutability or the immutability of the data. That is the theme of Principle #3.

PRINCIPLE #2 Represent application data with generic data structures.

A.2.1 Illustration of Principle #2

In DOP, data is represented with generic data structures (like maps and arrays) instead of instantiating data via specific classes. In fact, most of the data entities that appear in a typical application can be represented with maps and arrays (or lists). But there exist other generic data structures (e.g., sets, lists, queues, etc.) that might be required in some use cases. Let's look at the same simple example we used to illustrate Principle #1 (data that represents an author).

An author is a data entity with a `firstName`, a `lastName`, and the number of `books` they have written. Principle #2 is broken when we use a specific class to represent an author as this listing reveals.

Listing A.12 Breaking Principle #2 in OOP

```
class AuthorData {
  constructor(firstName, lastName, books) {
    this.firstName = firstName;
    this.lastName = lastName;
    this.books = books;
  }
}
```

Principle #2 is followed when using a map (a dictionary or an associative array) as a generic data structure that represents an author. The following listing illustrates how we can follow this principle in OOP.

Listing A.13 Following Principle #2 in OOP

```
function createAuthorData(firstName, lastName, books) {
  var data = new Map;
  data.firstName = firstName;
  data.lastName = lastName;
```

```
  data.books = books;
  return data;
}
```

In a language like JavaScript, we can also instantiate a map via a data literal, which is a bit more convenient. The following listing shows an example.

Listing A.14 Following Principle #2 with map literals

```
function createAuthorData(firstName, lastName, books) {
  return {
    firstName: firstName,
    lastName: lastName,
    books: books
  };
}
```

A.2.2 Benefits of Principle #2

Using generic data structures to represent data has multiple benefits. We cover these benefits in greater detail in the following sections:

- The ability to use generic functions that are not limited to our specific use case
- A flexible data model

Using functions that are not limited to a specific use case

Using generic data structures to represent data makes it possible to manipulate data with a rich set of functions that are available on those data structures natively in our programming language. Additionally, third-party libraries also provide more of these functions. For instance, JavaScript natively provides some basic functions on maps and arrays, and third-party libraries like Lodash (https://lodash.com/) extend the functionality with even more functions. There is a famous quote by Alan Perlis that summarizes this benefit:

> *It is better to have 100 functions operate on one data structure than to have 10 functions operate on 10 data structures.*
>
> —Alan Perlis ("Epigrams on Programming," 1982)

When an author is represented as a map, the author can be serialized into JSON using `JSON.stringify()`, which is part of JavaScript. The following listing provides an example.

Listing A.15 [#serialize-klipse-js],reftext="A.1"

```
var data = createAuthorData("Isaac", "Asimov", 500);
JSON.stringify(data);
// → "{\"firstName\":\"Isaac\",\"lastName\":\"Asimov\",\"books\":500}"
```

Serializing author data without the number of books can be accomplished via Lodash's `_.pick()` function. The following listing uses `_.pick()` to create an object with a subset of keys.

Listing A.16 Manipulating data with generic functions

```
var data = createAuthorData("Isaac", "Asimov", 500);
var dataWithoutBooks = _.pick(data, ["firstName", "lastName"]);
JSON.stringify(dataWithoutBooks);
// → "{\"firstName\":\"Isaac\",\"lastName\":\"Asimov\"}"
```

TIP When adhering to Principle #2, a rich set of functionality is available for data manipulation.

FLEXIBLE DATA MODEL

When using generic data structures, the data model is flexible, and data is not forced into a specific shape. Data can be created with no predefined shape, and its shape can be modified at will.

In classic OOP, when *not* adhering to Principle #2, each piece of data is instantiated via a class and must follow a rigid shape. When a slightly different data shape is needed, a new class must be defined. Take, for example, `AuthorData`, a class that represents an author entity made of three fields: `firstName`, `lastName`, and `books`. Suppose that you want to add a field called `fullName` with the full name of the author. If we fail to adhere to Principle #2, a new class, `AuthorDataWithFullName`, must be defined. However, when using generic data structures, fields can be added to (or removed from) a map *on the fly* as the following listing shows.

Listing A.17 Adding a field on the fly

```
var data = createAuthorData("Isaac", "Asimov", 500);
data.fullName = "Isaac Asimov";
```

TIP Working with a flexible data model is particularly useful in applications where the shape of the data tends to be dynamic (e.g., web apps and web services).

Part 1 of the book explores in detail the benefits of a flexible data model in real-world applications. Next, let's explore the cost for adhering to Principle #2.

A.2.3 Cost for Principle #2

As with any programming principle, using this principle comes with its own set of trade-offs. The price paid for representing data with generic data structures is as follows:

- There is a slight performance hit.
- No data schema is required.
- No compile-time check that the data is valid is necessary.
- In some statically-typed languages, type casting is needed.

COST #1: PERFORMANCE HIT

When specific classes are used to instantiate data, retrieving the value of a class member is fast because the compiler knows how the data will look and can do many optimizations. With generic data structures, it is harder to optimize, so retrieving the value associated to a key in a map, for example, is a bit slower than retrieving the value of a class member. Similarly, setting the value of an arbitrary key in a map is a bit slower than setting the value of a class member. In most programming languages, this performance hit is not significant, but it is something to keep in mind.

TIP Retrieving and storing the value associated to an arbitrary key from a map is a bit slower than with a class member.

COST #2: NO DATA SCHEMA

When data is instantiated from a class, the information about the data shape is in the class definition. Every piece of data has an associated data shape. The existence of data schema at a class level is useful for developers and for IDEs because

- Developers can easily discover the expected data shape.
- IDEs provide features like field name autocompletion.

When data is represented with generic data structures, the data schema is not part of the data representation. As a consequence, some pieces of data might have an associated data schema and other pieces of data do not (see Principle #4).

TIP When generic data structures are used to store data, the data shape is not part of the data representation.

COST #3: NO COMPILE-TIME CHECK THAT THE DATA IS VALID

Look again at the `fullName` function in the following listing, which was created to explore Principle #1. This function receives the data it manipulates as an argument.

Listing A.18 Declaring the `fullName` function

```
function fullName(data) {
  return data.firstName + " " + data.lastName;
}
```

When data is passed to `fullName` that does not conform to the shape `fullName` expects, an error occurs at run time. With generic data structures, mistyping the field storing the first name (e.g., `fistName` instead of `firstName`) does not result in a compile-time error or an exception. Rather, `firstName` is mysteriously omitted from the result. The following listing shows this unexpected behavior.

Listing A.19 Unexpected behavior with invalid data

```
fullName({fistName: "Issac", lastName: "Asimov"});
// → "undefined Asimov"
```

When we instantiate data via classes with a rigid data shape, this type of error is caught at compile time. This drawback is mitigated by the application of Principle #4 that deals with data validation.

TIP When data is represented with generic data structures, data shape errors are caught only at run time.

Cost #4: The need for explicit type casting

In some statically-typed languages, explicit type casting is needed. This section takes a look at explicit type casting in Java and at dynamic fields in C#.

In a statically-typed language like Java, author data can be represented as a map whose keys are of type `string` and whose values are of types `Object`. For example, in Java, author data is represented by a `Map<String, Object>` as the following listing illustrates.

Listing A.20 Author data as a string map in Java

```
var asimov = new HashMap<String, Object>();

asimov.put("firstName", "Isaac");
asimov.put("lastName", "Asimov");
asimov.put("books", 500);
```

Because the information about the exact type of the field values is not available at compile time, when accessing a field, an explicit type cast is required. For instance, in order to check whether an author is prolific, the value of the `books` field must be type cast to an integer as the next listing shows.

Listing A.21 Type casting is required when accessing a field in Java

```
class AuthorRating {
  static boolean isProlific (Map<String, Object> data) {
    return (int)data.get("books") > 100;
  }
}
```

Some Java JSON serialization libraries like Gson (https://github.com/google/gson) support serialization of maps of type `Map<String, Object>`, without requiring the user to do any type casting. All the magic happens behind the scenes!

C# supports a dynamic data type called `dynamic` (see http://mng.bz/voqJ), which allows type checking to occur at run time. Using this feature, author data is represented as a dictionary, where the keys are of type `string`, and the values are of type `dynamic`. The next listing provides this representation.

Listing A.22 Author data as a dynamic string map in C#

```
var asimov = new Dictionary<string, dynamic>();
asimov["name"] = "Isaac Asimov";
asimov["books"] =  500;
```

The information about the exact type of the field values is resolved at run time. When accessing a field, no type cast is required. For instance, when checking whether an author is prolific, the books field can be accessed as though it were declared as an integer as in this listing.

Listing A.23 Type casting is not needed when accessing dynamic fields in C#

```
class AuthorRating {
  public static bool isProlific (Dictionary<String, dynamic> data) {
    return data["books"] > 100;
  }
}
```

A.2.4 Summary of Principle #2

DOP uses generic data structures to represent data. This might cause a (small) performance hit and impose the need to manually document the shape of data because the compiler cannot validate it statically. Adherence to this principle enables the manipulation of data with a rich set of generic functions (provided by the language and by third-party libraries). Additionally, our data model is flexible. At this point, the data can be either mutable or immutable. The next principle (Principle #3) illustrates the value of immutability.

DOP Principle #2: Represent data with generic data structures

To comply with this principle, we represent application data with generic data structures, mostly maps and arrays (or lists). The following diagram shows a visual representation of this principle.

DOP Principle #2: Represent data with generic data structures

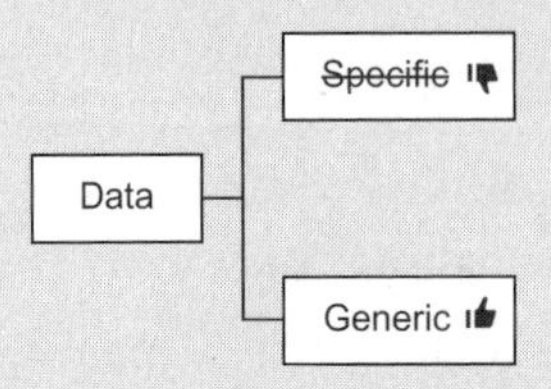

- Benefits include
  - Using generic functions that are not limited to our specific use case
  - A flexible data model
- The cost for implementing this principle includes
  - There is a slight performance hit.
  - No data schema is required.
  - No compile time check that the data is valid is necessary.
  - In some statically-typed languages, explicit type casting is needed.

A.3 Principle #3: Data is immutable

With data separated from code and represented with generic data structures, how are changes to the data managed? DOP is very strict on this question. Mutation of data is not allowed! In DOP, changes to data are accomplished by creating new versions of the data. The *reference* to a variable may be changed so that it refers to a new version of the data, but the *value* of the data itself must never change.

> PRINCIPLE #3 Data is immutable.

A.3.1 Illustration of Principle #3

Think about the number 42. What happens to 42 when you add 1 to it? Does it become 43? No, 42 stays 42 forever! Now, put 42 inside an object: `{num: 42}`. What happens to the object when you add 1 to 42? Does it become 43? It depends on the programming language.

- In Clojure, a programming language that embraces data immutability, the value of the `num` field stays `42` forever, no matter what.
- In many programming languages, the value of the `num` field becomes `43`.

For instance, in JavaScript, mutating the field of a map referred by two variables has an impact on both variables. The following listing demonstrates this.

Listing A.24 Mutating data referred by two variables impact both variables

```
var myData = {num: 42};
var yourData = myData;

yourData.num = yourData.num + 1;
console.log(myData.num);
// → 43
```

Now, `myData.num` equals `43`. According to DOP, however, data should never change! Instead of mutating data, a new version of it is created. A naive (and inefficient) way to create a new version of data is to clone it before modifying it. For instance, in listing A.25, there is a function that changes the value of a field inside an object by cloning the object via `Object.assign`, provided natively by JavaScript. When `changeValue` is called on `myData`, `myData` is not affected; `myData.num` remains `42`. This is the essence of data immutability!

Listing A.25 Data immutability via cloning

```
function changeValue(obj, k, v) {
  var res = Object.assign({}, obj);
  res[k] = v;
```

```
  return res;
}

var myData = {num: 42};
var yourData = changeValue(myData, "num", myData.num + 1);
console.log(myData.num);
// → 43
```

Embracing immutability in an efficient way, both in terms of computation and memory, requires a third-party library like Immutable.js (https://immutable-js.com/), which provides an efficient implementation of persistent data structures (aka immutable data structures). In most programming languages, libraries exist that provide an efficient implementation of persistent data structures.

With `Immutable.js`, JavaScript native maps and arrays are not used, but rather, immutable maps and immutable lists are instantiated via `Immutable.Map` and `Immutable.List`. An element of a map is accessed using the `get` method. A new version of the map is created when a field is modified with the `set` method.

Listing A.26 shows how to create and manipulate immutable data efficiently with a third-party library. In the output, `yourData.get("num")` is `43`, but `myData.get("num")` remains `42`.

Listing A.26 Creating and manipulating immutable data

```
var myData = Immutable.Map({num: 42})
var yourData = myData.set("num", 43);
console.log(yourData.get("num"));
// → 43
console.log(myData.get("num"));
// → 42
```

TIP When data is immutable, instead of mutating data, a new version of it is created.

A.3.2 *Benefits of Principle #3*

When programs are constrained from mutating data, we derive benefit in numerous ways. The following sections detail these benefits:

- Data access to all with confidence
- Predictable code behavior
- Fast equality checks
- Concurrency safety for free

BENEFIT #1: DATA ACCESS TO ALL WITH CONFIDENCE

According to Principle #1 (separate code from data), data access is transparent. Any function is allowed to access any piece of data. Without data immutability, we must be careful when passing data as an argument to a function. We can either make sure the function does not mutate the data or clone the data before it is passed to the function. When adhering to data immutability, none of this is required.

TIP When data is immutable, it can be passed to any function with confidence because data never changes.

BENEFIT #2: PREDICTABLE CODE BEHAVIOR

As an illustration of what is meant by *predictable*, here is an example of an *unpredictable* piece of code that does not adhere to data immutability. Take a look at the piece of asynchronous JavaScript code in the following listing. When data is mutable, the behavior of asynchronous code is not predictable.

Listing A.27 Unpredictable asynchronous code when data is mutable

```
var myData = {num: 42};
setTimeout(function (data){
  console.log(data.num);
}, 1000, myData);
myData.num = 0;
```

The value of `data.num` inside the timeout callback is not predictable. It depends on whether the data is modified by another piece of code during the 1,000 ms of the timeout. However, with immutable data, it is guaranteed that data never changes and that `data.num` is always `42` inside the callback.

TIP When data is immutable, the behavior of code that manipulates data is predictable.

BENEFIT #3: FAST EQUALITY CHECKS

With UI frameworks like React.js, there are frequent checks to see what portion of the UI data has been modified since the previous rendering cycle. Portions that did not change are not rendered again. In fact, in a typical frontend application, most of the UI data is left unchanged between subsequent rendering cycles.

In a React application that does not adhere to data immutability, it is necessary to check every (nested) part of the UI data. However, in a React application that follows data immutability, it is possible to optimize the comparison of the data for the case where data is not modified. Indeed, when the object address is the same, then it is certain that the data did not change.

Comparing object addresses is much faster than comparing all the fields. In part 1 of the book, fast equality checks are used to reconcile between concurrent mutations in a highly scalable production system.

TIP Immutable data enables fast equality checks by comparing data by reference.

BENEFIT #4: FREE CONCURRENCY SAFETY

In a multi-threaded environment, concurrency safety mechanisms (e.g., mutexes) are often used to prevent the data in thread `A` from being modified while it is accessed in thread `B`. In addition to the slight performance hit they cause, concurrency safety mechanisms impose a mental burden that makes code writing and reading much more difficult.

TIP Adherence to data immutability eliminates the need for a concurrency mechanism. The data you have in hand never changes!

A.3.3 *Cost for Principle #3*

As with the previous principles, applying Principle #3 comes at a price. The following sections look at these costs:

- Performance hit
- Required library for persistent data structures

COST #1: PERFORMANCE HIT

As mentioned earlier, implementations of persistent data structures exist in most programming languages. But even the most efficient implementation is a bit slower than the in-place mutation of the data. In most applications, the performance hit and the additional memory consumption involved in using immutable data structures is not significant. But this is something to keep in mind.

COST #2: REQUIRED LIBRARY FOR PERSISTENT DATA STRUCTURES

In a language like Clojure, the native data structures of the language are immutable. However, in most programming languages, adhering to data immutability requires the inclusion a third-party library that provides an implementation of persistent data structures.

The fact that the data structures are not native to the language means that it is difficult (if not impossible) to enforce the usage of immutable data across the board. Also, when integrating with third-party libraries (e.g., a chart library), persistent data structures must be converted into equivalent native data structures.

A.3.4 *Summary of Principle #3*

DOP considers data as a value that never changes. Adherence to this principle results in code that is predictable even in a multi-threaded environment, and equality checks are fast. However, a non-negligible mind shift is required, and in most programming languages, a third-party library is needed to provide an efficient implementation of persistent data structures.

DOP Principle #3: Data is immutable

To adhere to this principle, data is represented with immutable structures. The following diagram provides a visual representation of this.

DOP Principle #3: Data is immutable

- Benefits include
  - Data access to all with confidence
  - Predictable code behavior
  - Fast equality checks
  - Concurrency safety for free
- The cost for implementing Principle #3 includes
  - A performance hit
  - Required library for persistent data structures

A.4 Principle #4: Separate data schema from data representation

With data separated from code and represented with generic and immutable data structures, now comes the question of how do we express the shape of the data? In DOP, the expected shape is expressed as a data schema that is kept separated from the data itself. The main benefit of Principle #4 is that it allows developers to decide which pieces of data should have a schema and which pieces of data should not.

> PRINCIPLE #4 Separate data schema from data representation.

A.4.1 Illustration of Principle #4

Think about handling a request for the addition of an author to the system. To keep things simple, imagine that such a request contains only basic information about the author: their first name and last name and, optionally, the number of books they have written. As seen in Principle #2 (represent data with generic data structures), in DOP, request data is represented as a string map, where the map is expected to have three fields:

- `firstName`—a string
- `lastName`—a string
- `books`—a number (optional)

In DOP, the expected shape of data is represented as data that is kept separate from the request data. For instance, JSON schema (https://json-schema.org/) can represent the data schema of the request with a map. The following listing provides an example.

Listing A.28 The JSON schema for an `addAuthor` request data

Data is expected to be a map (in JSON, a map is called an object).

Only firstName and lastName fields are required.

```
var addAuthorRequestSchema = {
  "type": "object",
  "required": ["firstName", "lastName"],
```

```
  "properties": {
    "firstName": {"type": "string"},
    "lastName": {"type": "string"},
    "books": {"type": "integer"}
  }
};
```

firstName must be a string.

lastName must be a string.

books must be a number (when it is provided).

A data validation library is used to check whether a piece of data conforms to a data schema. For instance, we could use Ajv JSON schema validator (https://ajv.js.org/) to validate data with the `validate` function that returns `true` when data is valid and `false` when data is invalid. The following listing shows this approach.

Listing A.29 Data validation with Ajv

```
var validAuthorData = {
  firstName: "Isaac",
  lastName: "Asimov",
  books: 500
};

ajv.validate(addAuthorRequestSchema,
  validAuthorData); //
// → true

var invalidAuthorData = {
  firstName: "Isaac",
  lastNam: "Asimov",
  books: "five hundred"
};

ajv.validate(addAuthorRequestSchema,
  invalidAuthorData);
// → false
```

Data is valid.

Data has lastNam instead of lastName, and books is a string instead of a number.

When data is invalid, the details about data validation failures are available in a human readable format. The next listing shows this approach.

Listing A.30 Getting details about data validation failure

```
var invalidAuthorData = {
  firstName: "Isaac",
  lastNam: "Asimov",
  books: "five hundred"
};

var ajv = new Ajv({allErrors: true});
ajv.validate(addAuthorRequestSchema, invalidAuthorData);
ajv.errorsText(ajv.errors);
// → "data should have required property 'lastName',
// →  data.books should be number"
```

By default, Ajv stores only the first data validation error. Set allErrors: true to store all errors.

Data validation errors are stored internally as an array. In order to get a human readable string, use the errorsText function.

A.4.2 Benefits of Principle #4

Separation of data schema from data representation provides numerous benefits. The following sections describe these benefits in detail:

- Freedom to choose what data should be validated
- Optional fields
- Advanced data validation conditions
- Automatic generation of data model visualization

Benefit #1: Freedom to choose what data should be validated

When data schema is separated from data representation, we can instantiate data without specifying its expected shape. Such freedom is useful in various situations. For example,

- Rapid prototyping or experimentation
- Code refactoring and data validation

Consider rapid prototyping. In classic OOP, we need to instantiate every piece of data through a class. During the exploration phase of coding, when the final shape of our data is not yet known, being forced to update the class definition each time the data model changes slows us down. DOP enables a faster pace during the exploration phase by delaying the data schema definition to a later phase.

One common refactoring pattern is split phase refactoring (https://refactoring.com/catalog/splitPhase.html), where a single large function is split into multiple smaller functions with private scope. We call these functions with data that has already been validated by the larger function. In DOP, it is not necessary to specify the shape of the arguments of the inner functions, relying on the data validation that has already occurred.

Consider how to display some information about an author, such as their full name and whether they are considered prolific. Using the code shown earlier to illustrate Principle #2 to calculate the full name and the prolificity level of the author, one might come up with a `displayAuthorInfo` function as the following listing shows.

Listing A.31 Displaying author information

```
class NameCalculation {
  static fullName(data) {
    return data.firstName + " " + data.lastName;
  }
}

class AuthorRating {
  static isProlific (data) {
    return data.books > 100;
  }
}

var authorSchema = {
  "type": "object",
```

```
  "required": ["firstName", "lastName"],
  "properties": {
    "firstName": {"type": "string"},
    "lastName": {"type": "string"},
    "books": {"type": "integer"}
  }
};

function displayAuthorInfo(authorData) {
  if(!ajv.validate(authorSchema, authorData)) {
    throw "displayAuthorInfo called with invalid data";
  };
  console.log("Author full name is: ",
    NameCalculation.fullName(authorData));
  if(authorData.books == null) {
    console.log("Author has not written any book");
  } else {
    if (AuthorRating.isProlific(authorData)) {
      console.log("Author is prolific");
    } else {
      console.log("Author is not prolific");
    }
  }
}
```

Notice that the first thing done inside the body of `displayAuthorInfo` is to validate that the argument passed to the function. Now, apply the split phase refactoring pattern to this simple example and split the body of `displayAuthorInfo` into two inner functions:

- `displayFullName` displays the author's full name.
- `displayProlificity` displays whether the author is prolific or not.

The next listing shows the resulting code.

Listing A.32 Application of split phase refactoring pattern

```
function displayFullName(authorData) {
  console.log("Author full name is: ",
    NameCalculation.fullName(authorData));
}

function displayProlificity(authorData) {
  if(authorData.books == null) {
    console.log("Author has not written any book");
  } else {
    if (AuthorRating.isProlific(authorData)) {
      console.log("Author is prolific");
    } else {
      console.log("Author is not prolific");
    }
  }
}
```

```
function displayAuthorInfo(authorData) {
  if(!ajv.validate(authorSchema, authorData)) {
    throw "displayAuthorInfo called with invalid data";
  };
  displayFullName(authorData);
  displayProlificity(authorData);
}
```

Having the data schema separated from data representation eliminates the need to specify a data schema for the arguments of the inner functions `displayFullName` and `displayProlificity`. It makes the refactoring process a bit smoother. In some cases, the inner functions are more complicated, and it makes sense to specify a data schema for their arguments. DOP gives us the freedom to choose!

BENEFIT #2: OPTIONAL FIELDS

In OOP, allowing a class member to be optional is not easy. For instance, in Java one needs a special construct like the `Optional` class introduced in Java 8 (http://mng.bz/4jWa). In DOP, it is natural to declare a field as optional in a map. In fact, in JSON Schema, by default, every field is optional.

In order to make a field not optional, its name must be included in the `required` array as, for instance, in the author schema in listing A.33, where only `firstName` and `lastName` are required, and `books` is optional. Notice that when an optional field is defined in a map, its value is validated against the schema.

Listing A.33 A schema with an optional field

```
var authorSchema = {
  "type": "object",
  "required": ["firstName", "lastName"],       <-- books is not included in required, as it is an optional field.
  "properties": {
    "firstName": {"type": "string"},
    "lastName": {"type": "string"},
    "books": {"type": "number"}       <-- When present, books must be a number.
  }
};
```

Let's illustrate how the validation function deals with optional fields. A map without a `books` field is considered to be valid as listing A.34 shows. Alternatively, a map with a `books` field, where the value is not a number, is considered to be invalid as listing A.35 shows.

Listing A.34 A valid map without an optional field

```
var authorDataNoBooks = {
  "firstName": "Yehonathan",
  "lastName": "Sharvit"
};

ajv.validate(authorSchema, authorDataNoBooks);       <-- The validation passes, as books is an optional field.
// → true
```

Listing A.35 An invalid map with an invalid optional field

```
var authorDataInvalidBooks = {
  "firstName": "Albert",
  "lastName": "Einstein",
  "books": "Five"
};

validate(authorSchema, authorDataInvalidBooks);   <-- The validation fails, as books is not a number.
// → false
```

BENEFIT #3: ADVANCED DATA VALIDATION CONDITIONS

In DOP, data validation occurs at run time. It allows the definition of data validation conditions that go beyond the type of a field. For example, validating that a field is not only a string, but a string with a maximal number of characters or a number comprised in a range of numbers as well.

JSON Schema supports many other advanced data validation conditions such as regular expression validation for string fields or number fields that should be a multiple of a given number. The author schema in listing A.36 expects `firstName` and `lastName` to be strings of less than 100 characters, and `books` to be a number between 0 and 10,000.

Listing A.36 A schema with advanced data validation conditions

```
var authorComplexSchema = {
  "type": "object",
  "required": ["firstName", "lastName"],
  "properties": {
    "firstName": {
      "type": "string",
      "maxLength": 100
    },
    "lastName": {
      "type": "string",
      "maxLength": 100
    },
    "books": {
      "type": "integer",
      "minimum": 0,
      "maximum": 10000
    }
  }
};
```

BENEFIT #4: AUTOMATIC GENERATION OF DATA MODEL VISUALIZATION

With the data schema defined as data, we can use several tools to generate data model visualizations. With tools like JSON Schema Viewer (https://navneethg.github.io/jsonschemaviewer/) and Malli (https://github.com/metosin/malli), a UML diagram can be generated from a JSON schema.

For instance, the JSON schema in listing A.37 defines the shape of a `bookList` field, which is an array of books where each book is a map, and in figure A.4, it is visualized as a UML diagram. These tools generate the UML diagram from the JSON schema.

Listing A.37 A JSON schema with an array of objects

```
{
  "type": "object",
  "required": ["firstName", "lastName"],
  "properties": {
    "firstName": {"type": "string"},
    "lastName": {"type": "string"},
    "bookList": {
      "type": "array",
      "items": {
        "type": "object",
        "properties": {
          "title": {"type": "string"},
          "publicationYear": {"type": "integer"}
        }
      }
    }
  }
}
```

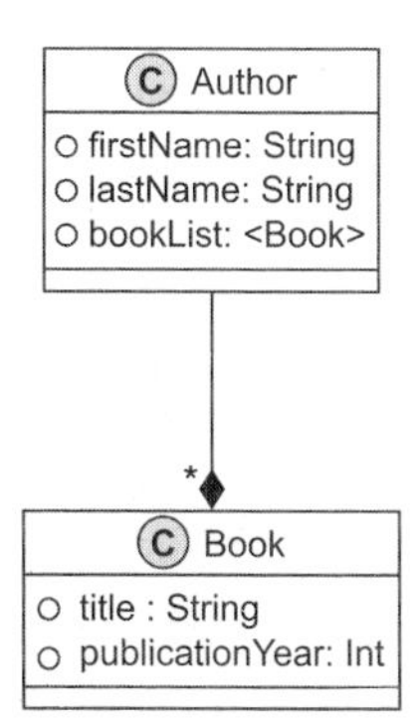

Figure A.4 A UML visualization of the JSON schema in listing A.37

A.4.3 Cost for Principle #4

Applying Principle #4 comes with a price. The following sections look at these costs:

- Weak connection between data and its schema
- Small performance hit

COST #1: WEAK CONNECTION BETWEEN DATA AND ITS SCHEMA

By definition, when data schema and data representation are separated, the connection between data and its schema is weaker than when data is represented with classes. Moreover, the schema definition language (e.g., JSON Schema) is not part of the programming language. It is up to the developer to decide where data validation is necessary and where it is superfluous. As the idiom says, with great power comes great responsibility.

Cost #2: Light performance hit

As mentioned earlier, implementations of JSON schema validation exist in most programming languages. In DOP, data validation occurs at run time, and it takes some time to run the data validation. In OOP, data validation usually occurs at compile time.

This drawback is mitigated by the fact that, even in OOP, some parts of data validation occur at run time. For instance, the conversion of a request JSON payload into an object occurs at run time. Moreover, in DOP, it is quite common to have some data validation parts enabled only during development and to disable them when the system runs in production. As a consequence, this performance hit is not significant.

A.4.4 Summary of Principle #4

In DOP, data is represented with immutable generic data structures. When additional information about the shape of the data is required, a data schema can be defined (e.g., using JSON Schema). Keeping the data schema separate from the data representation gives us the freedom to decide where data should be validated.

Moreover, data validation occurs at run time. As a consequence, data validation conditions that go beyond the static data types (e.g., the string length) can be expressed. However, with great power comes great responsibility, and it is up to the developer to remember to validate data.

DOP Principle #4: Separate between data schema and data representation

To adhere to this principle, separate between data schema and data representation. The following diagram illustrates this.

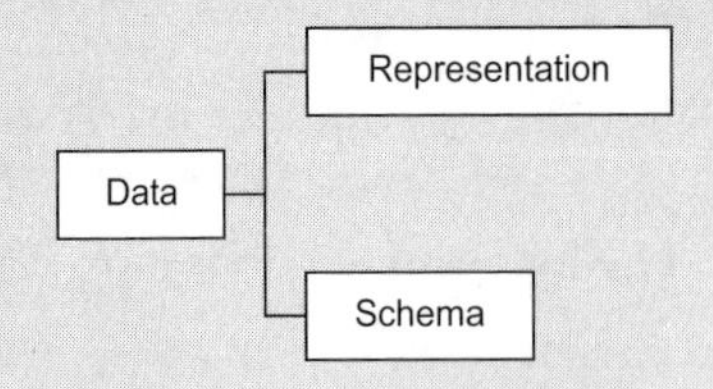

- Benefits include
  - Freedom to choose what data should be validated
  - Optional fields
  - Advanced data validation conditions
  - Automatic generation of data model visualization

- The cost for implementing Principle #4 includes
  - Weak connection between data and its schema
  - A small performance hit

Conclusion

DOP simplifies the design and implementation of information systems by treating data as a first-class citizen. This is made possible by adhering to four language-agnostic core principles (see figure A.5):

- Separating code from data.
- Representing application data with generic data structures.
- Treating data as immutable.
- Separating data schema from data representation.

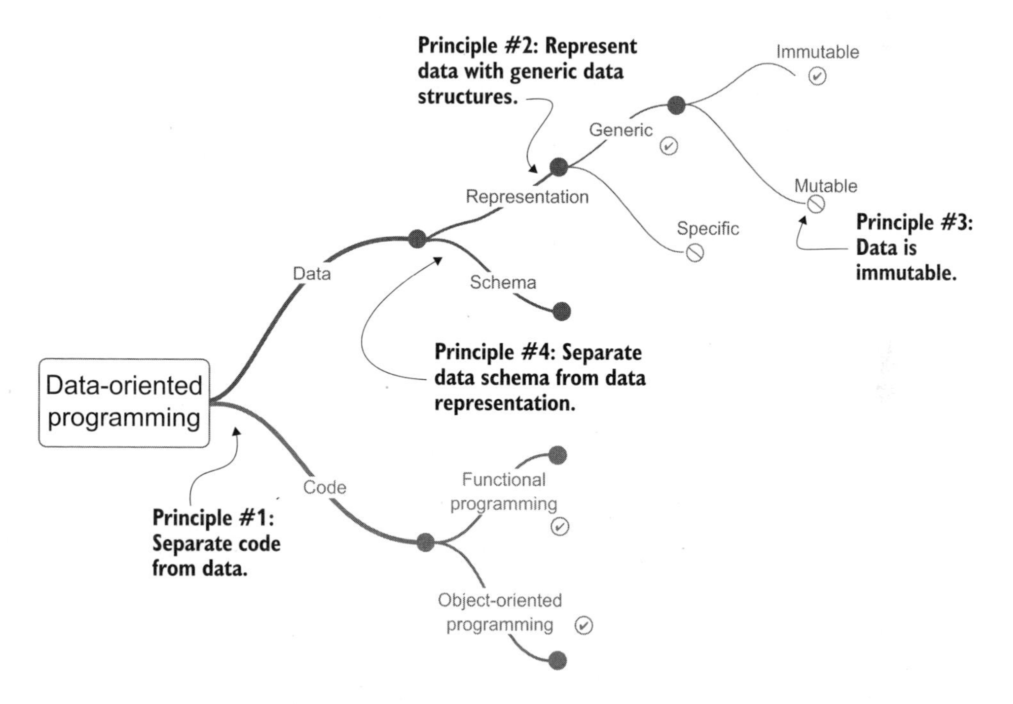

Figure A.1 The principles of DOP

This appendix has illustrated how each principle can be applied both in FP and OOP languages. It also describes at a high level the benefits of each principle and the costs of adherence to it.

appendix B
Generic data access in statically-typed languages

Representing data with generic data structures fits naturally in dynamically-typed programming languages like JavaScript, Ruby, or Python. However, in statically-typed programming languages like Java or C#, representing data as string maps with values of an unspecified type is not natural for several reasons:

- Accessing map fields requires a type cast.
- Map field names are not validated at compile time.
- Autocompletion and other convenient IDE features are not available.

This appendix explores various ways to improve access to generic data in statically-typed languages. We'll look at:

- Value getters for maps to avoid type casting when accessing map fields
- Typed getters for maps to benefit from compile-time checks for map field names
- Generic access for classes using reflection to benefit from autocompletion and other convenient IDE features

B.1 Dynamic getters for string maps

Let's start with a refresher about the approach we presented in part 1. Namely, we represented records as string maps and accessed map fields with dynamic getters and type casting.

▶ **NOTE** Most of the code snippets in this appendix use Java, but the approaches illustrated can be applied to other object-oriented statically-typed languages like C# or Go.

B.1.1 Accessing non-nested map fields with dynamic getters

Throughout this appendix, we will illustrate various ways to provide generic data access using a book record. Our record is made of these parts:

- `title` (a string)
- `isbn` (a string)
- `publicationYear` (an integer)

Listing B.1 shows the representation of two books, *Watchmen* and *Seven Habits of Highly Effective People*, in Java. These string maps contain values that are of type `Object`.

Listing B.1 Two books represented as maps

```
Map watchmenMap = Map.of(
  "isbn", "978-1779501127",
  "title", "Watchmen",
  "publicationYear", 1987
);

Map sevenHabitsMap = Map.of(
  "isbn", "978-1982137274",
  "title", "7 Habits of Highly Effective People",
  "publicationYear", 2020
);
```

The map fields can be accessed generically using a dynamic getter. The following listing shows the implementation.

Listing B.2 The implementation of dynamic getter for map fields

```
class DynamicAccess {
  static Object get(Map m, String k) {
    return (m).get(k);
  }
}
```

The drawback of dynamic getters is that a type cast is required to manipulate the value of a map field. For instance, as shown in listing B.3, a cast to `String` is needed to call the `toUpperCase` string method on the `title` field value.

Listing B.3 Accessing map fields with a dynamic getter and type casting

```
((String)DynamicAccess.get(watchmenMap, "title")).toUpperCase();
// → "WATCHMEN"
```

Dynamic getters provide generic data access in the sense that they do not require specific knowledge of the type of data the string map represents. As a consequence, the name of the field can be received dynamically (e.g., from the user) as listing B.4 shows. This works because, in order to access a book data field in a string map, it is not necessary to import the class that defines the book.

Listing B.4 Mapping a map field with a dynamic getter and type casting

```
var books = List.of(watchmenMap, sevenHabitsMap);
var fieldName = "title";

books.stream()
.map(x -> DynamicAccess.get(x, fieldName))
.map(x -> ((String)x).toUpperCase())
.collect(Collectors.toList())
// → ["WATCHMEN", "7 HABITS OF HIGHLY EFFECTIVE PEOPLE"]
```

Another aspect of the genericity of dynamic getters is that they work on any type of data. For instance, the dynamic getter for `title` works not only on books, but on any piece of data that has a `title` field.

B.1.2 Accessing nested map fields with dynamic getters

Listing B.5 presents an example of search results. Suppose that the search results represent as a string map, where

- Keys are book ISBNs.
- Values are book data represented as string maps as in the previous section.

Listing B.5 Search results represented as a map

```
Map searchResultsMap = Map.of(
  "978-1779501127", Map.of(
    "isbn", "978-1779501127",
    "title", "Watchmen",
    "publicationYear", 1987
  ),
  "978-1982137274", Map.of(
    "isbn", "978-1982137274",
    "title", "7 Habits of Highly Effective People",
    "publicationYear", 2020
  )
);
```

Book fields are nested in the search result map. In order to access nested map fields, a `get` method is added to the `DynamicAccess` class in listing B.6. This `get` method receives a list of strings that represents the information path of the nested map field.

Listing B.6 The implementation of dynamic getter for nested map fields

```
class DynamicAccess {
  static Object get(Map m, String k)  {
    return (m).get(k);
  }

  static Object get(Map m, List<String> path) {
    Object v = m;
    for (String k : path) {
```

```
      v = get((Map)v, k);
      if (v == null) {
        return null;
      }
    }
    return v;
  }
}
```

As with non-nested map fields in the previous section, type casting is required to manipulate a nested map field. Listing B.7 shows how to access these nested map fields. In the next section, we will look at how to avoid type casting when manipulating values in string maps.

Listing B.7 Nested map fields with a dynamic getter and type casting

```
((String)DynamicAccess.get(searchResultsMap,
  List.of("978-1779501127", "title"))).toUpperCase();
// → "WATCHMEN"
```

B.2 Value getters for maps

The simplest way to avoid type casting when manipulating the value of a string map field is to use a dynamic data type (see appendix A). Dynamic data types are supported in languages like C#, but not in languages like Java. Next, we'll illustrate how value getters make it possible to avoid type casting.

B.2.1 Accessing non-nested map fields with value getters

In this section, books are still represented as string maps with values of type `Object`. The following listing shows this representation.

Listing B.8 Two books represented as maps

```
Map watchmenMap = Map.of(
  "isbn", "978-1779501127",
  "title", "Watchmen",
  "publicationYear", 1987
);

Map sevenHabitsMap = Map.of(
  "isbn", "978-1982137274",
  "title", "7 Habits of Highly Effective People",
  "publicationYear", 2020
);
```

The idea of value getters is quite simple. Instead of doing the type casting *outside* the getter, it is done *inside* the getter. A value getter is required for every type: `getAsString` for strings, `getAsInt` for integers, `getAsFloat` for float numbers, `getAsBoolean` for Boolean values, and so forth.

The value getter approach is used by Java libraries like Apache Wicket (http://mng.bz/wnqQ) and Gson (https://github.com/google/gson). Listing B.9 shows an implementation for `getAsString` that retrieves a map field value as a string.

Listing B.9 The implementation of value getter for map fields

```
class DynamicAccess {
  static Object get(Map m, String k) {
    return (m).get(k);
  }

  static String getAsString(Map m, String k) {
    return (String)get(m, k);
  }
}
```

A map field can be accessed without type casting. For instance, we can use `getAsString` to manipulate a book title as in the next listing.

Listing B.10 Accessing non-nested fields with value getter

```
DynamicAccess.getAsString(watchmenMap, "title").toUpperCase();
// → "WATCHMEN"
```

Mapping over books with a value getter is a bit more convenient without type casting. Look at the following listing, for example.

Listing B.11 Mapping over a list of maps with a value getter

```
var books = List.of(watchmenMap, sevenHabitsMap);

books.stream()
.map(x -> DynamicAccess.getAsString(x, "title"))
.map(x -> x.toUpperCase())
.collect(Collectors.toList())
// → ["WATCHMEN", "7 HABITS OF HIGHLY EFFECTIVE PEOPLE"]
```

B.2.2 Accessing nested map fields with value getters

The value getter approach applies naturally to nested map fields. As in the dynamic getter section, suppose that search results are represented as a string map as in listing B.12. Book fields are nested in the search results map, where

- Keys are book ISBNs.
- Values are book data represented as string maps as in the previous section.

Listing B.12 Search results represented as a map

```
Map searchResultsMap = Map.of(
  "978-1779501127", Map.of(
```

```
    "isbn", "978-1779501127",
    "title", "Watchmen",
    "publicationYear", 1987
  ),
  "978-1982137274", Map.of(
    "isbn", "978-1982137274",
    "title", "7 Habits of Highly Effective People",
    "publicationYear", 2020
  )
);
```

In order to access nested map fields without type casting, we added a `getAsString` method to the `DynamicAccess` class. This class receives a list of strings that represents the information path of the nested map field as in the following listing.

Listing B.13 The implementation of value getter for nested map fields

```
class DynamicAccess {
  static Object get(Map m, String k)  {
    return (m).get(k);
  }

  static Object get(Map m, List<String> p) {
    Object v = m;
    for (String k : p) {
      v = get((Map)v, k);
      if (v == null) {
        return null;
      }
    }
    return v;
  }

  static String getAsString(Map m, String k) {
    return (String)get(m, k);
  }

  static String getAsString(Map m, List<String> p) {
    return (String)get(m, p);
  }
}
```

With the nested value getter, book titles can be manipulated inside search results without type casting. The following listing demonstrates this.

Listing B.14 Accessing nested map fields with value getter

```
var informationPath = List.of("978-1779501127", "title");

DynamicAccess.getAsString(searchResultsMap, informationPath)
.toUpperCase();
// → "WATCHMEN"
```

Value getters make data access a bit more convenient when avoiding type casting. The next section shows how typed getters make it possible to benefit from compile-time checks, even when data is represented as string maps.

B.3 Typed getters for maps

The typed getter approach is applicable in statically-typed languages that support generic types like Java and C#. In this section, we will illustrate the typed getter approach in Java.

B.3.1 Accessing non-nested map fields with typed getters

As in the previous sections, we'll use the representation of two books, *Watchmen* and *Seven Habits of Highly Effective People*, in Java as string maps. The following listing shows the maps, whose values are of type `Object`.

Listing B.15 Two books represented as maps

```
Map watchmenMap = Map.of(
  "isbn", "978-1779501127",
  "title", "Watchmen",
  "publicationYear", 1987
);

Map sevenHabitsMap = Map.of(
  "isbn", "978-1982137274",
  "title", "7 Habits of Highly Effective People",
  "publicationYear", 2020
);
```

The idea of typed getters is to create a generic object. This object would then contain information about:

- The field name
- The type of the field value

Now, we can use this object on a string map to retrieve the typed value of the field in the map. For example, in listing B.16, there is a typed getter named `TITLE` that retrieves the value of a field named `title` as a string. The implementation of typed getter is in listing B.17.

Listing B.16 Accessing map fields with a typed getter

```
Getter<String> TITLE = new Getter("title");
TITLE.get(watchmenMap).toUpperCase();
// → "WATCHMEN"
```

Listing B.17 The implementation of a typed getter

```
class Getter <T> {
  private String key;
```

```
  public <T> Getter (String k) {
    this.key = k;
  }

  public T get (Map m) {
    return (T)(DynamicAccess.get(m, key));
  }
}
```

TIP Typed getters are generic objects. Unlike value getters from the previous section, it is not necessary to provide an implementation for every type.

In a sense, typed getters support compile-time validation and autocompletion. If the name of the typed getter `TITLE` is misspelled, the compiler throws an error. Typing the first few letters of `TITLE` into an IDE provides autocompletion of the symbol of the typed getter. However, when you instantiate a typed getter, the field name must be passed as a string, and neither compile-time checks nor autocompletion are available. Mapping over a list of maps with a typed getter is quite simple as you can see in the following listing.

Listing B.18 Mapping over a list of maps with a typed getter

```
var books = List.of(watchmenMap, sevenHabitsMap);

books.stream()
.map(x -> TITLE.get(x))
.map(x -> x.toUpperCase())
.collect(Collectors.toList())
// → ["WATCHMEN", "7 HABITS OF HIGHLY EFFECTIVE PEOPLE"]
```

B.3.2 Accessing nested map fields with typed getters

The typed getter approach extends well to nested map fields. As in the value getter section, suppose that search results, presented in listing B.19, are represented as a string map, where

- Keys are book ISBNs.
- Values are book data represented as string maps as in the previous section.

Listing B.19 Search results represented as a map

```
Map searchResultsMap = Map.of(
  "978-1779501127", Map.of(
    "isbn", "978-1779501127",
    "title", "Watchmen",
    "publicationYear", 1987
  ),
  "978-1982137274", Map.of(
    "isbn", "978-1982137274",
    "title", "7 Habits of Highly Effective People",
    "publicationYear", 2020
  )
);
```

In order to support nested map fields, a constructor is added to the `Getter` class, which receives a list of strings that represents the information path. The following listing shows this implementation.

Listing B.20 A nested typed getter

```
class Getter <T> {
  private List<String> path;
  private String key;
  private boolean nested;

  public <T> Getter (List<String> path) {
    this.path = path;
    nested = true;
  }

  public <T> Getter (String k) {
    this.key = k;
    nested = false;
  }

  public T get (Map m) {
    if(nested) {
      return (T)(DynamicAccess.get(m, path));
    }
    return (T)(DynamicAccess.get(m, key));
  }
}
```

Nested map fields are manipulated with typed getters without any type casting. The following listing provides an example.

Listing B.21 Accessing nested map fields with typed getter

```
var informationPath = List.of("978-1779501127",
  "title");

Getter<String> NESTED_TITLE = new Getter(informationPath);
NESTED_TITLE.get(searchResultsMap).toUpperCase();
// → "WATCHMEN"
```

Why use typed getters? Typed getters provide several benefits:

- No required type casting
- No need for implementing a getter for each and every type
- Compile-time validation at usage time
- Autocompletion at usage time

However, at creation time, map fields are accessed as strings. The next section illustrates how to provide generic access when data is represented not as string maps but as classes.

B.4 Generic access to class members

Providing generic access to class members is a totally different approach. With this technique, we represent data with classes as in traditional OOP and use reflection in order to provide generic data access.

▶ **NOTE** The generic access to class members approach is applicable in statically-typed languages that support reflection like Java and C#. This section illustrates the approach in Java.

B.4.1 Generic access to non-nested class members

Instead of representing data as string maps, data can be represented as classes with data members only, providing generic access to the class members via reflection. This approach is interesting as only read data access is needed. However, when creating new versions of data or adding new data fields, it is better to represent data with maps as in part 1 of the book.

▶ **NOTE** The approach presented in this section is applicable only for read data access.

Here are a few guidelines in order to represent a book as a class. Make sure that

- The class has only data members (no methods).
- The members are public.
- The members are immutable.
- The `hashCode()`, `equals()` and `toString()` methods are properly implemented.

For instance, in Java, mark the members with `public` and `final` as in listing B.22. In the listing, the implementation of the `hashCode()`, `equals()`, and `toString()` methods are omitted for the sake of simplicity.

Listing B.22 Representing books with a class

```
public class BookData {
  public final String isbn;
  public final String title;
  public final Integer publicationYear;
  public BookData (
    String isbn,
    String title,
    Integer publicationYear) {
      this.isbn = isbn;
      this.title = title;
      this.publicationYear = publicationYear;
    }

  public boolean equals(Object o) {
    // Omitted for sake of simplicity
  }
```

```
  public int hashCode() {
    // Omitted for sake of simplicity
  }

  public String toString() {
    // Omitted for sake of simplicity
  }
}
```

Since Java 14, there is a simpler way to represent data using data records (http://mng.bz/q2q2) as listing B.23 displays. Data records provide

- Private `final` fields
- Public read accessors
- A public constructor, whose signature is derived from the record component list
- Implementations of `equals()` and `hashCode()` methods, which specify that two records are equal if they are of the same type and their record components are equal
- Implementation of `toString()`, which includes the string representation of the record components with their names

Listing B.23 Representing books with a record

```
public record BookData (String isbn,
  String title,
  Integer publicationYear
) {}
```

Let's create two objects (or records) for *Watchmen* and *Seven Habits of Highly Effective People*. The following listing provides the code for the two objects.

Listing B.24 Two book records

```
BookData watchmenRecord = new BookData(
  "978-1779501127",
  "Watchmen",
  1987
);

BookData sevenHabitsRecord = new BookData(
  "978-1982137274",
  "7 Habits of Highly Effective People",
  2020
);
```

The traditional way to access a data member is via its accessor (e.g., `watchmen.title()` to retrieve the title of *Watchmen*). In order to access a data member whose name comes from a dynamic source like a variable (or as part of a request payload), we need to use *reflection*. In Java, accessing the `title` field in a book looks like the code snippet in the following listing.

Listing B.25 Accessing a data member via reflection

```
watchmenRecord
.getClass()
.getDeclaredField("title")
.get(watchmenRecord)
// → "watchmen"
```

Listing B.26 shows how reflection can be used to provide access to any data member. The listing provides the implementation of dynamic access to non-nested class members.

Listing B.26 Accessing non-nested class members dynamically

```
class DynamicAccess {
  static Object get(Object o, String k)  {
    if(o instanceof Map) {
      return ((Map)o).get(k);
    }
    try {
      return (o.getClass().getDeclaredField(k).get(o));
    } catch (IllegalAccessException | NoSuchFieldException e) {
      return null;
    }
  }

  static String getAsString(Object o, String k) {
    return (String)get(o, k);
  }
}
```

Now, data members are accessible with the same genericity and dynamism as fields in a string map. The code in the next listing shows how this is done.

Listing B.27 Accessing a class member dynamically

```
((String)DynamicAccess.get(watchmenRecord, "title")).toUpperCase();
// → "WATCHMEN"
```

Without any code modification, value getters (presented earlier in this appendix in the context of string maps) can now work with classes and records. The following listing uses value getters in this way.

Listing B.28 Accessing a class member with a value getter

```
DynamicAccess.getAsString(watchmenRecord, "title").toUpperCase();
// → "WATCHMEN"
```

It is possible to map over a list of objects without having to import the class definition of the objects we map over. This is shown in the following listing.

Listing B.29 Mapping over a list of objects with a value getter

```
var books = List.of(watchmenRecord, sevenHabitsRecord);

books.stream()
.map(x -> DynamicAccess.getAsString(x, "title"))
.map(x -> x.toUpperCase())
.collect(Collectors.toList())
// → ["WATCHMEN", "7 HABITS OF HIGHLY EFFECTIVE PEOPLE"]
```

The typed getters we introduced earlier in the appendix can be used on objects. Take a look at the following listing to see how this is carried out.

Listing B.30 Mapping over a list of objects with a typed getter

```
var books = List.of(watchmenRecord, sevenHabitsRecord);

books.stream()
.map(x -> TITLE.get(x))
.map(x -> x.toUpperCase())
.collect(Collectors.toList())
// → ["WATCHMEN", "7 HABITS OF HIGHLY EFFECTIVE PEOPLE"]
```

B.4.2 Generic access to nested class members

The previous section showed how to provide the same data access to classes as we used for string maps. This becomes powerful when we combine classes and maps. For example, listing B.31 represents search results as a map, where

- Keys are book ISBNs (strings).
- Values are book data represented as data classes (or records) as in the previous section.

Listing B.31 Search results represented as a map of records

```
Map searchResultsRecords = Map.of(
  "978-1779501127", new BookData(
    "978-1779501127",
    "Watchmen",
    1987
  ),
  "978-1982137274", new BookData(
    "978-1982137274",
    "7 Habits of Highly Effective People",
    2020
  )
);
```

For this implementation, it is necessary to add two additional methods. We need to declare the static `get` and `getAsString()` methods that receive a list of strings as the next listing shows.

Listing B.32 The implementation of value getter for nested class members

```
class DynamicAccess {
  static Object get(Object o, String k)  {
    if(o instanceof Map) {
      return ((Map)o).get(k);
    }
    try {
      return (o.getClass().getDeclaredField(k).get(o));
    } catch (IllegalAccessException | NoSuchFieldException e) {
      return null;
    }
  }

  static Object get(Object o, List<String> p) {
    Object v = o;
    for (String k : p) {
      v = get(v, k);
    }
    return v;
  }

  static String getAsString(Object o, String k) {
    return (String)get(o, k);
  }

  static String getAsString(Object o, List<String> p) {
    return (String)get(o, p);
  }
}
```

Now, a data member that is nested inside a string map can be accessed through its information path as, for instance, in listing B.6. The following listing provides the code to access the data member with a value getter.

Listing B.33 Accessing a member of a class nested in a map

```
var informationPath = List.of("978-1779501127", "title");
DynamicClassAccess
.getAsString(searchResultsRecords, informationPath)
.toUpperCase();
// → "WATCHMEN"
```

There is a second kind of nested data member when a data member is itself an object. For instance, listing B.34 shows how a bookAttributes field can be made from a BookAttributes class, and listing B.35 shows an example of the nested class.

Listing B.34 Representing book attributes with a nested class

```
public class BookAttributes {
  public Integer numberOfPages;
  public String language;
  public BookAttributes(Integer numberOfPages, String language) {
```

```
    this.numberOfPages = numberOfPages;
    this.language = language;
  }
}

public class BookWithAttributes {
  public String isbn;
  public String title;
  public Integer publicationYear;
  public BookAttributes attributes;
  public Book (
    String isbn,
    String title,
    Integer publicationYear,
    Integer numberOfPages,
    String language) {
      this.isbn = isbn;
      this.title = title;
      this.publicationYear = publicationYear;
      this.attributes = new BookAttributes(numberOfPages, language);
    }
}
```

Listing B.35 An instance of a nested class

```
BookData sevenHabitsNestedRecord = new BookWithAttributes(
  "978-1982137274",
  "7 Habits of Highly Effective People",
  2020,
  432,
  "en"
);
```

Value getters work without any modification on nested data members. We can do this with the code in the following listing.

Listing B.36 Accessing a nested class member with a value getter

```
var informationPath = List.of("attributes",
  "language");
DynamicClassAccess.getAsString(sevenHabitsNestedRecord, informationPath)
.toUpperCase();
// → "EN"
```

B.4.3 Automatic JSON serialization of objects

An approach similar to the one illustrated in the previous section is used by JSON serialization libraries like Gson (https://github.com/google/gson) in order to serialize objects to JSON automatically. Gson uses reflection to go over the class members, generating a JSON representation of each member value. Listing B.37 displays an example of Gson in action.

Listing B.37 JSON serialization of an object with Gson

```
import com.google.gson.*;
var gson = new Gson();

BookData sevenHabitsRecord = new BookData(
  "978-1982137274",
  "7 Habits of Highly Effective People",
  2020
);

System.out.println(gson.toJson(sevenHabitsRecord));
// → {"title":"7 Habits of Highly Effective People", …}
```

Listing B.38 shows how it also works with objects nested in maps. Listing B.39 then provides an example with objects nested in objects.

Listing B.38 JSON serialization of objects nested in a map with Gson

```
Map searchResultsRecords = Map.of(
  "978-1779501127", new BookData(
    "978-1779501127",
    "Watchmen",
    1987
  ),
  "978-1982137274", new BookData(
    "978-1982137274",
    "7 Habits of Highly Effective People",
    2020
  )
);

System.out.println(gson.toJson(searchResultsRecords));
// → {"978-1779501127":{"isbn":"978-1779501127","title":"Watchmen", …}}
```

Listing B.39 JSON serialization of an object nested in an object with Gson

```
BookData sevenHabitsNestedRecord = new BookWithAttributes(
  "978-1982137274",
  "7 Habits of Highly Effective People",
  2020,
  432,
  "en"
);

System.out.println(gson.toJson(sevenHabitsNestedRecord));
// → {"isbn":"978-1982137274",
// →  "title":"7 Habits of Highly Effective People", …}
```

Summary

This appendix has presented various ways to provide generic data access in statically-typed programming languages. Table B.1 summarizes the benefits and drawbacks of each approach. As you incorporate DOP practices in your programs, remember that data can be represented either as string maps or as classes (or records) and benefits from generic data access via:

- Dynamic getters
- Value getters
- Typed getters
- Reflection

Table B.1 Various ways to provide generic data access in statically-typed programming languages

Approach	Representation	Benefits	Drawbacks
Dynamic getters	Map	Generic access	Requires type casting
Value getters	Map	No type casting	Implementation per type
Typed getters	Map	Compile-time validation on usage	No compile-time validation on creation
Reflection	Class	Full compile-time validation	Not modifiable

appendix C
Data-oriented programming: A link in the chain of programming paradigms

Data-oriented programming (DOP) has its origins in the 1950s with the invention of the programming language Lisp. DOP is based on a set of best practices that can be found in both functional programming (FP) and object-oriented programming (OOP). However, this paradigm has only been applicable in production systems at scale since the 2010s with the implementation of efficient persistent data structures. This appendix traces the major ideas and discoveries which, over the years, have led to the emergence of DOP (see figure C.1).

C.1 Time line

C.1.1 1958: Lisp

With Lisp, John McCarthy had the ingenious idea to represent data as generic immutable lists and to invent a language that made it natural to create lists and to access any part of a list. That's the reason why Lisp stands for *LISt Processing*.

In a way, Lisp lists are the ancestors of JavaScript object literals. The idea that it makes sense to represent data with generic data structures (DOP Principle #2) definitely comes from Lisp.

The main limitation of Lisp lists is that when we update a list, we need to create a new version by cloning it. This has a negative impact on performance both in terms of CPU and memory.

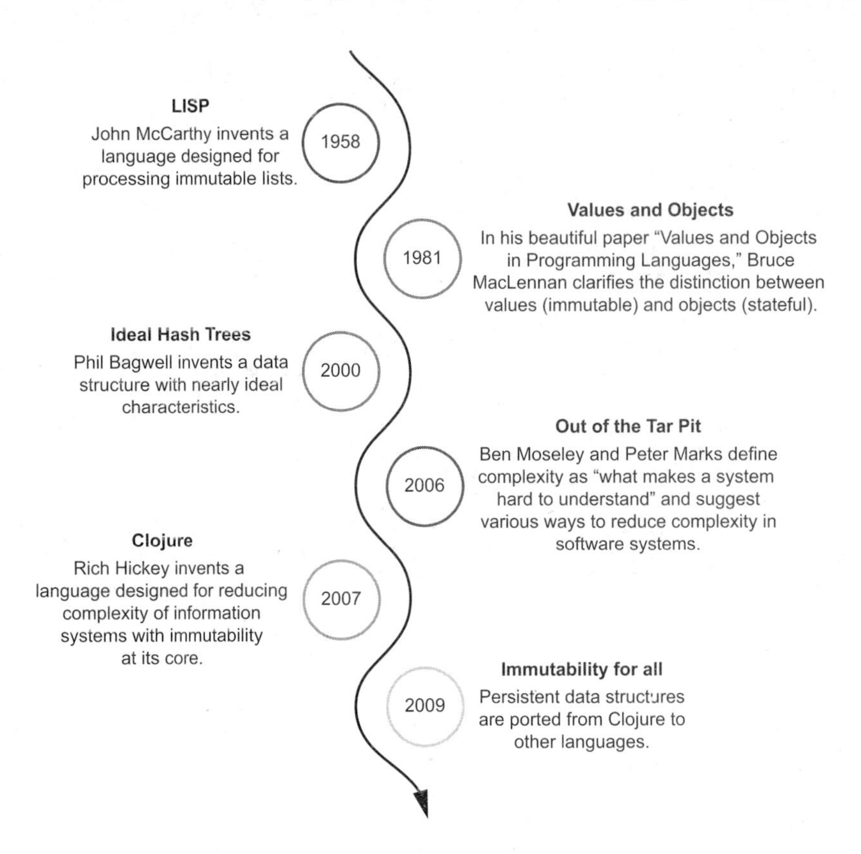

Figure C.1 DOP time line

C.1.2 1981: Values and objects

In a short and easy-to-read paper, named "Values and Objects in Programming Languages," Bruce MacLennan clarifies the distinction between values and objects. In a nutshell,

- Values (for instance, numbers) are timeless abstractions for which the concepts of updating, sharing, and instantiation have no meaning.
- Objects (for instance, an employee object in a human resource software system) exist in time and, hence, can be created, destroyed, copied, shared, and updated.

▶ **NOTE** The meaning of the term *object* in this paper is not exactly the same as in the context of OOP.

The author explains why it's much simpler to write code that deals with values than to write code that deals with objects. This paper has been a source of inspiration for DOP as it encourages us to implement our systems in such a way that most of our code deals with values. You can read the full text of this paper at http://mng.bz/7WNy.

C.1.3 2000: Ideal hash trees

Phil Bagwell invented a data structure called Hash Array Mapped Trie (HAMT). In his paper, "Ideal Hash Trees," he used HAMT to implement hash maps with nearly ideal characteristics both in terms of computation and memory usage. As we illustrated in chapter 9, HAMT and ideal hash trees are the foundation of efficient persistent data structures. See https://lampwww.epfl.ch/papers/idealhashtrees.pdf to read his technical paper.

C.1.4 2006: Out of the Tar Pit

In their paper, "Out of the Tar Pit," Ben Moseley and Peter Marks claim that complexity is the single major difficulty in the development of large-scale software systems. In the context of their paper, complexity means "that which makes large systems hard to understand."

The main insight of the authors is that most of the complexity of software systems in not essential but accidental: the complexity doesn't come from the problem we have to solve but from the software constructs we use to solve the problem. They suggest various ways to reduce complexity of software systems.

In a sense, DOP is a way to get us out of the tar pit. See http://mng.bz/mxq2 to download a copy of this term paper.

C.1.5 2007: Clojure

Rich Hickey, an OOP expert, invented Clojure to make it easier to develop information systems at scale. Rich Hickey likes to summarize Clojure's core value with the phrase, "Just use maps!" By maps, he means immutable maps to be manipulated efficiently by generic functions. Those maps were implemented using the data structures presented by Phil Bagwell in his paper, "Ideal Hash Trees."

Clojure has been the main source of inspiration for DOP. In a sense, this book is a formalization of the underlying principles of Clojure and how to apply them in other programming languages.

C.1.6 2009: Immutability for all

Clojure's efficient implementation of persistent data structures has been attractive for developers from other programming languages. In 2009, these structures were ported to Scala. Over the years, they have been ported to other programming languages as well, either by organizations like Facebook for Immutable.js, or by individual contributors like Glen Peterson for Paguro in Java. Nowadays, DOP is applicable in virtually any programming language!

C.2 DOP principles as best practices

The principles of DOP as we have presented them through the book (and formalized in appendix A) are not new. They come from best practices that are well known among software developers from various programming languages. The *innovation* of

DOP is the combination of those principles into a cohesive whole. In this section, we put each of the four DOP principles into its broader scope.

C.2.1 Principle #1: Separate code from data

Separating code from data used to be the main point of contention between OOP and FP. Traditionally, in OOP we encapsulate data together with code in stateful objects, while in FP, we write stateless functions that receive data they manipulate as an explicit argument.

This tension has been reduced over the years as it is possible in FP to write stateful functions with data encapsulated in their lexical scope (https://developer.mozilla.org/en-US/docs/Web/JavaScript/Closures). Moreover, OOP languages like Java and C# have added support for anonymous functions (lambdas).

C.2.2 Principle #2: Represent data with generic data structures

One of the main innovations of JavaScript when it was released in December 1995 was the ease of creating and manipulating hash maps via object literals. The increasing popularity of JavaScript over the years as a language used everywhere (frontend, backend, and desktop) has influenced the developer community to represent data with hash maps when possible. It feels more natural in dynamically-typed programming languages, but as we saw in appendix B, it is applicable also in statically-typed programming languages.

C.2.3 Principle #3: Data is immutable

Data immutability is considered a best practice as it makes the behavior of our program more predictable. For instance, in the book *Effective Java* (O'Reilly, 2017; http://mng.bz/5K81), Joshua Bloch mentions "minimize mutability" as one of Java best practices. There is a famous quote from Alan Kay, who is considered by many as the inventor of OOP, about the value of immutability:

> *The last thing you wanted any programmer to do is mess with internal state even if presented figuratively. Instead, the objects should be presented as sites of higher level behaviors more appropriate for use as dynamic components. . . . It is unfortunate that much of what is called "object-oriented programming" today is simply old style programming with fancier constructs. Many programs are loaded with "assignment-style" operations now done by more expensive attached procedures.*
>
> —Alan C. Kay ("The Early History of Smalltalk," 1993)

Unfortunately, until 2007 and the implementation of efficient persistent data structures in Clojure, immutability was not applicable for production applications at scale. As we mentioned in chapter 9, nowadays, efficient persistent data structures are available in most programming languages. These are summarized in table C.1.

Table C.1 Persistent data structure libraries

Language	Library
Java	Paguro (https://github.com/GlenKPeterson/Paguro)
C#	Provided by the language (http://mng.bz/y4Ke)
JavaScript	Immutable.js (https://immutable-js.com/)
Python	Pyrsistent (https://github.com/tobgu/pyrsistent)
Ruby	Hamster (https://github.com/hamstergem/hamster)

In addition, many languages provide support for read-only objects natively. Java added record classes in Java 14 (http://mng.bz/q2q2). C# introduced a `record` type in C# 9. There is a ECMAScript proposal for supporting immutable records and tuples in JavaScript (https://github.com/tc39/proposal-record-tuple). Finally, Python 3.7 introduced immutable data classes (https://docs.python.org/3/library/dataclasses.html).

C.2.4 Principle #4: Separate data schema from data representation

One of the more virulent critiques against dynamically-typed programming languages was related to the lack of data validation. The answer that dynamically-typed languages used to give to this critique was that you trade data safety for data flexibility. Since the development of data schema languages like JSON Schema (https://json-schema.org/), it is natural to validate data even when data is represented as hash maps. As we saw in chapters 7 and 12, data validation is not only possible, but in some sense, it is more powerful than when data is represented with classes.

C.3 DOP and other data-related paradigms

In this section, we clarify the distinction between DOP and two other programming paradigms whose names also contain the word *data*: data-oriented design and data-driven programming.

> *There are only two hard things in Computer Science: cache invalidation and naming things.*
>
> —Phil Karlton

Each paradigm has a its own objective and pursues it by focusing on a different aspect of data. Table C.2 summarizes the objectives, and we'll dive into each a bit more in the following sections.

Table C.2 Data-related paradigms: Objectives and main data aspect focus

Paradigm	Objective	Main data aspect focus
Data-oriented design	Increase performance	Data layout
Data-driven programming	Increase clarity	Behavior described by data
Data-oriented programming	Reduce complexity	Data representation

C.3.1 *Data-oriented design*

Data-oriented design is a program optimization approach motivated by efficient usage of the CPU cache. It's used mostly in video game development. This approach focuses on the data layout, separating and sorting fields according to when they are needed, and encourages us to think about data transformations. In this context, what's important is how the data resides in memory. The objective of this paradigm is to improve the performance of the system.

C.3.2 *Data-driven programming*

Data-driven programming is the idea that you create domain specific languages (DSLs) made out of descriptive data. It is a branch of declarative programming. In this context, what's important is to describe the behavior of a program in terms of data. The objective of this paradigm is to increase code clarity and to reduce the risk of bugs related to mistakes in the implementation of the expected behavior of the program.

C.3.3 *Data-oriented programming (DOP)*

As we have illustrated in this book, DOP is a paradigm that treats system data as a first-class citizen. Data is represented by generic immutable data structures like maps and vectors that are manipulated by general-purpose functions like map, filter, select, group, sort, and so forth. In this context, what's important is the representation of data by the program. The objective of this paradigm is to reduce the complexity of the system.

Summary

In this appendix, we have explored the ideas and trends that have inspired DOP. We looked at the discoveries that made it applicable in production systems at scale in most programming languages.

appendix D Lodash reference

Throughout the book, we have used Lodash (https://lodash.com/) to illustrate how to manipulate data with generic functions. But there is nothing unique about Lodash. The exact same approach could be implemented via other data manipulation libraries or custom code.

Moreover, we used Lodash FP (https://github.com/lodash/lodash/wiki/FP-Guide) to manipulate data without mutating it. By default, the order of the arguments in immutable functions is shuffled. The code in listing D.1 is needed when configuring Lodash in order to ensure the signature of the immutable functions is exactly the same as the mutable functions.

Listing D.1 Configuring immutable functions

```
_ = fp.convert({
  "cap": false,
  "curry": false,
  "fixed": false,
  "immutable": true,
  "rearg": false
});
```

This short appendix lists the 28 Lodash functions used in the book to help you, in case you are looking at a code snippet in the book that uses a Lodash function that you want to understand. The functions are split in to three categories:

- Functions on maps in table D.1
- Functions on arrays in table D.2
- Function on collections (both arrays and maps) in table D.3

Each table has three columns:

- *Function* shows the function with its signature.
- *Description* provides a brief description of the function.
- *Chapter* is the chapter number where the function appears for the first time.

Table D.1 Lodash functions on maps

Function	Description	Chapter
`at(map, [paths])`	Creates an array of values corresponding to `paths` of `map`	10
`get(map, path)`	Gets the value at `path` of `map`	3
`has(map, path)`	Checks if `map` has a field at `path`	3
`merge(mapA, mapB)`	Creates a map resulting from the recursive merges between `mapA` and `mapB`	3
`omit(map, [paths])`	Creates a map composed of the fields of `map` not in `paths`	10
`set(map, path, value)`	Creates a map with the same fields as `map` with the addition of a field `<path, value>`	4
`values(map)`	Creates an array of values of `map`	3

Table D.2 Lodash functions on arrays

Function	Description	Chapter
`concat(arrA, arrB)`	Creates an new array that concatenates `arrA` and `arrB`	5
`flatten(arr)`	Flattens `arr` a single level deep	14
`intersection(arrA, arrB)`	Creates an array of unique values both in `arrA` and `arrB`	5
`nth(arr, n)`	Gets the element at index `n` in `arr`	10
`sum(arr)`	Computes the sum of the values in `arr`	14
`union(arrA, arrB)`	Creates an array of unique values from `arrA` and `arrB`	5
`uniq(arr)`	Creates an array of unique values from `arr`	14

Table D.3 Lodash functions on collections (both arrays and maps)

Function	Description	Chapter
`every(coll, pred)`	Checks if `pred` returns `true` for all elements of `coll`	14
`filter(coll, pred)`	Iterates over elements of `coll`, returning an array of all elements for which `pred` returns `true`	3
`find(coll, pred)`	Iterates over elements of `coll`, returning the first element for which `pred` returns `true`	15
`forEach(coll, f)`	Iterates over elements of `coll` and invokes `f` for each element	14
`groupBy(coll, f)`	Creates a map composed of keys generated from the results of running each element of `coll` through `f`. The corresponding value for each key is an array of elements responsible for generating the key.	10
`isEmpty(coll)`	Checks if `coll` is empty	5
`keyBy(coll, f)`	Creates a map composed of keys generated from the results of running each element of `coll` through `f`. The corresponding value for each key is the last element responsible for generating the key.	11
`map(coll, f)`	Creates an array of values by running each element in `coll` through `f`	3
`reduce(coll, f, initVal)`	Reduces `coll` to a value which is the accumulated result of running each element in `coll` through `f`, where each successive invocation is supplied the return value of the previous	5
`size(coll)`	Gets the size of `coll`	13
`sortBy(coll, f)`	Creates an array of elements, sorted in ascending order by the results of running each element in `coll` through `f`	14
`isEqual(collA, collB)`	Performs a deep comparison between `collA` and `collB`	6
`isArray(coll)`	Checks if `coll` is an array	5
`isObject(coll)`	Checks if `coll` is a collection	5

index

D

U

V

W